# Are We Really Living In The Last Days?

## More Than 175 Fulfilled Prophecies

Roger Liebi

*Dedicated to my beloved mother
in affectionate thankfulness
for conveying and modeling
genuine biblical faith to me*

# Are We Really Living In The Last Days?

## More Than 175 Fulfilled Prophecies

Dr. Roger Liebi

Christlicher Medienvertrieb Hagedorn
Germany

1st English edition 2012

© CMV
Christlicher Medienvertrieb Hagedorn
Postfach 300430
40404 Düsseldorf
Germany

www.cmv-duesseldorf.de
info@cmv-video.de

Title of the original German edition:
"Leben wir wirklich in der Endzeit?"
© 2012 Verlag Mitternachtsruf

Translation: Barbara Gentry-Schmidt, Timothy Capes
Design & Layout: Susanne Martin
Print: Prospektus Nyomda, Hungary
Picture credits cover: fotolia.com/bluedesign

ISBN  978-3-943175-08-0

# Contents

# Bible Book Abbreviations

## Old Testament

| | | | |
|---|---|---|---|
| Gen | Genesis | Eccles | Ecclesiastes |
| Exod | Exodus | Song of Sol | Song of Solomon |
| Lev | Leviticus | Isa | Isaiah |
| Num | Numbers | Jer | Jeremiah |
| Deut | Deuteronomy | Lam | Lamentations |
| Josh | Joshua | Ezek | Ezekiel |
| Judg | Judges | Dan | Daniel |
| Ruth | Ruth | Hos | Hosea |
| 1 Sam | 1 Samuel | Joel | Joel |
| 2 Sam | 2 Samuel | Am | Amos |
| 1 Kings | 1 Kings | Obad | Obadiah |
| 2 Kings | 2 Kings | Jon | Jona |
| 1 Chron | 1 Chronicles | Mic | Micah |
| 2 Chron | 2 Chronicles | Na | Nahum |
| Ezra | Ezra | Hab | Habakkuk |
| Neh | Nehemia | Zeph | Zephaniah |
| Esth | Esther | Hag | Haggai |
| Job | Job | Zech | Zechariah |
| Ps | Psalms | Mal | Malachi |
| Prov | Proverbs | | |

## New Testament

| | | | |
|---|---|---|---|
| Matt | Matthew | 1Tim | 1 Timothy |
| Mark | Mark | 2Tim | 2 Timothy |
| Luk | Luke | Titus | Titus |
| Joh | John | Philem | Philemon |
| Acts | Acts | Heb | Hebrews |
| Rom | Romans | Jas | James |
| 1 Cor | 1 Corinthians | 1 Pet | 1 Peter |
| 2 Cor | 2 Corinthians | 2 Pet | 2 Peter |
| Gal | Galatians | 1 John | 1 John |
| Eph | Ephesians | 2 John | 2 John |
| Phil | Philippians | 3 John | 3 John |
| Col | Colossians | Jude | Jude |
| 1 Thess | 1 Thessalonians | Rev | Revelation |
| 2 Thess | 2 Thessalonians | | |

**Bible Quotes**

Bible translations used in this book are indicated in brackets after each Bible quote. Translations include: King James Version (*KJV*), New King James Version (*NKJV*; copyright © 1982 by Thomas Nelson, Inc.), Darby Translation (*Darby*; A.J. Holman Company, 1980) and American Standard Version (*ASV*).

Square brackets within the text of Bible indicate an insertion which is not part of the Bible text. In contrast, sentences or phrases between parentheses are part of the Bible text.

Poetic texts have been made apparent by the use of verse arrangements.[1]

The Hebrew name of God "YHWH" has been mostly rendered by "LORD," but in certain instances by "the ETERNAL ONE."

---

1  For Hebrew poetry cf.: LIEBI: Poesie im Alten Testament; LIEBI: Introduction à la poésie hébraïque.

# I. Introduction

## 1. More than 175 Prophecies

Never before in the long history of mankind has there been an age which fully conforms to what the Bible describes as the "End Times" or the "Last Days." Naturally, on occasion there have been eras in which enthusiastic but mistaken people have asserted that they were living in The Last Days. However, the sober proof that the End Time prophecies of the Holy Scriptures had been fulfilled could not be provided in a single case. The arguments were always weak and unsupportable. They never fulfilled the indications of the Biblical statements about The Last Days.

The world has always seen catastrophes and wars. Such events are, in and of themselves, not evidence for The Last Days. According to the Bible, The Last Days will be fundamentally characterized by the Jews' return to the Land of their Forefathers from the worldwide Diaspora and by the re-establishment of the State of Israel after an interruption of almost 2,000 years. Catastrophes and wars in human history alone are not evidence for The Last Days, as long as they do not coincide with the return of the Jews and with all the scores of other End Time events announced in the Bible.

The combination of events is of prime importance! When many specific events, which will occur in the same period according to prophecy, actually take place, one can, in view of mathematical probability, reasonably exclude coincidence!

What does the subject "The Last Days" look like today? All around the world, innumerable Bible expositors emphasize that we are presently living in The Last Days. This raises the question: Is it now really possible to prove this rationally, so that others can logically follow it? Or is that which has been rehearsed often enough by fantacists in other eras merely repeating itself?

We may stress this clearly: Our era – I speak especially of the time from 1882 until today – is unique in this regard! Indeed, there are concrete proofs that our era is that which the Bible prophetically describes as the age of the return of Jesus Christ! No-one has yet succeeded in factually refuting these arguments for The Last Days, as put forward in this book.

In the following chapters, we will be examining more than 175 Biblical prophecies altogether which have to do with the "The Last Days." These prophecies have all been verifiably fulfilled in our era of world history, i.e. beginning with the time of the first modern wave of Jewish immigration to the Land of their Forefathers (1882) until today. With this, definite proof can be given that we really are living in "The Last Days"! As stated, appalling wars and terrible catastrophes are, of themselves, no evidence of The Last Days. However, when they are coupled with the fulfilment of many other, very precise prophecies of very specific End Time events, naturally, the matter looks very different!

Subsequently, I will demonstrate that the days in which we live are exactly what the ancient Biblical prophets described in their prophecies as the "Last Days." Accordingly, the logically compelling conclusion is: Jesus Christ will soon come again!

Thus, more than 175 fulfilled End Time prophecies help us to evaluate soberly and clearly the signs of the age (cf. Matt. 16:1-3, Luke 12:54-56).

*Fig. 1: The Mount of Olives, as seen from the Temple Mount. According to Zechariah 14:4 Jesus Christ will come again on this mountain in "The Last Days" as Messiah and King of the world. The arrow points to the summit of the Mount of Olives.*

# 2. What is the Meaning of the Term "Last Days"?

Before we speak about The Last Days in detail, we must be clear about what the Biblical term "Last Days" actually means.

We find the term "Last Days" in a number of expressions. Here is a selection:

- Ezekiel 38:8: *"the latter years"*
- Daniel 8:17: *"time of the end"*[2]
- Daniel 8:19: *"the latter time of the indignation"*
- Daniel 12:13: *"the end of the days"*
- Hosea 3:5: *"in the latter days"*
- Joel 3:1: *"those days and at that time"*
- Isaiah 19:18: *"in that day"*[3]
- Jeremiah 30:3: *"behold, the days"*

---

2 Dan. 8:19; 11:35,40; 12:4,9.

3 The Hebrew term *bayom hahu'* always means "in that day" or "in that epoch". As a fixed term, there is no relationship to a 24-hour day, just as the term "today" has nothing to do with a calendar day, but rather defines the present time of the speaker, for example. See e.g. this often-used term in Zech. 12–14.

- Jeremiah 3:17: *"at that time"*
- Ezekiel 35:5: *"the time of their calamity, when their iniquity came to an end"*[4]
- Matthew 24:3 *"the end of the age"*
- 2 Timothy 3:1: *"in the last days"*
- 1 John 2:18: *"the last hour"*
- Jude 1:18: *"in the last time"*

When all the chapters of the Bible which deal with the theme "Last Days" are studied, one sees, perhaps with astonishment, that in contrast to accepted assumptions, there is absolutely nothing about an immediate, impending "end of the world." The Biblical term "Last Days" refers plainly and simply to the period of time in which the Messiah will come and, particularly, when He will appear as "King of kings" to rule here on Earth in peace and righteousness (cf. Rev. 19:11-20:11).[5]

# 3. The Suffering and the Reigning Messiah

Here I have used an important and very central keyword in Biblical prophecy: "the Messiah." Who is the Messiah? In the Old Testament (OT), the writings of the Bible written between 1606 and

---

4 Ezek. 21:25,29.

5 Sometimes it is asserted that The Last Days, according to the Bible, began with the Coming of Christ 2,000 years ago. When so stated, without additional explanation, this is not correct. Heb. 1:1-2 states, "[1] God, who at various times and in various ways spoke in time past to the fathers by the prophets, [2] has **in these last days** spoken to us by *His* Son, ..." Here the term "these last days" is used. However, in order to differentiate this expression from The Last Days in relationship to the Coming of the Messiah as Judge of the world, the term *these* last days is used. The Coming of the Messiah was the completion of the long, Old Testament time of waiting for the Saviour. His Coming was the end of these days of waiting. In most cases the term "Last Days" is not used for the completion of the Old Testament epoch, but rather for the completion of the long time between the First and the Second Coming of the Messiah, or rather for the completion of "the times of the Gentiles" (Luke 21:24). Cf. Roger Liebi: Die Bibel in der Vogelschau. Die 7 Bündnisse und die 7 Heilszeitalter (audio lecture on www.sermon-online.de).

420 BC,[6] the coming of a Saviour is announced, for Israel and also for all other peoples of the world. But let the following important conclusion be noted in this connection: The Hebrew prophets spoke about the Messiah in two completely different ways:

Many OT verses deal with the "suffering Messiah" who will come to deal with the problem of our guilt before God by dying as a sacrifice, the Righteous for the unrighteous, so that He might bring us to God (cf. e.g. Isa. 53; Ps. 22; Dan. 9:25).

On the other hand, the prophets have painted a picture in their texts of the "reigning Messiah." He will come as King of kings and Lord of Lords in order to establish a worldwide reign of peace and righteousness here on Earth (cf. e.g. Isa. 11; Dan. 7:13,14,18,22,27; Zech. 14).

How can we reconcile these two very different depictions? Quite simply! They deal with two different aspects of one and the same Messiah.

He came the first time to solve the problem of our personal guilt by His sacrifice on the cross. The Messiah will appear a second time in the future in order to abolish all political, social and economic problems of the world.

There is a remarkable interpretative key which can be helpful to the Bible reader in distinguishing these two different phases of the Messiah's coming: The prophets prophesied that the "suffering Messiah" would be rejected and discarded by the greater part of His people. As a consequence of the rejection of the One sent by God, the Jewish people would be torn out of the Land of Israel and scattered among all the nations of the world. In connection with the coming of the "reigning Messiah," the prophets foretold that the Jewish people would be brought back to the Land of their Forefathers, out of worldwide dispersion, in the time period immediately prior to the Second Coming.

---

6 A strict chronology of Bible history in which all dates are unified in a self-contained system gives a very early date for the Exodus (cf. LIEBI: Chronologie der Könige Israels und Judas; these notes will be sent free of charge on request from info@rogerliebi.ch; free to download at www.rogerliebe.ch). This chronology agrees impressively with the archaeological facts in Egypt and in Canaan/Israel (cf. the following audio lectures by the author at www.sermon-online.ch:
 · Hazor und Tel Dan – Zeugen der Glaubwürdigkeit der Bibel
 · Archäologie in der Davidsstadt
 · Israel in Ägypten – Realität oder Fiktion?

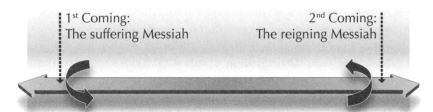

**The Two Appearances of the Messiah**

1st Coming:
The suffering Messiah

2nd Coming:
The reigning Messiah

*Fig. 2: In the period after the Messiah's First Coming the Jewish people would be scattered worldwide. In contrast, in the period before the Messiah's Second Coming, the Jewish people will be brought back from all over the world to the Land of their Forefathers.*

# 4. Consequences of Rejecting the Messiah

Jesus Christ fulfilled the prophecies of the "suffering Messiah" with His Coming a little more than 2,000 years ago. We are thereby in the position to prove[7] that Jesus Christ is the Messiah. More than 300 prophecies in connection with the promised Saviour have been fulfilled![8]

The rejection of the suffering Messiah by His own people would result in a national catastrophe. The OT prophets stated this in advance. I want to illustrate this connection directly from Bible texts and in such a way that each reader is able to understand this fact. It is possible to do this with, for example, Isaiah 8:14-15:[9]

---

7  Cf. Acts 9:22; 18:28

8  Cf. extensively to this theme: LIEBI: Der verheissene Erlöser. Messianische Prophetie – ihre Erfül-
lung und historische Echtheit, Bielefeld 2007; FRUCHTENBAUM: Jesus was a Jew. See also the
following audio lecture by the author at www.sermon-online.de :
· The Promised Savior
· Isaiah 53: The suffering servant of God
· The Messiah in Psalms
· The Messiah in the Old Testament

9  Incidentally, rabbis, the teachers in Judaism pointed to the Messiah with this verse already in
antiquity (cf. BABYLONIAN TALMUD, Sanhedrin 38a). In the NT this verse in 1 Peter 2:8 refers to
Jesus Christ.

*"14 He [the Messiah] ... will be a stone of stumbling and a rock of
offense
To both the houses of Israel,
As a trap and a snare to the inhabitants of Jerusalem.
15 And many among them shall stumble;
They shall fall and be broken,
Be snared and taken."* (NKJV)

The greater part of the Jewish people rejected Jesus of Nazareth as Messiah. He was for them a rock of offense. In 70 AD – a
few years after the crucifixion of Jesus – the Romans destroyed
Jerusalem, the Jewish capital, including the majestic Temple on
Mount Zion, in a brutal and bloody war. The Jewish sacrificial system came to an end. Following crushing defeats of the two Jewish
revolts against Rome (66–73 and 132–135 AD), the Jewish state
came to an end. The magnificent country of Israel, at one time
flowing with milk and honey (Deut. 6:3), became, in a centuries-
long process, an unsightly desert. This development reached its
climax in the 19th century. Likewise in a long process over many
centuries, the Jewish people were scattered throughout all five
continents of the world. For two thousand years, the Jews were
hated, rejected, slandered, ostracized, persecuted and slaughtered all over the world. The total dead of this afflicted nation
from 70 AD into the 20th century comprises some 13 million who
are to be mourned. Moses had already prophesied these things
with absolute precision in 1606 BC. Through him God declared
(Lev. 26:31-33):

*"31 I will lay your cities waste and bring your sanctuaries to
desolation, and I will not smell the fragrance of your sweet aromas. 32 I will bring the land to desolation, and your enemies who
dwell in it shall be astonished at it. 33 I will scatter you among
the nations and draw out a sword after you; your land shall be
desolate and your cities waste."* (NKJV)

In 1566 BC Moses prophesied in his farewell speech
(Deut. 28:64-67):

*"⁶⁴ Then the Lᴏʀᴅ will scatter you among all peoples, from one end of the earth to the other, and there you shall serve other gods, which neither you nor your fathers have known—wood and stone. ⁶⁵ And among those nations you shall find no rest, nor shall the sole of your foot have a resting place; but there the Lᴏʀᴅ will give you a trembling heart, failing eyes, and anguish of soul. ⁶⁶ Your life shall hang in doubt before you; you shall fear day and night, and have no assurance of life. ⁶⁷ In the morning you shall say, 'Oh, that it were evening!' And at evening you shall say, 'Oh, that it were morning!' because of the fear which terrifies your heart, and because of the sight which your eyes see."* (NKJV)

# 5. The Gentile Nations' Great Opportunity

What is the significance of the long period of time between the First and the Second Coming of the Messiah? This question was answered in the book of the prophet Isaiah (around 700 BC). In Isaiah 49:6 God tells His Messiah, that His mission will not be limited to Israel, and that He will, rather, bring blessing to the Gentile nations:

*"⁶ Indeed He says, ...*
*I will also give You as **a light to the Gentiles**,*
*That You should be My salvation to the ends of the earth."*
(NKJV)

This prophecy has been strikingly fulfilled: Throughout the past 2,000 years the Good News of the suffering Messiah has been spread over all five continents, even to the Eskimos, the Tierra del Fuegans the Tasmanian Aborigines and the Maoris of New Zealand at the "ends of the earth." This means to the farthest parts of the Earth, as seen from Jerusalem. Jerusalem was indeed the geographical starting point for world mission (Acts 1:18). During the course of church history, millions of Gentiles have acknowledged

Jesus of Nazareth as the God-sent Saviour and accepted Him as Master and Lord (John 1:12). They have acknowledged their personal guilt before God in repentance (1 John 1:9) and have claimed for themselves the substitutionary, atoning sacrifice of Jesus on the cross (Rom. 3:23-26). In this way, millions of people have found peace with God (Rom. 5:1).

# 6. The Long Period of Statelessness

During the same period of time in which the Gospel of Jesus Christ was spread among all nations on the five continents of the world, the Jews were a stateless people in the worldwide Dispersion.

This long period of statelessness had been recorded long ago in the book of the prophet Hosea (8th century BC). The people of Israel would, for a long time, be "without a king" and also "without a prince" (Hos. 3:4-5):

> *"4 For the children of Israel shall abide **many days without king** or **prince**, without sacrifice or sacred pillar, without ephod or teraphim. 5 **Afterward** the children of Israel shall **return** and seek the LORD their God and David their king. They shall fear the LORD and His goodness **in the latter days**."* (NKJV)

Let us take note of some further details in Hosea 3:4: The period of statelessness would also be characterized by the absence of sacrifices. In keeping with God's Law in Deuteronomy 12:13-14, the Jewish people are only allowed to sacrifice at the Temple in Jerusalem. However, the Temple was destroyed by the Romans in 70 AD. The mount on which this sanctuary once stood was taken away from the nation of Israel. The Jewish sacrificial system came to an end at that time and remains so to this day. Only in 1967, during the course of the Six Day War, the Jewish people gained control of Temple Mount once more. Since then various organisations have been active in reconstructing the Temple instruments and preparing for a future sacrificial system. Yet in view of the militant Muslim claim to 144,000 m² of the Temple area, the Jewish people are still unable to offer sacrifice to this day.

The office of High Priest ceased with the destruction of the Temple in 70 AD. During these many centuries, the Jewish people have lacked the High Priestly garments, to which the breastplate on the ephod, decorated with twelve precious stones, belonged (cf. Exod. 28). Only recently has this been reproduced, for the first time, at a cost of some $1.5 million. The author of these lines has seen these garments in Jerusalem with his own eyes, together with the ephod.[10]

Beginning with the Exodus from Egypt, Israel's Old Testament history was tragically characterized time and again by a relapse into idolatry. The religions of the Sumerians, Egyptians, Canaanites, Babylonians and Assyrians were always a tremendous challenge for the Chosen People. Ornamented columns (to honour Baal or Ashera, for example) and ancestor worship (Hebr. *teraphim*) constantly played a tragic role, since the first two laws of the Torah (Exod. 20:1-6) were repeatedly broken in a severe way through this alone. During a time when Israel was very guilty of idolatry, Hosea prophesied that the long period of statelessness (coming as a result of the nation's rejection of the Messiah) would be characterized by the absence of this idolatry. This was fulfilled exactly. Even though, during the past 2,000 years, the mass of the Jewish people have rejected the Messiah (Jesus Christ), they have not lapsed into the adoration of ornamented columns and ancestor worship, completely in contrast to professing Christendom, with its regrettable adoration of statues and images connected with the cult of Mary and the Saints.

# 7. The Return of the Jews and the Coming of the Messiah

According to Hosea 3:4-5, the period of Jewish statelessness would not go on forever, but would rather be limited to a long period,

---

10   Cf. www.temleinstitute.org (as of: 24.10.2011).

"many days." After this long period of statelessness, there would be a turn of events, and this would occur in The Last Days ("in the latter days"). Then the Jewish people would again return to the Land of their Forefathers and ultimately seek the rejected Messiah. The designation "David, your King" is applied in the standard rabbinic literature to the Messiah.[11]

Here we have an astounding prophecy. Almost 1,000 years before the complete fall of the Jewish nation in 135 AD, the long period of Jewish statelessness, as well as the following return and re-establishment of their nation, is prophesied here. (v. 5: *"Afterward the children of Israel shall return ..."*). It was certainly *"many days"* which made up the period from 135 AD to 1948.

Since it has been made clear that the Jewish people would be scattered as a result of rejecting the Messiah, I wish also to show directly from the Bible that the Messiah will appear in the period when the Jewish people return from their dispersion.

Ezekiel 38 deals with an enemy from the extreme north[12] which will attack Israel in The Last Days, in the period in which the Messiah will come as King. The reigning Messiah is described in Ezekiel 37:24-28. In Ezekiel 38:8 the enemy from the north is addressed:

> *"8 ... **In the latter years** you will come into the land of those brought back from the sword [as one people] and **gathered from many people** on the mountains of Israel, which had long been desolate; **they were brought out of the nations...**"* (NKJV)

As has just been pointed out, the expression "in the latter years" is one of the many terms used to express The Last Days. On the basis of this one verse alone it can be shown that the period of the regathering of the Jewish people to the Land of their Forefathers will take place within the Biblical Last Days. Furthermore, it

---

11 Cf. Metzudath David, Hosea 3:5, in: BAR ILAN'S JUDAIC LIBRARY, Bar Ilan University, Responsa Project, CD-Rom, Version 5; or in: *MIQRA'OTH GEDOLOTH*, Vols. I - VIII, *yerushalayim* 1972 (Hebrew Bible with Aramaic translation (Targumim), medieval Standard-Commentaries and Prayers).

12 As seen from Israel.

becomes clear from Ezekiel 37 and 38 that this corresponds to the time in which the reigning Messiah will come.

I will provide yet another proof in the following. In Joel 3:1-2 (8th century BC) the voice of the Messiah is heard:

*"¹ For behold, in those days and at that time,*
**When** *I bring back the captives of Judah and Jerusalem,*
*² I will also gather all nations,*
*And bring them down to **the Valley of Jehoshaphat**;*
*And **I** will enter into judgement with them **there***
*On account of My people, My heritage Israel,*
*Whom they have scattered among the nations; ..."* (NKJV)

I have already explained that the phrase "in those days and at that time" is a technical expression which refers to The Last Days. It is precisely during this time that the Messiah, according to Joel 3:2, will be here on Earth, in the Valley of Jehoshaphat (this being another name for the Kidron Valley which lies between the Mount of Olives and the Temple Mount in Jerusalem).[13] Here the Messiah will judge the nations and will raise the issue of what they have done with His people Israel in the past. From Joel 3:1-2 it follows that The Last Days concern a period in which the destiny of the Jews, and of Jerusalem, will see a positive turn of events.

Although the fate of the Jews' homelessness from the 1st to the 19th century seemed so hopeless, a decisive turn of events began in 1882. At that time, the first wave of Jewish immigration to the Land of their Forefathers became reality. Under pressure of persecution by the last Russian Czars, thousands of Jews left Russia for "Palestine" between 1882 and 1904. Wave after wave followed, so that today millions of Jews from all five continents have returned to the Land of their Forefathers.

---

13  In Gen. 14:17 this valley is called "the King's Valley", or rather, "Valley of Shaveh."

# 8. "The Last Days" and "the Time of the Beginning"

Since The Last Days deal with the period in which the Jews return to the Land of Israel, we can say justifiably that The Last Days is a period which has already encompassed 130 years. But what are 130 years in view of the past 2,000 years? These 130 years can be seen as a phase in the preparation for the coming of the Messiah.

In connection with the First Coming of the Messiah, there was a Messianic period analogous to this, in fact totalling 135 years, which preceded centuries of dispersion and statelessness: Jesus Christ was born in Bethlehem a little more than 2,000 years ago. In 32 AD the Romans crucified Him; in 70 AD the Second Temple and the city of Jerusalem were destroyed. With the defeat of the Second Revolt against Rome (132–135 AD), the Jewish state was finally crushed. All in all, the time from the First Coming of the suffering Messiah until the final demise of the state of Israel encompassed 135 years. In contrast to "The Last Days," this period may be called the "time of beginning."[14]

The beginning of The Last Days is designated by the first massive immigration of Jews into the Land of their fathers (1882). The Last Days is a period, an interval of time, which is continually developing and, ultimately, will result in the appearance of the Messiah Jesus, who will establish His worldwide Kingdom of peace and righteousness here on Earth.

---

14 The time of the coming of Jesus Christ 2,000 years ago is in 1 John 1:1 reported as the "beginning" (cf. additionally 1 John 2:7,13,14,24; 3:11; 2 John 1:5,6; Heb. 6:1.

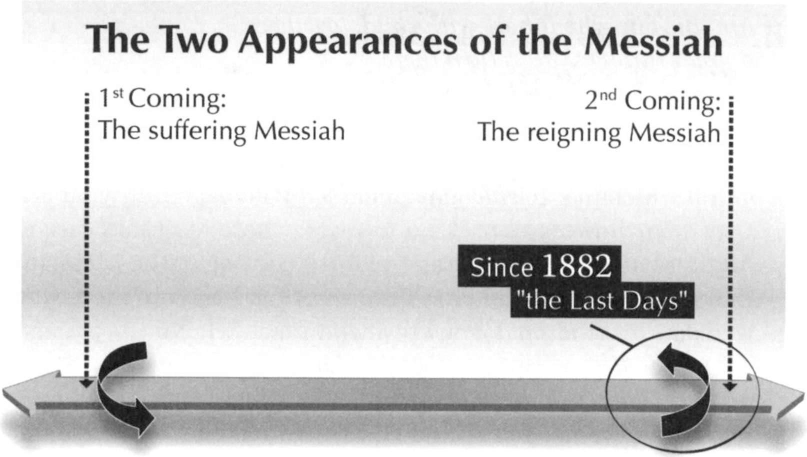

# The Two Appearances of the Messiah

1st Coming:
The suffering Messiah

2nd Coming:
The reigning Messiah

Since 1882
"the Last Days"

*Fig. 3: The Jewish fate of dispersal and statelessness began to reverse in 1882 with the first modern wave of immigration. Thus, the period from 1882 until today is what the Bible calls the "Last Days."*

It is very important when studying the prophetic texts of the Bible to notice that the term "Last Days" deals with an epoch and not just one moment in time. The Last Days is the time of change in Jewish destiny (Amos 9:14; Joel 3:1). Israel will become fully restored in one ongoing process. This development, which according to the vision in Ezekiel 37:1-14 will be accomplished in several phases, will come to completion and perfection when the Messiah appears as King of the world. Certain prophetic sections of the Bible speak about single events which will occur during this period; other sections describe the whole in a summarized view. In the sections where such a summarized view is found, it can be seen perhaps, how a particular event or even the greater part has been fulfilled, but not yet all of it. We can only speak of a complete fulfilment when the Messiah returns. Following is an example (Jer. 31):

*"⁸ Behold, I will bring them from the north country,*
*And gather them from the ends of the earth,*
*Among them the blind and the lame,*
*The woman with child*

*And the one who labors with child, together;*
*A great throng shall return there.*
*⁹ They shall come with weeping,*
*And with supplications I will lead them.*
*I will cause them to walk by the rivers of waters,*
*In a straight way in which they shall not stumble;*
*For I am a Father to Israel,*
*And Ephraim is My firstborn.*
*¹⁰ Hear the word of the* Lord, *O nations,*
*And declare it in the isles afar off, and say,*
*'He who scattered Israel will gather him,*
*And keep him as a shepherd does his flock.'"* (NKJV)

The gathering of Jews in great numbers from the land of the north (verse 8) is being fulfilled today because, since 1882, more that 1 million Jews have immigrated to Israel from Russia and the territories of the former Soviet Union. Also verse 10 is understandable today. It is being discussed all over the world that the Jews were a people scattered worldwide, but in our day they have experienced a unique return and assembly in the Land of their Forefathers. Still, the statement that the Messiah will care for them (verse 10b) and lead them (verse 9) as a good shepherd, can only be fulfilled when the Messiah comes again. We must keep this clearly in view: We are living in The Last Days, but we have not yet come to the end. "The End" is not yet (cf. Matt. 24:6). We are experiencing the progression of this period as it advances to its goal, but the ultimate goal has not yet been reached.

In the following, as stated at the outset, we will look at the more than 175 prophecies from the Bible which have been fulfilled over the years and decades from 1882 through to 2012, all of which deal with the "Last Days." It will thus be clearly and irrefutably demonstrated that we are actually living in the period of The Last Days and that Jesus Christ will come again soon!

With these more than 175 prophecies we will not be dealing with an exhaustive account of Biblical prophecy which has been fulfilled in our time, but an extensive, comprehensive treatment nevertheless.

# The End Times:
## Already a period of 130 years

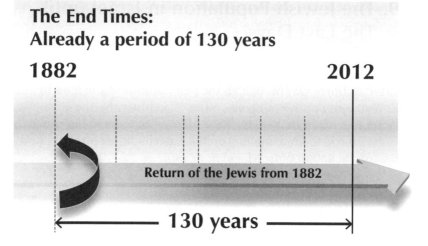

*Fig. 4:* The Last Days is a period, which encompasses the years beginning with the first Jewish wave of immigration until the Messiah's reign. Scores of End-Time events will occur in this epoch. More than 175 prophecies have already been verifiably fulfilled. The short lines signify the individual events which will be fulfilled during The Last Days.

## Time of the Beginning: A period of 135 years

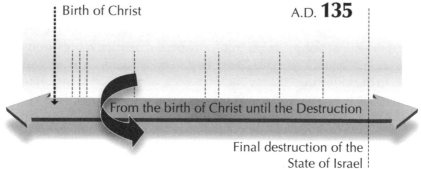

*Fig. 5:* The "Time of the Beginning" is a period which encompasses the coming of the Messiah as a baby in Bethlehem (birth of Jesus) till the complete demise of the Jewish state in 135 AD. The short lines signify the individual events prophesied in the OT which had been fulfilled during the "Time of the Beginning."

# 9. The Jewish Population in Israel until The Last Days

In spite of the fact of the worldwide dispersion of the Jewish people beginning in 70 AD, there remained a permanent Jewish population in the land. Through all the persecutions of the Jews by the Romans, Byzantines and, since the 7ᵗʰ century, by the Muslims, Israel was made "judenrein" [free of Jews] in an ongoing process. In Isaiah 6:9-10 God announced the judgement of spiritual blinding for the nation of Israel:

> *⁹ And He said, "Go, and tell this people:*
> *'Keep on hearing, but do not understand;*
> *Keep on seeing, but do not perceive.'*
> *¹⁰ Make the heart of this people dull,*
> *And their ears heavy,*
> *And shut their eyes;*
> *Lest they see with their eyes,*
> *And hear with their ears,*
> *And understand with their heart,*
> *And return and be healed."* (NKJV)

Following this announcement of a time of blindness for the Chosen People, the prophet wanted to know how long this period would be (Isa. 6):

> *¹¹ Then I said, "Lord, how long?"'* (NKJV)

Isaiah immediately received the following answer (Isa. 6):

> *¹¹ᵇ ... and He answered: "**Until** the cities are laid waste and without inhabitant,*
> *The houses are **without a man**,*
> *The land is utterly desolate,*
> *¹² The LORD has removed men far away,*

*And the forsaken places are many in the midst of the land.*
*[13] But yet **a tenth** will be in it,*
*And **will return and be for consuming,***
*As a terebinth tree or as an oak,*
*__Whose stump remains__ when it is cut down.*
*So the holy **seed** shall be its stump." (NKJV)*

The divine answer said this: The population of Jews in the Land will be reduced in an ongoing process. Even 1/10 of the former inhabitants would be far too many. But Israel would never be totally depopulated. There would always be a remnant population in the Land, analogous to the situation of a felled tree: the stump remains in the earth. This stump will finally – like scattered seed on a field – hold glorious hope for the future. Just as a stump sprouts anew and a tree grows, so it will be the case for the people of Israel from the remnant remaining in the Promised Land.

Jewish history of the past 2,000 years confirms exactly what was prophesied in Isaiah Chapter 6 in 700 BC: Beginning in 70 AD the Land of Israel was gradually depopulated due to the dispersion of the Jews. This process reached its climax at the beginning of the 19th century: At that time there were only about 6,700 Jews in the Land.[15] With the emergence of Zionism, the number increased somewhat. By the middle of the 19th century, there were about 10,000 Jews in the Land, of which 8,000 were residents of Jerusalem.[16] The fundamental change came with the massive waves of immigration beginning in 1882.

The most important Jewish cities in connection with the continuing Jewish presence in the Land since the fall of the state in 135 AD were: Jerusalem (including East-Jerusalem), Hebron, Safed and Tiberias.[17] In this connection, it should be noted that Hebron and East-Jerusalem are today significant cities in the so-called occupied West Bank which the world organisation, the UN, claims the Jews should part with, since it doesn't belong to them!

According to Isaiah 6, the Jewish people would be struck with

---

15   http://en.wikipedia.org/wiki/Zionism (as of: 24.10.2010).

16   GILBERT: Israel, A History, p. 3.

17   GILBERT: The Arab-Israeli Conflict, p. 2.

spiritual blindness during the period of depopulation of the Promised Land. However, afterward, the situation would change. In the 1st century AD tens of thousands of Jews came to the conclusion that Jesus of Nazareth was the Messiah of Israel prophesied in the OT.[18] Over the intervening centuries, very few Jews have come to faith in the Messiah Jesus. Beginning in Europe in 1517, as a mighty revival broke out with the Reformation, thousands and thousands discovered the Bible and, with it, God's mercy. The reformer Martin Luther thought that this would also mean a break-through, a turning point, among the Jews. But this did not happen at all. Tragically, Luther later became bitter and made reprehensible statements about the Jews. However, the prophetic period had not yet begun at that time. Israel was still in the process of Jewish depopulation, according to Isaiah 6. The turning point for the depopulation only came in the 19th century. The turning point with respect to the Messiah also occurred at that time. Hundreds of thousands of Jews have found the Messiah since the 19th century. The break-through was triggered by the "Hebrew Christian" movement.[19] Today, there are many hundreds of thousands of Messianic Jews worldwide.[20] There has never been anything like this in the past 2,000 years! In the past decade alone, the number of Messianic Jews in the USA has grown to a quarter of a million.[21] When such growth is related to the total number of Jews worldwide, approx. 14 million, this is considerable. Today in the West, say in Germany and Switzerland, if by percentage, so many Gentiles were to come to a living faith in Jesus Christ, and not only that but also came from a non-Christian background, this would be considered a revival. Unfortunately, this is not the case. However, the turn-point among the Jewish people prophesied in Isaiah 6, coming immediately after the completed process of depopulation in the Holy Land, is an astounding fact!

---

18  When Paul came to Jerusalem in 57 AD, this was reported to him concerning the believing Jews (Acts 21:20): *"You see, brother, how many myriads (Greek myriades) of Jews there are who have believed, and they are all zealous for the law."*

19  http://en.wikipedia.org/wiki/Messianic_Judaism (as of: 24.10.2010).

20  http://www.messianicjewish.net/messianic-judaism.html (as of: 24.10.2010).

21  http://en.wikipedia.org/wiki/Messianic_Judaism (see esp. footnotes 24 and 27; as of: 24.10.2010).

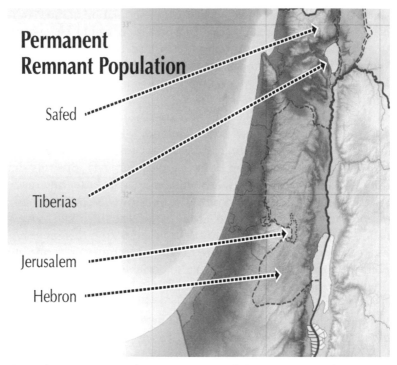

**Fig. 6:** *The most important places in connection with the permanent Jewish remnant population in the Promised Land were: Jerusalem, Hebron, Safed and Tiberias. (source: Eric Gaba GNU 1.2 or later).*

# II. A People Returns Home

## 1. Gathering and Return to the Land of Israel: 1882 until Today

In 600 BC Jeremiah announced the return of the Jewish people which had been dispersed worldwide. This event would be so significant someday that it would be made known to the most remote nations (Jer. 31:10).

> *"¹⁰ Hear the word of the LORD, O nations,*
> *And declare it in the isles afar off, and say,*
> *'He who scattered Israel will gather him, ..."* (NKJV)

The Jewish nation will be gathered again! In this verse of Jeremiah 31 it is not stated, however, to which place the Jewish people would be gathered. From this passage the fact simply emerges that the scattered members of this nation will one day be gathered together. Many other Bible verses answer the question of where on the Earth the Jewish people will again be united. God revealed through the prophet Ezekiel, amongst others, in the 6ᵗʰ century BC that the Jews would return "to their Land," to "the Land of Israel" in The Last Days.

> Ezekiel 11:17:
> *"¹⁷ Therefore say, 'Thus says the Lord GOD: "I will gather you from the peoples, assemble you from the countries where you have been scattered, and I will give you **the land of Israel**."'*
> (NKJV)

> Ezekiel 36:24:
> *"²⁴ For I will take you from among the nations, gather you out of all countries, and bring you **into your own land**."* (NKJV)

Ezekiel 37:21:
*"²¹ Then say to them, 'Thus says the Lord GOD: "Surely I will take the children of Israel from among the nations, wherever they have gone, and will gather them from every side and bring them **into their own land**; ..."'* (NKJV)

The Jewish dream of a return to the Land of Israel appeared to have been impossible throughout nearly two millennia. Every day – and this over centuries – there has been prayer in Judaism for a return.[22] However, this prayer has been unanswered for a long time. In earlier times, a mass-immigration from all over the world would have meant certain death for many people before they were able to reach their goal. Earlier attempts have shown this often enough. Not until modern times could such an undertaking be at all thinkable, thanks to modern technical achievements in the field of mobility. In the years from 1882 until today, more than 3 million Jews out of approx.130 different countries, from all five continents, have returned to the Land of their Forefathers.[23] According to statistics from 2011, almost 6 million Jews live in the Land of Israel. Today we are eye witnesses of the fulfilment of the ancient Biblical prophecies about the End-Time return home of the Jewish people![24]

## 1.1 Alternatives to the Land of Israel

There were numerous suggestions, plans and offers for the homeless Jews to establish a home somewhere in the world where they would find rest from all persecution. In the past four centuries, there were 17 plans altogether to establish a home for them in the following places (the years in brackets specify the date of each plan):[25]

1. Dutch West Indies (Curacao, 1652)
2. Surinam (1654)

---

22 Cf. the Eighteen Benedictions (*shmoneh 'esreh*), Text in: SIDDUR SHMA QOLENU, p. 57-66.
23 http://www.goisrael.com/Tourism_Eng/Tourist+Information/Discover+Israel/Population.htm (as of: 8.11.2011).
24 NACHRICHTEN AUS ISRAEL, 11/2011, p. 8.
25 GILBERT: Jewish History Atlas, p. 102-103.

3. French West Indies (Cayenne, 1659)
4. South America (1730)
5. on the Mississippi and the Missouri (1819)
6. Asia Minor (modern Turkey, 1820)
7. Grand Island (by the Niagara Falls, 1825)
8. Crimea (1841)
9. Argentina (1892)
10. Cyprus (1880–1902)
11. Kenya (on the Guas Ngishu Plateau, 1903 the so-called "Uganda-Project")
12. Brazil (Recife, 1904)
13. Southern Mesopotamia (modern southern Iraq, 1908–1909)
14. Australia (Melbourne, 1927)
15. Birobidzhan (on the Amur River, between Russia and China, 1928)
16. Madagascar (1940)
17. Vietnam (1946)

If any one of these plans had become reality, the prophetic word of the Bible would not have been fulfilled. Actually the prophecies stating that the Jewish people would be gathered *and brought together* from all over the world would have been fulfilled; however, the statement that there would be a return *to the Land of their Forefathers* would not have been fulfilled. For various reasons, all the different plans came to nothing and were never implemented. In our era, however, Jews from all over the world have found a home *in the Land of Israel*, exactly as it was prophesied in the Bible.

## 1.2 Must all the Jews Return Home?

Time and again we hear the question: Must *all* Jews return to the Land of the Fathers *before* the Messiah comes? From Ezekiel 39:28 it emerges that not until after the return of the Messiah Jesus will the last Jew still scattered among the nations be brought back. Ezekiel 39:21-29 deals with the time when the Messiah will ultimately deliver Israel from all trouble at His coming. It is in this context that the verses 28 and 29 (Ezek. 39) say:

*"28 ... then they shall know that I am the LORD their God, who* **sent them into captivity** *among the nations,* **but also brought them back to their land, and left none of them captive any longer.** *29 And I will not hide My face from them anymore; for I shall have poured out My Spirit on the house of Israel,' says the Lord GOD."* (NKJV)

Matthew 24:29-31 speaks explicitly about the gathering of the "elect," those who will be returned from all over the world to the Promised Land *after* the return of Jesus Christ.

## 1.3 Enemies in the Land

The Bible makes it clear that the Jews would not arrive in an unoccupied country at their return to their land in The Last Days. The prophecy we have already discussed in Lev. 26:31-33 makes it clear that enemies of the Jews would take up residence in the Land of Israel during the time of their dispersion:

*"31 I will lay your cities waste and bring your sanctuaries to desolation, and I will not smell the fragrance of your sweet aromas. 32 I will bring the land to desolation,* **and your enemies who dwell in it** *shall be astonished at it. 33 I will scatter you among the nations and draw out a sword after you; your land shall be desolate and your cities waste."* (NKJV)

The text of Lev. 26:32 states that enemies of the Jews will take the place of the dispersed Jews. The Arabian conquest and colonization of the Land of the Bible began in 636 AD – shortly after Mohammad's death in 632.

The Arabs from the Arabian peninsula, who had become Muslim only shortly before, did not content themselves with the reign of Islam in their country. Immediately following the death of their prophet, they quickly began to Islamize and "Arabize" all of the Middle East and North Africa. This included their expansion into the Jews' Holy Land.[26] The colonization of the Land of Israel by

---

26  The only passage in which the Land of Israel is so named occurs in Zech. 2:12.

Arabian Muslims was an important reason for the expulsion of the Jews from their own country in the centuries following 636 AD.

The Koran contains many verses which characterize the Jews as a people worthy of hatred and abuse.[27] It is on this foundation that anti-Semitism deeply rooted in the Islamic world today is still developing. (For example, let it be noted in this connection that, Hitler's book "Mein Kampf" is still a bestseller in the Arabian world today!) During the modern era Islamically motivated anti-Semitism led to the Middle East conflict in the course of the Jewish re-settlement of the Land of Israel. The conflict was pre-programmed by the fact that *enemies* would live in the Land of Israel.

# 2. Return from all over the World

As the first song in the 5th book of the Psalms, Psalm 107 gives an overview of the entire ways of God with Israel, from the time of the Exodus from Egypt until the reign of the Messiah at the End of Days.[28] The introductory verses 1-3 take the reader into the time of completion, the period of the Messianic kingdom when God will have brought together His scattered people from all over the world – from all four corners – into the Land of Israel. Here Israel is called upon to praise the LORD for kindness expressed in it (Ps. 107):

*"¹ Give ye thanks unto Jehovah; for he is good; for his loving-kindness (endureth) for ever.*
*² Let the redeemed of Jehovah say so, whom he hath redeemed*

---

27  Sura 2,85-86; 2,88-90; 4,160-161; 5,32-34; 5,41; 5,51; 5,64; 9,29-30; 47,4-6. Cf. THIEDE/STING-ELIN: Die Wurzeln des Antisemitismus, p.161ff.

28  A brief outline of Ps. 107:
   · Verse 1-3: praise in the Messianic Kingdom
   · Verse 4-9: desert wandering after the Exodus from Egypt
   · Verse 10-16: freedom from the Babylonian captivity (cf. Isa 44:28-45:7)
   · Verse 17-22: period of the First Coming of the Messiah Jesus (cf. „*He sent His Word ...*" with John 1:1 3,14)
   · Verse 23-32: dispersion of the Jews among all peoples and End-Time return to the desired havens (cf. Isa. 17:11-12: "seas" as picture of the restless people)
   · Verse 33-38: build up of the Land of Israel in The Last Days
   · Verse 39-40: future tribulation of Israel (cf. Matt 24:21)
   · Verse: 41-43: deliverance of Israel by the Messiah and the blessing of the Messianic Kingdom

*from the hand of the oppressor,*
*³ and gathered out of the countries, from the east and from*
*the west, from the north and from the [Red] sea. [i.e. from the*
*south]."* (Darby)

The words from Isaiah 43:5-6 confirm the Psalm verses quoted:
*"⁵ Fear not, for I am with you;*
*I will bring your descendants **from the east**,*
*And gather you **from the west**;*
*⁶ I will say to **the north**, 'Give them up!'*
*And to **the south**, 'Do not keep them back!'*
*Bring My sons from afar ..."* (NKJV)

Zechariah also spoke about the east and the west (Zech. 8:7-8):
*"⁷ Thus says the LORD of hosts:*
*"'Behold, I will save My people from the **land of the east***
*And from **the land of the west**;*
*⁸ I will bring them back,*
*And they shall dwell in the midst of Jerusalem.*
*They shall be My people*
*And I will be their God,*
*In truth and righteousness.'"* (NKJV)

As stated, in the years from 1882 until today, over 3 million Jews out of approx. 130 different countries, on all five continents – yes, even from North, Central and South America, from Africa, Asia and Australia – have returned to the Land of their Forefathers. In the period from 15 May 1947 to 31 December 1951 alone, Jews from 70 different countries immigrated home to Israel, most by ship.

When 130 years of Jewish immigration history is examined, it is clear that we are seeing an absolutely unique phenomenon in world history! There is no parallel to this type of migration of a people in the history of mankind, whether in ancient or in modern times! The prophetic words of Psalm 107:1-3, and of many other verses, have been fulfilled, virtually before our eyes, in this extremely spectacular way. God prophesied this wonderful return through the prophet Ezekiel with the following words:

Ezekiel 36:24:

*"24 For I will take you **from among the nations**, gather you **out of all countries**, and bring you into your own land."* (NKJV)

Ezekiel 11:17:

*"17 Therefore say, 'Thus says the Lord God: "I will gather you **from the peoples**, assemble you **from the countries where you have been scattered**, and I will give you the land of Israel."'* (NKJV)

Please notice how clear the text is. It needs no decoding. This is a millennia-old prophecy in plain language.

# 3. Fishermen and Hunters

In 600 BC it was prophesied in Jeremiah 16:14-16 that the return of the Jews would be characterized by two great phases:

- First, there will be *"a time of many fishermen"* and afterwards *"a time of many hunters."* The End-Time return of the Jews would firstly undergo a preliminary stage, which could be termed an "enticement-phase." In this phase there will be "fishermen" who move the Jews to return to the Holy Land.
- In the next phase, "hunters" will drive the Jews with violence to return home.

Jeremiah 16:14-16:

*"14 Therefore behold, the days are coming," says the Lord, "that it shall no more be said, 'The Lord lives who brought up the children of Israel from the land of Egypt,' 15 but, 'The Lord lives who brought up the children of Israel from the land of the north and from all the lands where He had driven them.' For I will bring them back into their land which I gave to their fathers.
16 Behold, I will send for many **fishermen**," says the Lord, "and they shall **fish** them; and **afterward** I will send for many **hunters**, and they shall **hunt** them from every mountain and every hill, and out of the holes of the rocks."* (NKJV)

The fulfilment of this prophecy occurred in this way: the early Zionist movement emerged in the 18th century. Looking back at the Jewish people's long period of statelessness with constant persecution and ostracism, great thinkers searched for an answer to the Jewish Problem with a return to the Land of their Forefathers. In this context we should mention the following Rabbis: Elijahu Ben Shlomo Zalman[29] (1720–1797; Lithuania), Menachem Mendel of Vitebsk (1730–1788; Russia), Jehuda Salomon Alkalay (1798–1878; Serbia), Zvi Hirsch Kalischer (1795–1874; Germany).

Kalischer even attempted to buy the Land of the Forefathers from Ibrahim Pasha, the king of Egypt, who at that time ruled over a completely devastated Palestine – yet without success.[30]

As important exponents of early Zionism, Mordechai Immanuel Noah (1785–1851), the one-time US Consul in Tunis, as well as Moses Montefiori (1784–1885) must certainly be mentioned.

The latter encouraged the return of the Jews to the Promised Land from 1827 onwards with financial support, by setting industrial and agricultural businesses on their feet.

Also worth mentioning in this context is the socialist Moses Hess (1812–1875). In 1862 he wrote the axiomatic work regarding the return of the Jews ("Rome and Jerusalem").

Later, people such as Leo Pinsker (1821–1891), Theodor Herzl (1860–1904) and Nathan Birnbaum[31] (1864–1937) built their work on the efforts of these early Zionists.

The impact of the great Zionist endeavors to entice the Jews home was, to be honest, disappointingly minimal. Worldwide it was difficult to get the Jews to move, to give up long-established homes and to begin from scratch in the Land of their Fathers, with virtually nothing.

However, after decades of Zionist appeals, came the extremely effective "hunter phase." Tsar Alexander II was murdered in 1881. That a Jewess was among the numerous suspects connected to this assassination was enough to unleash terrible persecution of the Jews in Russia during the years 1881–1884. This led to the flight of

---

29  He is known by the name Gaon Vilna.

30  ARIEL: The Odyssey of the Third Temple, p. 70-71.

31  Birnbaum first used the term "Zionism" in 1886.

thousands of Russian Jews who found refuge in Palestine, as the Land of Israel was called at that time. This was the first wave of Jewish immigration.

This wave gradually came to an end in 1903. However, Jewish persecution in connection with the communist revolution from 1905–1907 brought about momentum in the second wave of immigration, which brought even more Jews to Palestine than the first wave. This ended with the outbreak of the First World War, however.

The October Revolution of 1917 in Russia and persecution in Ukraine gave impetus to the third and fourth waves of immigration. At length, over 100,000 Jews returned to the Land of their Fathers. With Hitler's takeover of power in 1933 a quarter of a million Jews were driven home in connection with the fifth wave of immigration.

Some 650,000 Jews were forced to flee to Israel due to persecution in Arab countries following the founding of the State of Israel in May 1948. We could go on listing more. But it is clear: The main reason for the return of Jews in our time was never Zionism, rather much more pursuit of the Jews. However, Zionism was an important, intellectual preparation for the return brought about by persecution. Jeremiah 16:15 was fulfilled exactly: The drama of the return falls into two main phases:

1. The period of the fishermen (preparation for return through Zionism): 1750–1882
2. The period of the hunters (an effective return due to persecution): 1882 till today

# 4. Return in Numerous Phases

In Psalm 126:4, amongst the fifteen Songs of Ascents, a prayer is found in view of the End-Time return of the Jews:

*"4 Bring back our captivity, O LORD,*
**As the streams [Hebr. nachal] in the South."** (NKJV)

Why does the psalmist compare the return of the Jews from exile with streams, and why especially with streams in the Negev (the South)? Why does he speak of streams in the plural?

To really understand the meaning of the statement in Psalm 126:4, it is important to know the characteristic differences between the streams in the Judean desert and the streams in the Negev.[32] The text of the Psalm speaks specifically of the streams in the Negev (South).

The characteristic landscape of the Negev consists of wide valleys, which lead to innumerable mountain ranges. Valleys such as Nachal Zin, Nachal Paran,[33] Nachal Shikma, Nachal Gaza and Nachal El-Arish[34] are incomparably wider and more rambling than the countless small valleys of the Judean Desert, except for the Arava. In the winter rainy season (October–April), water in the Negev valleys pours forth from many small streams into larger rivers, which in turn release the precious liquid in powerful streams which can sometimes be several hundred metres wide.[35] In contrast to these broad valleys of the Negev, water flows into the narrow valleys of the Judean Desert in *one* raging winter torrent through the landscape.

As the Jews returned from the exile in Babylon in 539/538 BC under Zerubbabel, they resembled a Judean desert stream. It was in *one* more stream that they returned to the Land of their Fathers. When women and children are considered in addition to the approx. 40,000 men, there were well over 200,000 returnees altogether (Ezra 1–2) at that time. Many years later, in 457 BC, a smaller influx of somewhat more than 5,000 persons came under Ezra (Ezra 7–8).[36]

According to Psalm 126, the return in The Last Days will occur in many phases and include intermediate stages, analogous to the many small and large streams in a typical Negev valley.

---

32  REUVENI: Desert and Shepherd in Our Biblical Heritage, pp. 89-90.

33  The water in Nachal Zin and Nachal Paran flows east.

34  The water in Nachal Shikma, Nachal Gaza and Nachal El-Arish flows west.

35  Cf. the allusion to such powerful rivers in Jer. 47:2.

36  In Ezra 8:1-14 some 2,000 men are listed. A projection which includes women and children gives somewhat more than 5,000 people.

Today we can look back over 130 years of modern Jewish immigration. Prophecy has been fulfilled exactly, just as it was presented millennia ago in Psalm 126. There has not been a return in *one* great flood. In fact its entire history occurred in numerous and various phases. The course of the Jews' return to the Land of their Forefathers is divided into a series of epochs in modern historiography. Various "waves of immigration" are distinguished (Hebr. "Aliyot").[37]

Following is a complete overview of all Aliya periods until the present day:[38]

- **1st Aliya (1882–1903):** approx. 25,000 Jews from Russia; ca. 1,000 Jews from Yemen[39]
- **2nd Aliya (1904–1914):** approx. 40,000 Jews mainly from Russia, but also from Poland[40]
- **3rd Aliya (1919–1923):** approx. 35,000,[41] mainly from Russia (53%), but also from Lithuania and Romania (36%). The rest came from other East European countries, except for 800 people who emigrated from Western Europe
- **4th Aliya (1924–1931):** approx. 80,000 from Poland (ca. 50%) and from the Soviet Union, Lithuania and Romania (ca. 50%)[42]
- **5th Aliya (1932–1938):** following Hitler's take-over of power: approx. 250,000 Jews, primarily refugees from Nazi Germany, Poland and Central Europe[43]
- **Aliya B (1934–1947):**[44] so-called "illegal" immigrants before, during and after the Second World War, in spite of massive British obstacles
- **Mass immigration from all over the world (1948–2012):** Return of some 2.7 million Jews from ca. 130 different coun-

---

37 *'aliyot* = pl. of *'aliya* (literally 'immigration').

38 HIRSCH: Israel von A-Z, p. 50-51; www.mfa.gov.il/MFA/MFAArchive/2000_2009/2001/8/Aliya (as of: 24.10.2011); http://en.wikipedia.org/wiki/Aliyah (as of: 24.10.2011).

39 http://en.wikipedia.org/wiki/Yemenite_Jews (as of: 25.10.2011).

40 http://www.goisrael.com/Tourism_Eng/Tourist+Information/Discover+Israel/Population.htm (as of: 8.11.2011); RANDALL: Fast Facts on the Middle East Conflict, p. 20.

41 http://de.wikipedia.org/wiki/Alija (as of: 10.11.2011).

42 http://en.wikipedia.org/wiki/Fourth_Aliyah (as of: 10.11.2011).

43 http://de.wikipedia.org/wiki/Alija (as of: 10.11.2011).

44 "Aliya B" denotes illegal immigration in contrast to legal immigration, called "Aliya A." This clarifies the time period over-lap of the Aliya B-Epoch with the 5th Aliya.

tries, from all five continents:[45]

- 1948–1957: Mass immigration from Arab countries around Israel: ca. 650,000 Jews
- 1948–1970: *Mass return from Europe*: 557,314 Jews. Most were victims of Nazi persecution who had lost family and homes.[46]
- 1984–1985: *Operation Moses*: 8,000 –11,000 Ethiopian Jews come to Israel.[47]
- 1985: *Operation Saba*: 1,000 Ethiopian Jews flown out[48]
- 1989: Mass immigration from Soviet Union/CIS: more than 1 million
- 1991: *Operation Salomon*: 14,000 Ethiopian Jews return home.[49]
- Year by year until today: Thousands come home from all over the world.[50]

---

45  In the period from 15 May 1947 till 31 December 1951 alone, Jews immigrated from 70 different countries home to the Land of their Forefathers, incidentally most by ship.

46  GILBERT: The Arab-Israeli Conflict, p. 49.

47  MAI: Von Saba nach Zion, p. 73.

48  MAI: Von Saba nach Zion, pp. 75-76.

49  MAI: Von Saba nach Zion, p. 91 and 93.

50  See the yearly immigration statistics: http://jewishagency.org/JewishAgency/English/About/Press+Room/Aliyah+Statistics (as of: 10.11.2011).

# Gathering in many phases:
# Like the wadi streams in the Negev

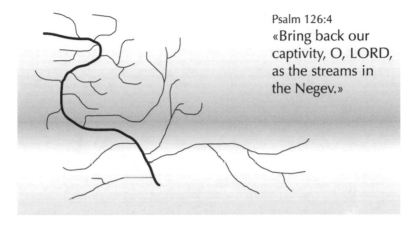

Psalm 126:4
«Bring back our captivity, O, LORD, as the streams in the Negev.»

**Fig. 7:** *The End-Time return of the Jews would resemble the picture of a stream in the Negev with many separate phases and occur with stops along the way.*

# 5. Return from the North

In contrast to the single return from Babylonian captivity in 539/538 BC, the Jewish people, in The Last Days, will return to Israel from all four corners of the Earth. In Psalm 107:1-3 Israel is summoned to praise God in the future End-Time Messianic Kingdom for gathering the Jews from all over the world, from all points of the compass:

> *"¹ Give ye thanks unto Jehovah; for he is good;*
> *for his loving-kindness (endureth) for ever.*
> *² Let the redeemed of Jehovah say so,*
> *whom he hath redeemed from the hand of the oppressor,*
> *³and gathered out of the countries, from the east and from the west,*
> ***from the north*** *and from the [Red] sea." (Darby)*

**Fig. 8:** *The Jewish return from the north has played a very crucial role in the past 130 years (source: CIA).*

Even though the Bible expressly names all four geographic directions in connection with the End-Time return of the Jews, the "land of the north" or very generally "the north" will play a very special role.

Jeremiah prophesied (c. 600 BC), that the End-Time event of the return of the Jews from the Land of the North and from all other countries would surpass the salvation-historical significance of the Exodus of the Israelites from Egypt under Moses (1606 BC). If earlier they had sworn by the living God who had exemplarily demonstrated His work in the history of mankind by the Exodus of the Israelites from Egypt, then in The Last Days, they would invoke the God who will have returned the Jews from all over the world to the Land their Forefathers (Jer. 16:14-15):

> *"14 Therefore behold, the days are coming," says the LORD, "that it shall no more be said, 'The LORD lives who brought up the children of Israel from the land of Egypt,' 15 but, 'The LORD lives who brought up the children of Israel **from the land of the north** and from all the lands where He had driven them.' For I will bring them back into their land which I gave to their fathers." (NKJV)*

Compare the parallel in Jeremiah 23:7-8
> *"7 Therefore, behold, the days are coming," says the LORD, "that they shall no longer say, 'As the LORD lives who brought up the children of Israel from the land of Egypt,' 8 but, 'As the LORD lives who brought up and led the descendants of the house of Israel **from the north country** and from all the countries where I had driven them.' And they shall dwell in their own land." (NKJV)*

Furthermore in Jeremiah 3:18
> *"18 In those days the house of Judah shall walk with the house of Israel, and they shall come together **out of the land of the north** to the land that I have given as an inheritance to your fathers." (NKJV)*

The prophet Isaiah (c. 700 BC) repeatedly mentions the return from the north in his prophecies (Isaiah 49:12):

*"12 Surely these shall come from afar;*
*Look! Those from **the north** and the west,*
*And these from the land of Sinim."* (NKJV)

Isaiah 43:5-7:
*"5 Fear not, for I am with you;*
*I will bring your descendants from the east,*
*And gather you from the west;*
*6 I will say to the **north**, 'Give them up!'*
*And to the south, 'Do not keep them back!'*
*Bring My sons from afar,*
*And My daughters from the ends of the earth—*
*7 Everyone who is called by My name,*
*Whom I have created for My glory;*
*I have formed him, yes, I have made him."* (NKJV)

Seen from Israel, Lebanon, Syria and Turkey are also countries in the north. Directly following the founding of the State of Israel in 1948, 4,000 Jews immigrated from Lebanon and 9,500 Jews from Syria.[51] Up to the present day over 62,000 Jews have come to Israel from Turkey.[52]

Jeremiah stresses that the return from the north will be accomplished even to "the ends of the earth" and in exceptionally great numbers (Jer. 31:8):

*"8 Behold, I will bring them **from the north country**,*
*And gather them from the ends of the earth,*
*Among them the blind and the lame,*
*The woman with child*
*And the one who labors with child, together;*
***A great throng** shall return there. "* (NKJV)

---

51 http://en.wikipedia.org/wiki/Aliyah (as of: 9.11.2011).
52 http://en.wikipedia.org/wiki/Aliyah (as of: 9.11.2011).

This verse was fulfilled in connection with the return of the Jews from Russia or, as the case may be, from the territories of the former Soviet Union.

As already stated, the course of the return of the Jews to the Land of their Forefathers is divided into a series of periods in modern historiography. Various waves of immigration are distinguished. In studying this, it is notable that Russia, or the Soviet Union, or the CIS, plays a very prominent role in this context as the "country in the far north," as seen from Israel:[53]

- The gathering of Jews from the entire world began in the "Land of the North."
- The first decades were characterized by Jews returning "from the north," from Russia and Poland.

The four first Aliyot (1882–1932) have already been dealt with. However, let us mention them again in this context, together with later waves:

- 1st wave (1882 –1903): ca. 25,000 Jews from Russia
- 2nd wave (1904–1914): ca. 40,000 Jews mainly from Russia, but also from Poland
- 3rd wave (1919–1923): ca. 35,000, mainly from Russia (53%), but also from Lithuania and Romania (36%). The rest came from other East European countries, except for 800 people who came from Western Europe.
- 4th wave (1924–1931): ca. 80,000 from Poland, the Soviet Union, Lithuania and Romania
- In the 1970s the Soviet Union allowed emigration to Israel. From 1971–1979 over 100,000 Soviet Jews reached Israel.[54]
- From 1989: With the break-up of the former Soviet Union, an evil prison was unlocked for a large part of world Jewry. It resulted in a great wave with some 1 million immigrants returning to Israel from this area.[55]

---

53 HIRSCH: Israel von A-Z, p. 49-52.

54 http://en.wikipedia.org/wiki/Aliyah (as of: 10.11.2011).

55 There were also those who were not Jewish, but wished to flee decades' long repression using falsified identity papers. Naturally, this was the minority. The greater mass of this more than 1 million people are true Jews.

And so it is clear: "The north" or the "Land of the North" at the "ends of the earth" (Jer. 31:8) has continually played a very outstanding role during the whole Last Days period of just 130 years! The Jews, particularly from the far north, came in overwhelming numbers back to Israel (cf. Jer. 31:8: "a great throng"). More than a third of all immigrant Jews – namely some 1.3 million - came from there.[56]

Additionally, it is very interesting to see that the capital of this "north country" at the "uttermost ends of the earth" (Russia/Soviet Union; Jer. 31:8) even lies approximately on the same longitude as Israel's capital Jerusalem:

- Moscow 37.5°
- Jerusalem 35.2°

# 6. Flight from the North

The return of Jews from the entire world resembles an avalanche which has got ever bigger, until finally, over 3 million people from all five continents have immigrated to Israel. The beginning was the 1st Aliya of 1882–1903, when 25,000 Jews left Russia as a result of the anti-Semitic persecution under Czar Alexander III in 1881–1884.

As the flow of immigrants from the 1st Aliya almost came to an end, persecution began anew in Russia. This was the motivation for the 2nd Aliya (1904–1919) which brought back many thousands of refugees to the Land of their Fathers.

The 3rd Aliya brought numerous refugees from the north to the Jews' homeland: This was especially instigated by the Russian Revolution of 1917 and the post-war persecution in the Ukraine.

Zechariah had already spoken prophetically about this wave of refugees from the Land of the North in 520 BC (Zech. 2:6):

*"6 Up, up! Flee from the land of the north," says the LORD; "for I have spread you abroad like the four winds of heaven," says the LORD."* (NKJV)

---

56 http://en.wikipedia.org/wiki/Aliyah ; http://jewishagency.org/JewishAgency/English/About/ Press+Room/Aliyah+Statistics/nov30.htm (10.11.2011).

Let us read this precisely: The text speaks of God's plan at one time to scatter the Jews to all four corners of the Earth, and then calls on them to return later as refugees from the north!

# 7. Return from the Islamic Countries Surrounding Israel

The founding of the State of Israel on 14 May 1948 worked like a magnet on the Jewish community in the Arab countries around Israel. A mass-movement was set in motion. The repressive measures and pogroms against the Jews in these countries proved to be a very decisive impetus for this exodus. Islamic hostility against the Jewish minority in these countries began anew exactly at the time of the founding of the State of Israel. There was widespread persecution and expulsion. Frequently the Jews were robbed of their homes and other possessions by the governments, so that many returned to the Land of Promise completely destitute. However, in Israel they were speedily and fully integrated into the community. In the years following May 1948, hundreds of thousands of Jews reached Israel from the Arab and Islamic countries of the Middle East and North Africa:[57]

* Morocco: 270,000[58]
* Algeria: 26,000[59]
* Tunisia: 54,000[60]
* Libya: 37,000[61]
* Egypt: 37,600[62]
* Lebanon: 4,000[63]

---

57 CARTA-REDAKTION/AUMANN: Geschichte Israels, p. 33.
58 GILBERT: The Arab-Israeli Conflict, Its History in Maps, p. 48; http://en.wikipedia.org/wiki/Aliyah (as of: 9.11.2011).
59 http://en.wikipedia.org/wiki/Aliyah (as of: 9.11.2011).
60 http://en.wikipedia.org/wiki/Aliyah (as of: 9.11.2011).
61 http://en.wikipedia.org/wiki/Jewish_exodus_from_Arab_lands ; http://en.wikipedia.org/wiki/Aliyah (as of: 9.11.2011).
62 http://en.wikipedia.org/wiki/Aliyah (as of: 24.10.2011).
63 http://en.wikipedia.org/wiki/Aliyah (as of: 9.11.2011).

- Syria: 9,500[64]
- Iraq: 150,000[65]
- Yemen: 51,000[66]
- Aden: 6,500[67]
- Iran: 100,000[68]

The exact numbers of Jewish immigrants vary somewhat in the literature on the subject. But what is important, is to have an idea of the scale.

The prophetic word in Ezekiel 37:21 was fulfilled by the return of the Jews from Egypt, Lebanon, Syria, and from somewhat more distant surroundings:

*"²¹ Then say to them, 'Thus says the Lord GOD: "Surely I will take the children of Israel from among the nations, wherever they have gone, and will **gather them from every side** and bring them into their own land; ..."* (NKJV)

Until the founding of the State of Israel in 1948, there were some 900,000 Jews in the Arab countries. Because of serious persecution beginning at this time, 99% of all Jews in these countries emigrated, often with huge material loss. The greater part – some 650,000 – of these Arabian Jews found a new and permanent home in Israel.[69]

---

64 http://en.wikipedia.org/wiki/Aliyah (as of: 9.11.2011).

65 HILLEL: Operation Babylon, p. 329 and passim.

66 http://en.wikipedia.org/wiki/Aliyah (as of: 9.11.2011); GILBERT: Jewish History Atlas, p. 106.

67 GILBERT: Jewish History Atlas, p. 106.

68 http://he.wikipedia.org/wiki/%D7%99%D7%94%D7%93%D7%95%D7%AA_%D7%90%D7%99%D7%A8%D7%90%D7%9F (as of: 24.10.2011).

69 http://en.wikipedia.org/wiki/Jewish_exodus_from_Arab_lands (as of: 24.10.2011).

# 8. Return from Northern and Southern Iraq

The detailed geographical information in Isaiah 11:11-12 is especially notable in relationship to the Jews' return from the Arab countries. We will first focus on the terms "Assyria" and "Shinar" (Isaiah 11):

> *"¹¹ It shall come to pass in that day*
> *That the Lord shall set His hand again the second time*
> *To recover the remnant of His people who are left,*
> ***From Assyria** and Egypt,*
> *From Pathros and Cush,*
> *From Elam and **Shinar**,*
> *From Hamath and the islands of the sea.*
> *¹² He will set up a banner for the nations,*
> *And will assemble the outcasts of Israel,*
> *And gather together the dispersed of Judah*
> *From the four corners of the earth."* (NKJV)

The names "Assyria" and "Shinar" refer to the area of modern Iraq. The nucleus of ancient Assyria, with the ancient cities of Nineveh, Ashura and Kalach is located in modern northern Iraq. The term "Shinar" describes the area of ancient Babylon (cf. Gen. 11:2; Isa. 11:11; Dan. 1:2) in modern southern Iraq where the famous cities Babel, Erech and Akkad used to be located.[70] In the Bible, this area was called "Land of the Chaldeans" (Jer. 50:8).

Practically all Jews, ca. 150,000 people, left Iraq between 1941 and 1991.[71] They left both the Assyrian area of northern Iraq[72] as well as the Babylonian area of southern Iraq.[73]

Thus various passages from Jeremiah 50–51 were fulfilled. These chapters deal with Babylon's Last Days. We will deal at length with

---

[70] The Hebrew name *shin'ar* corresponds to the cuneiform term *shanhar* in the texts of the Hittite and Syrian scribal schools of the 2nd century BC (WISEMAN: Shinar).

[71] Cf. HILLEL: Operation Babylon.

[72] Cf. here also Zech. 10:10.

[73] GILBERT: Jewish History Atlas, p. 109 (Identification of Jewish cities in northern and southern Iraq).

this in Chapter IV of this book.

In Jeremiah 50–51 God appealed to His people Israel to leave Babylon without fail in The Last Days:

Jeremiah 50:8:
*"⁸ Move **from the midst of Babylon,***
*Go out of the land of the Chaldeans; ..."* (NKJV)

Jeremiah 51:6:
*"⁶ Flee **from the midst of Babylon,***
*And every one save his life!*
*Do not be cut off in her iniquity,*
*For this is the time of the LORD's vengeance;*
*He shall recompense her."* (NKJV)

Jeremiah 51:45:
*"⁴⁵ My people, go out **of the midst of her [i.e. out of Babylon]***!
*And let everyone deliver himself from the fierce anger of the LORD."* (NKJV)

The prophet Zechariah, with prophetic insistence, summoned his people (whom he identified with Zion, the royal seat in Jerusalem, in contrast to the city of Babylon) to leave Babylonia (Zech. 2:7):

*"⁷ Up, Zion! Escape, you who dwell with the daughter of Babylon."* (NKJV)

Zechariah also spoke about an End-Time return of the Jews from Assyrian northern Iraq (Zech. 10:10):

*"¹⁰ I will also bring them back from the land of Egypt,*
*And gather them **from Assyria**.*
*I will bring them into the land of Gilead and Lebanon,*
*Until no more room is found for them."* (NKJV)

# 9. Return from Upper and Lower Egypt

Next, we will look at the words "Mizrayim" and "Pathros" in Isaiah 11:11:

> *"¹¹ It shall come to pass in that day*
> *That the Lord shall set His hand again the second time*
> *To recover the remnant of His people who are left,*
> *From Assyria and **Egypt [Mizrayim]**,*
> ***From Pathros** and Cush,*
> *From Elam and Shinar,*
> *From Hamath and the islands of the sea."* (NKJV)

The geographical term "Pathros" corresponds to the Egyptian word *p't'-rs* (read: *peteres*), which means something like "the southern land."[74] It identifies the area of Upper Egypt, in other words, the Nile Valley, which stretches in a north-south direction between Cairo and Aswan.

"Mizrayim" is the normal Hebrew designation for Egypt, especially for "Lower Egypt."[75]

When the words "Mizrayim" and "Pathros" appear as a pair in a text, such as in the verse from Isaiah quoted above, "Mizrayim" denotes Lower Egypt.

Isaiah 11:11 states that Jews would emigrate to Israel from Upper as well as from Lower Egypt.

"Lower Egypt" designates the Egyptian area from Cairo northwards. "Upper Egypt" is the area south of Cairo.

Most of the 75,000–80,000 Jews living in Egypt in 1948[76] resided in Cairo and Alexandria. However, it is worth mentioning the following towns in which Jewish population made up thriving communities in 20th century Egypt:[77]

- Lower Egypt: Damanhur, Damietta, Port Said, Mansoura,

---

74 KÖHLER/BAUMGARTNER: Hebräisches und aramäische Lexikon zum Alten Testament, III, p. 930.

75 GESENIUS/BUHL: Hebräisches und Aramäisches Wörterbuch zum Alten Testament, p. 454.
KÖHLER/ BAUMGARTNER: Hebräisches und aramäische Lexikon zum Alten Testament, IV, p. 591.

76 http://zionismus.info/antizionismus/arabisch-7.htm; http://www.sephardicgen.com/egypt_sites.htm (as of: 8.11.2011).

77 GILBERT: Jewish History Atlas, p. 114.

Zifta, Benha, Mahalla, Kubra, Tanta
• Upper Egypt: Faiyum, Beni Suef, Minya, Aswan and Qena

The prophecy of Isaiah 11:11-12 was fulfilled when, beginning in 1948, practically all Egyptian Jews left the Land of the Pharaohs.[78] They left their homes in "Mizrayim" (Lower Egypt) as well as "Pathros" (Upper Egypt) behind. In the Land of the Nile terrible persecution of the Jews, with massacres, internment, expulsion and awful indignities[79] followed the founding of the modern State of Israel. This all led to a modern exodus from Egypt. Today, there are only a few dozen Jews in Egypt. These are mainly old people. They will die out soon.[80]

The Exodus under Moses occurred in 1606 BC when the ETERNAL ONE freed Israel with "a strong hand" from slavery in Egypt (Exodus 13:3). In referring to this, Isaiah stated in 700 BC concerning the Messianic period mentioned in 11:11, "That the Lord shall set His hand again the second time" to free his people from Egypt! Part of these 75,000–80,000 Jews found refuge in various countries such as Brazil, Argentina, France and USA. The country which absorbed the most Egyptian Jews – some 37,600[81] altogether – was Israel.[82]

Incidentally, the prophet Zechariah also spoke about an End-Time return of the Jews from Egypt (Zech. 10:10):

*"[10] I will also **bring them back from the land of Egypt**,*
*And gather them from Assyria.*
*I will bring them into the land of Gilead and Lebanon,*
*Until no more room is found for them." (NKJV)*

---

78 http://www.jewishvirtuallibrary.org/jsource/anti-semitism/egjews.html (as of: 24.10.2011); http://www.jewsofegyptfoundation.com/index.php/Jewish-Presence-in-Egypt.html (as of: 24.10.2011).

79 GILBERT: Jewish History Atlas, p. 114.

80 http://www.jewsofegyptfoundation.com/index.php/Jewish-Presence-in-Egypt.html (as of: 24.10.2011).

81 http://en.wikipedia.org/wiki/Aliyah (as of: 24.10.2011).

82 http://en.wikipedia.org/wiki/History_of_the_Jews_in_Egypt (as of: 24.10.2011); GILBERT: The Arab-Israeli Conflict, Its History in Maps, p. 48.

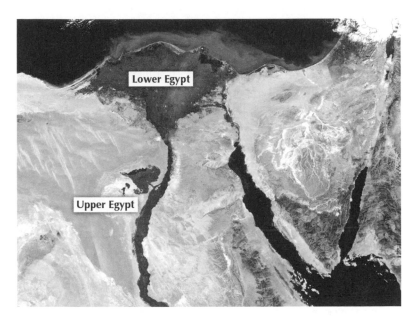

*Fig. 9: Upper and Lower Egypt (source: NASA).*

# 10. Return from Iran

The gathering from "Elam" is also mentioned in Isaiah 11:11:

> *"[11] It shall come to pass in that day*
> *That the Lord shall set His hand again the second time*
> *To recover the remnant of His people who are left,*
> *From Assyria and Egypt,*
> *From Pathros and Cush,*
> ***From Elam** and Shinar,*
> *From Hamath and the islands of the sea."* (NKJV)

"Elam" designates the large area of an ancient oriental kingdom in the south-west of modern Iran.[83] It lay north of the Persian Gulf

---

[83] KÖHLER/BAUMGARTNER: Hebräisches und aramäische Lexikon zum Alten Testament, III, p. 772-773.

and east of the Tigris River. Susa, the one-time capital and winter residence of the king of the Persian Empire, was in Elam.

It is clear that Isaiah foretold the return of Persian Jews in the verse quoted above. Around 70,000 Jews left Iran (Persia) in the years of 1948–1978.[84] Tens of thousands more fled this country in dramatic circumstances following the Islamic Revolution of 1979.

Altogether, in the 20th century, some 100,000 Jews emigrated from Iran and found a new home in Israel.[85]

# 11. Return from Syria

Before we grapple with the return of the Jews from "Cush," we will turn to the geographical term "Hamath" in Isaiah 11:11:

> *"[11] It shall come to pass in that day*
> *That the Lord shall set His hand again the second time*
> *To recover the remnant of His people who are left,*
> *From Assyria and Egypt,*
> *From Pathros and Cush,*
> *From Elam and Shinar,*
> ***From Hamath** and the islands [Iyim] of the sea."* (NKJV)

The name "Hamath" refers to both the present-day city "Hama" on the Orontes River, as well as the land in northern Syria, which was once ruled by this city, surrounding it in a wide radius.[86]

Since the name "Hamath" is mentioned in Isaiah 11:11 together with a list of *countries* rather than cities, it is easy to see that, in this context, the prophet meant the *country* of "Hamath" and not the city.

Therefore, it is clear that Isaiah was refering to the area of modern Syria with his use of the term Hamath. The End-Time return of Syrian Jews was announced in 11:11 of his scroll.

---

84  http://www.jewishvirtuallibrary.org/jsource/anti-semitism/iranjews.html (as of: 24.10.2011); http://en.wikipedia.org/wiki/History_of_the_Jews_in_Iran (as of: 24.10.2011); GILBERT: Jewish History Atlas, p. 106.

85  http://he.wikipedia.org/wiki/%D7%99%D7%94%D7%93%D7%95%D7%AA_%D7%90%D7%99%D7%A8%D7%90%D7%9F (as of: 24.10.2011).

86  BROWN/DRIVER/BRIGGS: The Brown-Driver-Briggs Hebrew and English Lexicon, p. 333.

Already in 1900, a community of Syrian Jews returned to the Land of their Forefathers and took up residence in Jerusalem.[87]

In 1947 there was a Jewish community of some 30,000 people in Syria.[88] Following the UN Resolution of 29 November of that year, there began an atrocious persecution of the Jews.[89] Hundreds of Jews were murdered. More than 200 houses, businesses and synagogues were destroyed. Some 15,000 fled the country, 5,000 to Israel and 10,000 to the USA.[90] In the following decades, the Syrian Jews were cruelly suppressed, afflicted and used as political hostages.[91]

Thousands of Jews left the country secretly in the following years.[92] Judy Feld Carr, a Canadian-Jewish musician and mother of six, managed to build up a highly secret network through which she was able to smuggle out more than 3,000 Jews from Syria by paying ransoms.[93]

In 1958 there were still some 5,000 Jews in Syria; ten years later the number was 4,000.[94] In 1976/1977 there was a relaxation of restrictions. Under certain conditions it was possible for some to leave the country.

As a result of strong pressure put on Syria by the US during the Madrid Peace Conference, all Jews who wished to do so were allowed to leave the country.[95] In the end, 1,262 people came to Israel through this open door at that time. The number of Jews who remain in Syria to this day is about 100.[96]

Altogether some 9,500 Jews from Syria have immigrated to Israel since 1948.[97]

---

87  http://en.wikipedia.org/wiki/Syrian_Jews (as of: 8.11.2011).

88  http://www.zionismus.info/antizionismus/arabisch-7.htm (as of: 8.11.2011).

89  http://www.zionismus.info/antizionismus/arabisch-7.htm (as of: 8.11.2011).

90  http://www.jewishvirtuallibrary.org/jsource/History/jewref.html (as of: 8.11.2011).

91  http://www.zionismus.info/antizionismus/arabisch-7.htm (as of: 8.11.2011).

92  http://en.wikipedia.org/wiki/Jewish_exodus_from_Arab_and_Muslim_countries (as of: 8.11.2011).

93  http://en.wikipedia.org/wiki/Judy_Feld_Carr ; http://www.jewishtoronto.com/page.aspx?id=52877 (as of: 8.11.2011).

94  http://www.zionismus.info/antizionismus/arabisch-7.htm (as of: 8.11.2011).

95  http://www.zionismus.info/antizionismus/arabisch-7.htm (as of: 8.11.2011).

96  http://www.zionismus.info/antizionismus/arabisch-7.htm (as of: 24.10.2011).

97  http://en.wikipedia.org/wiki/Aliyah (as of: 9.11.2011).

# 12. Return from the South: Yemen, Aden, Ethiopia and Sudan

As already discussed, the first song in the 5th book of Psalms, Psalm 107, gives an overview of all God's dealings with Israel, from the time of the Exodus from Egypt until the reign of the Messiah at the End of Days. The introductory verses 1-3 bring the reader into the time of consummation, the time of the Messianic Kingdom, when God will have brought His scattered people – from all four corners of the Earth – back to the Land of Israel. Israel is called upon to praise the LORD for the coming goodness expressed here (Psalm 107):

> *"¹ Give ye thanks unto Jehovah; for he is good; for his loving-kindness [endureth] for ever.*
> *² Let the redeemed of Jehovah say so, whom he hath redeemed from the hand of the oppressor,*
> *³ And gathered **out of the countries**, from the east and from the west, from the north and **from the [Red] sea**."* (Darby)

The alert Bible reader realises here that the Red Sea in this passage stands for the southern direction alongside the explicit reference to "east", "west" and "north". The conclusion of Psalm 107:3 has been fulfilled exactly in connection with the return of the Jews from *Yemen, Aden and Ethiopia* – countries neighbouring the Red Sea.

## 12.1 Return from Yemen, Aden, Djibouti and Eritrea

During the years 1881–1914 more than 1,000 Yemeni Jews immigrated from the southern tip of the Arabian peninsula to "Palestine," as the Land of Israel was called at that time.[98] Even today, in the Silwan district of East Jerusalem, the caves can be seen in which the Yemeni Jews made their homes in the most primitive and pitiable circumstances during the period of the First Aliya. It

---

98 http://en.wikipedia.org/wiki/Yemenite_Jews (as of: 24.10.2011); http://en.wikipedia.org/wiki/Operation_Magic_Carpet_%28Yemen%29 (as of: 24.10.2011).

was obvious where their priorities lay: the most important thing was to be in the Land of Promise!

Persecution broke out against the Jews in Yemen following the founding of the State of Israel. In a strictly secret operation between June 1949 and September 1950, almost the entire Jewish community of Yemen, some 49,000 people, were flown in 378 flights to the Land of their Forefathers.[99] Additionally, some 6,500 Jews were flown from Aden to Israel.[100] Some 500 Jews from Djibouti and from Eritrea were also brought to the Promised Land in this operation.[101] This sensational rescue was conducted with help from American and British transport aircraft.

It is striking that all these countries, Yemen, Aden, Djibouti and Eritrea, border the Red Sea. Psalm 107 has been literally fulfilled, since they came out of the countries of the Red Sea:

*"3 ... and gathered **out of the countries**,*
*... from the north and **from the [Red] sea.**"* (Darby)

## 12.2 Return from Sudan and from Ethiopia

The return of thousands of Jews from Ethiopia and Sudan was no less spectacular:

During the 20th century Ethiopian Jews experienced terrible persecution and suppression. Beginning in 1977, a great number of Jews from Ethiopia crossed the border into Sudan under extremely dangerous conditions. "Operation Moses" began on 21 November 1981[102] and ended on 5 January 1985. Jewish refugees were brought by bus from the Sudanese refugee camps to a military airport close to Khartoum. Some 8,000 to 11,000 Jews[103] were flown out of the region in a strictly secret mission. This rescue was revealed to the media through an indiscretion, leading to a premature abortion of the operation. The Arab world responded with outrage upon learning about this evacuation.

99  http://www.jewishvirtuallibrary.org/jsource/anti-semitism/yemenjews.html (as of: 24.10.2011);

100  GILBERT: Jewish History Atlas, p. 106.

101  http://de.wikipedia.org/wiki/Operation_Magic_Carpet_%28Jemen%29 (as of: 6.9.2007).

102  http://en.wikipedia.org/wiki/Operation_Moses (as of: 24.10.2011).

103  MAI: Von Saba nach Zion, p. 73.

The Arab League condemning it as "an act of piracy and racial discrimination."

In spite of this opposition from the Islamic world, the USA secretly negotiated with Khartoum to bring the remaining Ethiopian Jews out of Sudan. A new rescue action, code-named "Operation Saba," flew ca. 1,000 Jews out of Sudan to the Promised Land during the night of 28 May, using 6 Turbo-prop machines, type 130C from the US Air Force base near Frankfurt, Germany.[104]

In 1991, Eritrean and Tigrinya rebels took control of Addis Ababa. The ruler, Mengistu Haile Mariam, had to flee. In this situation "Operation Salomon" began on 24 May. 36 Hercules c-130s of the ELAL transported more than 14,000 Jews out of Ethiopia within 36 hours. In order to make full use of the capacity, the seats were removed from the planes. At times there were up to 28 airplanes in the air. The flight route took its course so that not one single Arab country was flown over. Inevitably the journey proceeded for the most part over the Red Sea, as it had been with the Jews from Yemen and Aden![105]

Thus Isaiah's prophecy about the return of the Jews from the Land of "Cush" has been most strikingly fulfilled (Isa. 11:11-12):

> *"[11] It shall come to pass in that day*
> *That the Lord shall set His hand again the second time*
> *To recover the remnant of His people who are left,*
> *From Assyria and Egypt,*
> *From Pathros and **Cush**,*
> *From Elam and Shinar,*
> *From Hamath and the islands [Iyim] of the sea.*
> *[12] He will set up a banner for the nations,*
> *And will assemble the outcasts of Israel,*
> *And gather together the dispersed of Judah*
> *From the four corners of the earth." (NKJV)*

---

104  MAI: Von Saba nach Zion, p. 75-76.
105  MAI: Von Saba nach Zion, p. 91 and 93.

The geographical name "Cush" designates the area south of Egypt, especially the country known today as *Sudan* (northern and southern Sudan), but also in an extended sense Ethiopia.[106] More than 84,000 Ethiopian Jews have reached the Promised Land since 1948.[107] Today more than 100,000 Jews with roots in the Land of Cush live in Israel.[108]

# 13. Return from Europe

We have not yet spoken about one of the geographical descriptions in Isaiah 11:11-12:

*"[11] It shall come to pass in that day*
*That the Lord shall set His hand again the second time*
*To recover the remnant of His people who are left,*
*From Assyria and Egypt,*
*From Pathros and Cush,*
*From Elam and Shinar,*
*From Hamath and **the islands [Iyim] of the sea.***
*[12] He will set up a banner for the nations,*
*And will assemble the outcasts of Israel,*
*And gather together the dispersed of Judah*
*From the four corners of the earth."* (NKJV)

The Hebrew word *'iyim*, translated "islands" in the text of Isaiah 11:11, deals with an extremely interesting geographical term. The scholars Carl Friedrich Keil and Franz Delitzsch were among the greatest specialists in Biblical Hebrew during the 19th century. In their multi-volume commentary on the entire OT, they clarify that the Hebrew term *'iyim* designates especially "the islands and costal lands of the Mediterranean on the European side, from Asia

---

106  KÖHLER/BAUMGARTNER: Hebräisches und aramäische Lexikon zum Alten Testament, Vol. II, p. 445.

107  http://www.jafi.org.il/JewishAgency/English/About/Press+Room/Aliyah+Statistics/jul27.htm (as of: 9.11.2011).

108  http://de.wikipedia.org/wiki/%C3%84thiopische_Juden (as of: 8.11.2011).

Minor to Spain."[109] Therefore, it can be said that the geographical term "Iyim" is an Old Testament word for "Europe!"

Hitler's take-over of power set the 5th wave of immigration in motion in which 250,000 Jews, mostly from Germany, returned to the Land of their Forefathers. During Aliya B (the 6th so-called illegal wave of immigration from 1939–1947), thousands of Jews from Europe managed to reach their home, in spite of massive barriers set up by the British government in "Palestine."

During the years 1948–2006 the return of around 700,000 Jews from Europe occurred. In the early period of this epoch many were victims of Nazi persecution who had lost homes and family:[110]

- Poland: 172,881
- Czechoslovakia: 24,256
- Romania: 275,856
- Bulgaria: 44,000
- Hungary: 31,350
- Yugoslavia or the former Yugoslavia: 10,594
- Austria: 4,120
- Germany: 19,136
- Switzerland: 3,706
- Italy: 4,589
- France: 40,601
- England: 29,101
- Belgium: 4,573
- Holland: 6,639
- Scandinavia: 4,364
- Spain: 1,604
- Greece: 3,936

In the same time period, over 62,000 Jews from Turkey, i.e. Asia Minor (which also belongs to the term "Iyim") reached the Land of Israel.[111]

---

109  KEIL/DELITZSCH: KEIL, C.F. /DELITZSCH, F.: Commentar über das Alte Testament, Erster Teil: Die fünf Bücher Moses, Vol. I: Genesis und Exodus, p. 134.

110  http://en.wikipedia.org/wiki/Aliyah#cite_note-29 ; http://www.cbs.gov.il/shnaton58/download/st04_04.xls (as of: 10.11.2011).

111  http://en.wikipedia.org/wiki/Aliyah (as of: 9.11.2011).

To date the figures given above have risen considerably higher. The numbers in each case can be seen at the homepage of the Israeli Central Bureau for Statistics.[112]

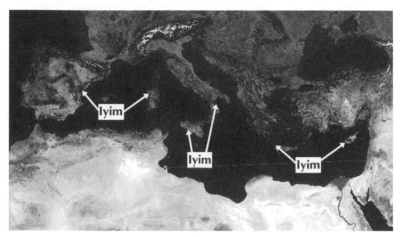

*Fig. 10: The Iyim as seen from outer space (source: NASA)*

# 14. Return from South Africa

God spoke to His people in Isaiah 43:5-7 about their return from all corners of the earth:

> *"⁵ Fear not, for I am with you;*
> *I will bring your descendants from the east,[113]*
> *And gather you from the west;[114]*
> *⁶ I will say to the north, 'Give them up!'*
> *And to the **south**, 'Do not keep them back!'*
> *Bring My sons **from afar**,*
> *And My daughters **from the ends of the earth**—*

---

112 http://www.cbs.gov.il/reader ; see also: http://en.wikipedia.org/wiki/Aliyah and the links found there (as of. 9.11.2011).

113 I.e. the "rising of the sun."

114 I.e. the "setting of the sun."

*⁷ Everyone who is called by My name[115],*
*Whom I have created for My glory;*
*I have formed him, yes, I have made him."* (NKJV)

Regarding the south, it is clearly stated that a return from the far reaches of the south is meant. As seen from Israel, the southern tip of the world is exactly located in South Africa. If you go down the globe from Israel, from the 32nd parallel, for example, you reach South Africa.

How did Diaspora Jews come to be on the southern end of the African continent? Even at the beginning of Dutch colonization of South Africa in 1652, Jews were making their way to South Africa.[116] Over time, the Jewish community there increased. From 1880–1910 it grew from 4,000 to 40,000.[117] Lithuanian Jews also found refuge from persecution in South Africa during those years. From 1920–1930 20,000 more Jews immigrated.[118] Following Hitler's takeover in Germany, South Africa opened its borders to unlimited Jewish immigration from 1933–1935.[119] During this period some 8,000 Jews were flown to the southern tip of the African continent.[120]

The return of the Jews from the south, from "the ends of the earth," proclaimed in Isaiah 43, has been fulfilled. Since the founding of the State of Israel in 1948, some 20,000 Jews from South Africa have immigrated to Israel.[121]

---

115 Verse 7 states that the returnees will be known by the name of their God. The Bible designates the decedents of patriarchs Abraham, Isaac and Jacob as "Israelites." The word for God (Hebrew *'el*) is contained in this word (Isra-el = God's warrior).

116 http://en.wikipedia.org/wiki/South_African_Jews (as of: 24.10.2011).

117 http://www.jewishvirtuallibrary.org/jsource/vjw/South_Africa.html (as of: 24.10.2011).

118 http://www.jewishvirtuallibrary.org/jsource/vjw/South_Africa.html (as of: 24.10.2011).

119 GILBERT: Jewish History Atlas, p. 98. Unfortunately, during the years 1936–1945 almost no Jews were taken in.

120 GILBERT: Jewish History Atlas, p. 98.

121 http://www.mio.org.il/en/node/289 (as of: 24.10.2011).

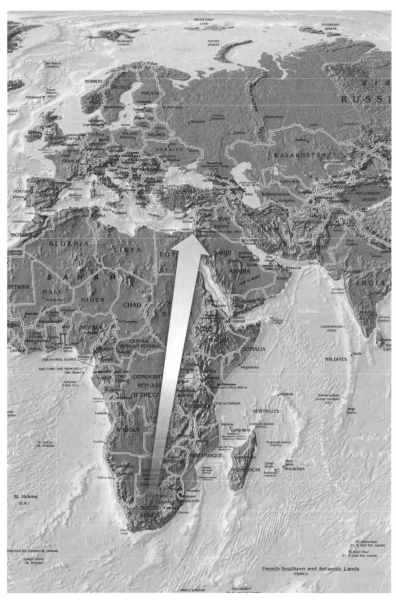

**Fig. 11** *The Jewish return from South Africa literally demonstrates the fulfilment of the prophetic announcement of the return from the farthest south in Isaiah 43:6 (source: CIA).*

# 15. Return from America

The passage from Isaiah 43 discussed above concerns the return from all four corners of the Earth. All the directions are presented in parallel in several verses of this poetic text. Since the south is explicitly the *farthest south*, it follows that the equivalent is meant by the other three directions.

*"⁵ Fear not, for I am with you;*
*I will bring your descendants from the east,[122]*
*And gather you **from the west**;[123]*
*⁶ I will say to the north, 'Give them up!'*
*And to the south, 'Do not keep them back!'*
*Bring My sons from afar,*
*And My daughters from the ends of the earth."* (NKJV)

Which country, as seen from Israel, lies farthest west? The USA! Since 1948, some 110,000 Jews have emigrated from North America (USA and Canada).[124] Thus the prophecy of return from the farthest west has also been fulfilled.[125]

# 16. Return from China

In Isaiah 49:12 the return from "the land of Sinim" is spoken about:

*"¹² Surely these shall come **from afar** [south];*
*Look! Those from the north and the west,*
*And these from the land of Sinim [east]."* (NKJV)

Here is a poetic text with three parallel lines of verse. The directions "north" and "west" are mentioned in the second line.

---

122  I.e. from the "rising of the sun."

123  I.e. from the "setting of the sun."

124  Cf. statistics until 2009: http://www.jafi.org.il/JewishAgency/English/About/Press+Room/ Aliyah+Statistics/jul27.htm (as of: .10.2011).

125  For the return from the west see also: Ps 107:3; Isa. 49:12; Zech. 8:7.

The first line "Surely these shall come from afar;..." is in contrast to "north" in the first half of the second line. Therefore, the first line concerns the south. The third line is in contrast to the last named direction in the second line, i.e. in contrast to "west." From this, it follows logically that the Land of Sinim must be sought for in the east, as seen from Israel. Not in the Near East, but rather, in the Far East. The term "from afar" in the first line makes it clear that the direction we have before us deals with a far distant country.

The suffix –*im* on the end of the word "Sinim" (Hebrew *sinim*) is a plural ending. "Sinim" means, therefore, the inhabitants of the Land "Sin" (Hebrew *sin*.) In good English "the Land of the Sinim" is nothing more than "the Land of the Sinese or rather, "the Land of the Chinese."[126] Franz Delitzsch noted in his Isaiah commentary that the western-most land of the feudal state of China in the period of 897–206 BC (i.e. exactly in Isaiah's time, 700 BC) was called "Tsin."[127] The Hebrew word "Sin" clearly designates the transcription of the Chinese name "Tsin" adapted to the Hebrew alphabet.

The usual word for "China" in Modern Hebrew is the word "Sin" (Hebr. *sin*).[128]

The history of the Chinese Jews has been long neglected. However, in the recent past this interesting subject has been increasingly studied.[129]

The existence of Jews in China can be established, at the very latest, since the beginning of the early Middle Ages (7th century AD).[130] An important Jewish community of the early period was based in Kaifeng.

Following the October Revolution of 1917 in Russia, thousands of Jews (many were anti-communists) fled to China. In the 1930s

---

126 China was called "Sina" in older German, and the Chinese "Sinesen" (cf. also the term "Sinaapfel" for "oranges").

127 KEIL/DELITSCH: Commentar über das Alte Testament, Dritter Teil, Die prophetischen Bücher Vol. I, Biblischer Commentar über den Prophet Jesaja, p. 487-489.

128 LAVY, J.: Langenscheidts Handwörterbuch Deutsch-Hebräisch, p. 130.

129 http://www.haruth.com/JewsChina.html (as of: 10.11.2011).

130 http://en.wikipedia.org/wiki/History_of_the_Jews_in_China ; http://he.wikipedia.org/wiki/%D7 %99%D7%94%D7%93%D7%95%D7%AA_%D7%A1%D7%99%D7%9F (as of: 10.11.2011).

and 1940s a further 20,000 Jews from Europe fleeing the Nazis found refuge in China. Following the Second World War and following the establishment of the Communist regime in China beginning in 1949, most Jews who had sought safety there during the 20<sup>th</sup> century left the Far East. So, in the end, the Chinese Jews also reached Israel!

# 17. Return by Ship

Ships played a special role in the Jews' return from all over the world to the Land of their Fathers. During the 20<sup>th</sup> century, hundreds of thousands of Jews, especially from Africa and Europe, reached harbours of the Promised Land via the Mediterranean Sea.

In Psalm 107, mentioned above, the one concise over-view of the whole history of Israel, beginning with the Exodus from Egypt to the Messianic Kingdom, verses 25–32 describe the End-Time return as a dramatic voyage over the sea:

*"25 For He commands and raises the stormy wind,*
*Which lifts up the waves of the sea.*
*26 They mount up to the heavens,*
*They go down again to the depths;*
*Their soul melts because of trouble.*
*27 They reel to and fro, and stagger like a drunken man,*
*And are at their wits' end.*
*28 Then they cry out to the LORD in their trouble,*
*And He brings them out of their distresses.*
*29 He calms the storm,*
*So that its waves are still.*
*30 Then they are glad because they are quiet;*
*So He guides them to their desired haven.*
*31 Oh, that men would give thanks to the LORD for His goodness,*
*And for His wonderful works to the children of men!*
*32 Let them exalt Him also in the assembly of the people,*
*And praise Him in the company of the elders."* (NKJV)

# 18. Return by Air

The return to the Land of Israel was not only by sea. Many thousands came home from all over the world by air. Especially noteworthy is "Operation On Wings of Eagles," which we have already looked at briefly. In this fantastic mission, the whole Jewish community of about 50,000 people were flown out of Yemen up until autumn 1949. Similarly dramatic was "Operation Babylon" in which far in excess of 100,000 Jews were flown out of Iraq.[131]

The prophecy of the OT foresaw the return home by air. Isaiah 60 deals with Israel's future Messianic Kingdom in The Last Days and the return of the Jews from the entire world. In this context the question is posed in two highly poetic lines in Isaiah 60:8:

*"8 Who are these who fly like a cloud,*
*And like doves to their roosts?"* (NKJV)

This verse has been known in Judaism from ancient times. It was known that, in the age of the Messiah, one would fly to the Land of Israel. It was thought that there would be a miracle in order for the prophecy from Isaiah 60 to be fulfilled.[132] But there was no need of a supernatural miracle. The return of the Jews by air in the 20th and 21st centuries would be a natural wonder.

# 19. Resurrection of Hebrew (1881–1922)

Hebrew, a Canaanite dialect, was still a living language in the Land of Israel 2,000 years ago.[133] However, with the destruction of Jerusalem in 70 AD and the heralded doom of the Jewish state following the brutal repression of the Second Jewish Revolt in 135 AD, Hebrew became less and less an everyday language. The holy

---

131  HILLEL: Operation Babylon.

132  RABOW: 50 Jewish Messiahs, pp. 21,43-44.

133  For history of Hebrew: HETZRON, R.: Hebrew, pp. 686-704; BERGSTRÄSSER: Einführung in die semitischen Sprachen, p. 36-59.

language was used for reading the OT in synagogue services and for reciting the OT. Hebrew was also used as the scholarly language of the rabbis, similar to Latin in the Middle Ages. Hebrew suffered the fate of becoming a dead language, like so many other languages in the world.

In the years 1881–1922, Hebrew was brought to life again especially through the efforts of Eliezer Ben-Yehuda – after some 1,600 years.[134] There has never been anything like this in the history of the world! There has never been a language which had been dead for over 1,000 years brought back to life as a fully functional national language. But this is exactly what had to happen in order for Isaiah 19:18 to be fulfilled:

*"*[18]* In that day [even] five cities in the land of Egypt will speak the language of Canaan [= Hebrew] ..."*(NKJV)

Isaiah 19 deals with prophecy regarding Egypt in The Last Days. In verse 14, it is prophesied that the language of Canaan – another name for Hebrew – would even be spoken in five Egyptian cities in The Last Days. Though Hebrew was a dead language for many centuries, it was known from this verse that in The Last Days Hebrew would again be spoken!

In this context some details regarding the history of the Hebrew language may be of use:

## 19.1 The History of Hebrew

Around 2,000 BC, Abraham, the ancestor of Israel, left Ur in Chaldea (in modern southern Iraq) to go to Canaan (Gen.12:1ff.). In Ur, an ancient Sumerian city, he spoke Babylonian (Akkadian). In those days Sumerian was already a dead language. His relatives in Haran, on the other hand, spoke Aramaic. In Canaan he learned another Semitic language: Canaanite, the language of the resident native population. So, Abraham began to speak "Hebrew"! His descendants continued speaking this language.

---

134 Cf. the extensive description of Eliezer Ben-Yehuda's life work in: ST. JOHN: Tongue of the Prophets the Life Story of Eliezer Ben Yehuda, and: PETERS: Die Sprache der Propheten, ethos, Nr. 2, 1990, p. 31ff.

Following the Exodus from Egypt (1606 BC), Moses wrote his five books in the Hebrew language.

The Babylonian Exile lasted from 606–539 BC. During this time the Jews acquired the then universal language: Aramaic.[135] This language is closely related to Hebrew.

The following portions of the OT were written in Aramaic: Jer. 10:11; Dan. 2:4-7; Ezra 4:9 – 6:18 and 7:12-26.

Following the return from Babylon beginning in 538 BC, both languages were spoken in the Land of Israel. For those who had difficulty with the public reading of the Hebrew OT, clarification in Aramaic was given (Neh. 8:8). In Jesus' time, both languages were in use, and, in addition, Greek, the universal language of the then Roman occupying power in Israel.[136] Latin was not so common. This is understood from the fact that very few Latin inscriptions have been found in Israel.

When Hebrew became a dead language following the destruction of Jerusalem in 70 AD, the Jews assumed the respective language of the country in which they lived. Dialects (Yiddish, Ladino, etc.) developed in certain places with the use of these languages restricted to ghetto life.

## 19.2 Eliezer Ben-Yehuda

Through the pioneering work of Eliezer Ben-Yehuda, born in 1858 in Luzhki, Lithuania, the fate of the Hebrew language experienced a fundamental change.[137] Ben-Yehuda arrived at Jaffa by steamship in October 1881. Sometime later, he made a home in Jerusalem, at that time one of the dirtiest and most run-down cities in the Ottoman Empire. The members of the Jewish colony there did not speak Hebrew, of course, but rather Russian, Yiddish and Arabic. Ben-Yehuda began to give Hebrew lessons at the Alliance Israelite Universelle in Jerusalem. Thus he broke away from all previous convention. This brought much hostility from the orthodox Jews, who considered the common use of the holy language to be

---

135 For Aramaic language of this time cf. ROSENTHAL: A Grammar of Biblical Aramaic.

136 MILLARD: Pergament und Papyrus, Tafeln und Ton, Lesen und Schreiben zur Zeit Jesu, passim.

137 Cf. Roger Liebi: Die dramatische Geschichte der hebräischen Sprache (audio lecture at www. sermon-online.ch).

a terrible desecration. Ben-Yehuda's safety was repeatedly threatened when stones were thrown at this alleged "heretic."

After his wife Deborah became pregnant, she had to promise that only Hebrew would be spoken to the child which would be born. Ben-Zion (= "son of Zion") was born in 1882. He only heard Hebrew in his first years. So it was that, since the demise of the Hebrew language, he was the first child in the history of the modern world to have Hebrew as his mother-tongue!

Beginning in 1884, Ben-Yehuda published his own Hebrew weekly journal named *ha-ziv*. ("The Glorious"; cf. Dan. 8:9). With this publication he taught his readers Hebrew. He created new words for all possible modern things and introduced them step-by-step in his newspaper.

The "Committee of the Hebrew Language" (Hebr. *va'ad ha-lashon ha-'ivrith*) was founded in 1890. This became the Academy of the Hebrew Language, founded by the Knesset in 1953.

In 1890, he began his monumental work creating the Modern Hebrew Lexicon. He turned his weekly journal into a daily newspaper in 1908. His dictionary appeared in five volumes until 1914. They were produced by the publisher Langenscheidt.

The situation in "Palestine" changed fundamentally because of the First World War. In 1917 the British conquered this country which had been under Islamic occupation since the 7th century. In the same year, Britain promised to champion the cause of "Palestine" becoming a "national home for the Jewish people" in the Balfour Declaration. Incidentally, the term "Palestine" at that time consisted of the whole of the modern Land of Israel, including the so-called occupied territories of Gaza, the West Bank and the Golan. Naturally, East Jerusalem, annexed in 1980, was also included. Furthermore, the whole area of modern Jordan was then, too, part of "Palestine."

In 1921, Ben-Yehuda moved the British High Commissioner Herbert Samuel to elevate Hebrew to the third official language in "Palestine" (alongside Arabic and English).

On 15 December 1922 Eliezer Ben-Yehuda died; 30,000 people attended his funeral. A three-day period of national mourning was for called in "Palestine." The goal had been reached: Hebrew was a living language again which was spoken day-to-day. The tiny alleys of Jerusalem again rang with the warm, throaty language of the ancient Hebrew prophets.

Following his death, Ben-Yehuda's as yet unpublished dictionary-notes were printed. Each volume consists of 600 pages.

Today, Hebrew is a fully functioning language. The morphology (the conjugation of verbs, declension of nouns and adjectives) corresponds to Ancient Hebrew in pronunciation, just as the Masoretes had vocalized the consonantal text of the OT in the Middle Ages. Most of the words of the OT were absorbed into the modern language. Whenever it was possible, new words for all the terms of modern life were formed from the Hebrew language system. Modern terms were formed which adapted to this Semitic language. Hebrew is fully functional in all areas, not only in the domain of every-day life, but even in every field of modern science and new literature.

# 20. Buying Back The Land: 1882–1940

The first decades of Jewish re-colonization of the Promised Land were characterized by extensive land purchases. Ruined regions, desert areas and malaria-infected swamps in the Galilee (northern Israel) and Judea (southern Israel) were bought up at inflated prices from European, Turkish, as well as the predominantly Arab big land owners living in Beirut and Damascus.[138] This corresponded exactly to Jeremiah's prediction for The Last Days when the fate of the Jewish people would finally change (Jer. 32:43-44):

> *[43] And **fields will be bought in this land** of which you say, "It is desolate, without man or beast; it has been given into the hand of the Chaldeans." [44] Men will buy fields for money, sign deeds and seal them, and take witnesses, **in the land of Benjamin, in the places around Jerusalem,** in the cities **of Judah,***

---

138 Gilbert: The Arab-Israeli Conflict, Its History in Maps, p. 32.

*in the cities **of the mountains**, in the cities **of the lowland**
**[Shephelah]**, and in the cities **of the South [Negev]**; for I will
cause their captives to return,' says the L*ORD*."* (NKJV)

The prophetic word *'and fields will be bought in this land'*, *"Men
will buy fields for money, sign deeds and seal them, and take witnesses,"* was literally fulfilled in a remarkable way.

There are many more prophetic details found in Jeremiah 32:44.
The focus of Jeremiah's prophecy is directed towards Judea. Today
we can trace the fulfilment of all these details with their astounding accuracy, because we know exactly where extensive land purchases were made:[139]

- *Benjamin's* tribal area was north of Jerusalem. Much land was
  bought just there, south of modern Ramallah.
- *Jerusalem* and the surrounding area was a region which was
  thickly settled by Jews. Real estate was purchased there as
  well.
- Land was bought *in the highland* ("in the cities of the mountains") in the tribal area of *Judah* ("in the cities of Judah"),
  actually in the area between Bethlehem and Hebron, as well
  as between Jerusalem and Ramla.
- The geographic term *"Shephelah"* (= "lowlands") describes
  the western slope of the Judean Mountains and the Judean
  Plains along the Mediterranean Sea. Especially large tracts
  were bought there, in the area between Gaza City and Jaffa/
  Tel Aviv, as well as north of Tel Aviv.
- In the Bible the word *"Negev"* (= the South) designates the
  desert area in southern Israel. Large areas of land were acquired in the area south and south-east of Beersheba, as well
  as south of the Rafah-Beersheba line.

The words of Jeremiah 32:43-44 hit the bull's-eye. Each word
has been fulfilled exactly, and this in our lifetimes, in combination
with all the further prophecies dealt with in this book (more than
170!).

---

139 Gilbert: The Arab-Israeli Conflict, Its History in Maps, p. 32.

Beginning in 1940, the British Mandate drastically limited the opportunity for Jews to buy land. The greater part of the Land of Israel was, for this reason, forbidden for Jews to purchase. A zone surrounding Jerusalem and a large part of the lowlands (the Shephelah) were exempted from this restriction, so that even after 1940 land could still be acquired there.[140] The Negev was, however, totally excluded from further land purchases from this time on. The Judean Mountains and the tribal area of Benjamin were declared as absolutely forbidden land.

# 21. Reconstruction of Old Testament Cities

Even in the 8th century, God announced through the prophet Amos that in The Last Days the Old Testament cities would be again built up and developed as Jewish cities (Amos 9:14-15):

> *"[14] 'I will bring back the captives of My people Israel;*
> *They shall **build the waste cities and inhabit them**;*
> *They shall plant vineyards and drink wine from them;*
> *They shall also make gardens and eat fruit from them.*
> *[15] I will plant them in their land,*
> *And no longer shall they be pulled up*
> *From the land I have given them,'*
> *Says the LORD your God."* (NKJV)

But first, a useful linguistic note of a technical nature regarding translation: The Hebrew word *banah*, translated here by "build," has a relatively wide meaning and can be translated: construct, establish, develop, reconstruct.[141] Thus, the text of Amos 9:14 means the following: When the Jews return in The Last Days, they

---

140 Gilbert: The Arab-Israeli Conflict, Its History in Maps, p. 32.

141 Cf. e.g. BAUMGARTNER/KÖHLER: Hebräisches und aramäisches Lexikon zum Alten Testament, Vol. I, p. 133-134; DAVIDSON: Analytical Hebrew and Chaldee Lexicon, p. 95; GESENIUS/MEYER/DONNER: Hebräisches und aramäisches Handwörterbuch über das Alte Testament, Vol. I, p. 158-159; KÖNIG: Hebräisches und aramäisches Wörterbuch zum Alten Testament, p. 42-43.

will build the OT cities anew. Additionally, they will beautify and develop the deteriorated cities.

Today we are eye-witnesses to the fact that innumerable OT towns have become vibrantly alive, modern Israeli cities. Permanent homes have been created for almost 6 million Jews by massive building activity throughout the whole country. According to Amos 9:14, the rebuilding of Biblical cities marks the turn in Israel's fate. The Chosen People were, for almost 2,000 years, characterized by the image of the homeless Jew, wandering from ghetto to ghetto, persecuted, hated and outlawed. This is past. Ancient cities from Biblical times are today progressive metropolises, areas of high population density, residential centres and settlements, and witnesses of God's faithfulness to the millennia-old promises in His Word.

# 22. Vineyards

Amos 9:14-15 also contains a prophecy about the planting of vineyards in the Land of Israel as an expression of the reversal of Jewish fate in The Last Days. God speaks:

> *"14 I will bring back the captives of My people Israel;*
> *They shall build the waste cities and inhabit them;*
> *They shall **plant vineyards and drink wine from them**;*
> *They shall also make gardens and eat fruit from them.*
> *15 I will plant them in their land,*
> *And no longer shall they be pulled up*
> *From the land I have given them,"*
> *Says the LORD your God."* (NKJV)

In OT times, vineyards were very important for Israel's agriculture.[142] Thus, in numerous places in the Bible, there is talk about grapevines, vineyards, planting vineyards, as well as blossoms,

---

142 Cf. for further detail on wine growing in Israel: http://en.wikipedia.org/wiki/Israeli_wine (as of: 24.10.2011), together with further extensive and detailed links given: GOLDFISHER/SACKS: The Wine Route of Israel.

grape harvest, grapes, grape treaders, grape honey, grape juice, wine, etc. Many vineyards were destroyed in the Romans' wars against the Jews (in 70 and 135 AD) because the Romans sought to ruin the country environmentally.[143] Following the Islamic conquest of the Holy Land in 636 AD, viticulture largely disappeared for more than 1,200 years. The returning Jews of the 1st Aliya, from 1882 onwards, were financially supported by Baron Edmond James de Rothschild, owner of the world-renowned Bordeaux vineyard Chateaux Lafite-Rothschild. At first, there were great difficulties: the ground was too stony and too sandy, grape buds could not bear the heat, and the first vineyards fell victim to the devastating vine fretter plague.

By importing grapevines from France, in accordance with the advice from Baron de Rothschild, the pests were also introduced which were destroying French viticulture at that time. Eventually, however, wine from Carmel was awarded a Gold Medal at the Paris World Fair of 1900. Admittedly, Israeli wine had, in general, the bad reputation of being too thick and too sweet well up until the 1960s. In the years following there was a real revolution in viticulture. Israeli wine was recognized internationally with a host of gold medals! Today, winegrowing is carried out on a large scale in the following areas: the Galilee, the Golan Heights, the Sharon Plain, Shamshon, the Judean Hills around Jerusalem and the Negev Desert.

Naturally, Israel's modern wine culture is only successful thanks to the introduction of foreign grape varieties. From France have come – to name just a few varieties - Cabernet Sauvignon, Merlot, Sauvignon Blanc, Syrah, Chardonnay, Pinot Noir, Cabernet Franc. Johannisberg Riesling comes from the Rhine Valley, Germany. Zinfandel originated in Croatia. What Isaiah prophesied some 2,700 years ago, regarding Israel in The Last Days, has been literally fulfilled (Isa. 17:10).[144]

---

143  NEGEV: Archaeology in the Land of the Bible, p. 36-37.

144  In the context of Isa. 17:10, the Jews are accused of activism while disregarding God. Many of the immigrating Jews, beginning in 1882, were agnostics or even atheists who wanted to build a better existence; God and His Word played no role for them.

*"10... therefore shalt thou plant pleasant plantations,
and shalt set them **with foreign slips...**"[145] (Darby)*

# 23. Fruit Plantations

The establishment of fruit plantations is spoken of in the fourth line of the text of Amos 9:14:

*"[14] I will bring back the captives of My people Israel;
They shall build the waste cities and inhabit them;
They shall plant vineyards and drink wine from them;
They shall also **make gardens and eat fruit from them**.
[15] I will plant them in their land,
And no longer shall they be pulled up
From the land I have given them,"
Says the LORD your God." (NKJV)*

During the past decades agriculture has been built up in Israel which is among the market leaders of the world.[146] Since the founding of the state, the area used for agriculture has tripled,

---

145 For the interested reader, I will here add a outline in note form, in order to better understand the prophetic context of Isa. 17:10:
  · Verses 1-4 were fulfilled in the 8th century BC:
    – VI: Prophecy about Damascus, capital of the Syrians / Arameans
    – VI-3: Tiglath Pileser conquered Syria in 733 BC. Ephraim's (10 tribes of Israel) judgement occurred in 722 BC. Syria and Ephraim threatened the House of David in the time of Ahaz (Isa. 7; Jas. 4:4)
  · The prophet jumps into the Last Days in verse 4. The adverbial term *beyom* ("in that day") is very typical for The Last Days. Afterward, it deals with the judgement on Israel, in the future, in which a portion of the people, the remnant, will come to repentance. Verses 10-11 speak about the End-Time return of the Jews/Israel, which is done in unbelief. It is noteworthy that the great effort of Zionism and reclamation of the land was accomplished by agnostics and atheists, who had forgotten the God of their Salvation and the Rock of their Strength!
  · v. 4: "In that day" (Hebr. *beyom* – to that time period, especially "period of The Last Days"; cf. v. 7 and v. 9; cf. e.g. Zech. 12-14: consistently: *beyom*)
  · v. 4-5: In The Last Days Israel goes through the Great Tribulation. But there is a remnant which will be saved (v. 6: "gleaning grapes").
  · v. 7-8: the remnant of Israel will trust in the LORD alone.
  · v. 9: During the Great Tribulation Israel will look as it did when Joshua conquered Canaan (Joel 2:3).
  · v. 10-11: Time of the return of the Jews in unbelief, foreign grapes from France (Bordeaux, Baron de Rothschild) and California were planted. But in the Tribulation, all will be destroyed.
  · v. 12-14: The mass of people raging against God will, in the end, come under God's judgement.

146 http://www.mfa.gov.il/mfa/facts%20about%20israel/economy/focus%20on%20israel-%20israel-s%20agriculture%20in%20the%2021st (as of: 24.10.2011).

while the harvest has multiplied sixteen times.[147] Fruit production plays an outstanding role in modern arable farming. Israeli production of citrus fruit such as oranges, clementines, mandarins, minneolas, yellow and red grapefruits, pomelos, etc., is renowned. About one-third of the yearly harvest of 900,000 tons is exported. The production of numerous other fruits besides citrus fruit plays an important role: e.g. dates, mangos, figs, pomegranates, persimmons, kiwis, bananas, etc.

Who, in the 19th century, could have imagined such a striking fulfilment of the Biblical prophecy? Today we are eye-witnesses of these things and can even taste fulfilled prophecy in all its sweetness, in the enjoyment of a world-famous Jaffa orange.

# 24. The Desert Blooms

In the last portion of his book (Ezek. 33-48) the prophet Ezekiel describes how the people of Israel and their land will experience a complete regeneration in a process consisting of several phases during The Last Days.[148] With the Land in mind, he wrote in the 6th century BC (Ezek. 36:34-35):

> *"34 The desolate land shall be tilled instead of lying desolate in the sight of all who pass by. 35 So they will say, 'This land that was desolate has become like the garden of Eden; and the wasted, desolate, and ruined cities are now fortified and inhabited.'"* (NKJV)

Beginning in 1882 the returning Jews gave themselves over to agriculture and began reclaiming the ravaged land of Israel. Kibbutzim (collective farms) and Moshavim (collective agricultural villages) were organized, with the goal of making the ruined land fruitful. Malaria-infested swamps were drained at huge cost of human life. Millions of trees were planted. The KKL (Keren Kay-

---

147  http://www.hagalil.com/01/de/Israel.php?itemid=2596 (as of 24.10.2011).

148  Cf.: LIEBI: Hesekiel, Ezra Studienreihe, CMV Hagedorn, Düsseldorf, Germany and CLKV,Pfäffikon, CH 2011.

emet LeYisrael), the Jewish National Fund, dedicated itself to the reforestation of the country. To this day, 80,000 hectares of land have been planted with over 230 million trees, thanks to contributions from all over the world. 2,000 hectares of new forest are planted with saplings every year throughout Israel. This has provided a substantial improvement in the climate in Israel and the Near East. When trees in desert areas have grown to be large, they provide shade, so that grass and other plants can grow which both strengthen the ground and provide sustenance for animals. This creates an ecological balance. The huge numbers of trees constitute Israel's "green lung," reducing pollution from the cities. In the mountains, the forests protect the earth from erosion during winter rains. Cliffs retain more stability by them, and, in addition, they prevent land-slides. Fields and gardens are effectively protected from sand storms. In the Negev Desert they prevent the expansion of sand dunes. Incidentally, in the Negev Desert 2,000 km$^2$ are used for agriculture, grazing land and forest today. The National Fund's extensive projects provide many meaningful jobs for new Jewish immigrants. As an ecological organization, the KKL also rehabilitates river-beds, giving new life to Israel's rivers. Israel's special knowledge in reclaiming the desert is made available to other countries, especially Israel's neighbours. Today the Promised Land has become a blossoming garden once again. Currently, 1.4 billion cut flowers are produced yearly and a significant portion of these is exported throughout the world. Israel has become a Land of Flowers, with flowers accounting for about 30% of agricultural export.[149] What a contrast this is to the situation Mark Twain encountered in 1867 when he visited this country a few years before the first Jewish wave of immigration! In his book "Innocents Abroad" (1869),[150] chapter LVI, as one of many "passing through" in earlier times, he wrote:[151]

---

149 http://www.mfa.gov.il/mfa/facts%20about%20israel/economy/focus%20on%20israel-%20israel-s%20agriculture%20in%20the%2021st (as of: 24.10.2011).

150 The German translation entitled "Die Arglosen im Ausland" appeared in 1875.

151 Following (German) quote: PETERSON: PLO kontra Israel, p. 63-64. The original English text is available free of charge: http://www.archive.org/details/theinnocentsabro03176gut (as of: 24.10.2011).

"Of all the lands there are for dismal scenery, I think Palestine must be the prince. The hills are barren, they are dull of color, they are unpicturesque in shape. The valleys are unsightly deserts fringed with a feeble vegetation that has an expression about it of being sorrowful and despondent. The Dead Sea and the Sea of Galilee sleep in the midst of a vast stretch of hill and plain wherein the eye rests upon no pleasant tint, no striking object, no soft picture dreaming in a purple haze or mottled with the shadows of the clouds. Every outline is harsh, every feature is distinct, there is no perspective -- distance works no enchantment here. It is a hopeless, dreary, heart-broken land. Small shreds and patches of it must be very beautiful in the full flush of spring, however, and all the more beautiful by contrast with the far-reaching desolation that surrounds them on every side. I would like much to see the fringes of the Jordan in spring-time, and Shechem, Esdraelon, Ajalon and the borders of Galilee -- but even then these spots would seem mere toy gardens set at wide intervals in the waste of a limitless desolation. Palestine sits in sackcloth and ashes. Over it broods the spell of a curse that has withered its fields and fettered its energies. Where Sodom and Gomorrah reared their domes and towers, that solemn sea now floods the plain, in whose bitter waters no living thing exists -- over whose waveless surface the blistering air hangs motionless and dead -- about whose borders nothing grows but weeds, and scattering tufts of cane, and that treacherous fruit that promises refreshment to parching lips, but turns to ashes at the touch. Nazareth is forlorn; about that ford of Jordan where the hosts of Israel entered the Promised Land with songs of rejoicing, one finds only a squalid camp of fantastic Bedouins of the desert; Jericho the accursed, lies a moldering ruin, to-day, even as Joshua's miracle left it more than three thousand years ago; Bethlehem and Bethany, in their poverty and their humiliation, have nothing about them now to remind one that they once knew the high honor of the Saviour's presence; the hallowed spot where the shepherds watched their flocks by night, and where the angels sang Peace on earth, good will to men, is untenanted by any living creature, and unblessed by any feature that is pleasant to the eye. Renowned Jerusalem itself, the stateliest name in history, has lost all its ancient grandeur, and is become a pauper village; the riches of Solomon are no longer there to compel the admiration of visiting Oriental queens; the wonderful temple which was the pride and the glory of Israel, is gone, and the Ottoman crescent is lifted above the spot where, on that most memorable day in the annals of the world, they reared the Holy Cross. The noted Sea of Galilee, where Roman fleets once rode at anchor and the disciples of the Saviour sailed in their ships, was long ago deserted by the devotees of war and commerce, and its borders are a silent wilderness; Capernaum is a shapeless ruin; Magdala is the home of beggared Arabs; Bethsaida and Chorazin have vanished from the earth, and the "desert places" round about them where thousands of men once listened to the Saviour's voice and ate the miraculous bread, sleep in the hush of a solitude that is inhabited only by birds of prey and skulking foxes. Palestine is desolate and unlovely. And why should it be otherwise? Can the curse of the Deity beautify a land? Palestine is no more of this work-day world. It is sacred to poetry and tradition -- it is dream-land."

Even in 1864, a few years before Mark Twain, H.B. Tristram could find no words of praise in describing "Palestine:"[152]
"... no indication of inhabitants, even where the valley is arable ... the monotony of non-use, bare of all life and movement."

The metamorphosis of the desert into a fertile country in Israel is a singular phenomenon in world history. There has never been anything like it. However, it had to happen because the prophetic word of the Bible had clearly announced that it would be so in The Last Days.

While the text of Psalm 107:33-34 describes the results of desolation beginning in 70 AD and continuing well into the 19th century, the following verses make us aware of the reverse process, beginning in 1882. Psalm 107:33-38:

---

152 The following quote is from: PETERSON: PLO kontra Israel, p. 63.

*"33 He turns rivers into a wilderness,*
*And the watersprings into dry ground;*
*34 A fruitful land into barrenness,*
*For the wickedness of those who dwell in it.*
*35 He turns a wilderness into pools of water,*
*And dry land into watersprings.*
*36 There He makes the hungry dwell,*
*That they may establish a city for a dwelling place,*
*37 And sow fields and plant vineyards,*
*That they may yield a fruitful harvest.*
*38 He also blesses them, and they multiply greatly;*
*And He does not let their cattle decrease."* (NKJV)

## 25. Founding of the State of Israel: 14 May 1948

The Jewish people were still without their own state during the first 66 years of the resettlement of the Land of their Forefathers. The founding of the state on 14 May 1948 is connected directly with the horrors of the Second World War (1939–1945). The annihilation of 6 million Jews made it clear that an answer to the Jewish Question was urgently needed. Deeply affected by the atrocities committed against the Jews, a majority of the nations of the recently founded UN exhibited the courage to defy Islamic opposition in the November Resolution and voted for the founding of a Jewish state. Immediately following, there were terrible bellicose conflicts in Palestine. It was the first phase of a war of annihilation against the Jews, beginning in December 1947, which would continue into 1949.[153] In the face of all this bloody opposition, on the unforgettable Friday afternoon of 14 May 1948, David Ben Gurion proclaimed to the new nation:

> "Here is the State of Israel. 2,000 years have passed. When the time for God has come, no one can withstand Him!"

---

153  http://de.wikipedia.org/wiki/Pal%C3%A4stinakrieg (as of: 24.10.2011).

In 700 BC this remarkable day was described by the prophet Isaiah in the following words (Isa. 66:8):

*"⁸ Who has heard such a thing?*
*Who has seen such things?*
*Shall the earth be made to give birth in one day?*
*Or shall a nation be born at once?*
*For as soon as Zion was in labor,*
*She gave birth to her children."* (NKJV)

Yes, the nation of Israel was born on 14 May 1948 in the middle of belligerent adversity. During the eve of the following Saturday total war broke out.

As soon as the British, as the Mandatory power, had completely withdrawn from Palestine, total war was declared by the surrounding enemy nations of Jordan, Syria, Iraq, Lebanon, Egypt, plus contingents from Saudi Arabia and Yemen. The verse quoted above states that the birth of the Jewish State would take place in the midst of extreme pain.

# 26. The Goal of the Enemy: The Obliteration of Israel

The nations around Israel tried to obliterate Israel, the Jewish State, three times through total war:

- 1948/1949: in the so-called Israeli War of Independence
- 1967: in the Six Day War
- 1973: in the Yom Kippur War

The prophetic Psalm 83 describes the enemies' objective precisely. The voice of the people of Israel is heard in this End-Time prayer-song, calling to God for help in the distress from their enemies:

*"¹ Do not keep silent, O God!*
*Do not hold Your peace,*

*And do not be still, O God!*
*² For behold, Your enemies make a tumult;*
*And those who hate You have lifted up their head.*
*³ They have taken crafty counsel against Your people,*
*And consulted together against Your sheltered ones.*
*⁴ They have said, "Come, and let us cut them off from being*
*a nation,*
*That the name of Israel may be remembered no more."*
(NKJV)

The following armies attempted to obliterate Israel in the first war of annihilation (1948/1949):

- Syria
- Lebanon
- Iraq
- Transjordan (known as "Jordan" after 1950)
- Egypt
- Saudi Arabia
- Yemen

These armies were supported by the ALA, Arab Liberation Army, in which Palestinians and other Arabs from various countries fought. [154] In addition, the Army of the Holy War also came under the leadership of Abd al-Qadir al-Husseini, nephew of the Grand Mufti of Jerusalem and Nazi collaborator.

- The armies of Egypt, Syria and Jordan fought in the second war of annihilation against Israel (1967). They were supported by troops from Iraq, Saudi Arabia, Sudan, Morocco, Algeria, Libya and Kuwait, as well as 10,000 soldiers from the PLO in the Gaza Strip.
- The Yom Kippur War, the third war of annihilation against Israel (1973), involved troops from Egypt, Syria and Jordan; support was given by Morocco, Algeria, Tunisia, Libya, Sudan, Uganda, Cuba, North Korea, Pakistan, Bangladesh,

---

154 The Arab Liberation Army was composed of volunteer fighters from Syria, Egypt, Lebanon, Iraq, and Transjordan. There were also Circassian, Yugoslav, German, English and Turkish deserters who fought. (cf. http://en.wikipedia.org/wiki/Arab_Liberation_Army [as of: 24.10.2011]).

Saudi-Arabia and Kuwait. The Palestinians also contributed soldiers.[155]

# 27. The Assembly of the Enemy: The Arab League

On 22 March 1945 the Arab League, an international organization of Arab nations, was founded. The original members included the following seven countries:

- Egypt
- Iraq
- Jordan
- Lebanon
- North Yemen
- Saudi Arabia
- Syria

These states considered themselves closely allied with the British administered "Palestine." One of their ostensible goals was to support the Palestinian Arabs in preventing the establishment of a Jewish nation, whatever the cost. However, once the nation of Israel was founded in 1948 in spite of their rabid resistance, the goal shifted to obliterating Israel and destroying its Jewish citizens.

The word "league" comes from the Latin verb *ligare*, which means "to bind" or "to unite." In the Cambridge On-line Dictionary/Thesaurus, league is defined as "union" or "conference." Psalm 83:5 states that the enemies, who demand Israel's total obliteration, form a confederacy, a league:

> *"5 For they have consulted together with one consent;*
> *They form a confederacy against You:*
> *6 The tents of Edom and the Ishmaelites;*
> *Moab and the Hagrites;*
> *7 Gebal, Ammon, and Amalek;*

---

155 http://en.wikipedia.org/wiki/Yom_Kippur_War (as of: 24.10.2011); http://de.wikipedia.org/wiki/Jom-Kippur-Krieg (as of: 24.10.2011).

*Philistia with the inhabitants of Tyre;*
*⁸Assyria also has joined with them;*
*They have helped the children of Lot."* (NKJV)

This League is said to turn against God. This can be explained by the fact that an attack on God's Chosen People is also always an attack on God Himself, corresponding to the word in Zechariah 2:8:

*"⁸ ... for he who touches you touches the apple of [My] eye."*[156]
(NKJV)

Today, the Arab League consists of 22 members in total. The Arab Palestinians joined in 1976, represented by the PLO. In addition, six countries have observer status.

Following is a list of the 22 members of the Arab League (with year of entry indicated in brackets).

- Egypt (1945; membership suspended 1979 to 1989 following peace treaty with Israel)
- Algeria (1962)
- Bahrain (1971)
- Djibouti (1977)
- Iraq (1945)
- Yemen (North Yemen: 1945; South Yemen: member from 1967–1990; since 1990 North and South have been united)
- Jordan (1945)
- Qatar (1971)
- Comoros (1993)
- Kuwait (1961)
- Lebanon (1945)
- Libya (1953)
- Marocco (1958)
- Mauretania (1973)
- Oman (1971)
- Palestinian Autonomous Area (1976, represented by the PLO)

---

156 The original and correct Hebrew text is *"my* eye," The incorrect text *"His* eye" is a *tiqunei sophrim,* i.e. one of the very few deliberate changes made by the ancient rabbis, all of which were carefully and explicitly denoted as such.

- Saudi Arabia (1945)
- Somalia (1974)
- Sudan (1956)
- Syria (1945)
- Tunisia (1958)
- United Arab Emirates (1971)

Observers:
- Turkey
- Iran
- Venezuela
- Pakistan
- India
- Eritrea

Several names of the members of this confederation against Israel are found in Psalm 83:5-8: Asaph, the author of this Psalm, uses the names of peoples and cities which were customary in his time, i.e. around 1000 BC. These terms can definitely be geographically identified with the help of a Bible atlas:

> *"⁵ For they have consulted together with one consent;*
> *They form a confederacy against You;*
> *⁶ The tents of **Edom** and the **Ishmaelites**;*
> ***Moab** and the **Hagrites**;*
> *⁷ **Gebal**, **Ammon**, and **Amalek**;*
> ***Philistia** with the inhabitants of **Tyre**;*
> *⁸ **Assyria** also has joined with them;*
> *They have helped **the children of Lot**."* (NKJV)

## 27.1 Jordan
- "Edom" was the name of an area in modern southern Jordan. The descendants of Jacob's brother Esau settled there.[157]
- "Moab" designates an area in modern central Jordan, principally beyond the Dead Sea. The Moabite tribe descended

---

157 Cf. Gen. 25:30; 32:3; 36:1ff.

from Abraham's nephew Lot. His son, fathered in incest, was the progenitor of this people.[158]

- "Ammon" is the area settled by the descendants of Lot's other son Ben Ammi.[159] It is found north of Moab. "Amman," the name of the Jordanian capital, goes back to the tribal name of the Ammonites. The term "the children of Lot" in Psalm 83:8 again refers to Ammon and Moab.

It follows from what has been said in the poetic language of Psalm 83, the three names Edom, Moab and Ammon refer to the area of modern Jordan. As stated, Jordan was a founding member of the Arab League and had a leading role in the first war of annihilation against Israel.

## 27.2 Saudi Arabia and North Yemen

The "Ishmaelites" of Psalm 83:6 go back to their tribal ancestor Ishmael, a son of Abraham and his maid-servant Hagar (cf. Gen. 16:1ff; 17:18 ff). From Ishmael came twelve princes (Gen. 25:12-16): Nebayoth, Kedar, Adbeel, Mibsam, Mishma, Dumah, Massa, Hadad, Tema, Yetur, Naphish and Kedemah. According to the Jewish historian Flavius Josephus (1st century AD), the Ishmaelite tribes settled in the Saudi peninsula, between the Euphrates and the Red Sea. Josephus makes it clear that the Ishmaelites nominally influenced the Arabs by their dominance.[160] The ethnic commingling of the Ishmaelites with other nomadic desert tribes finally led to Mohammed, and the Muslim Arabs generally, referring to Ishmael as their ancestor. The mention of the Ishmaelites in Psalm 83 refers us to the area of the Arabian peninsula. Saudi Arabia and North Yemen were founding members of the Arab League in 1945.

## 27.3 Syria

The Hagrites are mentioned in Psalm 83:6.[161] According to 1

---

158 Cf. Gen. 19:30-38; for the geographical specifications of the land of the Moabites cf. Num. 21:11ff; Deut. 1:5.

159 Cf. Gen. 19:30-38.

160 JOSEPHUS: Jewish Antiquities, I,12.4.

161 Further Verses: 1Chr 5:10,19,20; 27:31.

Chronicles 5:10 this was a tribe which lived east of Gilead. They were bordered to the north by the Gadites, whose territory ran from the land of Bashan to the southern Syrian city, Salkhad (Biblical "Salcah"; 1 Chron. 5:11). This tribe was mentioned, together with the Arameans (Syrians) on an inscription by Tiglath-Pileser III (8th century BC).[162] Thus, the Hagrites refer us to the area of the modern State of Syria, in accordance with the rhetorical device *pars pro toto* (a part stands for the whole). Syria was also a founding member of the Arab League.

## 27.4 Lebanon

Two cities are named in Psalm 83:7: Gebal (= Arab. Jibail)[163] and Tyre. Here, also, we must refer to the rhetorical device of *pars pro toto*.[164] These two cities stand as representatives for Lebanon. Tyre represents the south; Gebal, the north. Lebanon was also a founding member of the Arab League.

## 27.5 Egypt

The Amalekites, named in Psalm 83:7 were a desert people who lived on the Egyptian Sinai Peninsula. From 1 Samuel 15:7, we understand that the settlement area of Amalek extended from Shur to Havila. Shur lies on the west side of the Sinai Peninsula. Immediately following the Exodus from Egypt, the people of Israel arrived in the "Wilderness of Shur" (Exod. 15:22). Shortly thereafter, there was a fierce military confrontation with the Amalekites (Exod. 17). The mention of the Amalekites in Psalm 83 refers us to the Sinai Peninsula and, thereby, to the territory of the state of modern Egypt. Egypt, too, was also one of the seven founding members of the Arab League.

## 27.6 Palestinian Autonomous Region

Palestine (Hebr. *pelesheth*) is the term for the "Land of the Phi-

---

162  BURKHARDT/GRÜNZWEIG/LAUBACH/MAIER (eds.): Das grosse Bibellexikon, Wuppertal, Vol. II, p. 506.

163  In antiquity this city was famous under the Greek name Byblos.

164  BÜHLMANN/SCHERER: Sprachliche Stilfiguren der Bibel, Von Assonanz bis Zahlenspruch, p. 81.

listines." From ancient times Philistine settlements have been in and around the modern Gaza Strip. In OT times, the five main cities of the Philistines were Gaza, Ashkelon, Gath, Ekron and Ashdod (1 Sam. 6:17). With the term "Philistia" in Psalm 83:7, we have very clear reference to the modern Palestinian Gaza Strip, or rather, in the greatest sense, to the areas under Palestinian administration. Incidentally, already in OT times the Philistines extended themselves far outside their own core area in the Land of Israel.[165] Especially in King Saul's era (11th century BC), the Philistines ruled areas which belong to the heartland of modern Israel and the so-called West Bank.[166] Since 1976 the Palestinians, represented by the PLO, have been members of the Arab League. It is interesting to note that the name Palestinian and Philistine are linguistically related. When Latinised, the term "Philistine" is rendered *Palestini* amongst others (Lat. Vulgate Bible, Gen. 26:14). Notable is the following: In Arabic, the exact same term is used for "Palestinian" as for "Philistine" (in the Arabic Bible): *philastini*.

## 27.7 Iraq

Finally, in Psalm 83:8, Assur is mentioned. Assur, or Assyria attained the dimensions of a monumental world empire during the period of the kings in Israel. The heart of Assyria, with the significant cities of Nineveh, Assur and Kalach lay in the area of modern northern Iraq. Here Asaph, the author of Psalm 83, refers us to this region by mentioning Assur. Iraq was also one of the seven founding members of the Arab League.

Although Jordan played a leading role in the devastating war against Israel in 1947–1949, Iraq, too, was involved in that it supported Jordan. This is exactly what Psalm 83:8 states:

> "[8] *Assyria also has joined with them;*
> *They have helped the children of Lot.*" (NKJV)

---

165  Cf. i.e. 1 Sam 7:14.
166  1 Sam 13–31.

# 28. Capture of Temple Mount: 7 June 1967

In the November Resolution of 1947, a clear majority of the UN members voted for the creation of a Jewish state in Palestine. However, the heart of the Promised Land, Temple Mount, was excluded, along with the Old City, from Israeli national territory. The United Nations had planned to internationalize all of East Jerusalem, including Temple Mount. But the Arab-Islamic war of annihilation, from the end of 1947 till July 1949, changed this. Jordan managed to capture, with the help of all its allied armies, the Temple Mount and East Jerusalem. The UN had no power to change anything about that. Consequently Jordan annexed the entire West Bank together with East Jerusalem and the Temple Mount. Thus facts were created which the world accepted, even though hardly any of the world's nations acknowledged Jordan's annexation of this territory. Hence, this annexation was, according to international law, not binding.

However, there was a decisive turn of events as the Arab countries, encouraged by a massive arms build-up and modernization of their armies, under the leadership of Egypt, planned a second attempt to annihilate the Jewish nation during the '60s. As soon as Jordan, in spite of a prior stern warning by Israel, began taking an active part in the Six Day War of 1967, this was judged by the Jewish government as justification for conquering the Old City of Jerusalem and the Temple Mount. Shortly after Jordan had begun shelling Israeli West Jerusalem over the dividing wall with heavy artillery, paratroopers stationed on Mount Scopus received the order: "Take the Old City and Temple Mount!" The aforesaid soldiers of the Israeli Army pushed into the Old City through the Stephen's Gate (also called the Lions' Gate) to the north and conquered it together with the Temple Mount.

As an outsider, it is hard to imagine what a historic moment this was in the history of the Jewish people! In 70 AD Judaism had suffered the loss of sovereignty over Temple Mount for almost two thousand years. Therefore since that time, there has never again been a Jewish Temple built. According to the Torah, a temple to offer sacrifice may only be built here on this place chosen by God (Deut. 12:13-14). Yet since that memorable Wednesday in June, 1967, the Temple Mount on Zion is again in Jewish hands! This fulfilled the following verses from Psalm 126:

> *"¹ When the LORD brought back the captivity of Zion,*
> *We were like those who dream.*
> *² Then our mouth was filled with laughter,*
> *And our tongue with singing.*
> *Then they said among the nations,*
> *"The LORD has done great things for them."*
> *³ The LORD has done great things for us,*
> *And we are glad."* (NKJV)

The fate of Temple Mount changed fundamentally after 1,897 years. The turnaround in 1967 was inconceivably dramatic: An immensely greater power, both in numbers and military might, attempted to destroy the State of Israel, but this danger was repulsed in just six days. The enemy was beaten on all three fronts. Rest came on Sunday. A people had survived. The Temple Mount was again in the hands of the Jews. Thousands of Israelis surged to the Wailing Wall, the western wall of the former Temple, to pray and to thank God for the over-whelming victory.

In the military history of mankind there had never been anything like this! Millions all over the entire world acknowledged that God's Hand was seen in this war for survival. The word was fulfilled (Ps. 126:2b):

> *"²ᵇ Then they said among the nations,*
> *'The LORD has done great things for them.'"* (NKJV)

The masses in Israel also recognized that the Most High was to be thanked for this victory. Those who did not directly experience these events can hardly imagine the euphoria among the population of Israel at that time. Psalm 126:3 expresses it this way:

"³ The LORD has done great things for us,
And we are glad." (NKJV)

Throughout all the centuries, the liberation of Jerusalem had been prayed for three times a day in Judaism and suddenly the reality exceeded their wildest dreams.

At this point, some readers may need a clarification of the term "Mount Zion": the hill south-west of the Old City of Jerusalem is today named "Mount Zion." This could cause confusion, since this is a neighbouring hill of the Temple Mount. The geographical term "Zion" for this neighbouring hill, was first common following the 1ˢᵗ century AD. In Biblical times, Temple Mount was always named "Zion." In order to differentiate, it is advisable to call Temple Mount "Zion I" and the south-western hill "Zion II."[167] In the Bible the Temple Mount was also called "Moriah" (2 Chron. 3:1; cf. Gen. 22:2).

**Fig. 12:** *The conquerors on Temple Mount (Psalm 126:2): "Then our mouth was filled with laughter, and our tongue with singing." (source: Military Archives, Israel/ASEBA, Switzerland)*

167  Zion II was also salvation-historically very significant. The original Christian quarter was found on this hill in the time of Acts and again following 70 AD. (cf. RIESNER: Essener und Urgemeinde in Jerusalem, Neue Funde und Quellen, passim).

# 29. The Roman Empire Re-emerges

Toward the end of Babylon's world domination (549 BC), the prophet Daniel had a dream in which he saw four different vicious, bloodthirsty beasts emerge from the sea one after the other (Dan. 7:1ff). It was made clear to him that these beasts represented different successive empires (cf. Dan. 7:23).[168]

The first beast, a majestic lion with eagle's wings, represented the empire of that time (Dan. 7:4): *Babylonia* (609–539 BC).

The second, a voracious bear symbolized the next world empire which would appear in history (Dan. 7:5): *Medo-Persia* (beginning in 539 BC).

Daniel then saw an especially swift beast: a leopard with four heads and four wings emerging from the sea of the nations (Dan. 7:6). This beast refers to *the Greek Empire* which Alexander the Great built-up in a phenomenally short period of some 13 years, from Greece over the African continent to the Indus (from 336 BC). The four heads refer to the four great factions into which the Greek Empire diverged following Alexander's death.

The fourth beast was extraordinarily strong and frightening (Dan. 7:7). It had iron teeth and ten horns. Here *the Roman Empire* is characterized which, following the victory over the remnants of Alexander's former realm at the Battle of Actium (40 BC), clearly constituted world power Number One.

Now we can make a link from the OT to the NT: In Revelation 13, the Apostle John, around 95 AD – at the time of the Roman Empire – saw in his vision on Patmos this fourth beast with ten horns from Daniel 7 once again (cf. Rev. 13:1-10). It was revealed to John that the fourth empire from the Book of Daniel would have 3 phases. Corresponding to the three grammatical tenses; past, present and future, this is expressed as follows in Revelation 17:8:[169]

---

168 For details to Dan 7 cf. LIEBI: Weltgeschichte im Visier des Propheten Daniel (English edition in progress by CMV Hagedorn, Germany); LIEBI: Das neue Europa – Hoffnung oder Illusion, p. 29ff.

169 There is a very pointed reason why the Roman Empire is so described. In Rev. 13:1-10, it is explained that this empire worships itself. The true God is named in Rev. 1:4: "... *who is and who was and who is to come.*" When Rev. 17:8 and 1:4 are compared, the contrast is clear. Compared to the Eternal One, what is a "*god*" who "*was*", but "*is not*" and further "*will ascend out of the bottomless pit*" and then have to "*go to perdition*"?

*"[8] The beast that you saw [a] **was,**
and [b] **is not,**
and [c] **will ascend out of the bottomless pit** and go to perdition."* (NKJV)

Throughout history everything has unfolded exactly according to the prophecies in the book of Daniel. Beginning with Nebuchadnezzar of Babylon, ancient world history initially proceeded in four great stages:

- Babylonian Empire (606–539 BC)
- Medo-Persian Empire (539–331 BC)
- Greek Empire (331–40 BC)
- Roman Empire (from 40 BC)

The Western Roman Empire collapsed in 476 AD due to the invasion of barbarians from the north and the east. However, with the crowning of Charlemagne by Pope Leo III, France was understood to be the continuation of the old Roman Empire. Through further developments in the Ottonian Dynasty during the 10th century, the so-called "Holy Roman Empire" came into being. After the 15th century, the term "Holy Roman Empire of the German Nation" was in common usage. The name explains itself as follows: *German* emperors were always crowned by the Pope from *Rome* over this empire.

The Eastern Roman Empire had been able to continue without interruption since Antiquity. It shrank bit by bit, however. This empire ceased to exist with the Turkish onslaught in 1453.

The Holy Roman Empire encompassed, at its height, a significant part of the European continent, namely almost all of Central and Southern Europe. However, following Napoleon's victories, it became unwieldy. With the abdication of Emperor Franz II on 6 August 1806 the "Holy Roman Empire of the German Nation" expired. Napoleon, who had crowned himself Emperor of France previously, in 1804, attempted to build up a type of Roman Empire with his monstrous wars of conquest, reaching into Russia, Africa and Asia (Egypt and Palestine). Nonetheless, with Napoleon's defeat in the Battle of the Nations at Leipzig in 1813, the fall of this empire was sealed. On 2 April 1814 he was deposed from being Emperor by the Senate.

From then on, there has been no empire worthy of the name "Roman Empire." The once united European continent was characterized in its later history by internal splintering. Europe divided into many nation states. This was a matter of honour. Indeed, this was the period of nationalism. There was pride in being, for example, "German" or "French" or "British." This inner unrest led ultimately to the catastrophe of the First World War. But that was not the end of the inner conflict. European discord reached a climax in the Second World War (1939–1945), in an unimaginable escalation of evil. Afterward, Europe lay bombed in ruins. Europe had sunk into the abyss! The dreadful result: 50–70 million dead.

In 1946 Winston Churchill came to Zurich and stated, in his famous speech at the University:[170]

"Let Europe arise!"

He was certain of one thing:
"… we must recreate the European Family in a regional structure called, it may be the United States of Europe."

He laid down the basic structure of how a new Europe should be built. In 1957, the Treaties of *Rome* (!) brought six nations closer together. As a consequence, the EEC came into being. More nations joined. and, through increasing integration, the EEC became the EU in 1993. Today, the EU has grown to a power bloc of 27 member nations.

What constitutes this Imperium? This question was answered long ago by the European visionary Emile Lousse. He wrote in the 50s of the 20th century:

"It is essentially so: Europe, European unity, does not need to be created, but rather, restored."[171]

The former Swiss Secretary of State, Dr. Franz Blankart, as a

170 The text is public under: http://portal.coe.ge/index.php?lan=en&id=million (as of: 24.10.2011).

171 LOUSSE, E.: Europa's erf en vermogen, Schriften voor Europeese gemeenschapszin, 1955, p. 5, quoted from: MEDEMA: Europa, Der Alptraum von einem Supermarkt, p. 91.

European advocate looking toward this new unity, stated:
"A Holy Roman Empire must be built."[172]

The EU has succeeded the Roman Empire. It emerged from the abyss into which Europe had fallen, the most devastating war in human history. This describes exactly phase c) in Revelation 17:8:

*"⁸... and will **ascend out of the bottomless pit** and go to perdition."* (NKJV)

The Greek word *abyssos*, translated "abyss" in English, is used in Romans 10:7 for the realm of the dead. Europe's emergence from the wreckage of Second World War, with its well up to 70 million dead, definitely describes an emergence from the Abyssos!

In this context, the following is very noteworthy: According to the book of Revelation Jesus Christ will return in the period that the Roman Empire emerges from the abyss (cf. Rev. 17:14; 19:11ff)!

A most astonishing fact is that Europe's reunification occurred at just the right time, namely, exactly in the epoch in which millions of Jews from the entire world returned to the Land of their Forefathers, and in which all of the further, more than 175 prophecies regarding The Last Days have been fulfilled!

# 30. List with 62 Fulfilled Prophecies (P1–P62)

All the fulfilled prophecies regarding The Last Days (P1–P62) which we have handled thus far are clearly and concisely compiled in the following list. This will give the reader a quick access to individual prophetic statements.

I have attempted to list each prophetic statement separately, paraphrased in concise words, together with the Biblical quotation and its fulfilment. Should individual paraphrases prove to be unclear, the more detailed treatment of these prophecies can be

---

172  LIETH: Die letzten 75 Tage, p. 7.

located in the text above without difficulty and reread.

At times, the reader may take two successive, separately listed points to be one statement. On the other hand, there are also cases which I count as a *one* prophecy that someone else would expand into two or more ideas.

I have, for example, treated the prophetic announcement that the Jews will be brought together from all over the world, not as one prophecy, but rather, depicted as two prophecies. Why? There were plans to bring the Jews together in quite different places, other than Israel, for instance, in Uganda or in Argentina. If this had happened, it could have been said that the prophecy of Jeremiah 31:10 was fulfilled. This verse speaks only about *the gathering*, without mentioning the place of gathering. However, Ezekiel 36:24 expressly names the *Land of Israel* as the place of reassembly. Here it is clear that we effectively have two distinct prophetic statements. With each of these prophecies, there is, theoretically the possibility of fulfilment or non-fulfilment. We may ask:

- Were the Jews *assembled out of the entire world to some place*? Yes/No
- Were the Jews *assembled out of the entire world to Israel*? Yes/No

Another example may be helpful to make clear the methodology by which the individual prophecies have been numbered:

Jeremiah 31:8 states that Jews will return from the Land of the North in great numbers. Isn't this one single prophecy? No, there are two prophetic statements here! When e.g., 10,000 Jews returned from Russia, or as the case may be, from the Soviet Union, the prophecy of the return out of the north could be seen as fulfilled. But the text stresses that this return would be in *"great numbers."* Therefore, that some 1.3 million – more than a third of all returnees from the entire world – have come from *"from the north country ... from the ends of the earth"* fulfils the second statement. To be exact, *two* prophecies are dealt with here. Theoretically each statement could have been fulfilled on its own or not. The fulfilment of the second statement does not automatically result from the first. The second statement pertains to an incident independent from the first.

In Chapter IV, I will handle the prophecies regarding the moral collapse in The Last Days. I count these predictions as *one* prophecy. In principle, it would be possible to count separately the individual details clearly mentioned in the Bible. If this were done, naturally, there would be many more than the 178 fulfilled prophecies listed here. I have not done so in this case because various details can result as a consequence of other details and therefore are directly dependent on one another. It was my wish in writing this book to list the events which are independent of one another. The number 178 has no particularly deep significance. It is used simply to give the reader an idea of the magnitude of the numerous Biblical prophecies fulfilled in our time. The listing of events which are as independent as possible simplifies considering the calculation of mathematical probability found at the end of the book. The evaluation of events, each dependent upon the other, would be enormously more complicated and its calculation would hardly be possible.

| Prophecy | Statement | Bible verse | Fulfillment |
|----------|-----------|-------------|-------------|
| P1 | **Israel's enemies** live in the country of Israel, instead of the Jews | Lev. 26:32 | From 638 AD: Conquest and settlement of the Land of Israel by Arab Muslims. The marked hatred of Jews among the Palestinians is motivated by the teaching of the Koran |
| P2 | Return **after a long time** | Hos. 3:5 | 70 AD–1882 = 1,812 years |
| P3 | Return after a long time of **statelessness** | Hos. 3:4 | 135 AD–1948: No State of Israel |
| P4 | Return after **a long time without sacrifice** | Hos. 3:4 | 70 AD–today: Time without Jewish Temple; therefore, also without animal sacrifice |
| P5 | Return after **a long time without the High-Priestly garments (Ephod)** | Hos. 3:4 | 70 AD–approx. 2000: No High Priest; no High-Priestly garments with the Ephod |
| P6 | Return after **a long time without idols and ancestor worship** | Hos. 3:4 | 70 AD–19th century: No idols and ancestor worship in Judaism |
| P7 | A **permanent** Jewish remnant in the Land | Isa. 6:9-13 | 70 AD–1882: A continual Jewish remnant in the Land of Israel; Low point: around 1800: 6,700 Jews. Afterward, the number increased again |

| Prophecy | Statement | Bible verse | Fulfillment |
|----------|-----------|-------------|-------------|
| P8 | **Blinding** of Israel **during** the depopulation of the Land | Isa. 6:8-13 | **70 AD–19th century: Very few Jewish believers in the Messiah Jesus** (19th century = beginning of the "Hebrew Christian Movement." From the 19th century until today: Very many Jews have come to belief in the Messiah Jesus |
| P9 | **Gathering** of Jews **from the entire world generally** | Ps. 107:1-3; Isa. 43:5-7; Jer. 16:14-15; 23:7-8; Ezek. 11:17; 36:24; 37:21 | 1882 until today: > 3 million Jews **from all five continents** brought together, **from some 130 countries** |
| P10 | Return to the **Land of Israel** | Jer. 3:19; 23:7-8; 31:8; Ezek. 11:17; 36:24; 37:21 | 1882 until today: > 3 million came to the **Land of their Fathers** |
| P11 | **Initially** Zionism (period of "fishermen") | Jer. 16:15 | Zionism prepares the way for immigration: 1750–1882 |
| P12 | **Subsequent** persecution (period of the "hunters") | Jer. 16:15 | Jewish persecution led to huge waves of immigration |
| P13 | Return in **many phases, like the streams in the Negev** | Ps. 126:4 | 1882 until today: Return in numerous waves of immigration |

| Prophecy | Statement | Bible verse | Fulfillment |
|---|---|---|---|
| P14 | Return with **intermediate stops, like the little streams, which flow into larger streams before they all reach the main stream** | Ps. 126:4 | 1882 until today: Many Jews go through other countries on the way back to Israel |
| P15 | Return from **"the north ... the ends of the earth"** | Jer. 31:8; 3:19; 16:15; 23:7 ; Isa. 49·12; 43:6; Zech. 2:6 | Return of approx. 1.3 million **from Russia/ the former Soviet Union/from the CIS** |
| P16 | Return from the farthest north (Russia/Soviet Union/ CIS) **in very great numbers** | Jer. 31:8 | Return of **approx. 1.3 million** from Russia / the Soviet Union/ from the CIS (comprising more than 1/3 of all returnees) |
| P17 | **Flight** from the land of the north (Russia) | Zech. 2:6 | Since 1882: Several waves of emigration from Russia due to persecution of Jews |
| P18 | Return from the countries **surrounding Israel** | Ezek. 37:21 | From 1948: Mass emigration **from Arab countries around Israel**. Approx. 650,000 come to Israel |
| P19 | Return from **Assyria (northern Iraq)** | Isa.11:11 | Since 1941: Return of a total of 150,000 Jews **from northern** and southern **Iraq** |

| Prophecy | Statement | Bible verse | Fulfillment |
|---|---|---|---|
| P20 | Return from **Shine'ar/ Babylon/ Land of the Chaldeans (southern Iraq)** | Isa. 11:11; Jer. 50:8; 51:6,45; Zech. 2:11 | From 1941: Return of altogether 150,000 Jews from northern and **southern Iraq** |
| P21 | Return from **Mizrayim (Lower Egypt)** | Isa. 11:11 | From 1948: Emigration of 75,000 −80,000 Jews from Egypt. **Return** of altogether 37,600 Jews from Upper and **Lower Egypt to Israel** |
| P22 | Return from **Pathros (Upper Egypt)** | Isa. 11:11 | From 1948: Emigration of 75,000 −80,000 Jews from Egypt. **Return** of altogether 37,600 Jews from **Upper** and Lower **Egypt** to Israel |
| P23 | Return from **Elam (Iran/Persia)** | Isa. 11:11 | 20th century: Return of 100,000 Jews from Iran to Israel |
| P24 | Return from **Hamath (Syria)** | Isa. 11:11 | 1948–1964: Return of 9,500 Jews from Syria |
| P25 | Return **from countries by the Red Sea** | Ps. 107:3 | 1949–1950: Return of approx. 56,000 Jews from **Yemen, Aden, Somalia and Eritrea**[T1] (for return from Sudan and Ethiopia see under P26) |

---

T1 The return of Jews from Sudan was also fulfilment of the prophecy concerning the countries of the Red Sea. Since the return from Cush (Sudan, Ethiopia, and Eritrea) is clearly mentioned in the prophecy, however, this return is dealt with in connection with the prophecy in Isa 11:11 concerning Cush. The return from Eritrea could be taken in context with the prophecy regarding Cush.

| Prophecy | Statement | Bible verse | Fulfillment |
|----------|-----------|-------------|-------------|
| P26 | Return from **Cush** (Sudan, Ethiopia) | Isa. 11:11 | From 1980: Rescue in several operations: altogether more than 84,000 Jews from **Sudan and Ethiopia** come to Israel |
| P27 | Return from Europe, from the "Iyim" | Isa. 11:11 | From 1933–present: **Around 1 million Jews from Europe** (excluding Russia) arrive in the Land of their Fathers, a large part of whom as refugees from the Nazis |
| P28 | Return from **the south, ... the ends of the earth** | Isa. 43:6 | From 1948: Immigration of around 20,000 Jews **from South Africa** |
| P29 | Return from the **farthest west** | Isa. 43:5-6 | From 1948: Return of approx. 110,000 Jews **from North America** |
| P30 | Return from the **Land of Sinese** | Isa. 43:12 | From 1949: Return of Jews **from China** |
| P31 | Return **by ship** | Ps. 107:25-32 | Especially from 1932–today: hundreds of thousands reach the Land of the Fathers by ship |
| P32 | **Return by air** like clouds and like doves | Isa. 60:8 | Especially in the period from 1948–present: Return of many thousands from the entire world **by plane** to Israel |

| Prophecy | Statement | Bible verse | Fulfillment |
|---|---|---|---|
| P33 | **Hebrew**: A **spoken language** | Isa. 19:18 | **Revival of Hebrew** by Elieser Ben-Yehuda (1881–1922); **since 1922: Hebrew = official language in the Land** |
| P34 | Land is purchased in Israel | Jer. 32:43-44 | 1882–1940: Extensive land bought in "Palestine" (in the Galilee and Judea) |
| P35 | Geographical specification: land bought in **Benjamin** | Jer. 32:43-44 | 1882–1940: Land bought south of modern Ramallah (tribal region of Benjamin) |
| P36 | Specification: land bought in the **areas surrounding Jerusalem** | Jer. 32:43-44 | 1882–1940: Land bought extensively around Jerusalem |
| P37 | Specification: land bought in the **Judean Hills** | Jer. 32:43-44 | 1882–1940: Land bought in the Judean Hills between Jerusalem and Hebron, as well as between Jerusalem and Ramla |
| P38 | Specification: land bought in the **Shephelah (lowlands)** | Jer. 32:43-44 | 1882–1940: Great tracts of land bought in the Shephela, between Gaza und Jaffa /Tel-Aviv as well as north of Tel-Aviv |
| P39 | Specification: land bought in the **Negev** | Jer. 32:43-44 | 1882–1940: Land bought to the south and south-east of Beersheba as well as south of the Rafah – Beersheba line |

| Prophecy | Statement | Bible verse | Fulfillment |
| --- | --- | --- | --- |
| P40 | Reconstruction and development of Old Testament cities | Amos 9:14 | 1882–today: Numerous OT cities are reconstructed or modernized |
| P41 | **Vineyards** planted | Amos 9:14 | From the end of the 19th century: vineyards of world renown re-established following Islamic destruction |
| P42 | Replanting of vineyards with **foreign vines** | Isa. 17:10 | 1882–today: Building up a wine industry **with grape varieties from France, Germany and Croatia** |
| P43 | The laying out of **fruit plantations** | Amos 9:14 | 1882–Present: Building up of an extensive agriculture with fruit production (citrus, exotic fruits, etc.) |
| P44 | **Transformation of the desert** into fertile land | Ezek. 36:34,35; Ps. 107:35-38 | 1882–today: Reforestation in Israel with over 230 million trees; development of most modern agriculture; production of 1.4 billion cut flowers annually |
| P45 | Birth of the State of Israel | Isa. 66:8 | 14 May 1948 |
| P46 | Founding of the state **in the midst of painful military conflict ("woes")** | Isa. 66:8 | **War in the Land** from December 1947 –July 1949; **total war** as of 15 May 1948– July 1949 |

| Prophecy | Statement | Bible verse | Fulfillment |
| --- | --- | --- | --- |
| P47 | The enemies' goal: **Total obliteration of Israel** | Ps. 83:1-4 | Three all-out wars of annihilation against Israel: 1948/1949, 1967, 1973 |
| P48 | **The confederacy/ the league** of Israel's enemies | Ps. 83:5 | Arab League founded 22 March 1945 |
| P49 | Confederacy members: **Edom, Moab, Ammon** | Ps. 83:6,7 | Jordan: founding member of the Arab League from 1945 |
| P50 | Member of the confederacy: **The Ishmaelites** | Ps. 83:6 | Saudi Arabia/North Yemen: founding members of the Arab League from 1945 |
| P51 | Member of the confederacy: **The Hagrites** | Ps. 83:6 | Syria: Founding member of the Arab League from 1945 |
| P52 | Member of the confederacy: **Gebal und Tyre** | Ps. 83:7 | Lebanon: Founding member of the Arab League from 1945 |
| P53 | Member of the confederacy: **Amalek** | Ps. 83:7 | Egypt: Founding member of the Arab League from 1945 |
| P54 | Member of the confederacy: **Philistia** | Ps. 83:7 | Palestinians: Member of the Arab League from 1976 (via the PLO) |
| P55 | Member of the confederacy: **Assur** | Ps. 83:8 | Iraq: Founding member of the Arab League from 1945 |

| Prophecy | Statement | Bible verse | Fulfillment |
|---|---|---|---|
| P56 | Assur **supports** the sons of Lot | Ps. 83:8 | Iraq supported Jordan in the war of 1948–1949; also in 1967 |
| P57 | The fate of **Temple Mount Zion** is reversed | Ps. 126:1 | Capture of Temple Mount Zion: Six Day War – June, 1967 |
| P58 | It is said among the **nations: The LORD has done great things for them!** | Ps. 126:2b | Millions worldwide acknowledge God's intervention in the Six Day War: June 1967. The superior power was beaten on all three fronts after only six days |
| P59 | Jews are like **those who dream**, their mouths filled with laughter | Ps. 126:1,2,3 | Indescribable joy and euphoria in Israel: June 1967 |
| P60 | Acknowledgement in **Israel: The LORD has done great things for us!** | Ps. 126:3 | Countless Israelis acknowledge God's help in the Six Day War of 1967 |
| P61 | The Roman Empire **re-emerges** | Rev. 17:8 | Europe unites anew to be a great power (1957 till today) |
| P62 | The Roman Empire emerges **out of the abyss/the realm of the dead** | Rev. 17:8 | Europe unites directly after the catastrophe of the Second World War with some 70 million dead |

# III. The West Bank in View of Biblical Prophecy

## 1. Introduction

The Israeli Army wrested the West Bank away from Jordan during the Six Day War of 1967. Since then this area has remained in the headlines of the international press. The entire world is focused on questions of international law and world politics connected with this issue. What does the Bible actually say about these questions? Millennia ago, at God's command, the prophets of the Bible announced both the details and the outcome!

### 1.1 Land Gained and Land Lost

In accordance with a rigorously calculated chronology, which also agrees remarkably with archaeological dating in Egypt and Canaan, the Exodus took place in 1606 BC. [173] Moses led the Israelites out of slavery (Exod. 1–15). After 40 years of wandering through the desert (Numbers and Deuteronomy), the Nation reached its goal: The Promised Land was taken possession of under Joshua's leadership (Josh. 1–24). The entire area, known today as the "West Bank," belonged to the land of the ancient State of Israel. The West Bank occupies the central area of Israel. As we have just seen in the first part of this book, the nation of Israel lost its Land following 70 AD. This was one of the consequences of rejecting the Messiah. Thus, Deut. 28:63–64 was fulfilled (prophecy from 1566 BC).

---

173 Cf. LIEBI: Zur Chronologie des AT.

*"63 ... and you shall be plucked from off the land which you go to possess. 64 "Then the LORD will scatter you among all peoples, from one end of the earth to the other; ..."* (NKJV)

## 1.2 The First World War and the Liberation of the Land

The First World War brought about a fundamental turn of events. The Turkish Ottoman Empire, which ruled large parts of the Middle East for centuries, including the Land of the Bible since 1517, aligned itself with Germany in the course of the war. The Ottomans brought upon themselves the fury of the so-called Entente Powers. Afterwards the Ottoman Empire disintegrated. Its last Sultan, Mehmed VI, finally abdicated.

The United Kingdom issued the Balfour Declaration in 1917[174] as thanks for the crucial contribution of the British Jew, Dr. Chaim Weizman, who helped bring about a total change in the World War by his unexpected chemical discovery which helped turn the tide, preventing Germany from being victorious. In Lord Balfour's Declaration, England committed itself to do everything in its power to ensure that a national home for the Jewish people could be created in Palestine. Through the adoption of the Balfour Declaration as the League of Nations' Mandate on 24 July 1922, this proclamation received international legal recognition.[175]

Palestine came under British Mandate power in 1920, shortly after the War. Great Britain was responsible for the management of this region until a reasonable solution for its future could be worked out. Only in 1922 did the League of Nations formally recognize Britain's Mandate powers.

The term "Palestine" at that time described the entire territory of the modern State of Israel, including the Gaza Strip and the West Bank and also encompassing the modern nation of Jordan.[176]

---

174 http://www.uni-protokolle.de/Lexikon/Balfour-Deklaration.html (as of: 24.10.2011).

175 For very extensive treatment of this and the questions of international law connected with it cf.: GAUTHIER: Sovereignty over the Old City of Jerusalem, A Study of the Historical, Religious, Political and Legal Aspects of the Question of the Old City, Thèse présenté pour l'obtention du grade de Docteur ès Science politiques (Droit international), Université de Genève, Institut Universitaire de Hautes Etudes Internationales, Thèse N° 725, Genève 2007.

176 GAUTHIER: Sovereignty over the Old City of Jerusalem, A Study of the Historical, Religious, Political and Legal Aspects oft the Question of the Old City, p. 393-406.

All inhabitants of the area east and west of the Jordan River were named "Palestinians," completely independent of their being Jew or Arab. The term "Palestinian" or "Palestinian people" was not at all used to differentiate Jews from Arab descendants at that time! Both Jews and Arabs were recorded as "Palestinian" on the identity cards handed out by the British. This also explains why the internationally known Jewish newspaper, "The Jerusalem Post" was known during the Mandate period as "The Palestine Post." Today's world-renowned "Israel Symphony Orchestra" carried the name "Palestine Symphony Orchestra" in the period before the founding of the state.

The Golan Heights were a part of the Mandate area which the League of Nations transferred to the victorious Entente state of France.

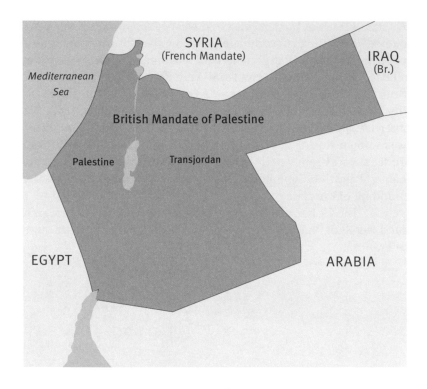

*Fig. 13: Palestine at the beginning of the 20ᵗʰ century.*

Britain implemented the first partition of Palestine in 1921. The area east of the Jordan River (the territory of modern Jordan) was separated and reserved for a projected Arab-Palestinian nation. The British government not only wanted to create a home nation for "Palestinian Jews," but also for the "Palestinian Arabs." This separated area was named "Transjordan" from then on.

On 22 March 1946 this area became totally independent from Britain. Its name was changed to "Jordan" on 24 May. It was clear that an Arab "Palestinian nation" was founded before a Jewish state was founded. This new state did not comprise 50% of the territory, which would have conformed to the Western sense of justice, but rather some 77% of Palestine!

**Fig. 14:** *The first partition of Palestine in 1921 (source: Doron, GNU 1.2 or later).*

The years of 1938–1945 brought a catastrophe of unimagined magnitude to the Jews in Europe: The Nazis and their allies annihilated 6 million Jews. Those who were somehow able, fled from their slaughterers. An escape to Palestine, the Land of their Fathers, seemed ideal to countless Jews. However, the British occupying power played an indescribably evil role in this period. In order to mitigate Muslim terrorism against the British, Britain locked the door to most Jews attempting to flee to Palestine. The quota for entry was drastically reduced. Thousands of Jews who, on their ships, wanted to dock in a safe harbour were sent back. Many of these Jews who had been returned fell into the hands of the Nazis again and were slaughtered.

## 1.3 The Second World War and the modern State of Israel

The entire horror of the Shoah[177] came to light when the concentration camps in Europe were opened at the end of the Second World War. The civilized world was in shock. This would have enormous consequences:

On 29 November 1947, when the UN voted on the second partition of Palestine and the creation of a Jewish nation, the majority of the nations responded with a bold "yes." The Islamic nations in the UN fell into a rage. They threatened that any future Jewish nation would be immediately destroyed. However, those who had voted "yes" would not be bullied. The shock of the latest Jewish annihilation was still too fresh to ignore. This "yes" came about on this remarkable day just in these special circumstances. This would be unthinkable today. Therefore, it can be said that the fact of the existence of the modern State of Israel is a direct consequence of the Second World War and the annihilation of over 6 million Jews connected with it! Isn't it astounding that the two most horrible wars in the history of mankind – there have been only two world wars – played key roles in the change in the Jews' fate after almost two millennia? The Land of Israel was freed for the Jews by the Second World War. The door to the Jews' modern state was thrown open by the Second World War.

The Palestinian Arabs had already obtained approximately 77% of Palestine. Now only 23% remained, in principle. However, the UN chose not to turn over all of the remainder to the Jews. No, Palestine would be divided a second time. In practice the vote regarding the second partition of Palestine and the creation of a Jewish state meant that, from the remaining territory of Palestine (approx. 23%), only 12.6% would be available for the founding of the modern State of Israel. This second partition was the UN's concession to the Islamic world raging in the Middle East.

A second (!) Palestinian nation was to be founded on the remaining 10.4% of the territory! However, this was incapable of placating the Islamic world at all. The explanation for this lies in the teach-

---

177 The Hebrew word sho'ah means "catastrophe." It is used today in German to designate the Nazi annihilation of the Jews. It can be used instead of the term "Holocaust."

ings of orthodox Islam. The theologian Al-Mawardi (975–1058 AD) divided the world, based on the Koran, in two parts:[178] The part of the earth which is under Islamic rule is described as *dar ul-islam* ("House of Islam"). The remaining part is *dar ul-harb* ("House of the Sword"). In the future, this area also would also come under Islamic law by means of Holy War. Al-Mawardi made it clear that once a country had become *dar ul-islam*, it may never again come under non-Muslim rule. Non-Muslims, such as Jews and Christians, in contrast to polytheists, may live as lesser subjects in such an area; but they may not independently rule over *dar ul-islam*. From this understanding, it is clear why, to this day in orthodox Islam, not only in fanatic Islam, it is not a question of how much land the nation of Israel is allowed to possess of the former Palestine. It is rather that, fundamentally, there may be no Jewish state between the Mediterranean and Jordan!

"Palestine" has been counted as *dar ul-islam* in Islam for more than 1,000 years. In 638, shortly after Mohammad's death (622), Muslims from the area of today's Saudi Arabia moved into Jerusalem as conquerors. Shortly afterward, the Dome of the Rock (682) and the Al-Aqsa Mosque (705) were built where the former Jewish Temple had stood, in order to seal the Islamic claim to power over the Holy Land.

The Jews accepted the UN's decision with both joy and disappointment. There was joy that the longing of two millennia would now become reality. The great disappointment was that actually the UN had only given them an amputated rump state by specifically excluding East Jerusalem, the heart of Judaism with Temple Mount and the City of David (Ir David). Even though the Arab Palestinians had been given 87.4% of Palestine in total and the Jews only 12.6%, the Islamic world in the Middle East was in a rage following the UN decision of November, 1947. How is this phenomenon to be explained? It can only be understood when Al-Mawardi's systemically formulated Islamic teaching of *dar ul-islam* and *dar ul-harb* is known!

The two partitions of Palestine by Britain and the UN were foreseen in the book of Joel (8th century BC). In chapter 3 verse

---

178 SCHIRRMACHER: Der Islam, Vol. I, p. 92-93.

1-3, the Messiah states that He will return in the period marking the change in the fate of Judah and Jerusalem. As Judge He will bring the nations to account according to what they have done to His people Israel and His Land. Among the accusations of wrongs done to His people is that of having scattered the Jews among the nations and of dividing up the Land of Israel, which is God's property, without authority[179] (Joel 3:1-3):

> *"¹ For behold, in those days and at that time,*
> *When I bring back the captives of Judah and Jerusalem,*
> *² I will also gather all nations,*
> *And bring them down to the Valley of Jehoshaphat;*
> *And **I will enter into judgement with them there***
> *On account of My people, **My heritage Israel**,*
> *Whom they have scattered among the nations;*
> ***They have also divided up My land.***
> *³ They have cast lots for My people ..."* (NKJV)

Historically speaking, when was the Land of Israel ever divided up by the nations of the world? Never in the far-reaching past has this happened. But in the 20th century, this has occurred twice in very fateful ways:
- The first partition of Palestine by Britain in 1921, approved by the League of Nations in 1922
- The second partition of Palestine by the UN in 1947

# 2. Founding of the State and Total War against Israel

On the basis of the UN decision, the State of Israel was founded on 14 May 1948. Ben Gurion stated on radio:
"Here is the State of Israel. 2000 years have passed. When the time for God has come, no-one can withstand Him."

---

179  Cf. also Lev. 25:23.

The British occupation force finally withdrew on this day. Waiting, massed on the borders, were troops from Jordan, Iraq, Syria, Lebanon and Egypt, supported by contingents from Saudi Arabia and Yemen, as well as the Arab Liberation Army (ALA) and the Army of the Holy War[180] in order to annihilate the Jewish state, newly come into existence, from midnight. Total war against the Jews began. For Israel it was a question of sheer survival. The Jewish state had very few planes and almost no heavy weapons at that time. The Haganah, the Jews' self-defence troop which came into being in the 1920s to combat Arab terrorism, together with the combat units Lehi, Palmach and Irgun, took on the task of the official army upon the founding of the state.

For the West, it seemed rather clear that the Jewish state would again perish. Easy come, easy go. Therefore, America tried in the last moment to prevent the founding of the State of Israel, but the Jews vehemently rejected this. A terrible period followed. Altogether, some 6,000 Jews were killed, both civilians and soldiers. However, Israel was soon gaining ground against the superior power and began winning additional land. The UN achieved a cease-fire in July, 1949.

## 2.1 Annexation of the West Bank by Jordan

Jordan was able to capture East Jerusalem, including the Wailing Wall and the Temple Mount. The Jews living there were slaughtered, expelled or taken as prisoners of war. The Jewish Quarter in the Old City was ravaged and defiled. Countless graves on the Mount of Olives were desecrated, many of which existed in antiquity. Finally, as once was the case in Berlin, a wall divided the east part of the city from the rest of the city. From then on, it was not possible for a Jew to pray at the Wailing Wall.

The UN protested against this, for by it the plan to internationalize East Jerusalem and the Temple Mount had fallen through. But they bowed to the facts created by Jordan.

With the help of its allies, Jordan was able to capture the entire West Bank for itself. Jewish communities there were seized, plun-

---

180 = Arab. Jaysh al-Jihad al-Muqaddas. They were deployed by Grand Mufti Amin Haj al-Husseini and one of his relatives within the Palestinian population.

dered and ravaged, the inhabitants slaughtered or expelled. In this way, the West Bank was then "judenrein" [free of Jews], to deliberately use a typical Nazi term.

Jordan went even further, however: Against the declared will of the UN, the West Bank was not only captured, but also annexed in 1950, i.e. incorporated into the state territory of Jordan. Even though this was never internationally recognized, it was so calm in the region during the following years that an additional Palestinian territory was of no importance in world politics. Egypt took control of the Gaza Strip. Also there, autonomy or the founding of a state by the Arab Palestinians was no longer an issue.

## 2.2 The Six Day War of 1967 and its Territorial Consequences

The fact that a superior power comprised of several armies lost the war to the poorly armed Jews was seriously humiliating for the Islamic world. But the plan to obliterate Israel was not given up. Over many years, the states around Israel continued to be supplied with the most modern weaponry by the Soviet Union. In the 1960s, this led to a growing conviction in the Arab world that absolute superiority had been achieved. Under the leadership of the then-Egyptian president Gamal Abdel Nasser, it was announced to the media (May 1967): "Our main goal is the annihilation of Israel!" The motto was that the Jews would be driven into the sea. This was an unmistakeable warning signal for Israel. Yet, before the Middle East Arab nations could strike an annihilating blow, Israel moved first against the aggressors. Within the first few hours, the air forces of Egypt and Syria and much of Iraq's had been wiped out. Israeli fighter jets in low-altitude flight destroyed enemy planes en masse before they were even occupied by enemy pilots. After a few hours the Israeli Army had achieved air supremacy over the neighbouring nations. King Hussein of Jordan had been warned insistently by Israeli leadership not to involve himself in the war, else there would be serious consequences for him. The warning fell on deaf ears. Jordan began shelling with heavy artillery over the separating wall into Israel. Thereupon a paratrooper unit received the order - as punitive measure for King Hussein - to capture East Jerusalem, including the Temple Mount. The order was carried out that same day. After almost 2000 years, all of Jerusalem was again in Jewish possession. Additionally, the entire West Bank was captured. The Golan Heights fell into Israel's hands in the fight against Syria. Along the Egyptian front, the Tzahal, the Israel Defence Forces, conquered the Gaza Strip, as well as the entire Sinai Peninsula. After six days, it was over. On this remarkable Sunday, there was rest on all three fronts. A people had survived. The second attempt to totally annihilate Israel had ended in a fiasco for the Islamic world.

Following the war, the State of Israel, under a leftist (!) government, encouraged its citizens to build settlements in the West Bank, with a clear, strategically-defined concept of security in view of future threats from Jordan's side. Over the years, more and more settlements were built. Today, there are over 200 Israeli settlements and outposts in the West Bank. Close to a half million Jewish citizens live in the West Bank area (including East Jerusalem).

*Fig. 15: Israeli settlements in the West Bank (source: Wikipedia).*

## 2.3 The Significance of the West Bank

What was the significance of the territorial conquest in the Six Day War?

The acquisition of all the tracts of land which would go down in history under the alleged, notorious name "Israeli occupied areas," was significant to Israel for various reasons: They would form buffer zones as protection against their deadly enemies: The Golan Heights are security against Syria, the West Bank against Jordan and the Gaza Strip, including the Sinai Peninsula, against Egypt. From the beginning, Israel also saw these territories as bargaining material, in the event that they would later need to be traded for peace. The principle of "land for peace" was a strategic consideration which had already been conceived of at that time.

The conquest of the West Bank had a yet more profound significance. In the period of the Old Testament, this territory formed the historical centre of the people of Israel. This was not a side show. In the Bible, the southern part is designated "Judea," the northern is called "Samaria." This is an area which was divided as property among the Israelite tribes of Issachar, Manasseh, Ephraim, Benjamin, Judah and Levi.[181] Many Old Testament localities of outstanding significance lie in the West Bank. Let a few significant examples taken from a plethora of towns be mentioned in the following:

### 2.3.1 Shechem

Shechem today is called Nablus and is the largest Palestinian city in the West Bank. In 2036 BC the covenant with Israel's patriarch Abraham was made there (Gen. 12:7). This covenant was established exactly 430 years before the covenant with Israel at Sinai (Gal. 3:17). Abraham built his first altar there as a token of thanks for this covenant of mercy (Gen. 12:7; Josh. 24:25). Shechem was also a home of the patriarch Jacob (Gen. 33:18-20).

Furthermore, the congregation of all the people of Israel took place here when Joshua renewed and confirmed the covenant (Josh. 24). Joshua set up a large memorial stone here (Josh. 24:26).

---

181 The tribe of Levi did not actually possess a tribal area of their own, nevertheless, they did possess a great number of cities and the surrounding land (Josh. 20-21).

It was in Shechem that Joseph's mummy was finally entombed (Josh. 24:32; cf. Gen. 50:25; Exod. 13:19; Heb. 11:22). This town was moreover the first royal city of the ten tribes (1 Kings 12:25).

### 2.3.2 Jericho
Jericho was the first city which fell into Israel's hands in the period of conquest of the land under Joshua (1566 BC). This place marks Israel's first and phenomenal military success in the Land of Promise (Josh. 6).

### 2.3.3 Shiloh
Already in the period of conquest of the land, the tabernacle, Israel's transportable Temple from the period of desert wandering (Exod. 25-40), was set up in Shiloh (Josh. 18:1). Shiloh became the centre of worship during the following centuries of Israel's history (cf. e.g. 1 Sam. 1).

### 2.3.4 Bethel and Ai
Abraham built his second altar between Bethel and Ai (Gen. 12:8; 13:3). He lived in this area for some time.

Bethel, the name meaning "house of God," was later the location of the divine promise to Jacob (Gen. 28). This is where Father Jacob had his prophetic dream of the ladder to Heaven. Later he also lived a long time in Bethel (Gen. 35).

### 2.3.5 Gibeah, or Gibeah-Saul
Saul came from Gibeah (1 Sam. 10:26; 11:4; 15:34; 14:2). When he became King, Gibeah was elevated to being the first royal city of Israel.

### 2.3.6 Tirzah
Tirzah was the royal city of the kingdom of the ten tribes under the Kings Jeroboam I, Baasha, Elah, Zimri and Omri (1 Kings 14:17; 15:21,33; 16:8,15,23).

### 2.3.7 Samaria
During the longest period of the kingdom of the ten tribes, Samaria

was the royal capital (1 Kings 16:24ff).

### 2.3.8 Jerusalem
Near the walls of Jerusalem, Abraham was blessed by Melchize-dek in the Name of God, the Most High (Gen. 14:18-20). Directly nearby, on one of the hills in the land of Moriah, Abraham was to offer up Isaac as a sacrifice to the LORD, after he had built his fourth altar there (Gen. 22:1-19).

Following David's conquest of Jerusalem in 1046 BC, this place was elevated to being Israel's eternal capital (2 Sam. 5:6ff, 2 Chron. 6:6; Mic. 4:7). At that time, Jerusalem was a walled city on the southern slope of Mount Zion, or rather Mount Moriah. Hence, Jerusalem's origins lie in today's contested East Jerusalem!

David's son Solomon built the First Temple on the mountain-top of Jerusalem (2 Chron. 3:1). From then on, Israel's sacrificial offer-ings could only take place at this chosen location (Deut. 12:13-14).

### 2.3.9 Hebron
Hebron was Abraham's home for many years (Gen.13:18). David reigned as king for seven and a half years at Hebron (2 Sam. 2:11). Only after this was Jerusalem elevated to being the capital (2 Sam. 5).

### 2.3.10 Bethlehem
The Israeli matriarch, Rachel, was buried near Bethlehem (Gen. 35:19; 48:7). King David grew up here as a shepherd boy (1 Sam. 16:4).

According to the prophecy of Micah from the 8th century BC, the Messiah would be born in Bethlehem (Mic. 5:1).[182]

## 2.4 The Yom Kippur War 1973
On 6 October 1973 Syria and Egypt once more commenced a war of extermination against Israel. By this surprise attack they hoped to recapture territories lost in the Six Day War. Both their armies were supported by contingents from Iraq, Saudi Arabia, Pakistan, Kuwait, Algeria, Tunisia, Sudan, Morocco, Lebanon, Jordan and

---

182 Cf. Targum Jonathan , Mi 5,1, in: MIQRA'OTH GEDOLOTH).

even Cuba (1,500 soldiers).

This war was deliberately begun on the holiest day in Israel, when most Jews were in the synagogue and no Israeli radio or television station was on the air. Initially, the war was a catastrophe for Israel. There were very many deaths, more than in any other war.

After a certain delay, however, they were actually able to mobilise the reserves within an unbelievably short time. The Israeli Army ultimately defeated all enemy troops. They pushed over the Suez Canal and set up position 120 km from Cairo. The Syrians, for their part, were pushed back to within 32 km of Damascus.

The Yom Kippur War made it clear again, what great strategic significance is accorded to the territories conquered in 1967.

# 3. Ezekiel 35 and 36

An astounding prophecy is found in Ezekiel 35 and 36 regarding the future of the West Bank. Before we go into the details of this prophecy, however, we should provide ourselves with a general overview of the background, as well as the layout and the structure of the book of Ezekiel. This is absolutely necessary, so as to correctly place the details in order.[183]

## 3.1 Historical Background

The book of Ezekiel begins with Israel's national catastrophe of Babylonian captivity and ends with the description of the glorious future of the Messianic Kingdom in The Last Days. It thereby proffers a prophetic overview which embraces a period of at least, 2,600 years.

Ezekiel lived in a period which was particularly turbulent in the Middle East. After the fall of the capital Nineveh (612 BC) and the final collapse of the Assyrian Empire afterwards, there were repeated violent clashes between Egypt and Babylon for regional dominance. After Nebuchadnezzar's victory at Carchemish over the army of the Pharaoh (605 BC), his troops subjugated the entire

---

183 Cf. in detail: LIEBI: Hesekiel, EZRA Sudienreihe, CMV Hagedorn, Düsseldorf, Germany and CLKV, Pfäffikon, Schweiz, 2011.

Fertile Crescent.[184] The Babylonians carried out several victorious wars against the kingdom of Judah during the entire period from 606 until 582 BC. The capital Jerusalem and the Temple were finally totally destroyed. The Jews were deported to Babylon in four successive stages:

606 BC: first deportation[185]
597 BC: second deportation[186]
586 BC: third deportation, following Jerusalem's destruction[187]
582 BC: fourth deportation[188]

How could Israel have ever come to this? The deportations were the consequence of the people's ever increasing faithlessness to the God of the Bible: Since the rule of King Manasseh of Judah (697–642 BC), the greater part of the Jews had turned away from the One True God and worshipped false gods instead. The result was that God turned away from His people which had terrible consequences: the collapse of Judah as an independent state, war and exile. In a sovereign act, God, the Lord over history, for a long time took away Israel's exalted position as the nation which should have ascended to global dominance (Deut. 28:13) and for some decades conferred it on the Babylonian Empire.

## 3.2 The Author

Ezekiel, the son of Buzi (Ezek. 1:3), was taken to Babylon on the occasion of the second deportation in the year 597 BC (Ezek. 1:2). There, he was put in a settlement of exiled Jews in Tel-Abib[189] on the Chebar River.[190]

---

184 The part of the Middle East designated by the term Fertile Crescent is that in which agriculture is possible. It reaches from the lower stretch of the Nile in Egypt to the Persian Gulf and forms a arc which encompasses Israel, northern Syria and the Euphrates and Tigris plains. Babylon (also called Chaldea) lay in the eastern part. Today, this area belongs to Iraq.

185 2 Chron. 36:5-8; Dan 1:1.2.

186 2 Chron. 36:9-16.

187 2 Chron. 36:17-21.

188 Jer. 52:30.

189 Or Tel-Aviv, not to be confused with the modern city of the same name founded in 1909 in Israel. Ezekiel's Tel-Abib lay close to Nippur, some 75 km south of Babylon. The name of the city means in Babylonian (Akkadian) something like "embankment against flooding."

190 The Chebar River was one of the most important irrigation canals from the Euphrates. In Babylonian, the name means "Great River."

Ezekiel lived in his own house (Ezek. 3:24; 8:1). He was married, but lost his beloved wife, "the desire of his eyes" (Ezek. 24:16) to a sudden stroke on the day the LORD revealed to him that the Babylonians would destroy the glorious Temple in Jerusalem as a judgement of God. Very few details are known of his life, but this is without a doubt willed by the Spirit of God: In contrast to the message, the person should stay in the background.

Ezekiel was called to be a prophet five years after his deportation in 593 BC. He was about 30 years old at that time (Ezek. 1:1).[191] Like his contemporary Jeremiah, Ezekiel was also a priest, a Cohen (Ezek. 1:3). Doubtless, this was a reason why Jerusalem and everything having to do with the Temple and the sacrifice play a central role in his book. The last dated revelation was 571 BC (Ezek. 29:17). This prophet's period of service lasted more than 22 years.

## 3.3 The Structure of the Book

The book of Ezekiel is divided in three main parts:

**First Part: Israel's Fall: Ezekiel 1–24**

I. The depopulation of the Land of Israel: 1–7
1. God's chariot-throne: 1:1-28
2. Ezekiel's calling: 2:1–3:27
3. Announcement of Jerusalem's destruction: 4:1–5:17
4. Announcement of the destruction of the land: 6:1–7:27

II. The glory of the LORD in the First Temple: 8–11
1. Idolatry in the Temple: 8:1-18
2. Judgement on Jerusalem's inhabitants: 9:1-11
3. The glory leaves the Temple: 10:1-22
4. Jerusalem, a cauldron: 11:1-13
5. The Sanctuary of the deportees: 11:14-25

III. Israel's path to destruction 12–24
1. Two symbolic actions: 12:1-20
2. The end of the false prophets: 12:21–14:11
3. Protection of the Righteous: 14:12-23
4. Parable of the vine: 15:1-8
5. Parable from Jerusalem's history: 16:1-63

---

191 The term "*in the thirtieth year*" has been interpreted various ways. The simplest and really most satisfying explanation is that it deals with Ezekiel's age at the time of his call to service as prophet.

6. Parable of the two eagles: 17:1-24
7. Personal responsibility: 18:1-32
8. Lamentation for the princes of Israel: 19:1-14
9. The story of unfaithful Israel: 20:1-44
10. God's sword over Israel: 21:1-27
11. Jerusalem's guilt: 22:1-31
12. Parable of the two unfaithful sisters: 23:1-49
13. Two signs for Jerusalem's end: 24:1-27

## Second Part: The Judgement of the Nations: Ezekiel 25–32

I. *Ammon: 25:1-7*
II. *Moab: 25:8-11*
III. *Edom: 25:12-14*
IV. *Philistia: 25:15-17*
V. *Tyre: 26:1–28:19*
VI. *Sidon: 28:20-26*
VII. *Egypt: 29–32*

## Third Part: The Restoration of Israel: Ezekiel 33–48

I. Israel's path to restoration: 33–39
1. The messenger is again confirmed: 33
2. A new shepherd: 34
3. A renewed Land: 35:1–36:15
4. A new heart: 36:16-38
5. A renewed people: 37
6. The destruction of the final enemy: Gog: 38–39

II. Glory of the LORD in the Third Temple: 40:1–47:12
1. The new Temple: 40:1–43:12
2. New worship: 43:13–47:12

III. Resettlement of the Land of Israel: 47:13–48:35

## Remarks on structure:
- **First Part:**
  **Israel's Fall: Chapters 1–24**
  Chapters 1 to 24 come before the destruction of Jerusalem

chronologically. God's irrevocable judgement is announced on Jerusalem, the Temple, the people, the kingdom of Judah and the Land of Israel. All was tragically fulfilled shortly thereafter.

- **Second Part:**
  **The Judgement on the Nations: Chapters 25–32**
  In the Chapters 25 to 32 God's judgement on seven Gentile nations, or cities, as the case may be, is announced. Israel, as the chosen people, had greater responsibility than the nations. Therefore, Israel's judgement is presented before that of the nations.

- **Third part:**
  **The Restoration of Israel: Chapters 33–48**
  Chapters 33 to 48 show God's glorious plan for a complete restoration of Israel in the Land of their Forefathers. Everything will be renewed: the Jewish people, the Land of Israel, the city of Jerusalem and the Temple.

Chapters 33 to 39 describe the course of the End-Time reestablishment of Israel until the coming of the Messiah as King of the World.

In Ezekiel 40 to 48 the perfect condition is described when the Messiah will have completely reordered the Land of Israel (during the 1,000-year reign).

While Part II forms a self-contained central section, Parts I and III constitute a contrast to one-another: Downfall – Reestablishment.

It is extremely common in the Bible that texts are structured symmetrically. This is different to Western texts, which often only proceed linearly; in a symmetric structure (the specialist term for which is "chiasmus") the first element corresponds to the last. An example for this is progressions such as ABA' or ABB'A'. Such constructions, and often even more complex arrangements, in addition to linear structures, chiefly appear as a principle of composition, be it in a single verse, a section, a large part of a book, the whole book or even in the order of several books of the Bible.

Symmetrical structures on all possible levels are found in the book of Ezekiel. Even a rough outline makes it clear that there is specific symmetry between the first and the third parts. The first part "Israel's Fall" stands in contrast to the last part "The Restoration of Israel." Also, the three subsections exhibit contrasting parallels, conceived as a mirror-image:

A. The depopulation of the Land of Israel (1–7)
B. Glory of the LORD in the First Temple (8–11)
C. Israel's path to destruction (12–24)

C'. Israel's path to restoration (33–39)
B'. The glory of the LORD in the Third Temple (40:1–47:12)
A'. Resettlement of the Land of Israel (47:13–48:35)

The chapters we will be examining, 35 and 36, belong to the section in Ezekiel which describes the progressive restoration of Israel. From Ezekiel 36:4 and 38:8, it is also clear that this epoch of restoration is in the "Last Days". In these verses we find the expression, *"time of their calamity, when their iniquity came to an end,"*[192] (35:5) as well as *"in the latter years"* (Ezek. 38:8). According to Ezekiel 36:24, this will be the period of the return of the Jews, or Israelites, from their worldwide dispersion:

*"24 For I will take you from among the nations, gather you out of all countries, and bring you into your own land."* (NKJV)

This verse has already been discussed in Part I of this book.

### 3.4 The Mountains of Israel Versus the Mountains of Seir

Between Ezekiel 35 and 36 there is a stark comparison: The promises of blessing for the Mountains of Israel stand in contrast to the fate of the Mountains of Seir in the Land of Edom. Chapter 35 is a prophecy *against* the Mountains of Seir, i.e. against the southern mountains of modern Jordan. The following Chapter 36, in con-

---

192 The term "time of their calamity, when their iniquity *came to an* end," is a Hebraism, which in English means something like "in The Last Days, which is governed by inequity."

trast to this, contains a prophecy in favour of the Mountains of Israel. Ezekiel 35:1-4:

> *"¹ Moreover the word of the LORD came to me, saying, ² "Son of man, set your face **against** Mount Seir and prophesy **against** it, ³ and say to it, 'Thus says the Lord GOD:*
> *"Behold, O Mount Seir, I am **against** you;*
> *I will stretch out My hand **against** you,*
> *And make you most desolate;*
> *⁴ I shall lay your cities waste,*
> *And you shall be desolate.*
> *Then you shall know that I am the LORD."* (NKJV)

In OT times, the Mountains of Seir in the Land of Edom were the home of Esau, Jacob's brother, and his decedents the Edomites (Idumeans). The Mountains of Edom were also called "Mount Seir" in the Bible (Ezek. 35:2,3,7,15) or "the mountains of Esau" (Obad. 1:8).

In Hebrew "Edom" means "red" or "red [land]" or a "red [person]."

These names hold much material for wordplay, especially loved in Hebrew:

When Esau, the older twin brother of Israel's patriarch, Jacob, was born, his skin was *"red"* (Gen. 25:25). Having been born first, he had not suffered so much from lack of oxygen. Immediately following delivery, babies are normally somewhat bluish.

Later, Esau developed a particular liking for *red* lentils. Therefore, he received his second name "Edom" (Gen. 25:29-34).

Following Esau's taking leave of his parent's home, he took up residence in the southern mountains of modern Jordan (Gen. 36:8-9). And so these heights became known as the "Mountains of Edom." These hillsides have a clearly *reddish cast*. This geographic name is doubly fitting.

Jacob's brother was especially hairy at birth. Because of this, he received the name "Esau," which means "hairy." I have just stated that the Mountains of Edom are also called the "Mountains of Seir." Here is another play on words. In Hebrew, "Seir" means something like "rough" or "hairy." The first meaning is appropriate to this wild region. The word "hairy," on the other hand, suits "Esau" perfectly, who found his home in the "Seir" Mountains.

While in Chapter 35 God's judgement against the mountains of Seir is pronounced, the prophet proclaims an encouraging prophecy to the mountains of Israel, which has the future well-being of this region in view (Ezek. 36:1):

> *"¹ And you, son of man, prophesy **to** the mountains of Israel, and say, 'O mountains of Israel, hear the word of the LORD!"* (NKJV)

The term "the mountains of Israel" is characteristic for Ezekiel. This term is found 18 times in this book. In the rest of the writings of the Bible, this expression is not to be found.[193]

Israel's most important range of mountains, populated and settled in OT times, ran north to south, and is found mainly in Samaria and Judea.

Israel's most northern outpost in Biblical times was the town of Dan, while the southern border was marked by the city of Beersheba on the edge of the Negev desert. The following examples make this clear:[194]

Judges 20:1:
> *"¹ So **all the children of Israel** came out, **from Dan to Beersheba**, as well as from the land of Gilead, and the congregation gathered together as one man before the LORD at Mizpah."* (NKJV)

1 Samuel 3:20:
> *"²⁰ And **all Israel from Dan to Beersheba** knew that Samuel had been established as a prophet of the Lord."* (NKJV)

---

193 All passages with the term "the mountains of Israel": Ezek. 6:2,3; 19:9; 20:40; 33:28; 34:13,14,14; 35:12; 36:1,1,4,8; 37:22; 38:8; 39:2,4,17.

194 All passages which name Dan and Beersheba together: Judg. 20:1; 1 Sam 3:20; 2 Sam 3:10; 17:11; 24:2,15; 1 Kings 4:25; 1 Chron. 21:2; 2 Chron. 30:5; Amos 8:14.

2 Chronicles 30:5:

*"⁵ So they resolved to make a proclamation **throughout all Israel, from Beersheba to Dan**, that they should come to keep the Passover to the LORD God of Israel at Jerusalem, since they had not done it for a long time in the prescribed manner."* (NKJV)

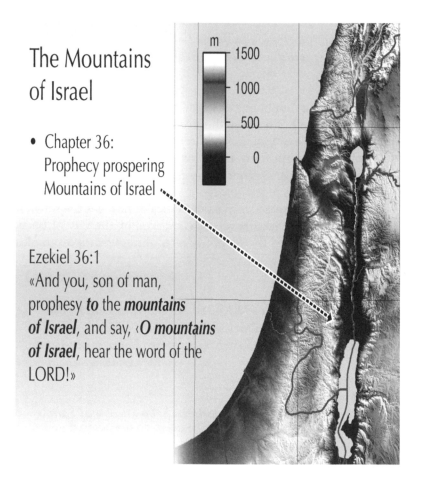

# The Mountains of Israel

- Chapter 36: Prophecy prospering Mountains of Israel

Ezekiel 36:1
«And you, son of man, prophesy **to the mountains of Israel**, and say, ‹**O mountains of Israel**, hear the word of the LORD!»

**Fig. 16:** *The Mountains of Israel in the region between Dan and Beersheba correspond to the modern "West Bank" (source: Wikipedia, I, Sadal-melik).*

Looking at Israel's mountainous land between Dan and Beer-sheba, it is clear that it corresponds with what is today called the "West Bank." When we keep in mind that the "West Bank" only recently became a singularly political term, namely through plans of Britain and the UN, it is even more astounding to realise that over 2,600 years ago the prophet Ezekiel uttered detailed prophecies, using the term "the mountains of Israel," about this region in connection with our own times!

It is worth mentioning that Ezekiel, in addition to the 18 places which speak of "the mountains of Israel," twice calls the Temple Mount in Jerusalem "the mountain height of Israel" (Ezek. 17:23; 20:40). Thus, the Temple Mount also belongs to the "mountains of Israel." This is the heart of Israel. Is it any wonder that this mountain is undeniably the focus of the conflict surrounding the West Bank?

The term "the mountain height of Israel" also occurs in the Bible only in the book of Ezekiel.

## 3.5 The Mountains of Seir and the Nations Surrounding Israel

When Ezekiel addresses the mountains of southern Jordan as if they were living persons, we must assume that these mountains in the message of the prophet represent the inhabitants of this region.

However, these distinctive mountains not only typify the Edomites in Jordan, but effectively all the nations surrounding Israel which, together with Edom, would become hostile to Israel in The Last Days. This is evident from Ezekiel 36:5, for example:

> ⁵ ... therefore thus says the Lord GOD: "Surely I have spoken in My burning jealousy against **the rest of the nations** and against **all Edom**, who gave My land to themselves as a possession, with wholehearted joy and spiteful minds, in order to plunder its open country.'" (NKJV)

Ezekiel 36:4 and 7 also addresses the nations allied with Edom:

*"4 ... therefore, O mountains of Israel, hear the word of the Lord GOD! Thus says the Lord GOD to the mountains, the hills, the rivers, the valleys, the desolate wastes, and the cities that have been forsaken, which became plunder and mockery to the rest of* **the nations all around**–*"*(NKJV)

*"7 ... the nations that are around* **you [i.e. Israel] shall ...**" (NKJV)

The mountains of Seir represent Israel's End-Time Arab neighbours who will turn against Israel in enmity. The prophet Ezekiel appealed to all of them with a stern message of warning and judgement. They are called "the rest of the nations all around" because they are, as the descendants of all the peoples who were Israel's neighbours in OT times, remnants in the modern age.

Naturally, the ancient people groups such as the Edomites, Ammonites, Moabites, Arameans, Phoenicians, Philistines, Babylonians, Assyrians, Ishmaelites, Amalekites, and Egyptians etc. mixed with one-another over the centuries. Most of these groups have not been able to retain such a singular identity as the Jewish people, as Israel.[195] But this does not mean that they have disappeared without a trace. There have been tremendous advances made in genetic testing in recent years to determine original people groups.[196] For example, every Swiss man can determine, with an inexpensive analysis of his marker in the Y-section of his DNA, passed on from the father to the *son*, whether the direct paternal line (collateral lines are left out of consideration) goes back to the Helvetians, the Germani, Vikings, Jews, etc. Today one can trace his ancestors to approximately 3,000 years in the past! Accordingly, it can be determined with the mitochondrial DNA that is passed from mother to sons *and* daughters, from which ancient people group one is descended on the direct maternal line. Again, the collateral lines are left out of consideration. This could also occur in the coming years. Thus these new scientific methods

---

195 For the astoundingly preserved genetic identity of the people of Israel cf. KLEIMAN: DNA & Tradition, The Genetic Link to the Ancient Hebrews.

196 Cf. for instance www.igenea.ch (as of: 24.10.2011).

make possible a more exact identification of the ancient people of the Biblical world.

## 3.6 Perpetual Hatred

We have already read the announcement of judgement in Ezekiel 35:1-4. Why should this still future (for us today) judgement come on the Mountains of Seir, or on the nations around Israel? In the following verse the "ancient hatred" is named (Ezek. 35:5):

> *"⁵ Because thou hast had a **perpetual hatred**, and hast given over the children of Israel to the power of the sword, in the time of their calamity, in the time of the iniquity of the end; ..."* (NKJV)

Edom's hatred of Israel goes back to the patriarch Esau who wished to kill his brother Jacob (Gen. 27:41). Esau's descendants have also lived out this enmity against Jacob's descendants (Israel, cf. Gen. 32:28) from Biblical times onwards (cf. for example Num. 20:14ff; 1 Sam. 14:47; 2 Sam. 8:14; 1 Kings 11:14; 2 Kings 14:10; Jer.: 49:7ff; Obad. 1:1-21; Amos 1:11). Ezekiel 35 makes it clear that this hatred will continue in The Last Days.

Even in the early days when the Jewish returnees came to the Land of their Forefathers on the occasion of the First Aliya, Arabic opposition was aroused.[197] The conflict became so dangerous in the following years that the Jews felt compelled to build up the unit called the Haganah in 1920 to defend against Arab attacks. In 1921, when the British partitioned East Palestine, the area of the later Jordan, for a future Palestinian nation, the entire territory east of the Jordan River was closed to Jews. No Jew would ever have the right to live there, even though the Balfour Declaration, in its very broad formulation, would have opened up such a opportunity. In OT times, a great deal of territory east of the Jordan River had belonged to the Land of Israel!

From this time on, essentially Jewish immigration was only possible in West Palestine. In the 1930s, the British Mandate

---

197  GIBERT: The Routledge Atlas of the Arab-Israeli Conflict, p. 4.

even imposed a limit on immigration for West Palestine, as a concession to Arab-Islamic terrorism directed at Britain. Jewish immigration was finally drastically reduced from 1939 on. This occurred precisely during the period of Jewish persecution by the Nazis. Just at the time when countless European Jews desperately needed a refuge in the Land of their Fathers, Britain, under Palestinian pressure, closed the door for the majority.

At this time, Amin Haj el-Husseini, a relative of Yasser Arafat, was Grand Mufti of Jerusalem. He was a leading anti-Semite in the Arab world, with powerful influence. As Grand Mufti of Jerusalem he was the Muslim religious leader of the Arabs in his region. He became Hitler's friend and ally in Palestine. He even visited Hitler in Germany. Conferring with the Nazi leader, he discussed how the plan for the annihilation of the Jews in Europe could be extended to the Middle East. When, on 14 May 1948, the fundamental change for the world's Jews regarding the opening up of the country came with founding of the State of Israel, the following day Jordan and its allies around Israel attacked with burning hatred.

When this total war did not bring the hoped-for annihilation of the Jews, however, Jordan was again present when the second total war against Israel raged in 1967. However, Jordan refrained from active participation in the Yom Kippur War, fearing further loss of territory.

When Jordan made its peace treaty with Israel in 1994, this was actually an agreement between King Hussein and Israel, not between the Jordanian nation and Israel. The people of Jordan have not renounced their hatred against Jews, or Israel. According to Islamic law, Muslims may not make peace with their enemies. There is one exception: the Hudna. A temporary peace treaty is meant by the Arabic word "Hudna," while the enemy is too strong. According to Islamic law, peace, Hudna, may be made with an opponent who is stronger in order to have time to gather strength so that the enemy can finally be beaten in the future, as soon as one is strong enough. When an "enemy of Islam" shows weakness, he must be fought and conquered.

In all the wars between 1948 and 1994, Israel was too strong.

Therefore, according to Islamic teaching, it was finally possible for Jordan to make a peace treaty with Israel. This is based on the legal practice from 628 AD, when Mohammad negotiated a peace treaty with the non-Muslim citizens of Mecca, which was set to last ten years. However, when Mohammad came to the conclusion the following year that he already had the sufficient prerequisites for a victory, he broke this treaty. For Muslims the principles of Hudna in Islamic teaching are derived from this obligatory example.

## 3.7 Surrender at the Time of Catastrophe

With Hitler's take-over in 1933, came the epoch in Jewish history which is best identified with the Hebrew word "Shoah" (catastrophe). More than 6 million Jews were murdered, simply because they were Jews, including some 1 million children. Thanks to the Arabs in Transjordan (East-Palestine), the doors to Palestine remained closed. Jewish immigration was drastically reduced in West Palestine in 1939. By their armed uprising the Arabs compelled the British to implement barbaric restrictions on Jewish immigration. This is recorded in the infamous MacDonald White Papers of 1 April 1939, half a year after the Nazis' terrible Night of Broken Glass. Ships with refugees from Nazi Europe were turned away at the border of the Promised Land. As an ultimate consequence of Britain's war against the immigrants, hundreds met a tragic death. Some refugees were beaten bloodily by British soldiers. Many were brought with armed force to British concentration camps on the islands of Cyprus and Mauritius.[198] It was exactly as Ezekiel 35:5 had prophetically described:

> "5 Because you have had an ancient hatred, and have shed the blood of **the children of Israel by the power of the sword at the time of their calamity [Hebr. 'ed]**, when their iniquity came to an end," (NKJV)

The Arab leadership in the Middle East was determined to give

---

198  http://en.wikipedia.org/wiki/Aliyah_Bet (as of: 10.11.2011).

the Children of Israel over to death by making their refuge in the Land of the Fathers impossible! This did not happen in just any epoch of history, but rather in the Nazi period, according to Ezekiel "at the time of their calamity, when their iniquity came to an end."[199] Exactly at the time when it was more necessary than ever for the Jews to have their own land of refuge, the door to the Land of their Fathers was bolted. Furthermore, there was barely another country in the world willing to accept Jews indiscriminately in large numbers. How many Jews in Europe were held back from seeking refuge in the Land of their Fathers by the knowledge that Palestine was closed to them? And so they were forced to surrender to the power of the sword and disappeared in the Nazi death machine!

**Fig. 17:** *Auschwitz concentration camp (source: Deutsches Bundesarchiv CC 3.0 Germany).*

---

199 The term "*at the time of their calamity*" is a Hebraism, which in English means something like "in the end time, which is governed by injustice."

## 3.8 The Future Judgement of Southern Jordan

Divine judgement as the consequence of the responsibility of Edom and all other peoples around Israel for their guilt in the period of the Shoah is described in Ezekiel 35:6-7:

> *"⁶ Therefore, as I live," says the Lord GOD, "I will prepare you for blood [Hebr. dm; cf. 'dm = Edom], and blood shall pursue you; since you have not hated blood, therefore blood shall pursue you. ⁷ Thus I will make Mount Seir most desolate, and cut off from it the one who leaves and the one who returns. ⁸ And I will fill its mountains with the slain; on your hills and in your valleys and in all your ravines those who are slain by the sword shall fall. ⁹ I will make you perpetually desolate, and your cities shall be uninhabited; then you shall know that I am the LORD."* (NKJV)

The judgement cited in this text is still in the future. According to Isaiah 63:1ff and Obadiah 1:21, it will take place in the time when Jesus Christ returns as Judge of the World.

The word "blood" (Hebr. *dam*) is found in a heaped form (4 times) in verse 6. According to its root, the word *dm*, written in the Hebrew consonantal script means "red" in the sense of "blood," while *'dm* (Edom) also means "red" in the geographical sense "red [land]." Here is another play on words. The term *dam* hints at the name "Edom," the land of the Red Mountains.

## 3.9 Judah and Samaria Captured and Annexed

The following verse gives further reason for future judgement (Ezek. 35:10):

> *"¹⁰ Because you have said, 'These **two nations** and these **two countries shall be mine, and we will possess them**,' although the LORD was there."* (NKJV)

In the war of 1947–1949, Jordan, supported by its allies Lebanon, Syria, Iraq, Egypt Saudi Arabia and Yemen, was able to conquer the entire region of the West Bank.

The war began, as stated above, actually immediately following the UN Resolution of 27 November 1947. The bloody Arabic conquest of the West Bank began at that point. Ezekiel 36:4 speaks about this defeat:

*"⁴ ... therefore, O mountains of Israel, hear the word of the Lord GOD! Thus says the Lord GOD to the mountains, the hills, the rivers, the valleys, the desolate wastes, and the cities that have been forsaken, which became **plunder and mockery to the rest of the nations all around**." (NKJV)*

Following the War of 1947–1949, the West Bank was firmly in Jordan's hands. It was not just a matter of conquest. The West Bank would not only be a spoil of war, but would rather more become a part of Jordan itself: *"'These two nations and these two countries shall be mine, and we will possess them,' although the LORD was there ..."* (Ezek. 35:10).

Even before the war, Jordan's King Abdullah I clearly stated that he had in mind to unite all of Palestine under his rule. The statement in verse 10 corresponds exactly to his language![200]

Jordan annexed the West Bank in 1950 and thereby enlarged its territory, assessed as 77% of Palestine by Britain. Most of the world's nations never acknowledged this annexation. Under international law, the West Bank was never part of Jordan. However, in the following years, world politics in general and the UN in particular did not further concern themselves with this issue. It went all quiet about the West Bank.

With the conquest and subsequent annexation of the West Bank, Jordan laid claim to both East Palestine (Jordan) as well as West Palestine, to the extent of the West Bank. Thus the claim on *"these two nations and these two countries"* mentioned in Ezekiel was fulfilled!

Jordan's King Abdullah I had the goal of uniting East and West Palestine under his rule. He wasn't able to do this entirely, but at least he brought the West Bank under his control. He was not

---

200 http://en.wikipedia.org/wiki/Abdullah_I_of_Jordan (as of: 22.11.2011).

interested in another Palestinian state, but rather to laying claim to "Palestine" east and west of the Jordan River.[201]

## 3.10 War Miracles through God's Presence

With the founding of the State of Israel, the former self-defense troops of the Haganah were elevated to the position of Israeli Army, as we have already seen. There were very few aircraft available, however. Initially there was almost no heavy weaponry. The Israelis were resisting nine armies which were all well supplied with heavy fire power. A superior force with 100 million people turned against a small nation of 650,000 people, who initially possessed virtually no heavy weapons and only very few planes.

From a purely human point of view, this war was totally hopeless for Israel. The USA tried at the last moment, shortly before 14 May 1948, to block the founding of the state, fearing that the Jewish state would be cut off at its roots and destroyed by an Arab attack. However, the Jews in Israel persisted, not wanting to pass up this one-time chance of founding the state. When the war came to an end in July 1949, stock was taken: Israel emerged victorious and had won land, as well. All the Arab armies had been beaten. This was contrary to all initial human expectations. What had happened could only have been a miracle. The Biblical explanation is given in Ezekiel 35:10: God's special presence was a protective shield for the nation of Israel.[202]

> *"[10] Because you have said, 'These two nations and these two countries shall be mine, and we will possess them,' although the LORD was there."* (NKJV)

This verse indicates that it was an especially foolhardy act for Jordan to annex the West Bank in 1950, because the war of 1947–1949 had shown well enough that God, indeed the God of Israel, the God of the Bible, proved his abiding presence, providing Israel's

---

201  http://en.wikipedia.org/wiki/Abdullah_I_of_Jordan (as of: 22.11.2011).

202  The Bible teaches that God is omnipresent. When it speaks in various places about God's presence at a particular place, however, the meaning is that God reveals Himself in a special way to mankind and makes His existence clear.

astounding protection. This was proof of his special presence! The experience of the war miracle of 1947–1949, as Israel survived, against all expectation, should have made Jordan understand that the God of the Bible exists and that His statements concerning the Land promises in favour of Israel must be acknowledged. Nonetheless, Jordan insisted on conquering and subsequently annexing the West Bank.

## 3.11 Anger and Envy Towards Israel

The following verse in Ezekiel ascribes two further motives, in addition to hatred, to Edom and its allies in their struggle against Israel, namely, anger and envy.

> Ezekiel 35:11:
> *"11 Therefore, as I live," says the Lord GOD, "I will do according to **your anger** and according to **the envy which you showed** in your hatred against them; and I will make Myself known among them when I judge you."* (NKJV)

The Bible promises Israel a lasting right to the Land of their Fathers. God promised to Abraham and his descendants the Land of Canaan, or rather, the Land of Israel, without limitations of time (Gen. 17:8):

> *"8 Also I give to you and your descendants after you the land in which you are a stranger, **all the land of Canaan, as an everlasting possession**; and I will be their God."* (NKJV)

This promise stands in glaring opposition to the teachings of Dar-ul-Islam by Al-Mawardi, as I have described them above. Jordan and its allies could not accept the Biblical claims to all the towns then settled by Jews in the West Bank, or the claim to the other places in Israel. This describes the accusation of *envy* exactly.

The rage discussed here showed itself especially clearly when the Islamic world of the Middle East was in uproar on the occasion when the majority of the UN, in the November Resolution of 1947, accepted the Partition Plan involving the creation of a Jewish

State in Palestine. This rage led directly to the devastating war of independence of 1947–1949.

## 3.12 Blasphemy against the Mountains of Israel

Jordan managed, with the help of its allies, to conquer and devastate all Jewish settlements in the West Bank which, according to the UN Partition Plan of 1947, were outside of Israel's entitled territory. All Jews living there were either killed or driven out. At the end of this war, Jordan could look at the mountains of Israel and say (Ezek. 35:12):

*'They are desolate; they are given to us to consume.'*

In Ezekiel 35:12-13 God describes this as blasphemy and as pride against Himself. It is known in the Islamic world that the Bible promises the Land of Israel, Canaan, to the Jews for eternity and not to Ishmael, whom Mohammad claimed as patriarch (e.g. Gen. 17:8,18-21). Yet all these texts are dismissed as intentional misrepresentations and falsifications.

The Biblical manuscripts found in the caves of Qumran on the Dead Sea have definitively documented that these assertions, based on certain Koran verses,[203] are totally false. The manuscripts from Qumran, Masada and from Wadi Muraba'at, some of which go back to the 3rd century BC, document that the Masoretic Bible text has been faithfully passed down to this day from antiquity. Nevertheless, in the Arab-Islamic world, the Bible is unequivocally rejected and disgracefully trampled under foot. Their talk against the Bible and God's land promises contained in it is *blasphemy* against God (Ezek. 35:12-13):

*"[12] Then you shall know that I am the LORD. I have heard all your **blasphemies** which you have spoken against the mountains of Israel, saying, 'They are desolate; they are given to us to consume.' [13] Thus with your mouth you have **boasted against Me** and **multiplied your words against Me**; I have heard them." (NKJV)*

---

203  For example, Surah 2:39,70; 3:72.

Hatred of the Bible and the promises contained in it is seen in the following example: To this day it is officially forbidden to be in the Palestinian Waqf-governed Temple area in East Jerusalem with a Bible in hand or even in one's baggage! Furthermore, prayer to the God of the Bible is there explicitly forbidden!

## 3.13 Horrible Devastation

The prophet Ezekiel announced in 35:14-15 that in the time when the Messiah comes again and establishes worldwide peace and justice, there will be joy in the entire world. Edom, however, will be a horribly devastated country:

> *"14 'Thus says the Lord GOD: "The whole earth will rejoice when I make you desolate. 15 **As you rejoiced because the inheritance of the house of Israel was desolate, so I will do to you;** you shall be desolate, O Mount Seir, as well as all of Edom—all of it! Then they shall know that I am the LORD."'* (NKJV)

From then on, Edom will be an uninhabited country, with no one passing through (cf. Isa. 34:1-17). The reason for this destiny, according to the context of Ezekiel 35-36, lies in the fact that Edom took part in and rejoiced in the devastation of Israel in such an evil manner.

In 1948, there were about 650,000 Jews in the Land of the Fathers. Some 6,000 Jews were killed in the devastating war following the UN Conference of 29 November 1947. This was about 1% of the population; men, women and children. If this were projected to the population of the EU today, it would mean over 400,000 deaths!

Although Israel finally won the war, Jordan and its allies wreaked terrible havoc. The joy taken in this devastation is illustrated by the harrowing destruction in the Jewish Quarter of the Old City in East Jerusalem: In this struggle against a superior army, the Quarter sank into a cloud of smoke, destruction, death and agony. The Jews entrenched there were killed or driven out. 350 people became prisoners of war. Dozens of synagogues were destroyed. There were the most disgraceful desecrations. Practically all houses were destroyed. Countless gravestones from the more than 2,000-year-old Jewish cemetery on the western slope of the Mount of Olives were torn out and defiled in most provocative ways.[204] The Quarter was thoroughly plundered.[205] The Old City of Jerusalem was separated from the west part by a wall.[206] Neve Yaakov, Kibbutz Kalya, Ataroth and Beith Ha-Arava und Kfar Etzion were destroyed.[207] The towns of Revadim, Massuot Yitzchak, Ein Tzurim und Kfar Etzion were completely flattened to the ground. Thousands of trees which had been planted by the Jews were destroyed.[208]

## 3.14 Derision and Scornful Laughter over the Mountains of Israel

We now come to Chapter 36 in our verse-by-verse examination:

> *"¹ And you, son of man, prophesy to the mountains of Israel, and say, 'O mountains of Israel, hear the word of the LORD! ² Thus says the Lord GOD: "Because the enemy has said of you, 'Aha! The ancient heights have become our possession,"' ³ therefore prophesy, and say, 'Thus says the Lord GOD: "Because they made you desolate and swallowed you up on every side, so that you became the possession of the rest of the nations, and you are taken up by the lips of talkers and slandered by the people—"* (NKJV)

The war with Jordan and its allies was accompanied by jeering war rhetoric, which is virtually unknown in democratic nations of the Western world. But the verses quoted above above denounce precisely this wrongdoing and the guilt of Jordan and its allies, especially in view of the capture of the West Bank together with all its Jewish towns.

---

204 http://en.wikipedia.org/wiki/Jewish_Quarter_%28Jerusalem%29 ; http://www.aish.com/jw/j/48954821.html ; http://www.jewish-quarter.org.il/atar-acharon.asp (as of: 22.11.2011).

205 http://en.wikipedia.org/wiki/Abdullah_el-Tell (as of: 21.11.2011).

206 http://en.wikipedia.org/wiki/Jerusalem (as of: 22.11.2011).

207 http://www.eifermanrealty.com/ShowNb.aspx?id=65 ; http://en.wikipedia.org/wiki/Kalya ; http://en.wikipedia.org/wiki/Atarot_Airport ; http://www.historama.com/online-resources/history-collecting-resources/eretz-israel/eretz_israeli_palestine_towns_cities_kibbutzim_moshavim (as of: 21.11.2011).

208 http://en.wikipedia.org/wiki/Gush_Etzion (as of: 21.11.2011).

Following the vote over the partition plan at the end of November 1947, an Arab representative gave the following statement:
"Any line drawn by the United Nations will be nothing but a line of blood and fire."[209]

Azzam Pasha, the Secretary-General of the Arab League, stated in a press conference 15 May 1948 in Cairo:
"... this will be a war of extermination and a momentous massacre which will be spoken of like the Mongolian massacres and the Crusades. "[210]

Matiel Mughannam, a representative of the Arab High Commission to Palestine, stated the following:
"The UN decision has united all Arabs, as they have never been united before, not even against the Crusaders. ... [A Jewish State] has no chance to survive now that the 'holy war' has been declared. All the Jews will eventually be massacred."[211]

The Arab world called for "Holy War," the Jihad, against the Jews.[212] Abba Eban wrote in connection with this war:
"On 17 January 1948, thirty-five young men of the Palmach and Chel Sadeh on their way to support the settlement of Etzion were ambushed and killed by Arab forces in the area. Their bodies were savagely mutilated; the Arabs would not even give the Jews the decent dignities of death."[213]

This illustrates the fulfilment of the prophecy of derision of the mountains of Israel (v.3).

The jeering laughter in verse 2 ('*Aha! The ancient heights have become our possession,*') describes precisely the typical Holy War rhetoric in the Islamic world.

209  EBAN: My Country: The Story of Modern Israel, p. 47.

210  New York Times, 16.5.1948; cited by: PFISTERER: Israel oder Palästina?, p.126.

211  http://de.wikipedia.org/wiki/Pal%C3%A4stinakrieg (as of: 15.11.2011).

212  King Abdullah Bin Hussein spured the war on with a nationalistic speech and praise of martyr-dom. (http://de.wikipedia.org/wiki/Arabische_Legion [as of: 15.11.2011).

213  EBAN: My Country: The Story of Modern Israel, p. 49.

## 3.15 The Whole World Chatters about the West Bank

The prophet speaks in Ezekiel 36 about two evils the Mountains of Israel must accept: on the one hand is the disgrace of mocking and conquest by Israel's enemies (Ezek. 36:1,3), on the other hand, the fact that generally people gossip and talk thoughtlessly about this region (Ezek. 36:3):

> *"3 Therefore prophesy, and say, 'Thus says the Lord GOD:*
> *"Because they made you desolate and swallowed you up on every*
> *side, so that you became the possession of the rest of the nations,*
> *and you are **taken up by the lips of talkers and slandered by the***
> ***people***—*" (NKJV)

Israel was forced to conquer the West Bank amongst others because of the Arabs' second attempt to destroy the Jewish State in 1967. Since that day, Israel has been seen as the villain. Today, the areas occupied by Israel, especially the West Bank, are presented as the main hindrance to peace in the Middle East. The entire world wants to have a say in this matter. Unfortunately, it is a clear fact that most people do not really know the background to the Middle East conflict. Many of the circumstances, which have been outlined above, escape them. Who among them know that there has long been a Palestinian nation (Jordan), founded before the Jewish nation (in 1946) which is in possession of 77% of Palestine? Who knows that, according to international law, the West Bank may not to be dealt with as a national territory? Who understands that the West Bank has been an inhabited homeland to Jews over the past 2,000 years? If all this is known, why is it not spoken of? Were it known, but nevertheless not spoken of, this would be much worse than if it were simply unknown. This would be absolutely unethical.

Now, who informs the majority of people in the media? For the most part it is precisely those who cannot be said to have knowledge of the material. Therefore, the man or woman on the street chatters away to a large extent in ignorance about the Mountains of Israel, as if they were the main problem for a comprehensive solution in the Middle East. It is simply not known to most people that the surrounding Arabic world has repeatedly attempted to radically destroy Israel, and that this evil plan has not been publically repented of to this day. The direct connection between Palestine and Nazi Germany is also not widely known, much less, that in the Arabic world – in contrast to Germany – there was no break with anti-Semitism following the Second World War.

The majority of people today talk about the West Bank without knowing what this area means for Israel's security from a strategic point of view.

Ezekiel 36:3b has been thus clearly fulfilled, and is being fulfilled anew daily!

## 3.16 Massacre and Plunder

In the following verse, the nations around Israel are accused of wrongfully taking possession of God's Land and plundering it. According to the text they have done this "with ... spiteful minds." (Ezek. 36:5):

> *"⁵ Therefore thus says the Lord GOD: "Surely I have spoken in My burning jealousy against the rest of the nations and against all Edom, who **gave My land to themselves as a possession**, with wholehearted joy and **spiteful minds**, in order to **plunder** its open country." (NKJV)*

The "spiteful minds" mentioned in Ezek.36:5 were fulfilled in a terrible way: Jews in the West Bank were killed, mercilessly massacred, men, women and children.[214] All Jewish towns, including all assets, were confiscated: East Jerusalem (the Jewish Quarter in the Old City), Kfar Etzion, Ein Tzurim, Massuot Yitzchak, Revadim, Kibbutz Kalya, Beit Ha-Arava, Neve Ya'akov and Atarot. Widespread plunder was carried out.[215] The tracts of land between Jerusalem and Ramallah (in Benjamin's tribal area) and in the Judean Hills between Jerusalem and Hebron (cf. Jer. 32:44) bought for a lot of money during the period of 1882 to 1940 were looted.

---

214 http://en.wikipedia.org/wiki/Kfar_Etzion_massacre ; http://en.wikipedia.org/wiki/Gush_Etzion (as of: 21.11.2011).

215 http://en.wikipedia.org/wiki/Gush_Etzion (as of: 21.11.2011).

## 3.17 Shame and Disgrace over the Mountains of Israel

In verse 6 God speaks about the fact that the Mountains of Israel have had to bear shame on the nations' part and, therefore, this judgement will come to the neighbouring nations: one day they will bear their own shame (Ezek. 36:6-7):

> *"⁶ Therefore prophesy concerning the land of Israel, and say to the mountains, the hills, the rivers, and the valleys, 'Thus says the Lord GOD: "Behold, I have spoken in My jealousy and My fury, **because you have borne the shame of the nations**." ⁷ Therefore thus says the Lord GOD: "I have raised My hand in an oath that surely the nations that are around you shall bear their own shame."* (NKJV)

We have seen that the Israeli Army conquered the West Bank in the Six Day War in order to achieve strategic distance from Jordan. This area had been annexed in 1950 by Jordan, but this annexation was never internationally acknowledged. Therefore, according to international law, at the time of its conquest in 1967, the West Bank did not have the status of a "national territory." This remains so today. Therefore, it is, to say the least, highly problematic, legally, to apply international law, which concerns the property of nation states, to the West Bank. While it is constantly asserted that Israel is breaking international law by its occupation of the West Bank, unjustified shame is brought upon the Mountains of Israel. Israel's occupation of the West Bank is scandalously termed a "war crime." In addition, the legal situation is very complex because Turkish, Jordanian and British law is applied. Now there is also Israeli military law.

The shame of Israel's mountains is also expressed by the call for the boycott of Jewish export products from the West Bank throughout the world.

Moreover, the Israeli settlement movement in the West Bank is internationally prohibited. "Aggressive settlement politics" and "the evil of settlements" are spoken of. The dwellings are described as "a threat to the entire peace process," regardless of the true roots of the Middle East conflict. The term "cancerous settlement activities" has also been used.

Why did the Israeli Army conquer the West Bank in 1967? By conquering the land the desire was to have something concrete in hand in order to later bargain in the "land for peace" negotiations. But the desire was to never again surrender all the land there to the Arabs. Therefore, following the Six Day War, the State of Israel encouraged its citizens to build settlements with enormous strategic importance on the east front, in order to be better prepared against invasions from this direction in the future. Other than the West Bank, Israel has no strategic depth. It is so narrow that an attack from the West Bank can hardly be defended against. One doesn't need to be a military specialist in order to understand this. The 1948 borders were totally precarious. The former Israeli Secretary of State, Abba Eban named them appropriately "the Auschwitz Borders."

The shamefulness of all these accusations against Israel's administration and settlement activities in the West Bank becomes even clearer against the background of all the facts.

Furthermore, it also needs to be said at this point that even if the West Bank were actually a foreign national territory, it would be legal, according to international law, for Israel to occupy it, for as long as it posed a threat to its citizens.

Since this threat still persists to this day, it would be legal in this case for Israel to continue to act as occupying power in the West Bank.

The West Bank does not have the status of a national territory. All of the accusations against Israel quoted above are therefore, in every regard, an injustice, whether from the purely human perspective of international law or from God's point of view, according to his promises to Israel recorded in the Bible.[216]

---

216 Regarding the question of international law in relation to East Jerusalem and the West Bank, the extremely significant and exhaustive doctoral dissertation of the Canadian Jaques Paul Gauthier deserves special recognition. It is a prerequisite for a discussion of this subject.

GAUTHIER, J.P.: Sovereignty over the Old City of Jerusalem, A Study of the Historical, Religious, Political and Legal Aspects of the Question of the Old City, Thèse présenté pour l'obtention du grade de Docteur ès Science politiques (Droit international), Université de Genève, Institut Universitaire de Hautes Etudes Internationales, Thèse No 725, Genève 2007.

## 3.18 Israel's Return to the West Bank

In Ezekiel 36:8, God promises that, following the period of occupation by the surrounding nations, the Jewish people would return to the mountains of Israel, and *"within a short time."* Then the Mountains of Israel will again prove fruitful for the chosen people (Ezek. 36:8):

> *"⁸ But you, O mountains of Israel, you shall shoot forth your branches and yield your fruit to My people Israel, **for they are about to come."** (NKJV)*

Twenty years had passed since 1948. Prior to the second attempt at Israel's total obliteration in 1967, King Hussein was earnestly warned against taking part in this war against Israel. He was threatened with severe consequences. When Jordan nonetheless opened a third front against Israel, the West Bank was conquered, including East Jerusalem and the Temple Mount. The Jewish people had returned to the mountains of Israel after the relatively short period of 19 years. What is 19 years in contrast to the almost 2000 years of loss of land in the past? It really was a short time! By this return coming *"soon"* after their loss, the Jewish people were able to enjoy the blossoming fruits of Israel's mountains.

## 3.19 Rebuilding the Ruins, Agriculture and Fertility

Following the Six Day War, Israeli citizens were encouraged to settle in the West Bank. Towns formerly conquered and destroyed by Jordan such as Kfar Etzion, Revadim, Massuoth Yitzchak, Ein Tzurim, Kibbutz Kalya, Beit Ha-Arava, Ataroth and Neve Ya'akov were rebuilt. The Jewish Quarter in the Old City of Jerusalem, found in a lamentable state, was reconstructed according to a uniform, highly aesthetic architectural plan. This followed excavations which brought a number of phenomenal archaeological treasures from Biblical times to light. Through the efforts of numerous, newly founded kibbutzim (collective agricultural settlements) and Moshavin (co-operative rural settlements) extensive agriculture was built up in the West Bank, arable farming as well as animal husbandry (especially cattle and poultry).

Beginning in 1882, in the first decades of the resettlement of the Land of their Fathers, socialistic-minded Jews played a key role in the agriculture and development of the country. This means that mainly non-religious, liberal, atheist or, at least agnostic, Jews were the driving force of the reconstruction. A significant change came in 1967 as the impetus in the resettlement of the West Bank came from especially religious, Orthodox Jews. Orthodox Jews have fundamentally a very positive out-look on marriage and family. They have a much higher birth-rate than their liberal countrymen. Settlement of the West Bank is not only characterized by immigration, but especially by natural population increase. The rate of growth in the West Bank was 5.6% in 2009, while it was 1.8% in the heartland of Israel.[217] Of this 5.6% growth rate, about 40% may be attributed to immigration. [218] The growth rate through children is still at a phenomenal 3.4%! This is a rate which is among peak rates worldwide.

All this was prophesied a long time ago in Ezekiel 36:9-11:

*"9 For indeed I am for you, and I will turn to you, and you shall be **tilled** and **sown**. 10 I will **multiply** men upon you, all the house of Israel, all of it; and **the cities shall be inhabited** and **the ruins rebuilt**. 11 I will multiply upon you **man and beast**; and they shall increase and **bear young**; I will make you inhabited as in former times, and do better for you than at your beginnings. Then you shall know that I am the LORD."* (NKJV)

In verse 10, the Bible text speaks about cities which will be rebuilt. This prophecy would by no means have been fulfilled by small settlements and outposts. In the West Bank since the resettlement of 1967, modern large towns pulsing with life have been built, such as Ariel (16,000 inhabitants), Mode'in Illit (30,000 inhabitants), Beitar Illit (28,000 inhabitants), Ma'ale Adumim (32,000 inhabitants) und Gush Etzion (60,000 inhabitants).

---

217  http://de.wikipedia.org/wiki/Westjordanland (as of: 24.10.2011).

218  http://de.wikipedia.org/wiki/Westjordanland (as of: 24.10.2011).

## 3.20 More Blessing Than at First

In the verse 11 just quoted we find the promise that the blessing following the Jews' return to the Mountains of Israel will be much greater than before (Ezek. 36:11).

> *"[11] I will multiply upon you man and beast; and they shall increase and bear young; **I will make you inhabited as in former times, and do better for you than at your beginnings.** Then you shall know that I am the LORD."* (NKJV)

There was a powerful breakthrough with the return to the West Bank in 1967. Earlier building appears modest by comparison. Numerous new villages and cities were built. Furthermore 250 factories, 70 high-tech industries and 16 institutions of higher education were constructed. Compared with the agricultural accomplishments following 1967, the efforts of the Kibbutzim before 1948 were very humble.

Naturally, the blessings of the coming Messianic Kingdom will be much greater. But the blessing since the return in 1967 is palpable.

## 3.21 Curse Because of Idolatry

In Ezekiel 36:12 Israel is explicitly promised that they will ultimately possess the Mountains of Israel as their inheritance intended by God. There follows a statement which sounds curious at first: *In the future Israel's mountains shall no more rob them of children (Ezek. 36:12-15):*

> *"[12] Yes, I will cause men to walk on you, My people Israel; they shall take possession of you, and you shall be their inheritance; **no more shall you bereave them of children.**" [13] 'Thus says the Lord GOD: "Because they say to you, 'You devour men and bereave your nation of children,' [14] therefore **you shall devour men no more, nor bereave your nation anymore,**" says the Lord GOD. [15] "Nor will I let you hear the taunts of the nations anymore, nor bear the reproach of the peoples anymore, **nor shall you cause your nation to stumble anymore,**" says the Lord GOD.'"* (NKJV)

In Old Testament times, when the Jewish people repeatedly fell away from worshipping the one true God of the Bible, they would honour the gods of the surrounding nations. Cultic practices were very often conducted at sacred sites on the mountain tops. Sacrifice of children played a significant role in connection with the Baal cult. According to Ezekiel 6 and 7, a particular curse from God came to "the Mountains of Israel" just because of this. This curse would continue into The Last Days. The West Bank, the land of the Mountains of Israel, is an especially afflicted area up until our own time. Yet Ezekiel 36 brings the encouraging message that God has good thoughts about this region and, with Israel's return to the West Bank, will finally bring blessing instead of cursing to this mountain range. Through the horrible deeds connected with the sacrifice of children, the mountains of the West Bank had "bereave(d) them of children." Yet everything will be different in The Last Days. There will be no renewal of the Baal cult in these mountains. These things will definitely be relegated to the past.

## 3.22 Return Home in Impurity

Prophecy about the West Bank includes the text from Ezekiel 35:1 to 36:15. From verse 16 on it deals, quite generally, with the return of the Jews from the whole world to the Land of their Fathers. We have already looked at verse 24 especially in Part I (Ezek. 36):

> *"24 For I will take you from among the nations, gather you out of all countries, and bring you into your own land."* (NKJV)

In verses 16-23 it is explained that Israel, scattered among the nations as a witness for God, had failed by being unfaithful. God's Name had been profaned by them. Furthermore God declares that He will, nevertheless, bring them home to their land. Not because they have earned this, but rather because of the honour of God's Name (Ezek. 36:21-23).[219] The nations shall have no grounds to

---

219 Furthermore, Jeremiah 31 teaches that because of His electing love, God will restore Israel and bring them back to their land in The Last Days.

speak against God: At one time He chose Israel and led them out of Egypt, but He has never brought their destiny to its completion. Ezekiel 36 shows this: God has a goal for Israel and will, at the end, gloriously conclude Israel's history. To God's honour the Jews will be returned home from the entire world. This is the actual statement of verse 24 as seen in its context!

The Jewish people would return home in an impure state. Verses 25-32 describe how God – still in the future from our perspective – someday will purify and revive His people. This corresponds to the statements in Isaiah 10:20-22 that God, in The Last Days, will bring a remnant to belief.[220] Consequently, the fact that the greater part of immigrant Jews in Israel is liberal and does not see the commandments of the Bible as binding on their lifestyle, corresponds exactly to the statements of the prophecy in Ezekiel 36! Many Israelis are atheists or agnostics; only some 30% call themselves Orthodox.

In addition, there is the fact that today only some 10,000 to 20,000 Jews in Israel acknowledge Jesus Christ as Messiah.[221]

### 3.23 The Separation Barrier

In Ezekiel 36:35 it is said that the country will bloom again. We have already dealt with this in Part I. But we should turn our attention to the statement "*cities are now fortified*" in reference to the issue of the West Bank (Ezek. 36:34-35):

> "*34 The desolate land shall be tilled instead of lying desolate in the sight of all who pass by. 35 So they will say, 'This land that was desolate has become like the garden of Eden; and the wasted, desolate, and ruined **cities are now fortified** and inhabited.'*" (NKJV)

---

220 This revival will come following the rapture of the church (1 Thess. 4:13-18). First of all a group of 144,000 will come to belief on the Messiah Jesus (Rev. 7:1-8), afterward in the great tribulation, ultimately 1/3 of the population of Israel (Zech. 13:8).

221 The proportion of Jews who believe in Jesus as the Messiah is considerably higher in the Diaspora. As already mentioned above, there are over 400,000 Messianic Jews, especially in the USA and Canada.

The word here translated "fortified" in Hebrew, *batzur* means "made inaccessible/cut off/held apart [by a steep wall/partition]."[222] The word does not refer to a curtain wall in particular, but rather fundamentally a construction which keeps enemies out and prevents access to the cities.

Following the outbreak of the Second Intifada in 2000, the number of Israeli victims rose devastatingly. Therefore, the then Sharon government ordered the building of a barrier over 750 km long facing the West Bank. On the whole this construction project is a separation fence, but in the areas around Qalqilya and Jerusalem there is a wall at least 25 km in length and up to 8 metres high made out of reinforced concrete. Palestinian terrorism has been drastically reduced by this gigantic project. This retentive structure continuously saves peoples' lives. Nevertheless, on 9 July 2004 the International Court of Justice at The Hague issued a legal opinion in which portions of the path of the barrier's route were condemned as a breach of the Fourth Geneva Convention. On 20 July 2004 a UN Resolution called for the demolition of the structure in the West Bank. However, defense experts on international law have emphatically pointed out the inconsistencies in this condemnation.[223]

Whatever the world decides about this wall remains to be seen. But the prophetic Word of the Bible was fulfilled in an astounding way with this issue which is of concern to the entire world.

### 3.24 The Prophet Obadiah's Warning

We have looked at the significance Edom has, according to Ezekiel 35 and 36, regarding all the events concerning the annihilation of the Jews from 1938–1945 and the attempt to obliterate the Jews in the Land of their Fathers in 1947–1949.

Obadiah devotes his entire book to the subject of Edom.[224]

---

222 BAUMGARTNER/KÖHLER: Hebräisches und aramäisches Lexikon zum Alten Testament, Vol. I, p.142; GESENIUS/MEYER/DONNER: Hebräisches und aramäisches Handwörterbuch über das Alte Testament, Vol. I, p.166-167; KÖNIG: Hebräisches und aramäisches Wörterbuch zum Alten Testament, p.46.

223 http://de.wikipedia.org/wiki/Israelische_Sperranlagen_%28Westjordanland%29 (as of: 24.10.2011).

224 See Roger Liebi: Das Buch des Propheten Obadja (audio lecture at www.sermon-online.de ).

God warned this country on the east side of the Jordan River with the following grave words, which would have been of utmost significance in precisely these aforesaid years of affliction and catastrophe for the Jews (Obad. 1:12-14):[225]

> *"[12] But you should not have gazed [maliciously] on the day[226] of your brother*
> *In the day of his captivity;*
> *Nor should you have rejoiced over the children of Judah*
> *In the day of their destruction;*
> *Nor should you have spoken proudly*
> *In the day of distress.*
> *[13] You should not have entered the gate of My people*
> *In the day of their calamity.*
> *Indeed, you should not have gazed [maliciously] on their affliction*
> *In the day of their calamity,*
> *Nor laid hands on their substance*
> *In the day of their calamity.*
> *[14] You should not have stood at the crossroads*
> *To cut off those among them who escaped;[227]*
> *Nor should you have delivered up those among them who remained*
> *In the day of distress."* (NKJV)

Unfortunately, Jordan did not heed this grave, millennia-old warning from the Bible and proceeded to violate each divine command.

---

225 Roger Liebi's translation of the Minor Prophets is available at: www.rogerliebi.ch .

226 The Hebrew *vav* expresses here, in view of the future, practical results from the historical events described in 1:11.

227 The same word as in Obadiah 1:10c.

# 4. List with 28 Fulfilled Prophecies (P63–90)

In the following list only those prophetic statements have been presented which have not been already introduced in the list at the end of Part I.

| Prophecy | Statement | Bible verse | Fulfillment |
|----------|-----------|-------------|-------------|
| P63 | Partition of the Land of Israel | Joel 3:2-3 | Palestine's partition by Britain in 1921; Palestine's partition by the UN in 1947 |
| P64 | **Perpetual hostility** from the surrounding countries against Israel | Ezek. 35:5 | Arab resistance from 1882; 1921: Transjordan = "judenrein;" 1939–1947: drastic reduction of Jewish immigration; 3 attempts to obliterate Israel (1947–1949; 1967; 1973) by the surrounding nations |
| P65 | Israelites **given over to the sword** | Ezek. 35:5 | From 1921: Transjordan completely closed as a refuge for Jews; 1930s: Reduction in immigration to Western Palestine due to Arabic pressure on the British (➔ given over to the sword of the Nazis); Amin Haj al-Husseini, Mufti of Jerusalem, allied with Hitler; given over to British military violence against "illegal" immigrants |
| P66 | Catastrophe for Jews | Ezek. 35:5 | Nazis in Europe annihilate 6,000,000 Jews (1938–1945) |
| P67 | Abandonment of the Israelites by Edom in The Last Days, "**at the time of their calamity**" | Ezek. 35:5 (cf. Deut. 4:30; 31:29) | Immigration reduction and deportation **exactly at the time of the annihilation of the Jews by the Nazis (1938–1945)** |

| Prophecy | Statement | Bible verse | Fulfillment |
|----------|-----------|-------------|-------------|
| P68 | **War miracles** through God's presence | Ezek. 35:10 | In spite of poor armament, Israel is victorious over 9 Arab armies (1948/49) |
| P69 | **Envy** of Israel's land | Ezek. 35:11 | Wars against Israel (1947–1949; 1967; 1973) = expression of envy of Israel's land because of Islamic doctrine of Dar ul-Islam |
| P70 | **Anger and snorting** against Israel | Ezek. 35:11; 36:1-3 | Nov. 1947: the Arab world riots in anger against the UN Resolution in favor of the Jews ➜ total war against Israel; war rhetoric in run-up: Assam Pasha, Arab League Secretary-General (15 May 1948): "This will be a war of extermination and a huge bloodbath which will be spoken of like the Mongolian massacres and the Crusades."[T2] Statement by an Arab representative following the UN Resolution at the end of Nov. 1947: "Any line drawn by the United Nations will be nothing but a line of blood and fire."[T3] Matiel Mughannam: "[A Jewish State] has no chance to survive now that the 'holy war' has been declared. All the Jews will eventually be massacred."[T4] |

[T2] NEW YORK TIMES, May 16, 1948; cited by: PFISTERER: Israel oder Palästina? p.126.

[T3] EBAN: My Country: The Story of Modern Israel, p. 47.

[T4] http://de.wikipedia.org/wiki/Pal%C3%A4stinakrieg (as of: 15.11.2011).

| Prophecy | Statement | Bible verse | Fulfillment |
|---|---|---|---|
| P71 | **Blasphemy** against God | Ezek. 35:12-13 | The Bible promises Israel the Land. The Arab world blasphemously rejects the Bible and its promises for Israel, treating the Bible disgracefully and dismissing it as perversion of the Jews and Christians |
| P72 | **Terrible destruction** in the region of "the mountains of Israel" | Ezek. 35:14-15 | Destruction and total ruin of Israeli settlements/residential areas in the West Bank, provocative desecration in East Jerusalem and in the historic cemetery on the Mount of Olives; extensive destruction of kibbutz orchards |
| P73 | **The entire world chatters** about the "Mountains of Israel" | Ezek. 36:3 | Israel criticized worldwide by politicians and the rank-and-file for the occupation and resettlement of the West Bank from 1967 on |
| P74 | **Conquest** and **plunder** of the "Mountains of Israel" by Edom and its allies | Ezek. 36:4-5 | Conquest of the West Bank by Jordan and its allies (1947–1949); extensive plundering of Jewish settlements in the West Bank, including East Jerusalem |
| P75 | Conquest of "the Mountains of Israel" = **"Edom" and "the nations all around"** | Ezek. 36:4 | Jordan, Syria, Iraq, Lebanon, Egypt, Saudi Arabia, Yemen, Palestinians |

| Prophecy | Statement | Bible verse | Fulfillment |
|---|---|---|---|
| P76 | **Leadership** of the surrounding nations: **Edom** | Ezek. 36:4; 35:1ff | Leadership of the coalition against Israel: **in 1948 Jordan possessed the strongest army of all its allies**[T5] **and received almost all of the spoils of war** |
| P77 | **Seizure** of the "Mountains of Israel" – Edom's **claim to "these two countries"** | Ezek. 35:10; 36:1-3 | King Abdullah of Jordan explicitly claimed East and West Palestine. **Annexation** of the West Bank by Jordan in 1950 (*conquest* and *annexation* are two clearly different terms!) |
| P78 | **Massacre** of the Israelites on the "Mountains of Israel;" no regard for life | Ezek. 36:5 | Massacre of Jews in the West Bank in the war of 1947–1949 |
| P79 | **Shame** over the "Mountains of Israel" | Ezek. 36:6-7 | Boycott of Jewish export products from the West Bank, worldwide ostracism of the settlement movement, shaming of Jewish settlements with terms such as "war crimes", "aggressive settlement policy," "obstacle to peace," "the evil of settlements," "cancerous growth," "cancerous settlement activity" |
| P80 | The "mountains of Israel" shall **bear fruit** for Israel. | Ezek. 36:8 | Israel's agricultural fruit production in the West Bank since 1967 |

---

[T5] http://fr.wikipedia.org/wiki/Guerre_isra%C3%A9lo-arabe_de_1948-1949 (as of: 31.10.2011).

| Prophecy | Statement | Bible verse | Fulfillment |
|---|---|---|---|
| P81 | **Return** of the Israelites to "the mountains of Israel" | Ezek. 36:8 | Return of the Jews to the West Bank following its conquest in 1967 |
| P82 | **Speedy** return ("they are about to come") | Ezek. 36:8 | Return after **only 19–20 years**: interruption: 1947/48 –1967 |
| P83 | The "Mountains of Israel" will **again be agriculturally "tilled" and "sown"** | Ezek. 36:9 | Development of numerous Kibbutzim (agricultural collectives) and Moshavim (co-operatively organized rural settlements) in the West Bank from 1967 |
| P84 | **Rebuilding the ruins** on "the mountains of Israel" | Ezek. 36:10 | Restoration of destroyed settlements: Jewish Quarter in East Jerusalem, Kfar Etzion, Revadim, Ein Tzurim, Massuot Yitzchak, Beit Ha-Arava, Kibbutz Kalya, Atarot, Neve Ya'akov |
| P85 | **Increase** of the Israelites on "the Mountains of Israel" | Ezek. 36:10 | Rate of growth high in the West Bank, 2009: 5.6% (2.2% through immigration; 3.4% through children); the remainder of Israel: not more than 1.8% growth through childbirth |
| P86 | Life in **cities** | Ezek. 36:10 | Development of large cities: Ariel (16,000 inhabitants), Mode'in Illit (30,000), Beitar Illit (28,000), Ma'ale Adumim (32,000), Gush Etzion (60,000) |

| Prophecy | Statement | Bible verse | Fulfillment |
|---|---|---|---|
| P87 | Livestock fertility | Ezek. 36:11 | Successful poultry and dairy farming in the West Bank |
| P88 | More blessing than at first | Ezek. 36:11 | Beginning of fulfillment: numerous kibbutzim, new villages and towns are built, 250 factories, 70 high-tech industries, 16 institutions of higher education. Development since 1967 greatly exceeds all activity before 1948 |
| P89 | Return in **impurity** | Ezek. 36:22-24 | The greater part of immigrant Jews in Israel is liberal, the commandments of the Bible are not binding for their lives and lifestyles. Many athiests and agnostics |
| P90 | The cities are **secured by partition** and **made inaccessible** (Hebr. *batzur*) | Ezek. 36:35 | From 2003: Construction of the separation structure more than 750 km long and reinforced concrete wall for the protection of the cities in the Israeli heartland |

***Fig. 18***: *The separation wall in the region of East Jerusalem (Picture by Roger Liebi).*

# IV. Israel and the Destiny of Iraq

## 1. 1. Southern Iraq in View of Prophecy

At the end of the 20th and beginning of the 21st centuries, Iraq posed a threat to the safety of the world in general and to the security of Israel in particular. This fact led to the Gulf Wars of 1991 and 2003.

These two wars, which deeply frightened and perplexed mankind, were immensely significant from the Biblical point of view. In Isaiah 13–14 (written in 740 BC) and Jeremiah 50–51 (from 582 BC) we discover detailed prophecies regarding Iraq's or Babylonia' End-Time destiny. In these texts we find remarkable prophecies about these conflicts mentioned above, which were decisive stages on the way to Babylonia's ultimate destiny: This territory in the south of Iraq is doomed to final and total destruction.[228]

These prophecies from the four chapters of the Bible just mentioned are over 2½ thousand years old, but have suddenly gained astounding currency in our time. We read in Jeremiah 50:

> *"45 Therefore hear the counsel of the LORD that He has taken against Babylon,*

---

228 In this connection, it must be clear that the "Babylon" of the Revelation, whose End-Times doom is foretold there, may not be confused with the Babylon of Isaiah and Jeremiah.

The *"whore Babylon"* in the last book of the Bible is the counterpart of *"the wife of the Lamb, the new Jerusalem."* Whereas *"new Jerusalem"* is not the capital of Israel; rather, the true church of God, "Babylon" is a competing false church based in the city of seven hills (Rev. 17:9,18).

Jerusalem in the OT is a spiritual allusion to the "new Jerusalem" without being identical to it. Comparably the city of Babylon in the OT is a typological allusion to "Babylon the Great." This explains also why there are so many references to Jer. 50-51 in Rev. 17-19 (cf. parallel verse index in: The Greek New Testament, p. 898).

*And His purposes that He has proposed against the land of the Chaldeans: ..."* (NKJV)

In the following, we will look closely at this counsel of the LORD. We want to know what is prophesied in the Bible about "Babylon, ... the land of the Chaldeans!"

## 1.1 Summary of Prophecy in Isaiah 13–14 and Jeremiah 50–51

The following summarized main points briefly clarify what will be dealt with in the prophetic chapters of Isaiah and Jeremiah, which describe the End-Times fate of Babylonia:

- Isaiah 13–14 and Jeremiah 50–51 portray the total demise of the land of Babylonia, so that it can no longer be inhabited (Isa. 13:17,18; Jer. 51:3,41,48).
- This will happen in the time when the Jewish people return to the Land of their Fathers from a worldwide dispersion (Isa. 14:1-2; Jer. 50:3).[229]
- The Jews in Babylonia are called to leave the country *before* this event, on one hand, through *flight* (Jer. 50:8,28; 51:6) and on the other hand, in an orderly withdrawal (Jer. 51:45).
- A coalition of many nations from far away will make war with Babylonia (Isa. 13:1-5).
- Babylonia's destruction will not happen in one fell swoop, but will rather occur after a number of successive phases (Jer. 51:33).
- The Medes (today's Kurds) and another powerful nation attacking from the north will play a special role in the final destruction (Isa. 13:17-18; Jer. 51:11,28; Jer. 50:3,41,48).
- The judgement of Babylonia is a warning for the entire world, which has likewise earned God's judgement. The example of Babylon is a warning for all of mankind to turn to the Living God.

---

[229] Isaiah 14:1a: *"For the LORD will have mercy on Jacob, and will still choose Israel, and settle them in their own land."*

Jeremiah 50:5: *"They shall ask the way to Zion, With their faces toward it."*

- The prophecy regarding Babylonia demonstrates the credibility of the Bible: it is God's Word to us humans!

## 1.2 A Preliminary Clarification

Were Isaiah 13–14 and Jeremiah 50–51 fulfilled in 539 BC when the Medo-Persians conquered Babylonia? Even though many commentaries, due to superficial handling of the text, answer "yes" to this question, this is, however, quite clearly wrong, as is documented by the following arguments:

- The Persians did not destroy the *city* of Babylon at that time. The conquest of the city by King Cyrus resembled more a coup. Cyrus was allied with the Babylonian priests. They opened the gates for their conquerors into the almost impregnable city. King Belshazzar was killed with a stroke of the sword at the end of his nocturnal party (cf. Dan. 5). The Persians did not destroy or wreck the *country*. There were only a few brief battles. The bureaucracy of Babylon was essentially taken over by the Medo-Persian rulers (cf. Dan.6).
- The region around the *city* of Babylon is inhabited to this day (the modern city Al Hillah has about 300,000 inhabitants).[230] The oft-found assertion that Babylon became an uninhabited region as a result of the Medo-Persian conquest in the 6th century is simply historically false.
- The country of Babylonia (southern Iraq) is inhabited to this day.
- The Jews did *not* need to flee from the country following the conquest of Babylon in 539 BC. They received permission from the government of the Persian King to leave in a dignified manner and return to the Land of their Fathers (cf. Ezra 1ff). However, in Jeremiah 50–51 the issue is that the Jews should leave the country hastily *before* a catastrophe which would come upon Babylon.
- The Jewish exodus in 539 BC occurred *after* the conquest of Babylon, *not before*. Jeremiah 50–51 deals not only with a *flight* from Babylonia but also an *orderly exodus*. Yet this

---

230  http://de.wikipedia.org/wiki/Al_Hilla (as of: 24.10.2011).

exodus would occur *before* a future judgement on Babylon.

- The Medo-Persian army conquered Babylon in 539 BC. The leading people at the time were the *Persians*, not the Medes. In Isaiah 13–14 and Jeremiah 50–51, however, the Persians are not even named. By contrast, the *Medes* are specifically mentioned as being significant in connection with the downfall of Babylon.[231] This already indicates that, in the chapters mentioned, Isaiah and Jeremiah were considering another event. When Daniel prophesied to Belshazzar of the coming conquest by Cyrus, he explicitly referred to *the Persians and the Medes* coming as invaders (Dan. 5:28).
- There is indeed a connection between Cyrus' judgement on Babylon and the final judgement prophesied in Isaiah 13–14 and Jeremiah 50–51: Cyrus' judgement was a harbinger, a foretaste of the final destruction. This is clear, for example, from the fact that Babylonia's final judgement is presented as retribution for what Nebuchadnezzar had at one time done to the Jews (Jer. 50:17-18,28; 51:34-37).

## 1.3 The Geography of Babylonia

The heartland of *"the land of Babylonia"* lies in modern Iraq. In antiquity it included the region of southern Iraq in the area of the Euphrates and Tigris Rivers to just north of Baghdad. Interestingly, today it corresponds to a large extent with the *territory of the Shiites* in Iraq.

The Bible also often speaks of *Assyria*. The heartland of Assyria with the ancient cities of Nineveh, Kalakh and Assur are found in modern northern Iraq. This corresponds to a large extent with the *region of the Sunnis*.

When Iraq is considered in the light of the Bible, *the Land of the Medes* has to be distinguished together with Babylonia and Assyria: The heartland of the Medes is *the modern Kurdish region* in north-east Iraq. It stretches on into north-west Iran. Today's Kurds proudly see themselves as descendants of the ancient Medes.

---

231  Isa. 13:17-18; Jer. 51:11,28.

174

Seen Biblically and prophetically, Assyrian and Median north-ern Iraq has a completely different future to the south. According to Isaiah 13–14 and Jeremiah 50–51, only Babylonia will undergo complete destruction.

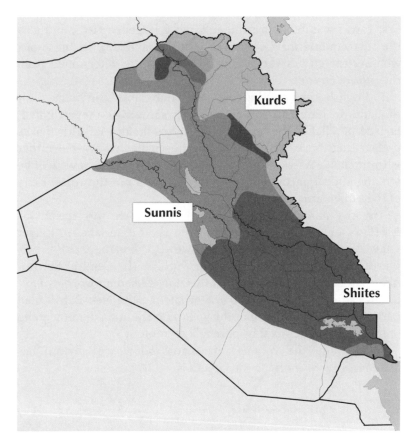

*Fig. 19:* Settlement regions of the Kurds, the Sunnis and the Shiites in Iraq (source: Wikipedia, Rafi, Creative Commons 3.0).

## 1.4 A Definition of Terms

In the OT, when "Babel" and "Babylon" are spoken of, the following must be kept in mind: "Babel" (Hebr. pronunciation: *bavel*; stress on the last syllable) is Hebrew and is equivalent in usage to the Greek word "Babylon."

Both terms (Babel and Babylon) denote both *the city* where the first tower was built in southern Iraq (cf. Gen. 11:1-9), and also the surrounding *land* (southern Iraq to Baghdad). In the Bible, whether the city or the land is meant must be determined from the *context* in each case.

In English, the unambiguous term "Babylonia" can be used for the land. In Jeremiah 50:1 and 45, for example, the term "Babel" is used parallel to the term "Land of the Chaldeans." This makes it clear that these verses are not dealing with the city, but rather with the land. As we will clearly see, the four chapters we will be looking at deal particularly with the land and not the ancient city of the same name.

The city name "Babel" is found in Sumerian inscriptions as *babillum* or *babilla*.[232] However, even the Sumerians no longer knew the origin or meaning of this word. The name *Babel* is neither a Sumerian nor an Akkadian word.[233] The Semitic Babylonians later attempted to explain this non-Akkadian word as *bab-ili* (Akkadian = "gate of God"),[234] or later in the Neo-Babylonian period as *bab-ilani* ("gate of the gods").[235] The Akkadian meaning of the name "Babel" is thus pure folk etymology. [236]

Incidentally, the very familiar name *babylon* (Babylon) has arisen from *bab-ilani* via the Greeks.[237]

---

232 GESENIUS/MEYER/DONNER: Hebräisches und aramäisches Handwörterbuch über das Alte Testament, p.122; VANGEMEREN: New International Dictionary of Old Testament Theology & Exegesis, Vol. IV, p.430.

233 BOTTERWECK/RINGGREN: Theological Dictionary of the Old Testament, Vol. I, p. 466-467.

234 This corresponds to the Sumarian term ka-dingir-ra (BOTTERWECK/RINGGREN: Theological Dictionary of the Old Testament, Vol. I, p.466.)

235 KÖHLER/BAUMGARTNER: Hebräisches und aramäisches Lexikon zum Alten Testament, Vol. I, p.103.

236 GESENIUS/MEYER/DONNER: Hebräisches und aramäisches Handwörterbuch über das Alte Testament, p.122.

237 In the Greek text of the NT, the word babylon is found in the following places: Matt. 1:11,12,17; Acts 7:43; 1 Pet 5:13; Rev 14:8; 16:19; 17:5; 18:2,10,21.

## 1.5 The Biblical Significance of Babylon

The Bible teaches: Babylon is *the cradle of mankind*. The original Pre-Sumerian society established the first civilization here following the Flood.[238] From there, the various tribes were scattered over the five continents as a result of the confusion of language (Gen. 10:1–11:9).[239]

Babylon is also *the cradle of Israel*. Over 4,000 years ago Abraham, the patriarch of the Chosen People, lived as a creation-worshipper in the Babylonian city of Ur (Gen. 11:27ff.; Josh. 24:2,14-15).[240] However, the God of Creation appeared to him (Gen.12:1-3; Acts 7:2-4) and Abraham experienced radical change: He turned his back on the worship of false gods and began to worship the God of Heaven. He abandoned worship of the moon god, customary in Ur. Then Israel's patriarch was called out of Babylon. In obedience to God, Abraham left this region and went to Canaan, later to be the Land of Israel (Heb. 11:8).

In our own time, the cradle of civilization, the cradle of Israel, has become a threat for the world generally and for Israel in particular.

## 1.6 The History of the City of Babylon: From Nebuchadnezzar to Saddam Hussein

Nebuchadnezzar was a mighty builder. He knew how to elevate the capital city of Babylon to a true world wonder of ancient architecture (cf. Dan. 4:30). Archeology has shown that Babylon was a city of almost indescribable majesty.[241] However, in the autumn of 539 BC, Babylon was conquered by the great king Cyrus' Medo-Persian army. Cyrus did not in any way ravage Babylon, as we already know. Rather he made this city the third capital of the Medo-Persian Empire. Henceforth, Cyrus was the *"King of Persia"* (Ezra 4:3)

---

238  BECK, H.W.: Genesis, Aktuelles Dokument vom Beginn der Menschheit, Neuhausen-Stuttgart 1983.

239  For the confusion of the languages cf. extensively: LIEBI: Herkunft und Entwicklung der Sprachen. Sprachwissenschaft contra Evolution.

240  Cf. Roger Liebi: Von Ur nach Salem (audio lecture at www.sermon-online.de).

241  MAIER: Das Buch Daniel, p. 193-194.

and also the *"King of Babylon/Babylonia"* (Ezra 5:13).[242]

At this point in time the prophecy concerning Babylonia in Daniel 7:4 was fulfilled. Babylonia, the "lion with eagle's wings," would be humbled and subjugated, but in no way destroyed or pillaged.[243]

Babylon continued to be a thriving city following its conquest by Cyrus. Under the rule of Darius I (522–486 BC) the citizens of the city of Babylon revolted against their overlords. Darius was able to put down the revolt. Subsequently he had the city gates and walls torn down.[244] In 478 BC, Xerxes I took drastic action against another rebellion.[245] In the process, he destroyed the Temple to Bel.

Alexander the Great conquered Babylon 331 BC. He was impressed with this city and entertained the plan to make Babylon the eastern capital of his empire. 10,000 soldiers were deployed to ensure that the city once again flourished. Alexander also set about rebuilding the Tower of Babel; however, he apparently fell victim to malaria and died before fulfilling his plans.[246]

In 312 BC, Seleucus I conquered Babylon. Sometime later he founded a new capital on the Tigris: Seleucia. Thus, Babylon lost her commercial and political might and deteriorated. However, she was still able to hold on to her religious power; various temples, e.g. the Marduk Temple, continued to operate. Even in 139 BC, when the Parthians ousted the Greeks, Babylon remained a religious center.[247]

The historian Cassius Dio has been cited many times, in order to advance the argument that Trajan, when he visited Babylon in 116 AD, saw nothing but "graves, stones and ruins." But Dio apparently only wanted to give an impression of disappointed expectations. According to Dio's statements, Trajan had gone to Mesopo-

---

242  Artaxerxes I. Longimanus (= Artasasta; 464–423 BC.) was also called "King of Babylon/ Babylonia" in the Bible.

243  LIEBI: Weltgeschichte im Visier des Propheten Daniel (English edition in progress by CMV Hagedorn, Germany).

244  DYER/HUNT: The Rise of Babylon: Sign of The End Times, p. 122-123.

245  ALEXANDER: Apocalypse, p. 306.

246  DYER/HUNT: The Rise of Babylon: Sign of The End Times, p. 123-124.

247  DYER/HUNT: The Rise of Babylon: Sign of The End Times, p. 124-125.

tamia with great hopes of viewing awesome, dazzling architecture. What a disappointment when the Roman emperor realized that he had come to Babylon too late! Dio obviously did not mean to express in his report that Babylon was deserted at this time.[248]

Dio's communications must definitely be seen in conjunction with Pausanias' report, in order to get a correct impression of Babylon's circumstances in this period. Pausanias came from Asia Minor and was active as a writer between 160 and 180 AD. He reported that the walls of Babylon and also the Tempel of Bel (= Bel-Marduk) were still standing in his time.[249]

The Jewish traveler Benjamin of Tudela visited Babylon in the Middle Ages, the 12th century. He referred to a synagogue there still functioning. According to his statements, it lay some two kilometres from the ruins of Nebuchadnezzar's temple (possibly he meant the Marduk Temple).[250]

When the German archaeologist Koldewey visited Babylon at the end of the century before last, Babylon was not uninhabited. He found several villages there near the ruins: Kweiresh, Djumdjumma, Sindjar und Ananeh.[251]

Worthy of mention is the fact that innumerable buildings of the city of Hillah, situated some six kilometres south of the Babylonian ruins, are built of bricks from the ancient ruins of Babylon.[252] Hillah had 75,000 inhabitants in 1965.[253] On 1 January 2005 the number of inhabitants was 289,714. [254]

We see that the city of Babylon has continued to exist throughout the many centuries and into our time – until the government of Iraq decided to revive the one-time metropolis and grant her new glory.

---

248  DIO: Roman History, 68.30.1. and also 68,26-27.

249  PAUSANIAS: Description of Greece, 8.33.3.

250  DYER/HUNT: The Rise of Babylon: Sign of The End Times, p. 128 and 227 (source: ADLER, M.N.: Itinary of Benjamin of Tudela, Jewish Quarterly Review 17 (1905), p. 514-530).

251  DYER/HUNT: The Rise of Babylon: Sign of The End Times, p. 129-130.

252  TITZE: Lexikon der Geographie, Vol. II, p. 398.

253  TITZE: Lexikon der Geographie, Vol. II, p. 397.

254  http://de.wikipedia.org/wiki/Al_Hilla (as of: 24.10.2011).

## 1.7 From Jerusalem to Babylon

The descendants of the patriarchs Abraham, Isaac and Jacob developed into a great nation during the course of the first half of the 2nd millennium BC. Around 1049 BC King David made Jerusalem the capital city of the Jews (2 Sam. 5).

His son Solomon built the First Temple on the peak of Mount Zion in Jerusalem (1 Kings 6-8).This *one* Jewish temple was to be a symbolic witness to the fact that there is only *one* true God.

At the end of his life, however, Solomon tragically turned away from the God of Abraham, Isaac and Jacob (1 Kings 11). He began to worship the nature gods of the surrounding pagan nations. His people then followed the example of their King (1 Kings 11ff.). Prophets arose and urged the Jewish people to repent. They promised a national catastrophe, unless there was a radical repentance. Jerusalem and the Temple would be destroyed and the Jewish people deported to Babylon. The masses ignored the earnest call of those sent by God to warn them (2 Chron.36:15-16). Moses had even foretold the Babylonian captivity of the Jews in 1546 BC (Deut. 28:36):

> "36 The LORD will bring you and the king whom you set over you to a nation which neither you nor your fathers have known, and there you shall serve other gods—wood and stone." (NKJV)

Exactly at the time the fullness of sins in Judah was reached, Babylon rose to World Power No. 1 and placed the nations of the Middle East under its authority. The beginning of this world dominion was marked in 609 BC by the fall of the Assyrian Empire.

The Babylonian army made war three times with the kingdom of Judah in the years of 606–582 BC. Ultimately, Jerusalem was destroyed; the Temple reduced to dust and ashes. The Jews were deported to Babylon in four phases (606, 597, 586 and 582 BC).

They had come full circle: Abraham, the patriarch of the Jewish nation, had been a creation-worshipper (Josh. 24:2, 14-15). He renounced the worship of false gods, however, and turned to the one Creator-God. Thereupon he left Babylon and went to the Land of Israel (Gen. 11:31 ff; Acts 7:2-4).

His descendants, in contrast, turned away from the Creator and gave themselves over to the worship of the creation (Judg. 3ff; 1 Kings 11ff). So, in the end, they had to leave Israel and return to Babylon, to the land of false gods (2 Chron. 36).

Jeremiah, a prophet in 600 BC, foresaw Babylon's heyday and its end (Jeremiah 25:11-12):

> *"¹¹ ... and these nations [in the Middle East] shall serve the king of Babylon seventy years. ¹² 'Then it will come to pass, when seventy years are completed, that I will punish the king of Babylon and that nation ..."* (NKJV)

## 1.8 From Babylon to Jerusalem

Babylon's empire lasted exactly 70 years, from 609–539 BC. In the autumn of 539 BC, the Persians and the Medes conquered the Babylonian Empire. King Cyrus gave the Jews permission to return to the Land of their Fathers and to rebuild the Temple on Zion (Ezra 1).[255] Approximately 200,000 people, including women and children, travelled home at that time (Ezra 2). Mainly, it was the poorer people who returned. Many of the rich wanted to remain in Babylon. In their abundance they had put roots down in the foreign country. They saw themselves, however, as sponsors for the semi-autonomous Persian province of Judea.[256] The returnees went back to the Promised Land to meet the Messiah, the promised Saviour, whose coming and appearance in Israel had been announced in detail by the prophets.

## 1.9 From Jerusalem to Babylon Again

A little more than 2,000 years ago, Jesus Christ was born in Bethlehem. He fulfilled more than 300 OT prophecies of the promised Messiah.[257] However, the majority of His people did not recognize him. At the command of the Jewish High Court, Jesus Christ

---

255 Cf. fulfilled prophecy from Isa. 44:26–45:7.

256 ENGEL: Die Juden in Babylon unter den persischen Königen während des zweiten Tempels bis nach dem barkochbäischen Kriege.

257 Cf. LIEBI: Der verheissene Erlöser, Messianische Prophetie – ihre Erfüllung und historische Echtheit (English edition in progress by CMV Hagedorn, Germany).

was sentenced to death in 32 AD and crucified by the Romans (Matt. 26–27).

Yet the prophets had also foretold the rejection of the Messiah (Isa. 53; 49:7; Ps. 22). They had also foretold its consequences: The Jewish people would be dispersed throughout the nations of the world. Moses prophesied in 1566 BC (Deut. 28:64):

> "*⁶⁴ Then the LORD will scatter you among all peoples, from one end of the earth to the other, ...*" (NKJV)

In 70 AD, when the Romans destroyed Jerusalem and ravaged the land of Israel, many Jews fled to Babylon, which was part of the Parthian Empire at that time.[258] Flight there was desirable because it was a relatively short distance away which made it possible to very quickly reach an area outside Rome's sphere of power.

When the Jewish Revolt under the leadership of Bar Kochba, a false messiah, was put down by the Romans (132–135 AD) there was a new wave of many Jewish refugees into Babylon.[259]

The number of Jews in Babylon grew at that time to some 1 million.[260] This strong Jewish concentration in this area had significant consequences, especially because there were great scribes among the refugees. Babylon became the spiritual center of Judaism and retained this uncontested position until the Middle Ages (10/11th century). Israel's greatest teachers were to be found in Babylon! The most important theological work of post-Biblical Judaism is the Babylonian Talmud, which for the most part is authored by rabbis from Mesopotamia.[261]

In the 10th and 11th centuries, however, there was a massive decline in the central status of the Jews in Babylon. This was caused, on one hand, by inner conflicts and arguments and, on the other hand, by Islamic suppression from the outside.

The spiritual leadership of world Judaism then moved to other areas: Cordoba in Spain, Narbonne in France, Alexandria in

---

258 LANDMANN: The Universal Jewish Encyclopedia, p. 13.

259 LANDMANN: The Universal Jewish Encyclopedia, p. 13.

260 LANDMANN: The Universal Jewish Encyclopedia, p. 13.

261 Cf. the statements in the bibliographic index in the appendix under BABYLONIAN TALMUD.

Egypt and to Kairouan in Tunisia.[262]

Throughout the centuries following the momentous year of 70 AD, suppression and persecution came again and again to the Jews in Babylonia. This repeatedly led to emigration to other regions.[263] However, not until the 20th and 21st centuries would the long Babylonian exile come to an end.

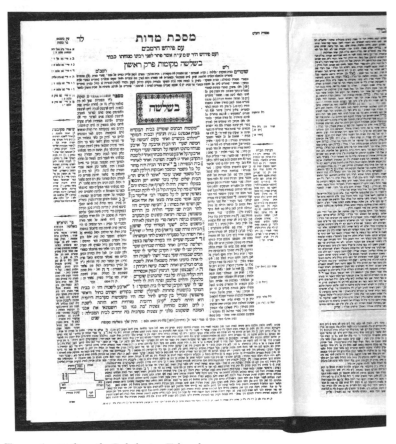

**Fig. 20:** *A page from the Babylonian Talmud*

---

262 LANDMANN: The Universal Jewish Encyclopedia, p. 17-18.

263 To the history of the Jews in Babylon cf. the informative article in: LANDMANN: The Universal Jewish Encyclopedia, p. 9-18. See also: GILBERT: Jewish History Atlas, p. 10.

## 1.10 Fate of the Jews in Babylonia

Babylonian Judaism went through many hardships. Here is a list of the especially important events:

- 581: Persecution of Jews in Babylonia and Persia
- 634: Islamic conquest of Babylonia
- 800/850: heavy taxation, restrictions on freedom of where to live, compulsion of wearing a yellow emblem on the clothing
- 1000: serious suppression, penalty taxation
- 1333: destruction of synagogues in Baghdad, much property stolen
- 1750–1830: (under Turkish/Ottoman rule) serious anti-Jewish measures. Many fled to Persia and India.

## 1.11 Babylonia in the 20th Century

The Ottoman Empire of the Turks, which had ruled the Middle East for centuries, was shattered by the Entente powers Britain and France in the First World War. Babylonia thus came under British rule. In their Mandate government, the British made Faisal I King in Mesopotamia (1923–1933).

The modern State of Iraq was founded in autumn of 1932. Britain then granted independence to Mesopotamia. Some 150,000 Jews lived in Iraq at this time.[264]

In the 1920s, Judaism was able to flourish under King Faisal I. But these golden years would last only a short time.

In 1933, shortly after the state was founded, under the leadership of Ghazi, Faisal's successor, Iraq enthusiastically turned to Arab Nationalism, which was very instrumental in promoting an anti-Semitic atmosphere. This development came at the same time as emergence of National Socialism in Germany! When Hitler came to power early in 1933, this was received by the Iraqi press and by the Iraqi people with great enthusiasm and gratification. Hitler's anti-Semitism had a major representative in Iraq, the German ambassador Fritz Grobba, who had significant popularity both in government circles and generally among Iraqi intellectuals.[265]

---

264  HILLEL: Operation Babylon, p. 329.
265  HILLEL: Operation Babylon, p. 20 und 165.

On 1 June 1941 there was a savage persecution of the Jews with massacres in Baghdad.[266] In the following years, too, there was terrible rioting.[267] The Jews in Iraq were confronted with the danger of their extermination. For this reason, in the following years, the fervent wish grew to leave Iraq and flee to "Palestine," the Land of their Fathers.

As a reaction to the persecution in June 1941, an underground Zionist organization was founded with the goal of helping Jews flee the country.[268]

In the following years, the number of Jews fleeing Iraq took on a completely unacceptable dimension from the point of view of the government. The Iraqis were simply not in a position to seal the borders completely to the Jews. This "outrage" (the fleeing Jews, for instance, no longer paid the taxes for the current year) led to the decision by the government in Baghdad to authorize free departure for the Jews, albeit with the condition that they give up their Iraqi citizenship.

Tawfiq Suweidi, the then Prime Minister, concluded that under such circumstances, only some seven to ten thousand Jews would leave Iraq, ... and then this unfortunate problem would be finally solved. Suweidi's assumptions were based on completely reasonable considerations. However, it would turn out very differently, as we will now see.[269]

When we look at these Iraqi events in their historical background, their drama is intensified immeasurably: during this period of upheaval in the years 1933–1945 over 6 million Jews were murdered in Europe. However, a direct result of this shock to the civilized world brought the founding of the modern State of Israel on 14 May 1948, shortly after the Second World War. Following the Nazi nightmare, the Allies wanted an immediate solution to the ancient Jewish-question.

Yet even on the day after the founding of the state, Iraq, together with Jordan, Syria, Lebanon, Egypt, Saudi Arabia and Yemen

---

266  HILLEL: Operation Babylon, p. 21.

267  http://www.zionismus.info/antizionismus/arabisch-7.htm (as of: 24.10.2011).

268  HILLEL: Operation Babylon, p. 21.

269  HILLEL: Operation Babylon, passim, especially p. 258ff.

attacked Israel. The goal was total annihilation. But one year later, the Jewish state emerged as victor from this catastrophe, with an increase of territory.

# 2. The Rescue of Iraqi Jews

## 2.1 Flight from Babylon: 1941–1950

Thousands of Jews fled Iraq in the years 1941–1950.[270] This agreed exactly with the divine call through the prophet Jeremiah:

Jeremiah 50:8:
*"⁸ Move from the midst of Babylon ..."* (NKJV)

Jeremiah 51:6:
*"⁶ Flee from the midst of Babylon,*
*And every one save his life!*
*Do not be cut off in her iniquity,*
*For this is the time of the Lord's vengeance;*
*He shall recompense her."* (NKJV)

This call to flee is also found in Zecheriah 2:
*"⁷ Up, Zion! Escape, you who dwell with the daughter of Babylon."* (NKJV)

This flight would protect the Jews from a catastrophe which would come upon Iraq (cf. Jer. 51:6b-c: *"Do not be cut off in her iniquity, for this is the time of the LORD's vengeance; He shall recompense her."*)

Jeremiah 50–51 does not just call for flight from Babylon. It is made clear in Jeremiah 50:28 that this call would actually take place:
*"²⁸ The voice of those who flee and escape from the land of Babylon*
*Declares in Zion the vengeance of the LORD our God,*
*The vengeance of His temple."* (NKJV)

---

270 HILLEL: Operation Babylon, passim.

## 2.2 Exodus from Babylon: 1950–1952

The Iraqi government simply was not able to close the borders completely against the Jews' flight. On 2 March 1950 – precisely on the day that the Jews in their synagogues worldwide were celebrating Purim in memory of the wonderful deliverance of their forefathers in Mesopotamia and the entire Persian Empire (cf. the book of Esther; 5th century BC) –, there was an unexpected turning point: the Iraqi government under Tawfik Suweidi announced that all Jews would be allowed to officially emigrate! They must first pay their taxes and relinquish their Iraqi citizenship. Additionally, they were allowed to sell their property at only 10% of its worth.[271]

This was, in spite of the extreme conditions, a double Purim-joy for the Iraqi Jews![272] As we have mentioned above, the government assumed, apparently after reasonable consideration, that only seven to ten thousand Jews would leave in this way and the refugee problem would be finally solved. But it turned out quite differently: 95% of the Jewish community registered for departure even though there was good reason to fear repression upon registration![273]

The whole issue had an additional catch: the emigration law would only be effective until 9 March 1951. At that time, to bring 104,000 people from Iraq by airplane actually seemed an impossibility, humanly speaking, for the young State of Israel, which had just survived a war for its very existence and had a very limited number of planes.[274]

## 2.3 Coup d'état in Iraq

At the beginning of September 1950, a terrible, unexpected turn of events struck like lightening: Tawfiq Suweidi was over-thrown and Nuri Said, a formidable Jew-hater came to power. This coup d'état led to incredible tension and immense fear among the Jews in Iraq. It was feared that the Jewish exodus would soon be stopped

---

271  HILLEL: Operation Babylon, passim.
272  HILLEL: Operation Babylon, p. 260.
273  HILLEL: Operation Babylon, p. 262-263.
274  HILLEL: Operation Babylon, p. 305.

again.[275] This would be a catastrophe for all the now-stateless Jews.

It was learned only afterwards that Nuri Said considered various vicious plans to inflict damage to the Jews in Iraq, or at least the young State of Israel. He considered, for example, the possibility of setting up concentration camps in the Iraqi desert in order to annihilate the Jews there.[276]

## 2.4 The Completion of "Operation Babylon"

Tension and fear in Iraq grew the closer it got to 9 March 1951. Thousands of Jews, who had given up their citizenship, did not know when they could emigrate. It was not clear how they would be able to get out of the country before the deadline. Additionally, the rumour was spread that the emigration would be completely stopped after 9 March. It is hard to imagine the fear and horror the Iraqi Jews experienced during those days.[277]

On 10 March 1951 Nuri Said issued a sadistic decree designed to drive the State of Israel to economic ruin: The Jews would be allowed leave, but all their possessions would be confiscated! This was a heavy blow for the Jews in Iraq and for the young State of Israel, which was already having financial difficulties and now needed to take in tens of thousands of destitute immigrants.[278]

While the Jewish year, which lasted from the New Year's Feast ("Rosh Hashanah") on 24 September 1949 to 11 September 1950, was characterized by the wonderful, almost unbelievable news of permission to emigrate, by contrast, the following year (which, according to the Jewish calendar, lasted from 12 September 1950 to 30 August 1951) was characterized by a contrary, worrying rumour. Nevertheless, in the end, all who had registered were able to leave for Israel! "Operation Babylon" was concluded by its last flight in February 1952.[279]

However, the tremendous event of the Jewish exodus from Iraq was overshadowed by tragedy: In 1951, the Iraqi secret police were

---

275 HILLEL: Operation Babylon, p. 303ff.

276 HILLEL: Operation Babylon, p. 303ff.

277 HILLEL: Operation Babylon, p. 305.

278 HILLEL: Operation Babylon, p. 305-306.

279 HILLEL: Operation Babylon, p. 323.

able to detect and bloodily smash the Zionist underground organization which had so successfully campaigned for the rescue of the Iraqi Jews.[280]

## 2.5 Amazement about the Precision of Biblical Prophecy

These events were all exactly foretold in Jeremiah 51:45-46:

> *"[45] My people, **go out** of the midst of her [i.e. from Babylonia]!*
> *And let everyone deliver himself from the fierce anger of the LORD.*
> *[46] And lest **your heart faint**,*
> *And **you fear for the rumour** that will be heard in the land*
> *(**A rumour will come one year**,*
> *And **after that, in another year***
> *A rumour will come,*
> *And **violence** in the land,*
> *Ruler against ruler)."* (NKJV)

In contrast to Jeremiah 50:8 and 51, these verses do not deal with a "flight," but rather with an "exodus" (*"My people, **go out** of the midst of her!"*). This verse refers to the mass exodus of the Jews, officially approved by the Iraqi government, from March 1950 to February 1952. At that time there was an orderly exodus from Iraq. Jeremiah 51:45-46 has nothing to do with the waves of immigration before this exodus nor afterwards. This orderly exodus is also mentioned in the following verses:

Isaiah 48:20:
*"[20] **Go forth** from Babylon!"* (NKJV)

Jeremiah 50:8b:
*"[8b] **Go out** of the land of the Chaldeans ..."* (NKJV)

This exodus, as well as the flight according to Jeremiah 51:6, was to protect the Jews from a *later catastrophe* which would come to Iraq

---

280 HILLEL: Operation Babylon, p. 298ff.

(*"every one **save** his life! Do not be cut off in her iniquity, for this is the time of the **LORD's vengeance**"*). This exodus occurred before the Gulf Wars of 1991 and 2003 and the future events which followed! It also occurred before the terrible Iran-Iraq War of 1980–1988, which claimed 1.7 million deaths in total and left hundreds of thousands crippled. The Iraqi Jews were protected from unimaginable suffering by this dramatic exodus!

The scary and terrifying news which spread in the country under Nuri Said is directly addressed in verse 46. However, Jeremiah said the Jews should not fear ([46]*"And **lest your heart faint, and you fear** for the rumour that will be heard in the land."*). In the end, everyone, who wanted to, was able to leave the country unhindered.

We have seen how one (Jewish) year under Suweidi was characterized by good news and the following (Jewish) year by contrary, bad news. Even these details were clearly prophesied in verse 46 (*"A rumour will come one year, and after that, in another year a rumour will come ..."*).

I have already explained how this period of emigration was affected by the sudden fall of the Tawfiq Suweidi government and Nuri Said's take-over. Even this is pointed to in verse 46: *"Ruler against ruler."*

The Iraqi Jews' joy over the possibility of escaping Babylonia's sphere of power was overshadowed by the destruction of the Zionist underground organization occurring at the same time. Jeremiah spoke about this as well: *"... and violence in the land."*

Don't we have every reason to stand in awe at the precision of the ancient prophecies in the Bible? Isn't this ancient book sensationally relevant for us in the 21st century?

## 2.6 Flight from Babylon: 1952–1991

Some 5,000 Jews remained in Iraq following the completion of "Operation Babylon." They hoped for better times and just would not be persuaded to leave. The Zionists' pleas that they ought to leave Iraq fell on deaf ears.

However, in the following decades they would be exposed to

further horrific suffering and terrors by the Iraqi government. [281]

The Ba'ath Party gained power through a coup in 1963. The consequence was that the Jews in Iraq were to suffer renewed waves of excruciating persecution.

The Six Day War took place in 1967. The Iraqi Army took part in this war to destroy Israel. When the war finally ended in humiliating defeat for Iraq and its allies, the Iraqi Jews had to serve as the object of their rage and endured terrible suffering.

Following a short interruption meanwhile, the Ba'ath Party returned to power in July 1968 and, once again, there was renewed persecution of the Jews.

These developments caused new waves of flight, until finally almost all the Jews had left Iraq. [282]

An official door opened again at the beginning of the '70s: Due to international pressure, Jews were allowed to leave the country. Most of those having stayed up to this point finally left at that time. [283]

By the autumn of 1990, there were reportedly still some 150 Jewish people remaining in Iraq, most of those living in Baghdad. [284] Practically all of Iraq's Jews had fled or moved out, before the catastrophe of the 1991 Gulf War came upon Babylonia.

In 1948, Jews had constituted a quarter (77,000) of Bagdad's population. Today there are still about 30 Jews there. On Friday, 25 July 2003, six of the last Baghdad Jews were flown out. The Jewish Agency had sought out Jews from the entire country in order to make their departure possible. [285]

## 2.7 Shlomo Hillel

A quintessentially important work about the drama of the Jews in Iraq and their rescue, which provides numerous historical data mentioned in this subsection, is the book by Shlomo Hillel: Opera-

---

281 http://www.zionismus.info/antizionismus/arabisch-7.htm (as of: 24.10.2011).

282 HILLEL: Operation Babylon, p. 324ff.

283 http://www.zionismus.info/antizionismus/arabisch-7.htm (as of: 24.10.2011).

284 HIZAK/EKEROTH: Hier in Israel, April 1992.

285 http://www.zionismus.info/antizionismus/arabisch-7.htm (as of: 24.10.2011).

tion Babylon. In it the rescue of the Jews from Iraq is presented in a lively and dramatic way.[286]

As an Israeli secret agent from 1946–1951, Hillel played a key role in the events which would finally lead to the rescue of over 100,000 Jews.

He was born in 1923 in Baghdad. The Hillel family can be traced back to Jews which were deported to Babylon by Nebuchadnezzar 2,600 years ago.

Little Shlomo immigrated to "Palestine" in 1934, before the founding of the State of Israel.

After working as a secret agent, he became a politician, serving several times in the position of minister in the government of Israel. In 1984 he became President of the Knesset.

His book "Operation Babylon" was first published in 1985. For reasons of safety and for the protection of Jews in other Arab countries, this topic was handled with utmost discretion for a long time. However, now that 95% of the Jews have been brought to safety from Arab countries, it seemed responsible to the author to go public with his sensational report.

When Hillel visited George Bush Sr. in Washington in December 1987 (Bush was the then vice-president), he gave him a copy of his book, "Operation Babylon."[287] Thus, Bush was informed of the Jews' history of suffering in Iraq before the Gulf War of 1991 began.

Hillel's book simply reports the facts regarding the rescue of Iraqi Jewry in the 20th century. There is absolutely no reference to fulfillment of the prophetic word of the Bible in this book. Hillel's stirring account is simply a presentation of the events which occurred.

# 3. Saddam Hussein and the New Babylon

Saddam Hussein was born in 1937. His mother Subha Talfa had conceived him out of wedlock. Therefore she wanted to kill him

---

286  The detailed bibliography is found in the appendix.

287  HILLEL: Le souffle du levant (see the photographs in the French version, which unfortunately are missing in the German version).

by abortion. She attempted to be rid of the child through extreme physical labour. Yet Saddam survived. It did not result in an abortion[288]

In order to overcome her shame, Subha Talfah also attempted suicide. She wished to do away with herself along with her unborn child. After throwing herself in front of a moving automobile, an Iraqi-Jew passing by was able to save her and her un-born child. The then unusual name "Saddam" (= bumper) which he received after the birth would be a reminder of this event which had almost cost the mother and child their lives. The word *saddam* is related to the word *saddma*, which in Arabic is synonymous with "collision." Only following the Gulf War of 1991, this became a common name for children in the Arab world.

Saddam committed his first murder when he was fourteen years old[289] and at nineteen, his second. This was the beginning of a bloody trail which followed him throughout life and eventually cost hundreds of thousands of lives.

Saddam's uncle, with whom he spent a great deal of his youth, taught him that Allah hated three things: flies, Persians and Jews.

In 1979 Saddam Hussein came to power. He identified himself positively with the Babylonian King Nebuchadnezzar II.[290] Just as this ruler of the Neo-Babylonian Empire, who is mentioned many times in the Bible, destroyed the Jewish state in 586 BC, Saddam wanted to someday destroy the modern Jewish state. This was the aim in his life. It is said that the older Saddam Hussein became, the more anxious he was regarding this "purpose."

Public depictions of Saddam Hussein attempted to portray their ruler as a modern "King of Babylon." On street murals, Saddam Hussein was portrayed together with Nebuchadnezzar. The ancient city of Babylon with its Ishtar Gate was to be seen in the background of the portrait of both rulers.[291]

To drive home this message, Saddam Hussein shied away from

---

288 http://de.wikipedia.org/wiki/Saddam_Hussein (as of: 24.10.2011).

289 L'EXPRESS, 20.3.2003, p. 88

290 Saddam Husseins Vorbilder: Die Herrscher von Mesopotamien, p. 134, in: Der Spiegel, Nr. 35, 27. Aug. 1990, p. 134.

291 L'EXPRESS, 20.3.2010, p. 90.

spending in order to have the ancient city of Babylon rise again symbolically from the ruins, even during the treasury-depleting war against Iran. He had city walls erected together with the famous Ishtar Gate, as well as various pagan sanctuaries such as the Temples of Ninmah, Ishtar and Nabu. Even Nebuchadnezzar's fabulous Southern Palace was raised from the dust.[292] On countless stones the inscription could be read: "Built in the days of Saddam Hussein." By February 1990, more than 60 million stones had been used for reconstruction.

Just one year after his take-over Saddam Hussein unleashed a horrible war with his Persian neighbour. The results of this conflict, which would last from 1980 to 1988, were devastating: 1.7 million dead and hundreds of thousands mutilated and crippled. Additionally, the nation's treasury was dangerously depleted.

# 4. The Gulf War of 1991

## 4.1 Babylon Trapped

Following the war with Iran Saddam Hussein sought to refill the nation's treasury. The hole needed to be filled in some way. Under these circumstances, the small, but unbelievably rich, oil-producing country of Kuwait in the south, which was at the same time hardly protected militarily, looked positively enticing.

On 25 July 1990 the US Ambassador April Glaspie visited Saddam Hussein.[293] According to the report in the New York Times, she said to him:

"We have no opinion on the Arab-Arab conflicts, like your border disagreement with Kuwait."[294]

---

292  Extremely good photos found in: Archéologia, No. 266, mars 1991, BP 90, 21800 Quétigny.

293  http://en.wikipedia.org/wiki/April_Glaspie (as of: 24.10.2011).

294  New York Times, 23 Sept. 1990. The extended text reads: "But we have no opinion on the Arab-Arab conflicts, like your border disagreement with Kuwait. I was in the American Embassy in Kuwait during the late 60's. The instruction we had during this period was that we should express no opinion on this issue and that the issue is not associated with America. James Baker has directed our official spokesmen to emphasize this instruction. We hope you can solve this problem using any suitable methods via Klibi (Chedli Klibi, General Secretary of the Arab League) via President Mubarak. All that we hope is that these issues are solved quickly."

Saddam Hussein apparently understood this as American invitation, even though Glaspie, at least according to her own later statements, did not intend it this way. One week later, on 2 August 1990, Iraq invaded Kuwait. Saddam Hussein conquered the weak country of Kuwait with 95,000 soldiers and numerous tanks and soon declared it to be the 19th province of Iraq. From a military point of view this was no heroic deed. There were terrible violations: internment, torture and executions. Kuwait was plundered on a grand scale. Kuwaiti citizens were carried off to Iraq. Gold in excess of €614 million was looted.[295] The entire world was horrified. This initially precipitated the Gulf Crisis of 1990/1991, leading to the Gulf War of 1991.

The state visit of April Glaspie had set a trap for Iraq. Whether Mrs. Glaspie was conscious of this or not is essentially of no consequence. In Jeremiah 50:24 God spoke to Babylonia:

> "[24] I have **laid a snare** for you;
> You have indeed been **trapped**, O Babylon,
> And **you were not aware**;
> You have been **found** and also **caught**,
> Because you have contended against the LORD." (NKJV)

The Iraqi President Saddam Hussein was trapped – and could not get free. He did not understand the seriousness of the situation, as Jeremiah had foretold. Iraq was "*found*" by the international community like a thief, which led to the Gulf Crisis of 1990; and finally Iraq was "*caught*" during the War of 1991.[296] Yet it could have happened that, following the surrender of Kuwait, Iraq would have been allowed to go free, in a manner of speaking. But this was not to be. Iraq became the international community's prisoner-of-war. A cruel embargo was imposed on Iraq which lasted until 2003 and cost the lives of 500,000 to 1.2 million children.[297]

---

295  http://de.wikipedia.org/wiki/Zweiter_Golfkrieg (as of: 24.10.2011).

296  The trapping of Iraq by the entire world community was not an obvious business. Syria's stealthy take-over of Lebanon over 15 years, beginning in 1975, was, in principle, the same as what Iraq had done with Kuwait. Generally, the world was oblivious to this, however, and so there were not the tragic consequences for Syria as there were for Iraq. Syria was neither "caught" nor "captured."

297  http://en.wikipedia.org/wiki/Gulf_War (as of: 24.10.2011).

## 4.2 Gulf Crisis of 1990

For six months the allied armed forces of over 43 different countries,[298] from all five continents, deployed almost 1 million soldiers in order to attack Iraq on 17 January 1991. Under a UN Mandate, the world community fell upon Iraq.

The grounds for the trap are stated in the book of Jeremiah:

*"24 Because you have contended against the LORD."* (NKJV)

First, we must ask: How can war be made against God? The Biblical answer is found in the book of the prophet Zechariah. Whoever molests a Jew, a member of the Chosen People of God, effectively assaults the "apple of His eye" (Zech. 2:8b):

*"8b ... for he who touches you touches the apple of [My] eye."* (NKJV)[299]

Three times Iraq attempted to annihilate Israel completely: in the War of Independence (1948/1949), the Six Day War (1967) and likewise in the Yom-Kippur War (1973). Iraq was the only Islamic country which, up to the time of the Gulf War of 1991, had never made a cease-fire agreement with Israel. Thus, Iraq had continued in a state of war with Israel for 55 years!

### 4.2.1 Pride and Rebellion

After the Iraqi army had marched into Kuwait on 2 August 1990, this grave offense was condemned on the same day by a UN Secu-

---

298 The following countries provided soldiers: Afghanistan, Egypt, Argentina, Australia, Bahrain, Bangladesh, Belgium, Denmark, France, Greece, Great Britain, Honduras, Italy, Canada, Kuwait, Malaysia, Morocco, the Netherlands, New Zealand, Niger, Norway, Oman, Pakistan, Portugal, Philippines, Poland, Portugal, Qatar, Romania, South Korea, Saudi Arabia, Sweden, Senegal, Sierra Leone, Singapore, Soviet Union, Spain, Syria, Czechoslovakia, Turkey, Hungary, the United Arab Emirates, Britain and the United States. Furthermore, Germany and Japan supported the war with financial contributions in the amount of $16.6 billion dollars (cf. e.g. http://en.wikipedia.org/wiki/Gulf_War ; http://de.wikipedia.org/wiki/Zweiter_Golfkrieg#Zusammensetzung_der_Koalitionsstreitkr.C3.A4fte [as of: 25.10.2010]).

299 The original Hebrew text is *"my* eyeball". The incorrect reading *"His* eye" is a *tiqunei sophrim*, i.e. one of the very few intentional alterations by the ancient rabbis, all of which are explicitly recorded as such.

rity Council Resolution. Iraq was challenged to immediately and unconditionally retreat from Kuwait. Consequently extreme sanctions were imposed. But this did not deter Saddam Hussein from putting up a thoroughly resolute front against the nations from across the world condemning him severely.

Even as the Allies began to build-up the huge machinery of war in the Gulf, derision and mockery were heard from the Iraqi leadership. Saddam Hussein was prepared to stand up to the entire world. Countless states attempted to bring the Iraqi leadership to terms. But all the warnings were of no use. It would be really difficult to find a parallel case of such provocation, willful rebellion and brazenness of one country against the international community. Under the aegis of the UN, the world confronted Iraq. But Mesopotamia showed itself to be completely unbending.

On top of this rebellion, the Iraqi leadership displayed outrageous arrogance and pride in its resistance. Even on the 17 January 1991, as the Gulf War had begun with the allied troops fighting against Iraq, Saddam Hussein announced in an appeal on television that "the mother of all battles" had begun, and that this war was "the beginning of the end of imperialism." That same evening the Revolutionary Council under Saddam Hussein met and declared that the "Iraqi army was convinced of their victory."[300]

Jeremiah spoke about the rebellious attitude, arrogance and pride of Babylonia. In Chapter 50:31-32 Babylonia is addressed by God:

*"³¹ Behold, I am against you,*
*O **most haughty one[or impudent]**!" says the Lord GOD of hosts;*
*"For your day has come,*
*The time that I will punish you.*
*³² **The most proud [or impudent]** shall stumble and fall,*
*And no one will raise him up;*
*I will kindle a fire in his cities,*
*And it will devour all around him." (NKJV)*

---

300  NIRUMAND: Sturm im Golf, p. 261.

In Jeremiah 50:21, Babylonia is called *"the land of Merathaim"* which means *"the land of double unruliness"* or *"the land of double rebellion."*

A linguistic explanation regarding the name *"land of Merathaim"* may be of interest: The Hebrew word *merathaim* is a word-play on the Akkadian (Babylonian) vernacular term for southern Babylonia *mat murrati* ("Land Murrati" or "land of lagoons").[301]

### 4.2.2 Special Weapons against Babylonia

The ancient Hebrew prophets spoke the language of their time. So Isaiah and Jeremiah used traditional words to denote weapons which would be raised against Babylonia in The Last Days, e.g. "spear" [*kidon*], "bow" [*qesheth*] and "arrow" [*chetz*] to describe firearms. In prophesying, the prophets had to describe things which did not even exist in their period of history, things of a future age from their perspective. How would it be possible to do this with words which would be understandable in the lifetimes of the Biblical prophets?

What was it actually like when the Hebrew language was revived and modern terms had to be reformulated linguistically in 1881–1920? In many cases, old terms were filled with new content in order to give names to things in the modern era. Yet there must be a very close, intrinsic relationship between an old term and a new term. This is best understood with the help of examples:

The word *kinnor*, which denoted the OT stringed instrument that David played (1 Sam. 16:23), a type of lute, now means "violin" in the modern language.

The Aramaic term *psanther*, from Daniel 3:5 (the fifth instrument mentioned in this verse), means "piano" in today's Hebrew.

In this connection, it is interesting to know that the ancient Hebrew word *chetz* (= "arrow") is used in modern Hebrew for an Israeli anti-missile system designed to intercept surface-to-surface missiles.[302] This illustrates how obviously modern things can be described with ancient terms. The underlying principle behind the

---

301 From ancient times the landscape of Southern Iraq was characterized by the innumerable wonderful marshes and canals between the Euphrates and the Tigris with impressive fauna and flora.

302 http://de.wikipedia.org/wiki/Arrow-Rakete (as of: 24.10.2011).

ancient and modern usage must be the same. "Bow" in this case corresponds to a modern launching platform and the "arrow" is today's "rocket."

Isaiah doubtlessly understood that he was speaking about very unusual weapons in his End-Time prophecy against Babylon as he wrote about their force directed to destroy an entire country (Isaiah 13:4-5):

*"⁴ The LORD of hosts musters*
*The army for battle.*
*⁵ They come from a far country,*
*From the end of heaven—*
*The LORD and **His weapons of indignation,***
***To destroy the whole land."*** (NKJV)

Regarding the prophetic use of arms against Babylonia, the statement in Jeremiah 50:25 also deserves our special attention:

*"²⁵ The LORD has opened His armory,*
*And has brought out the weapons of His indignation;*
*For this is the work of the Lord GOD of hosts*
*In the land of the Chaldeans."* (NKJV)

This passage indicates that this is special weaponry which will be deployed against Babylonia. The Hebrew term *'otzar*, which is translated "armory," can also be rendered "treasury." "God's armory" is also spoken of here. That alone makes it clear that these weapons are to be considered as something outstanding.

It is a fact that in the Gulf War the allies had assembled a concentration of weapons of such high technological standards never before seen in military history. In this "air-land-sea-war," there was an enormously powerful combination of infantry, armored units, amphibious forces, combat helicopters, land-attack, air defense and altitude reconnaissance aircraft, as well as surveillance and navigation satellites in low Earth orbits (up to 36,000 km). It was precisely because of the incredible high-technology, which was employed, that the strikes against Iraq were of an especially fearsome effectiveness. With laser-guided precision weapons target accuracy was achieved which far exceeded anything ever used before. In Jeremiah 50:9b we find agreement:

> *"9b Their arrows shall be like **those of an expert warrior;** **None shall return in vain.**" (NKJV)*

Sometimes the "modern" meaning of an ancient term is made especially clear, such as when traditional terms are combined in stark comparison making the new term clearer. One example of this is the mention of "horses" in Jeremiah 51:27:

> *"27 Set up a banner in the land,*
> *Blow the trumpet among the nations!*
> *Prepare the nations against her,*
> *Call the kingdoms together against her:*
> *Ararat, Minni, and Ashkenaz.*
> *Appoint a general against her;*
> *Cause the horses to come up **like the bristling locusts.**" (NKJV)*

In this verse "horses," the normal means of transportation for soldiers in earlier times, are compared to *"bristling locusts."* The analogy between *"bristling locusts"* and modern means of transportation in war is striking and easy to understand, as it were!

There are statements which can be said to apply both to ancient as well as modern warfare, as, for example, in Jeremiah 50:32:

> *"32 The most proud shall stumble and fall,*
> *And no one will raise him up;*
> *I will **kindle a fire in his cities,**
> *And it will **devour all around him.**" (NKJV)*

However, there are numerous prophetic passages which can only apply to modern warfare, e.g. in such cases as when the destruction being spoken will have the consequence that the devastated land can no longer be traveled through, much less inhabited:

Isaiah 13:19-20:
*"19 And Babylon, the glory of kingdoms,*
*The beauty of the Chaldeans' pride,*
*Will be as when God overthrew Sodom and Gomorrah.*
*20 **It will never be inhabited,***
***Nor will it be settled from generation to generation;***
***Nor** will the Arabian pitch tents there,*
***Nor** will the shepherds make their sheepfolds there."* (NKJV)

Jeremiah 50:39-40:
*"39 It shall **be inhabited no more forever,***
***Nor shall it be dwelt in from generation to generation.***
*40 As God overthrew Sodom and Gomorrah*
*And their neighbors," says the LORD,*
*"**So no one shall reside there,***
***Nor son of man dwell in it."*** (NKJV)

In the time of Isaiah and Jeremiah (8th–6th centuries BC), it was impossible to conceive how such statements would be fulfilled. Nevertheless, this is exactly what the prophets wrote. Today, we have no trouble imagining such devastation because we are familiar well enough with the effectiveness of atomic, biological and chemical weapons of mass destruction which have been invented only in modern times.

### 4.2.3 Foreigners Escape

On 9 August 1990, a few days after Saddam Hussein's invasion of Kuwait, Iraq's borders were closed. Countless foreigners were thereby trapped in the enemy's country, seemingly with a sword of Damocles hanging over them. Through long, tedious international mediation, thousands of hostages were finally able to flee Iraq and reach safety before the outbreak of the Gulf War. The prophet Jeremiah spoke of such an international flight (50:16b):

*"16b For fear of the oppressing sword*
*Everyone shall turn **to his own people,***
*And everyone shall **flee to his own land."*** (NKJV)

## 4.3 Kuwait's Liberation

Saddam Hussein was not willing to yield to the international community. He did not want to give up Kuwait. He had sunk his teeth into it and couldn't escape this stranglehold. So the world attacked Iraq. The war began on 17 January 1991 and ended on 28 February after 40 days of air warfare and 100 hours of ground offensive. The goal set forth by the UN was defined exactly: Kuwait's liberation.

We will now deal with the opening words of judgement upon Babylonia as they are presented in Isaiah 13.

Verse 1 contains the title which the prophet himself gave to the following statements (Chapters 13 and 14) - (Isaiah 13:1):

*"¹ The burden against Babylon which Isaiah the son of Amoz saw."* (NKJV)

At first sight, verse 2 seems somewhat mysterious:
*"²Lift up **a banner** on the high mountain,*
**Raise your voice to them;**
*Wave your hand, that they may **enter the gates of the nobles."***
(NKJV)

We must, first of all, ask some legitimate questions about this text:
- Why would a banner be raised,
- Who shall call whom,
- What is meant with the wave of the hand,
- Who shall go into the city of nobles,
- Which city is actually meant?

On 27 February 1991, the day Kuwait City was liberated, the world saw what Isaiah had beheld long before in his vision: as the victorious forces of the Allies entered the city of the noble family of the Emir Jaber as-Sabah,[303] acclaimed in celebration as the great liberators, they were greeted by the Kuwaitis with loud and enthusiastic cheers and cries. They waved to them, they sounded their

---

303 Emir = Prince.

car horns and American and Kuwaiti flags were seen everywhere as a sign of the victory celebration.

Isaiah's prophecy about Babylonia in The Last Days begins with the description of the international community's (UN's) advance toward the clearly defined goal of the 1991 Gulf War!

The liberators were perfectly described by Isaiah in verses (3-5). God Himself speaks:

> *"³ I have commanded My sanctified ones;*
> *I have also called My mighty ones for My anger—*
> *Those who rejoice in My exaltation."*
> *⁴ The noise of a multitude in the mountains,*
> *Like that of many people!*
> *A tumultuous noise of the kingdoms of nations gathered together!*
> *The LORD of hosts musters*
> *The army for battle.*
> *⁵ They come from a far country,*
> *From the end of heaven—*
> *The LORD and His weapons of indignation,*
> *To destroy the whole land."* (NKJV)

How relevant are the words of the prophet Isaiah! Those who have seen the Gulf War photos of 27 February 1991 know how the Allied forces, "rejoicing in exaltation," entered Kuwait City.[304]

The sounds of war of these gathered nations captured the attention of the entire world. Allied ground troops, made up of soldiers from more than 40 countries, formed a number of fronts. Altogether, more than ten different convoys were deployed. The majority crossed the hills of southern Iraq, going from Saudi Arabia in numerous ranks (cf. Isa. 13:4: *"The noise of a multitude in the mountains, like that of many people! A tumultuous noise of the kingdoms of nations gathered together!"*) and finally entered Kuwait, turning to the south, coordinated with the other fronts which were thrusting directly into Kuwait.

---

304 The title page photo of the TIME edition of 11 March 1991 (Vol. 137. Nr. 10), together with the photography on pp. 20-21 and 32-33, is a phenomenal documentation of the actual fulfillment of Isa. 13:2-3!

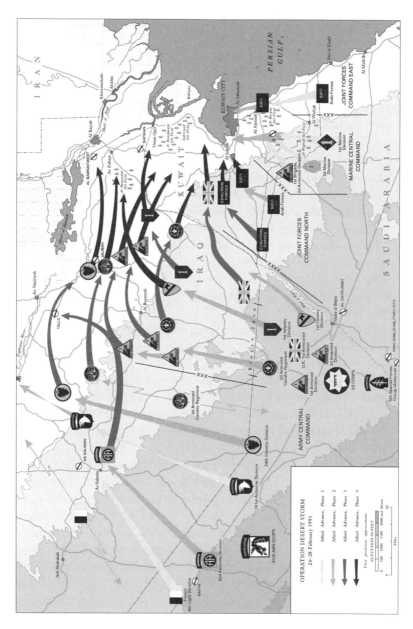

**Fig. 21:** *The 100-hour ground war (source: Jeff Dahl, GNU 1.2 or later).*

The lion's share of the Anti-Iraq-Coalition with some 660,000 soldiers (74%) came from the USA![305] As seen from Iraq and Israel, they actually come *"from a far country, from the end of heaven,"* from the most distant part on planet Earth. This figure of speech, *"from the end of heaven"* (= an extremely distant region geographically), typical of classic Hebrew, applies precisely to the USA. With Biblical geography, it must always be remembered that the Land of Israel, at the junction of the three continents, Asia, Africa and Europe, is viewed by God as the centre of the world (Ezek. 5:5; 38:12). Geographical terms in the Bible must always be considered from this perspective. In principle, this corresponds to the standard depiction of the Earth's continents on a world map. As such, Europe is positioned at the centre of the map. But according to the Bible, the Land of Israel is the centre of the Earth, at the junction of the three continents Europe, Asia and Africa.

In the Bible, terms such as *"end of the Earth,"*[306] *"end of the world,"*[307] *"end of heaven"*[308] are used in many verses to describe the remote parts of the landmass on the planet Earth, as seen from the Land of Israel.

Naturally, it can be argued that for a person in Antiquity – with a more limited view of the Earth than we have today – these expressions sometimes describe a relatively far distant part of the landmass. This can only be partially claimed, since there are enough Biblical instances which clearly designate objectively the most distant regions of the continents, for example, Deut. 28:64 which relates to the worldwide Diaspora of the Jews. Its fulfillment shows that the Jews had been dispersed from Canada to Australia and New Zealand, as well as from Argentina and Chile to the east coast of China and from Scandinavia to South Africa.

With 100,000 air strikes, the Allies decimated the land of Babylonia in accordance with Isaiah 13:4. Generally, we have no true conception of this kind of destruction! The reporting of the entire war was heavily censored then (in contrast to the Gulf War of

---

305  http://de.wikipedia.org/wiki/Zweiter_Golfkrieg (as of: 24.10.2011).

306  For example: Deut. 13:7; 28:49,64; Ps. 46:10; 61:3; Isa. 24:16 etc; "Earth" = Hebr. *'eretz*.

307  Ps. 19:4. "World" = Hebr. *thevel* = inhabited land.

308  For example: Deut. 4:32; 30:4; Neh. 1:9; Isa. 13:5.

2003) so that the public had only a little idea of what transpired. In this conflict, not only was the Iraqi army thrown out of Kuwait, but also Iraq was bombed with full force. The Allies comprehensively destroyed the infrastructure and the economy of the country.[309]

Kuwait's liberation occurred on 27/28 February. These days fell exactly on the Jews' Purim Festival in that year. The terrible Scud-rocket attacks on Israel ended with the liberation of Kuwait. The fortune of the Jews was, once again, turned against their oppressors. Let this be compared to the account in the book of Esther which explains the origin of Purim in the 5th century BC!

What is described in the outline of Isaiah 13:1-5 – a self-contained section – precisely corresponds to the then UN Mandate:

- war with Iraq
- and the liberation of Kuwait!

Allied Commander General Schwarzkopf wanted to continue the assault on Baghdad, and in so doing overrun Iraq. President Bush (senior) vehemently blocked him at that time. Iraq was not conquered and Saddam Hussein was not overthrown. Only the goal prophesied in Isaiah 13:1-5 was achieved then.

Iraq was a prisoner of war of the UN for years. Sanctions were designed to force the state to disarm. This did not suit Saddam Hussein at all, who still saw himself as successor to Nebuchadnezzar, King of Babylon. The destruction of Israel remained an important goal in life. So there was an unprecedented game of cat and mouse for 12 years, to which the United States wanted to put an abrupt end in 2003.

For the liberation of Kuwait, for the fulfilment of the opening words of Isaiah 13:1-5, it required 40 days of air strikes and a ground offensive of 100 hours. Thus, the war was over.

## 4.4 Cruelty

Jeremiah 50:42 describes Iraq's opponents as *"cruel and shall not show mercy"* (NKJV).

---

309  http://en.wikipedia.org/wiki/Gulf_War (as of: 24.10.2011).

Here are a few facts from 1991 which illustrate the appalling fulfilment of this statement:[310] The Allies deployed "Daisy Cutters." These are unbelievably brutal 15,000 pound bombs with a lethal radius of 100 metres.

According to experts' statements, the US Marine Infantry also deployed some 500 MK-77 incendiary bombs against Iraqi targets.[311] Upon impact with the ground huge areas are engulfed by fire.

The greater proportion of the bombs dropped was unleashed in the form of carpet bombing by B-52 bombers, as was once done in the Vietnam War.

There were also cluster bombs used which, again, for their part scatter smaller bombs ("bomblets").

Ammunition enriched with uranium was also used, which is responsible for many long-term injuries to the Iraqi population. The number of children with deformities rose drastically following the war. With this type of ammunition it is possible, for example, to penetrate heavily armored tanks easily and set them ablaze. The occupants were burned immediately in temperatures of some 1,000° C.

As a huge convoy of the Iraqi Army, together with many civilians, was withdrawing hastily along the main highway between Kuwait and Iraq, it was mercilessly bombed for hours by the Allies. This retreat later became known under the name "Highway of Hell." Many experts have condemned this event as an Allied war crime.

Regarding all these cruelties of war, let us consider what is said in Jeremiah 50:32:

*"32 The most proud [or the impudent] shall stumble and fall,*
*And no one will raise him up;*
**I will kindle a fire in his cities,**
**And it will devour all around him."** (NKJV)

---

310 http://de.wikipedia.org/wiki/Zweiter_Golfkrieg (as of: 24.10.2011).

311 http://www.sueddeutsche.de/politik/kriegsfuehrung-usa-warfen-umstrittene-feuerbomben-auf-den-irak-1.743915 (as of: 23.11.2011).

The world community's strangle-hold on Iraq, led by the UN, continued in the years following the war of 1991. The intention was to bring Iraq to submission through the use of an embargo. The sanctions brought unspeakable suffering to the Iraqi people in the following years. According to UN estimates between 500,000 and 1.2 million children died as a harrowing consequence.[312]

It could be said in criticism that the prophecy concerning cruelty and ruthlessness is a statement that in any event would have been fulfilled with a probability rate of 1:1. All conflicts are cruel and merciless. But when we consider that, following the Second World War, the UN developed a catalogue of human rights and also established many international laws in regard to warfare, it would have been expected that this war, under UN leadership, with countries signed to these conventions, would never have been allowed to exceed the degree of horrors necessary, in such a brutal and conspicuous manner. When one considers that Israel, in its modern warfare, goes to enormous and unprecedented lengths to protect the civilian population to the best of their ability, this is a rather flagrant contrast.

## 4.5 Iraq's War against Israel

The Gulf War was also Iraq's war against Israel. In the spring of 1990, before the Gulf crisis, Saddam Hussein stated that, should he be attacked, he would "burn up" Israel "with poison gas", or turn the Jewish State "into a crematorium."[313] During the Gulf War, the Iraqi Army launched 39 Scud rockets at Israel. These resulted in losses of buildings totalling billions in value, but hardly any deaths. This was a miracle of divine protection, since under normal conditions a Scud rocket can claim thousands of deaths. Israel had to remain calm and was not allowed to react, lest the coalition of Western and Arab states should fall apart.

---

312 http://en.wikipedia.org/wiki/Gulf_War (as of: 24.10.2011).

313 http://www.welt.de/politik/article1018616/Wallraff_schwimmt_gegen_den_Strom.html (as of: 23.11.2011).

# 5. Gulf War of 2003

The Gulf War of 2003 was the continuation of the 1991 war. According to the Jewish calendar, the 1991 war came to an end exactly on the two days of Purim (27/28 February). The 2003 war began precisely on the day after Purim. In 2003 Purim fell on 18 and 19 March according to the Gregorian calendar.[314] The US ultimatum to Saddam Hussein came during these days. It was short and to the point: Saddam, leave!

Saddam Hussein was not prepared to be submissive. So the war was renewed. On the day following the ultimatum, 20 March 2003, the new war began – according to the Jewish-Biblical calendar exactly on that day after 12 years interruption. In contrast to 1991, the phase of *conquering the country* prophesied by Jeremiah would now begin.

Now, though, the circumstances were fundamentally different to those in 1991. The UN was not willing to legitimize this war. Therefore, the USA circumvented the world organization and independently brought together its "Coalition of the Willing," which more than 60 nations joined to give support militarily and/or politically as America's allies. This was many more nations than had participated in the 1991 war under UN leadership. The following countries took part:[315]

Afghanistan, Albania, Angola, Armenia, Azerbaijan, Ethiopia, Australia, Bahrain, Bulgaria, Costa Rica, Denmark, Dominican Republic, El Salvador, Eritrea, Estonia, Fiji, Georgia, Great Britain, Honduras, Iceland, Italy, Japan, Jordan, Kazakhstan, Qatar, Colombia, Kuwait, Latvia, Lithuania, Macedonia, the Marshall Islands, Micronesia, Moldova, Mongolia, New Zealand, Nicaragua, the Netherlands, Norway, Oman, Palau, Panama, the Philippines, Poland, Portugal, Romania, Rwanda, Saudi Arabia, the Solomon Islands, Singapore, Slovakia, Slovenia, Spain, South Korea, Thailand, Tonga, Czech Republic, Turkey, Uganda, Ukraine, Hungary, Uzbekistan, the United Arab Emirates and of course the

---

314 The Biblical method of calculating years, used even today by Judaism, follows a lunisolar calendar. Therefore, Jewish holidays fall a little differently each year in the Gregorian calendar.

315 http://de.wikipedia.org/wiki/Koalition_der_Willigen (as of: 24.10.2011).

USA, which led the Coalition.

In addition to troops from official armies from all over the world, an extremely high proportion of mercenaries[316] from some 30 nations, who were active in private security and military firms.[317] The significance of so-called PMFs [Paramilitary Forces] was a new phenomenon in warfare. Soldiers who had become unnecessary to their respective national armies were now working in such PMFs.

In addition to all these armies and PMFs Israel took part, which is not realised by most people! Their participation was kept under-cover in deference to the Arab states. President George President George Bush did not want Israel to engage openly in war, because he must have feared loss of support for the Americans from Muslim countries. However, Israel worked in the background deploying the ultra-modern technology and weapon systems which were used against Iraq during the 2003 war.[318] In this connection, the statement in Jeremiah 50:21, directed at Israel, is very noteworthy:

*"21 Go up against the land of Merathaim,[319] even against it,*
*and against the inhabitants of Pekod:[320]*
*waste and utterly* ***destroy after them*** *[the other army],*
*saith the LORD,*
*and do according to all that I have commanded thee." (KJV)*

## 5.1 Babylonia – A Shock for the World

In Jeremiah 50:22-23 the prophet announces that the nations of world will be horrified by the End-Time events in Babylonia:

---

316  http://de.wikipedia.org/wiki/Zweiter_Golfkrieg (as of: 24.10.2011).

317  http://www.brookings.edu/articles/2004/0415defenseindustry_singer.aspx (as of: 24.10.2011).

318  http://www.usatoday.com/tech/world/iraq/2003-03-24-israel-tech_x.htm ; http://de.wikipedia.org/wiki/Koalition_der_Willigen (as of: 14.10.2011).

319  The land of double unruliness" or "the land of Merathaim" is a poetic term for Babylonia. The Hebrew word *merathayyim* is a word-play on the Akkadian (Babylonian) vernacular term for South Babylonia, mat *murrati* ("Murrati Land" or "Land of the Lagoons").

320  Hebr. *pakod* = devastating punishment. This is a linguistic allusion to the Akkadian name of the East Babylonian tribe Pakudu (Ezek. 23:23).

*"²² A sound of battle is in the land, and great destruction.*
²³ *...* **How is Babylon become an astonishment among the**
**nations!***"* (Darby)

Many millions of people worldwide went out on the streets horrified and outraged in protest against the Iraq War. Yet, as they demonstrated, Babylonia was being destroyed by the US Alliance with some 30,000 air strikes. [321]

After just 25 days, Iraq's military power was brought to an end by the unimaginable violence of the enemy armies. Baghdad was surrounded on all sides and finally captured. The Tigris River crossings were occupied. Numerous palaces of Saddam Hussein's were in flames. At the time the shocking pictures of this went around the world. At first, the Iraqi soldiers fought like lions. But the tactic, used especially by the USA, of psychologically destroying the Iraqi army by the hardest and most devastating shock strikes led quickly to success. Suddenly, the Iraqi army's will to fight was broken.

This is vividly foretold in Jeremiah 51:30-32:

*"³⁰ The mighty men of Babylon have ceased to fight, they are sitting in the fortresses; their might hath failed, they are become as women: they have set her dwelling places on fire; her bars are broken.*
³¹ *Courier runneth to meet courier, and messenger to meet messenger, to announce to the king of Babylon that his city is taken from end to end;*
³² *and the passages are seized, and the reedy places [fortresses] [Hebr. 'agammim] are burnt with fire, and the men of war are affrighted."* (Darby)

The *"strongholds"* and *"[the mighty men's] dwelling places"* in the text above are terms for the soldiers' shelter and living quarters during war time, which were bombed and thus set on fire.

The term *"the king of Babylon"* in the Bible text quoted above

---

321 http://de.wikipedia.org/wiki/Irakkrieg (as of: 17.10.2010).

clearly applies to Saddam Hussein in this passage. In this context, *"his city"* identifies the capital Baghdad.

The *"seized passages"* are the bridges over the Tigris in the Iraqi metropolis, which fell under Allied control.

The Hebrew word *'agammim* (singular: *'agam*) that was rendered in the quoted text by *"lagoon/reeds"* can also mean *"fortresses."*[322] A translation of *"lagoon/reedy places"* would not be relevant in this context. Lagoons do not burn, only the reeds along the bank could go up in flames. Therefore, in Jeremiah 51:32, "fortresses" gives the most appropriate sense. The fulfillment of these verses made it quite clear: in 2003 it was not lagoons burning, but rather many of Saddam Hussein's magnificent palaces which would have given him protection as fortresses and strongholds!

## 5.2 Babylonia's Oil Riches

Through their conquest of Iraq it was possible for Saddam Hussein's enemies to gain access to the country's treasures. This is a country that is rich in water resources and possesses fertile valleys. However, its real economic significance lies in its enormous oil riches. Iraq has one of the greatest crude oil reserves of the world.[323] This wealth is the focus of the prophecy in Jeremiah 51:13. God speaks to Babylonia, the land between the Euphrates and the Tigris, with the following words (Jeremiah 51):

> *"13 O you who dwell by many waters,*
> ***Abundant in treasures,***
> *Your end has come,*
> *The measure of your covetousness."* (NKJV)

Jeremiah foresaw that the enemies of Babylonia, or Chaldea, would enrich themselves with the treasures of the country (Jer. 50:10):

> *"10 And Chaldea shall become plunder;*

---

322 GESENIUS/BUHL: Hebräisches und aramäisches Wörterbuch, p. 8 ("castle"/"citadel"); GESENIUS/ MEYER: Hebräisches und aramäisches Handwörterbuch, Vol. I, p. 12 ("bulwark"); KÖHLER/ BAUMGARTNER: Hebräisches und aramäisches Lexikon zum AT, Vol. I, p. 10 (reference to the related Arab word 'uğum = castle).

323 http://de.wikipedia.org/wiki/Irak#Wirtschaft (as of: 24.10.2011).

All who **plunder** her shall be satisfied," says the LORD.' (NKJV)

Jeremiah 51:2 confirms with other words that the riches of Babylon will fall into the hands of others:

*"2 And I will send winnowers to Babylon,*
*Who shall winnow her and empty her land.*
*For in the day of doom*
*They shall be against her all around."* (NKJV)

Since the war of 2003, many western firms in Iraq have become rich through their involvement in oil production.

It was not possible that the final destruction of Babylon would happen all at once, or else this prophecy would not have been fulfilled. The prophecy of Isaiah 13–14 and Jeremiah 50–51 would necessarily have to happen in phases. This fulfillment in phases is pointed to in Jeremiah 51:33:

*"33 For thus saith Jehovah of hosts, the God of Israel: The daughter of Babylon is like a threshing-floor, at the time of its being trodden; yet a little while, and the time of harvest shall come for her."* (Darby)

First, a few remarks on this analogy from daily life in Biblical times used in this verse:

A "threshing-floor" is an open place in a field which has been flattened and prepared by pounding the earth well.

The harvested grain is spread out on such a place for threshing. The terms "to stamp/ pound," "to harvest," and "to thresh" are used in many cases in the Bible as pictures of judgement (cf. Hab. 3:12; Mic. 4:12-13; Joel 3:12-13).

Jeremiah 51:33 contains the following statement: Babylonia would first be "pounded flat" by a severe judgement. Only then, sometime later, would final judgement come to this country ("harvest and threshing").

Clearly there are two phases, separated from one another in time, differentiated in this verse:

The first phase, "being trodden down," was fulfilled in the terrible Gulf Wars of 1991 and 2003. The Iraqis and their country were horribly "trodden" upon by some 100,000 air attacks in 1991 and 30,000 attacks in 2003.

The completely devastating end phase is still to occur. While the prophet Isaiah deals with the *two phases consecutively*, the book of Jeremiah depicts the two phases as *a unity*.

## 5.3 The Structure of Isaiah 13–14

The very easily understandable structure of Isaiah 13–14 appears as follows:

**Chapter 13**

- **verses 1-5:** Gulf War of 1991[324]
- **verses 6-16:** Worldwide judgement on the "Day of the LORD"[325]
- **verses 17-22:** Babylonia's final destruction[326]

**Chapter 14**

- **verses 1-2:** The End-Time return of the Jews to their land and their complete restoration
- **verses 3-23:** The fall of the King of Babylonia in The Last Days[327]

---

324 V. 1-5: Judgement of Babylonia by a coalition of many nations, which destroys the entire country (Gulf War 1991, liberation of Kuwait City ["Gate of the Nobles"], the city of the Emir Jabir al-Ahmad al-Jabir as-Sabah, the Allied forces greeted with applause, following 40 days of air warfare (c. 100,000 air strikes) against the Iraqi Army and the 100-hour land war.

325 V. 6-16: God's judgement of the whole world on the "Day of the LORD" (cf. Zeph. 1:14-18: Great Tribulation and the return of Jesus as Judge of the world). The judgement, in verses 1-5, of Babylon, the cradle of mankind, will be a foretaste of the worldwide judgement on the Day of the LORD.

326 Verses 17-22: v.17 is connected to v.5. Babylonia's judgement is taken up again here. V. 17: Medes = Kurds, campaign of vengeance against Babylon. V. 20: complete destruction on Babylonia is imminent (cf. Jer. 50–51).

327 V. 3-23: When Israel comes to perfect rest in the Messianic Kingdom, the poem about the End-Time "King of Babylon" will be recited: his dramatic fall from the throne to the grave (v. 13-15), his death: fall into the realm of the dead (v.8-15), many see the fallen one (v. 16), he horrified the world (v. 16), he shook kingdoms (v. 16), he made the country a desert (v. 20), he demolished the cities (v. 17), he did not allow prisoners to return home (v. 17), he was buried, but his body was defiled afterwards (v. 18-19), he destroyed his own country (v. 20), and murdered his own people (v. 20), his sons would be slaughtered (v.21). V. 12-15: the End-Time King of Babylon will be identified with Satan (possession, cf. Ezek. 28:12ff), therefore these verses speak of the fall of Lucifer (= Lat. shining star, v. 12).

## 5.4 The Structure of Jeremiah 50–51

The structure of Jeremiah 50–51 is divided into numerous strophes of differing lengths. Unlike in Isaiah 13–14, the text does not detail the course of events in sequence. The individual strophes form numerous, self-contained poetic reflections on the events in Babylonia, from completely different view-points. The various phases of judgement are always presented in a *synopsis*:

**Chapter 50**
- **verse 1:** Title
- **verses 2-3:** Introductory summary of the judgement on Babylonia
- **verses 4-5:** The time of Israel's restoration in The Last Days
- **verses 6-7:** Israel's guilt and enemies in Jeremiah's time
- **verses 8-10:** The international anti-Babylonian coalition
- **verses 11-13:** Babylonia, deceived in its aspirations
- **verses 14-16:** Vengeance on Babylonia
- **verses 17-20:** Israel between judgement and mercy
- **verses 21-32:** Judgement of Babylonia's rebelliousness and pride
- **verses 33-40:** God supports Israel's cause
- **verses 41-46:** God's plans are fulfilled

**Chapter 51**
- **verses 1-6:** Judgement will come upon God's adversaries
- **verses 7-10:** Babylonia will be irremediably destroyed
- **verses 11-14:** Medes as executors of judgement
- **verses 15-19:** The greatness and majesty of the only true God
- **verses 20-26:** Babylonia: once judge, now judged
- **verses 27-33:** Babylonia and the two phases of its judgement
- **verses 34-58:** Israel's plea for revenge and God's answer
- **verses 59-64:** Instructions for the reading in Babylonia (prose)

The closing verses 51:49-64 explain the historical background of the prophecy concerning Babylon: In 582 BC Jeremiah sent Chapters 50–51 as a separate scroll to Babylonia with Seraiah, who was the marshall among the Jews being deported into exile at that time. In Babylonia Seraiah solemnly read aloud this scroll in public. Afterwards he threw it into the Euphrates River, and declared that Babylonia would one day sink, just as the scroll had then sunk into the River Euphrates.

## 5.5 Who are Babylonia's Enemies in The Last Days?

Babylon's enemies are listed in the prophetic texts of Isaiah 13–14 and Jeremiah 50–51 in such a way that we can classify them in eight groups:

- a great gathering of various nations (Isa. 13:4/lines 1 + 2)
- *one* powerful nation from the end of heaven (Isa.13:5/lines 1 + 2)
- *many* nations from the uttermost ends of the Earth (Jer. 50:41/ lines 2 + 3)
- desolators from the North (Jer. 51:48)
- *one* mighty nation from the North (Jer. 50:3; 50:41/lines 1 +2)
- a gathering of mighty nations from the land of the North (Jer. 50:9)
- the Medes from Media, the land of their dominion (Isa. 13:17; Jer. 51:11; 51:28)
- the kingdoms of Ararat, Minni and Ashkenaz (Jer. 51:27)

We have already seen that the Biblical prophecy of Isaiah 13:4 clearly speaks of "kingdoms of nations" which will advance together against Babylonia in The Last Days.

This was fulfilled by the Gulf War of 1991 when over 40 nations joined the war alliance. It was even more impressive in 2003 when more than 60 nations in total associated with the Allies. Isaiah 13:4 – this verse clearly refers, as we have seen, to the war of 1991 – speaks of a huge army (*"a great people"*), composed of *"nations assembled together"* in lines 1 and 2:

*"⁴ The noise of a multitude on the mountains, as of **a great people**; a tumultuous noise of the kingdoms of **nations assembled together**: Jehovah of hosts mustereth the host of the battle.*
*⁵ They come from a far country, **from the end of the heavens***

*-- Jehovah, and the weapons of his indignation -- to destroy the whole land."* (Darby)

In the 3$^{rd}$ line *a* "host of the battle" is mentioned which would come from a far country, *"from the end of the heaven."* The fulfillment made it clear that the USA is referred to here, the country which by far supplied the most soldiers.

Now, it is significant that further participants in the war are also mentioned in Jeremiah, who would likewise come from the most distant parts of the Earth (Jeremiah 50:41):

*"⁴¹ Behold, a people cometh from the north, and a great nation. And many kings shall arise **from the uttermost parts of the earth**."* (Darby)

The expression *"many kings ... from the uttermost parts of the earth"* was strikingly fulfilled when the following nations from extreme points of the Earth's continents, which supported the campaign against Iraq by sending soldiers (in 1991 and 2003), are considered:

Australia, Dominican Republic, El Salvador, Estonia, Fiji, Great Britain, Honduras, Japan, Latvia, Lithuania, Micronesia, New Zealand, the Netherlands, Spain, the Philippines, Portugal, South Korea and Thailand

In Jeremiah 51:48 enemies which would come from the north are spoken of in the plural:

*"⁴⁸ And the heavens and the earth, and all that is therein, shall shout aloud over Babylon; **for out of the north the spoilers shall come against her, saith Jehovah**."* (Darby)

In the Gulf War of 1991 those involved with the northern enemies were: Turkey and Syria, as well as the Soviet Union.

In the Gulf War of 2003, there were even more nations from the north involved: Turkey, Azerbaijan, Armenia, Georgia and Ukraine. Of all these northern Allies, however, one nation stands out which was not only of nominal significance. This was Turkey. In 1991 Turkey was already very important. Some 100,000 soldiers were deployed by Turkey in the region of the northern border with Iraq. Therefore, Iraq was forced to station a sufficient number of soldiers in the north. It was not known on the Iraqi side just how the war would develop. In this way, many Iraqi soldiers were diverted from taking part in the fighting in southern Iraq and in Kuwait, clearly weakening the Iraqi position there. Turkey also played an important logistical role: Turkey provided an important base for a certain contingent of troops and especially for the airforce. Since 1990 the air base in Incirlik had been a very important launching pad for the US Air Force.[328] Other towns in Turkey, as well as Incirlik, namely Batman and Diyarbakir,[329] also served as airforce bases for the US. Up to 90 nuclear weapons, type B61, were stored there![330]

Even though the Bible speaks of a number of desolators from the north, "*a great nation*" is especially mentioned (Jer. 50:41):

> "*41 Behold, **a people cometh from the north, and a great nation**. And many kings shall arise from the uttermost parts of the earth.*" (KJV)

In the prophecy which has thus far been fulfilled this statement applies to Turkey. So, in this context we need to keep in mind that a nation from the north will clearly play a special role in the prophecy yet to be fulfilled (Jer. 50:3):

> "*3 **For out of the north there cometh up a nation** against her, **which shall** make her land desolate, and none shall dwell therein: both man and beast are fled; they are gone.*" (Darby)

In Isaiah 13–14 and Jeremiah 50–51, we find a people which is especially highlighted. These are the "Medes" (Isa. 13:17; Jer. 51:11; 51:28). They will play a critical role in the future, final destruction of Babylon.

---

328   http://de.wikipedia.org/wiki/Incirlik_Air_Base (as of: 24.10.2011).
329   DER SPIEGEL, 12/2003, p. 102, 112.
330   http://de.wikipedia.org/wiki/Incirlik_Air_Base (as of: 24.10.2011).

## 5.6 The Medes are Coming

Who are the Medes today? For the Kurdish people the answer is easy. The Kurds proudly identify themselves as descendants of the ancient Medes.[331] Naturally, this does not mean that there are no other ethnic minorities which stem from the Medes. This also does not mean that there has not been a mixing of various peoples with the Medes throughout the course of history.

The language of the Kurds, which is divided into various dialects, belongs to the so-called Northwest Iranian language group, which was also the origin of the ancient Median language.[332] The Kurds hold stubbornly to the fact that they have resided in Kurdistan for 3,000 years. They recall with pride that their ancestors, together with the Persians under King Cyrus, conquered the ancient Babylonian Empire in 539 BC (Dan. 5:28; cf. also Esther 1:19; 10:2).

While the Persian Cyrus exercised sovereignty over the Medo-Persian Empire, "Darius the Mede" was the subordinate King of Babylon (Dan. 5:31 – 6:28; 9:1).

In this context Kurdish readers in particular may be referred to the fact that, according to Biblical statements, the Medes stem from the Japhethite ancestor Madai (Gen. 10:2; 1 Chron. 1:5).

The term "Mede" is also used in the New Testament in connection with the Median Jews who had come to Jerusalem as visitors for Pentecost (Acts 2:9).

Today, the Kurdish population is estimated at approximately 36 million.[333] They are the fourth largest ethnic group in the Middle East, following Arabs, Persians and Turks. According to the CIA Factbook, Kurds in Turkey make up 20% of the population, in Iraq 15-20%, in Syria possibly 8%, in Iran 7%, and in Armenia 1.3%.[334] Kurds are the second-largest ethnic group in Turkey. There they must take part in national military service. It follows therefore, that the role of the Medes can partially overlap the role of Turkey in prophecy.

---

331 MOORE: Pass the Word, p. 137; http://fr.wikipedia.org/wiki/Histoire_du_peuple_kurde (as of: 24.10.2011). For the results of genetic testing on the Kurds cf.: http://en.wikipedia.org/wiki/History_of_the_Kurdish_people (as of: 24.10.2011).

332 http://en.wikipedia.org/wiki/Western_Iranian_languages (as of: 24.10.2011).

333 http://en.wikipedia.org/wiki/Kurdish_people (as of: 24.10.2011).

334 http://en.wikipedia.org/wiki/Kurdish_people (as of: 24.10.2011).

Firstly, we will look at the prophet Isaiah's statements in connection with the Medes: Chapter 13:1-5 refers to the war of 1991. Verses 6-16 form, as will be explained further below, an excursus dealing with the "day of the Lord." The description of the final phase of the judgement on Babylonia begins at verse 17. God, the LORD, is speaking (Isaiah 13:17-20a):

> *"[17] Behold, I will stir up **the Medes** against them, who do not regard silver, and as for gold, they have no delight in it.*
> *[18] And [their] bows shall dash the young men to pieces, and they shall have no pity on the fruit of the womb: their eye shall not spare children.*
> *[19] And Babylon, the glory of kingdoms, the beauty of the Chaldeans' pride, shall be as when God overthrew Sodom and Gomorrah.*
> *[20] It shall never be inhabited, neither shall it be dwelt in, even to generation and generation."* (Darby)

It is especially important to notice the following in these verses:
1. The Medes or the Kurds shall be stirred up against Babylon. This was fulfilled in this way: After the Ottoman Empire had been destroyed by the Allies in First World War, the Kurds were given cause to nurture hopes of having their own state in Kurdistan.[335] However, in the negotiations following this terrible large-scale war, the Kurds were given nothing. This people felt cheated and justifiably so. This caused the Kurds to awake from their long slumber and to fight for their ethnic rights, unfortunately, not always in legal ways. Since the 1920s they have pursued their demands using all possible means. They have been driven by their distinctive nationalism since that time.
2. The abhorrent genocide perpetrated against them in past years by Saddam Hussein, sending hundreds of thousands of Kurds

---

335 http://en.wikipedia.org/wiki/History_of_the_Kurdish_people (as of: 24.10.2011); http://en.wikipedia.org/wiki/Treaty_of_S%C3%A8vres (as of: 19.10.2010); for the Kurds in general cf.: SCHIRRMACHER: Die Kurden: Ein staatenloses Volk als Spielball islamischer Mächte, factum, May 1991.

to their deaths, in which he did not once shrink back from using poison gas against them, caused them to rise up especially against Iraq, modern Babylonia. The prophet Jeremiah also spoke of the "stirring up of the Medes" (Jeremiah 51:11):

*"11 Sharpen the arrows; take the shields. **Jehovah hath stirred up the spirit of the kings of the Medes**; for his purpose is against Babylon, to destroy it."* (Darby)

3. According to Isaiah 13:17, the Medes will not attack Babylon in order to enrich themselves. Their attitude in war in verse 18 is paraphrased as: *"... they are cruel and merciless ..."* Isaiah makes clear that their final destructive blow against Babylonia will not have to do with "gold" or "silver." Their interest will not be in booty, but much more as a cruel, bitter and merciless revenge for, as we know today, the indescribable injustice done to them by Babylonia.

4. The Medes will be aligned with Babylonia's enemies. Already during the Gulf War of 2003, the Kurds in northern Iraq were important allies of the Anti-Iraq Coalition. The Kurds were armed. Thus they played an important role in the conquest of the country. In 2003 Iraq was conquered from three fronts, the north, west and south. Northern Iraq was subdued by a joint action of the US army together with the Kurds![336] Here we have already seen what is presented in Isaiah 13:17-18:

*"17 Behold, I will stir up the Medes against them, who do not regard silver, and as for gold, they have no delight in it.
18 And [their] bows shall dash the young men to pieces, and they shall have no pity on the fruit of the womb: their eye shall not spare children."* (ASV)

That which follows in verses 19-20 is still completely preserved for the future.

From Jeremiah 51:27-29 it follows that there would be extensive

---

336 http://en.wikipedia.org/wiki/Iraqi_Kurdistan (as of : 24.10.2011).

cooperation between the Anti-Iraq Coalition and the Kurds. The Kurds would be moved to participate in the war:

> "*27 Lift up a banner in the land, blow the trumpet among the nations, prepare nations against her [i.e. against Babylonia]; call together against her the kingdoms of Ararat, Minni, and Ashkenaz; appoint a captain against her; cause the horses to come up as the bristly caterpillars.*
> *28 Prepare nations against her, **the kings of the Medes, their governors and all their rulers, yea, all the land of their dominion.***
> *29 And the land trembleth and is in pain; for the purposes of Jehovah against Babylon do stand, to make the land of Babylon a desolation, without inhabitant.*" (Darby)

In reference to the term "*all the land of their dominion*" let it be noted that the Kurds in northern Iraq have enjoyed far-reaching autonomy since 1991. Also the new Iraqi constitution gave the Kurds in the north of the country substantial rights of self-determination.

## 5.7 The Kingdoms of Ararat, Minni and Ashkenaz

In Jeremiah 51 three participants in the war against Babylonia are emphasized by name:

> "*27 Lift up a banner in the land, blow the trumpet among the nations, prepare nations against her; call together against her the kingdoms of Ararat, Minni, and Ashkenaz; appoint a captain against her; ...*" (Darby)

In the Bible, the name "*Ararat*" defines (a) *a mountain range*, the region where Noah's Ark landed (Gen. 8:4), as well as (b) *a country* (2 Kings 19:37; Isa. 37:38) or a Kingdom (Jer. 51:27).

2 Kings 19:37 and Isaiah 37:38 report that the sons of Assyrian King Sennacherib fled to the land of "Ararat" following the murder of their father. In the Assyrian language this land was called "Urartu," as follows from discovered cuneiform tab-

lets.[337] In the 1ˢᵗ century BC the Urartian Kingdom encompassed large areas of land in the Caucasia,[338] in the region of ancient Armenia between the Black and the Caspian Seas. In the Septuagint,[339] the earliest translation of the OT in Greek from the 3ʳᵈ century, the expression *"land of Ararat"* in Isaiah 37:38 was rendered *"Armenia."* It must be kept in mind that the Armenia of Antiquity was much larger than the present-day shrunken nation.[340]

The Republic of Armenia[341] was a member of the "Coalition of the Willing" in the Gulf War of 2003 and contributed soldiers to the Iraqi war-zone.[342]

*"Minni"* describes a region between the Van and the Urmia Lakes where the Mannaeans settled in the 1ˢᵗ millennium BC. The central region with the ancient Mannaean cities of Hasanlu[343] and Mahabad[344] was located in the province of Azerbaijan in Iran and extended north to the Kura River which flows through the Republic of Azerbaijan.[345] The area of the ancient kingdom of Minni corresponds to the somewhat larger region of the Azerbaijani people.[346] West Azerbaijan is simply a province of Iran,[347] but the Azerbaijanis now possess their own sovereign state in the Republic of Azerbaijan.

In the Gulf War of 2003 the Republic of Azerbaijan[348] was part of the "Coalition of the Willing" and sent soldiers to the Iraqi war-zone.[349]

---

337 KÖHLER/BAUMGARTNER: Hebräisches und aramäisches Lexikon zum Alten Testament, Vol. I, p. 88; GESENIUS/MEYER/DONNER: Hebräisches und aramäisches Handwörterbuch über das Alten Testament, Vol. I, p. 103.

338 http://de.wikipedia.org/wiki/Kaukasien (as of: 24.10.2011).

339 See in the bibliography in the appendix: SEPTUAGINTA.

340 http://fr.wikipedia.org/wiki/Mahabad ; http://fr.wikipedia.org/wiki/Mann%C3%A9ens (as of: 24.10.2011).

341 http://de.wikipedia.org/wiki/Armenien (as of: 24.10.2011).

342 http://de.wikipedia.org/wiki/Koalition_der_Willigen (as of: 24.10.2011).

343 http://fr.wikipedia.org/wiki/Hasanlu ; http://fr.wikipedia.org/wiki/Mann%C3%A9ens (as of: 24.10.2011).

344 http://fr.wikipedia.org/wiki/Mann%C3%A9ens ;

345 http://fr.wikipedia.org/wiki/Mann%C3%A9ens (as of: 24.10.2011).

346 http://de.wikipedia.org/wiki/Aserbaidschaner (as of: 24.10.2011).

347 http://en.wikipedia.org/wiki/West_Azerbaijan_Province (as of: 24.10.2011).

348 http://en.wikipedia.org/wiki/Azerbaijan (as of: 24.10.2011).

349 http://de.wikipedia.org/wiki/Koalition_der_Willigen (as of: 24.20.2011).

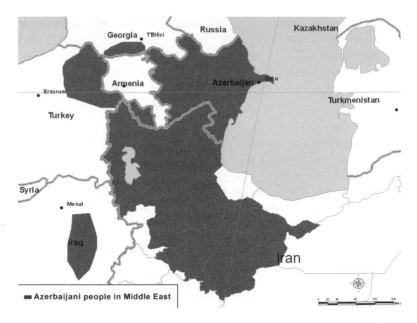

*Fig. 22*: Present area of settlement of the Azerbaijani people (source: Wikipedia, Ebrahimi-amir, CC 3.0 BY-SA).

The name *"Ashkenaz"* is the name for the Scythians as testified in cuneiform inscriptions (cf. Col. 3:11) "Aschguzi" or "Ishkuzai" are associated with this name.[350] In the time of the prophet Isaiah, the wild Scythian horsemen settled in the territory of modern Ukraine and southern Russia[351] between the Black and Caspian Sea.[352]

In the Gulf War of 2003 Ukraine was also a member of the USA's alliance against Iraq under Saddam Hussein and sent soldiers to the war-zone.[353]

---

350  KÖHLER/BAUMGARTNER: Hebräisches und aramäisches Lexikon zum Alten Testament, Vol. I, p. 92; GESENIUS/MEYER/DONNER: Hebräisches und aramäisches Handwörterbuch über das Alten Testament, Vol. I, p. 108.

351  http://de.wikipedia.org/wiki/S%C3%BCdrussland (as of: 24.10.2011).

352  http://de.wikipedia.org/wiki/Skythen (as of: 24.10.2011).

353  http://de.wikipedia.org/wiki/Koalition_der_Willigen (as of: 24.20.2011).

# 6. The End-Time King of Babylonia

The fall and the consequent death of the End-Time King of Babylon are described in Isaiah 14:3-23. This powerfully eloquent description could not have applied to a king from ancient times. There was no ruler from ancient Babylon whom this description would fit in any way. Isaiah spoke of the ruler whose fall is connected with the final destruction of Babylon.

The prophet called the poem in verses 4b-23 a *"proverb against the king of Babylonia"* (Isaiah 14:4). In the Messianic Kingdom,[354] when Israel and the entire world will completely be in peace under the Prince of Peace, Jesus Christ (Isa. 14:3-4,7), this poem will be solemnly recited (Isaiah 14:4), remembering all the pain Babylonia had meant to Israel.

## 6.1 A Satanic Person

In verses 12-15 the prophet goes – without a pause – from the description of the King of Babylon to the description of Satan's fall (cf. 1 John 3:8; 1 Tim. 3:6). The same device is, in principle, is found in Ezekiel 28. This chapter deals with the Prince, or King, of Tyre. Surprisingly, in verses 14 and 16 the ruler of Tyre is suddenly spoken of as a *"cherub."* Cherubim[355] are some of the mightiest angels whose purpose in creation was to function as guardians of the Throne of God in the heavenly sanctuary.[356]

Behind the earthly monarch a supernatural prince was concealing himself, who filled the Tyrian king's heart with pride and sinful self-confidence, causing him to defy God as the Creator and Lord of the universe (v. 2). The King of Tyre was possessed by Satan. Possession means identification (being one with) with an evil spirit. Therefore, the human ruler of Tyre in the 6th century BC, Ethbaal II, is equated with Satan. This identification means there is no longer any distinction between the two persons.[357]

---

354  I.e. in the 1,000-year Reign of Peace (cf. Rev. 20).

355  *"Cherubim"* (Hebr. pronunciation: *keruvim*) is the plural of "Cherub" (*keruv*) in Hebrew.

356  Cf. Exod. 25:18ff; 1Sam 4:4; Ps. 80:1; 99:1; Col. 1:16.

357  Cf. Mark 3:11: the demons fell down before Christ, the possessed people bowing the knee.

Isaiah 14 also deals with identification through possession. Here, the End-Time King of Babel is under discussion. Since this is a possessed person, the prophet also moves, without pause, from the description of the "human" to the description of "Satan's" fall in this passage (Isa. 14:12ff; cf. 1 Tim. 3:6; 1 John 3:8).

Saddam Hussein was one of the most notably satanic people in history, which include others such as Hitler, Stalin, Mao and many others, people who have fully identified themselves with evil one. Saddam Hussein was animated by the spirit of Lucifer. Therefore, we see very striking parallels between Satan's fall and the fall of Saddam Hussein.

## 6.2 Self-idolisation

In one of Saddam Hussein's palaces a self-glorifying inscription in gold letters was found. It stated, "You are the glory."[358] This is nothing more than self-idolatry. According to the "Lord's Prayer," worship belongs to God, the Father – using the Majority Text (Matt. 6:13b):[359]

> *"13 For thine is the kingdom, and the power, and the glory, for ever. Amen."* (KJV)

To God alone be the glory! HE is *"the God of glory"* (Psalm 29:3). Saddam Hussein's self-worship equates to the original sin of Lucifer who wanted to be like the most High (Isa. 14:13-14):

> *"13 For thou hast said in thine heart, I will ascend into heaven, I will exalt my throne above the stars of God: I will sit also upon the mount of the congregation, in the sides of the north:*
> *14 I will ascend above the heights of the clouds; I will be like the most High."* (KJV)

---

358 http://community.seattletimes.nwsource.com/archive/?date=20021203&slug=webpalace03 (as of: 23.11.2011).

359 Cf. 1 Chron. 29:11.

## 6.3 The Fall into the Pit

On 13 December 2003, according to US reports, Saddam Hussein was pulled out of a tightly walled hole in the ground, not to mention a dirty hole in the ground near a pitiable hut by soldiers of the occupation forces. He surrendered himself wearily and without a fight when soldiers, brandishing their firearms, tracked him down in his pit in the village of Dur, 15 km from his home village of Tikrit.[360] This sensational find was described in the German magazine Focus of 20 December 2003 on p. 161 as follows:

"Saddam fell from his throne of power literally into the dust."

It is astounding what a double meaning Isaiah's words yield regarding Lucifer's fall and the fall of the "King of Babylon" (Isaiah 14:12,15):

*"12 How art thou fallen from heaven, O Lucifer, son of the morning! How art thou cut down to the ground, which didst weaken the nations! ...*
*15 Yet thou shalt be brought down to hell, to the sides of the pit."*
(KJV)

The term "son of the morning" (Hebr. *heilel*) was rendered *Lucifer* in the Latin Vulgate translation (c. 400 AD). That is why the term "Lucifer" is sometimes used for Satan in English.

## 6.4 Everyone Beholds Him

On 14 December 2003 photographs taken of Saddam Hussein's arrest the previous day were distributed around the world. I still remember seeing those first pictures that Sunday morning before the church service. "Is that really Saddam Hussein?" – this question was asked worldwide, somewhat sceptically and with good reason as one had to take a more careful look. "That cannot be him!" – the scruffy face of an aged man with a beard was critically inspected. Saddam Hussein had never been seen looking like this.

---

360 http://de.wikipedia.org/wiki/Saddam_Hussein (as of: 24.10.2011).

Yet, apparently, the DNA analysis was able subsequently to provide the necessary proof. It was Saddam Hussein himself!

*Fig. 23: Saddam Hussein following his arrest on 13 December 2003 (source: USA).*

These verses in Isaiah 14 follow the words about the fall:

*"16 **They that see thee shall narrowly look upon thee, and consider thee, saying, Is this the man** that made the earth to tremble, that did shake kingdoms;*
*17 That made the world as a wilderness, and destroyed the cities thereof; that opened not the house of his prisoners?"* (KJV)

## 6.5 Horror for the World

Saddam Hussein was a horror for the world. He was the man who, in Isaiah 14:16, 2nd line, is said to have *"made the earth to tremble."* On the eve of the Gulf War of 1991 there was worldwide anxiety that a Third World War could arise from the crisis of that time. And toward the end of the war, as hundreds of oil fields burned, the world feared an incalculable ecological catastrophe for the blue planet. These are only two examples from Saddam Hussein's life which document the fulfillment of the Bible's words:

*"16 They that see thee shall narrowly look upon thee, and consider thee, saying, Is this **the man that made the earth to tremble,** ..."* (KJV)

## 6.6 Nations Shaken

The third line in Isaiah 14:16 describes how the King of Babylon shook kingdoms:[361]

*"[16] They that see thee shall narrowly look upon thee, and consider thee, saying, Is this the man that made the earth to tremble, **that did shake kingdoms**; ..."* (KJV)

It can certainly be said that Saddam Hussein shook Iran in the dreadful war of 1980 – 1988. That was a war which killed 1.7 million and left hundreds of thousands crippled altogether. Saddam Hussein repeatedly employed chemical weapons of mass destruction during this war.[362]

This same man shook the country of Kuwait in 1990 as he overcame it with an overwhelmingly superior military force and swallowed it up into his sphere of influence.

Isaiah 14:5-6 refers to this:

*"[5] The LORD hath broken the staff of the wicked, and the sceptre of the rulers.*
*[6] **He who smote the people in wrath with a continual stroke, he that ruled the nations in anger**."* (KJV)

The term "nations" (Hebr. *goyim*) is more encompassing than the term *"peoples"* (Hebr. *'ammim*). It defines a larger social entity. Therefore, it can be said that line 2 (in 14:6), with the term "nations" applies to the wars against Iran and Kuwait, while the term "people" applies to ethnic groups attacked by Saddam Hussein such as the Kurds and the Shiites in southern Iraq which belong as subgroups to the nation of Iraq.

## 6.7 The Land Turned into a Desert

In verse 17 the End-Time King of Babylon is accused of ravaging the land (Isaiah 14:17):

---

361 Cf. also Isaiah 14:6-7.
362 http://de.wikipedia.org/wiki/Irak (as of: 24.10.2011).

*"17 ... that made the world*[363] *as a wilderness, and destroyed
the cities thereof; that opened not the house of his prisoners?"*
(KJV)

Verse 20 makes the accusation even more clear, saying he has
destroyed his own country:

*"20 Thou shalt not be joined with them in burial, **because thou
hast destroyed thy land**, and slain thy people: the seed of evildoers shall never be renowned."* (KJV)

The marshy region of southern Iraq between the Euphrates and
Tigris Rivers had been from ancient times a wonderful habitat
especially worth protecting, having a huge variety of fauna and
flora. Yet following the Gulf War of 1991, Saddam Hussein took
bitter, cruel revenge against the Shiite rebels in the south of Iraq.
Using a scorched-earth policy, he caused an ecological catastrophe on a devastating scale. By the end of 1993, 9/10 these marshes
had been turned into a barren wasteland through channeling and
canalization of the river waters. Furthermore the vegetation was
systematically burned, together with villages and fields. Numerous species of animal were threatened with extinction. 2/3 of the
inhabitants of the marshlands lost their livelihood through this
and had to flee for their lives.[364]

In the 1980s, Saddam Hussein cut off, ravaged and laid mines in
large areas of the Kurdish regions in northern Iraq.[365]

## 6.8 Towns and Villages Demolished

During the 1980s Saddam Hussein led a campaign of annihilation
against the Kurdish population in northern Iraq. He levelled some
4,500 villages and towns and poisoned the drinking water sources.
He destroyed 90% of Kurdish rural region and, in this way, devastated their material and socio-cultural foundations.

---

363  Re. translation of *thevel* as "world" cf. HARRIS/ARCHER/WALTKE: Theological Wordbook,
      *thevel*; DAVIDSON: Analytical Hebrew and Chaldee Lexicon, p. 291 (under *yaval*).
364  NEUE ZÜRCHER ZEITUNG, 9 September 1994, p. 5; MITTELLAND-ZEITUNG, 9 September
      1994, p. 2.
365  http://www.ag-friedensforschung.de/regionen/Irak/kurden.html (as of: 21.10.2010).

Following the Gulf War of 1991, Saddam Hussein, as stated, also destroyed the Shiite villages in southern Iraq.[366] In a terrible way, the 2nd line of Isaiah 14:17 was fulfilled:

*"17 That made the world as a wilderness,*
*and destroyed the cities thereof;*
*that opened not the house of his prisoners?"* (KJV)

The word Hebrew word *'ir,* rendered here as "cities," designates, in an all-encompassing way, all types of settlements from encampments to villages and on to fortified cities.[367]

## 6.9 Murdering His Own People

Verse 20 speaks of the End-Time King of Babylon having murdered his own people.

*"20 Thou shalt not be joined with them in burial,*
*because thou hast destroyed thy land,*
**and slain thy people:**[368]
*the seed of evildoers shall never be renowned."* (KJV)

Altogether, no less than 1 million Iraqi citizens from all ethnic groups fell victim to Saddam Hussein's regime.[369]

In the 1980s, he fostered a destructive war against his own Kurdish population in northern Iraq. He raged unimaginably against this afflicted people. It is estimated that he killed some 180,000 of his Kurdish-Iraqi citizens.[370] He executed, bombed and gassed them on a massive scale.

There are estimates that, during the entire 35 years of his reign of terror, Saddam Hussein killed some ½ million Kurds.[371]

Following the Gulf War of 1991, the Shiite population in the south of the country believed that their time of liberation from Saddam

---

366  NEUE ZÜRCHER ZEITUNG, 9. September 1994, p. 5.

367  GESENIUS/BUHL: Hebräisches und aramäische Wörterbuch über das Alte Testament, p. 584.

368  Cf. also Isa. 14:6a.

369  http://www.rojava.net/02.07.2005menschenrecht3.htm (as of: 24.10.2011).

370  http://en.wikipedia.org/wiki/1988_Anfal_campaign#cite_note-hang-7 (as of: 24.10.2011).

371  http://www.rojava.net/02.07.2005menschenrecht3.htm (as of: 24.10.2011).

Hussein had come. They staged an uprising, but were deserted by the UN and the Anti-Iraq Coalition. Saddam Hussein attacked the Shiites in the marshlands and anihilated some 100,000 citizens of his own country.[372] According to other estimates, there were about 300,000 people who were killed at that time.[373]

Concerning this Isaiah 14:5-6 reads:

> *"5 The LORD hath broken the staff of the wicked,*
> *and the sceptre of the rulers.*
> *6 **He who smote the people in wrath with a continual stroke**,*
> *he that ruled the nations in anger, is persecuted, and none hindereth."* (KJV)

The term "nations" (Hebr. *goyim*) is, as already stated, more encompassing that the term "people" (Hebr. *'ammim*). Many peoples can make up a nation, as in India or Russia, for example. *goy* (plural *goyim*) designates a larger social entity. Therefore, it can be said that line 1 in verse 14:6 applies especially to the destruction of the Kurds in the north and the Shiites in the south of the country.

## 6.10 His Prisoners Not Released

When Saddam Hussein committed genocide against the Kurds in the 1980s, he not only killed thousands upon thousands of his citizens, but also deported innumerable others. Hundreds of thousands were put in huge "resettlement camps" and "collective cities." It is estimated that a further 400,000 people, mostly men, were carried off. Some 180,000 disappeared without a trace. They never returned home.[374]

In Isaiah 14:17 we read:

> *"17 ... that made the world as a wilderness,*
> *and destroyed the cities thereof;*
> ***that opened not the house of his prisoners?"*** (KJV)

---

372 http://www.rojava.net/02.07.2005menschenrecht3.htm; http://www.guardian.co.uk/world/2007/aug/22/iraq.ianblack (as of: 24.10.2011).

373 http://www.rojava.net/02.07.2005menschenrecht3.htm (as of: 24.10.2011).

374 http://www.ag-friedensforschung.de/regionen/Irak/kurden.html (as of: 23.11.2011).

During Saddam Hussein's rule there were also hundreds of thousands more Iraqis arrested by the duplicitous secret services and never returned home.[375] In 1997 Amnesty International demanded clarification regarding the hundreds of thousands of Iraqi citizens who had disappeared without trace since the 1980s.[376]

## 6.11 Uday and Qusay Killed

Saddam Hussein's sons, Uday and Qusay, among the most wanted criminals of Saddam Hussein's regime, were still free until mid-2003. Both were greatly feared for their cruelty. The ex-dictator had chosen the younger son, Qusay, to be his successor. He had risen to be head of all secret services before his father's fall. In addition, he was the commander of the elite "Republican Guards."

Uday was notorious in his lifetime for his murders, excessive alcohol use, immorality as a sex offender and his luxury cars.[377]

On 22 July 2003, these two men died during an attack by US Forces on their hideout in a luxury villa in Mosul. This happened after fierce fighting involving helicopters, machine guns, rockets, rocket propelled grenades and bombs.[378] Shortly afterward, in order to put their minds at rest, U.S. Secretary of Defense Rumsfeld announced to Iraqis on television: "...they're dead ... and they're not coming back." Shocking photographs of the dead and older x-rays demonstrated to the Iraqi population that the report of the end of these wicked sons was authentic. In this way Isaiah 14:21 was fulfilled:

*"21 Prepare slaughter for his children for the iniquity of their fathers;*
*that they do not rise, nor possess the land."* (KJV)

---

375  http://www.rojava.net/02.07.2005menschenrecht3.htm (as of: 24.10.2011).

376  http://www.rojava.net/02.07.2005menschenrecht3.htm (as of: 24.20.2011).

377  http://de.wikipedia.org/wiki/Saddam_Hussein (as of: 24.20.2011); http://www.wsws.org/de/2003/jul2003/huss-j26.shtml (as of: 24.10.2011).

378  http://de.wikipedia.org/wiki/Saddam_Hussein (as of: 24.10.2011); http://www.wsws.org/de/2003/jul2003/huss-j26.shtml (as of: 24.10.2011).

## 6.12 Saddam's Death

Following his capture on 13 December 2003, Saddam Hussein was kept in the high security prison Camp Cropper. On 30 June 2004, two days after the US transferred power to the Iraqi interim government, Saddam Hussein was handed over as a criminal to the Iraqi courts.

Afterwards he appeared before a special tribunal, denying all his guilt. The trial began on the 19 October 2005. On 5 November 2006 he was sentenced to death by hanging. During the reading of the verdict Saddam Hussein recited verses from the Koran, war slogans and shouted abuse in the courtroom. He demanded that he not be hanged like a common criminal. His request was to be shot. This request was not granted and on 30 December 2006 the sentence was carried out.[379] The murderer was given over to death, thus, fulfilling the poetic description of Isaiah 14:9-11:

> *"⁹ Hell from beneath is moved for thee to meet thee at thy coming: it stirreth up the dead for thee, even all the chief ones of the earth; it hath raised up from their thrones all the kings of the nations.*
> *¹⁰ All they shall speak and say unto thee, Art thou also become weak[380] as we? art thou become like unto us?*
> *¹¹ Thy pomp is brought down to the grave, and the noise of thy viols: the worm is spread under thee, and the worms cover thee."*
> (KJV)

The phrase, *"art thou also become weak?"* (14:10b; Hebr. *chulletha*) is an intensive form of the passive (Pual) of the verb *chalah*. This form signifies the violent death which this End-Time "King of Babylon" would experience.

## 6.13 His Burial

Following the execution of the death sentence, Saddam Hussein's corpse was buried under the dome of a tomb in his native village,

---

379 http://de.wikipedia.org/wiki/Saddam_Hussein (as of: 25.10.2011).

380 Hebr. *chulletha* (Pual of *chalah*) points to the violent death of the King of Babylon.

Al-Awja, not far from Tikrit. He had built this tomb for himself during his lifetime, directly next to the mosque named after him, Saddam Mosque.[381]

The statements regarding the End-Time King of Babylonia in Isaiah 14 have been fulfilled in phenomenally precise ways. Only one single point remains: the future desecration of his grave and his mortal remains. In Isaiah 14:18-20 we find:

> *"[18] All the kings of the nations, even all of them, lie in glory, everyone in his own house.[382]*
> *[19] **But thou art cast out of thy grave [Hebr. miqirbekha]** like an abominable branch, and as the raiment of those that are slain, thrust through with a sword, that go down to the stones of the pit; as a carcase trodden under feet.*
> *[20] Thou shalt not be joined with them in burial, because thou hast destroyed thy land, and slain thy people: the seed of evildoers[383] shall never be renowned."* (KJV)

# 7. The Final Destruction of Babylonia

The prophecy regarding Babylonia is being fulfilled in phases. Today we can look back over the fulfilled prophecy from Isaiah 13–14 and Jeremiah 50–51 in everything which has already been fulfilled since 1882 until now. The final phase of total destruction is yet to come. Babylonia, southern Iraq, will be so devastated that the area will no longer be inhabitable.

Isaiah 13:19-20:
> *"[19] And Babylon, the glory of kingdoms,*
> *the beauty of the Chaldees' excellency,*
> *shall be as when God overthrew Sodom and Gomorrah.*
> *[20] It shall never be inhabited,*
> *neither shall it be dwelt in from generation to generation:*

---

381 http://de.wikipedia.org/wiki/Saddam_Hussein (as of: 25.10.2011).

382 I.e. in his grave.

383 His descendants (= "his seed") will not be mentioned favourably in the future.

*neither shall the Arabian pitch tent there;*
*neither shall the shepherds make their fold there."* (KJV)

Jeremiah 50:39-40:
*"39 And it shall be no more inhabited for ever; neither shall it*
*be dwelt in from generation to generation. 40 As God overthrew*
*Sodom and Gomorrah and the neighbour cities thereof, saith*
*the LORD; so shall no man abide there, neither shall any son of*
*man dwell therein."* (KJV)

Sodom and Gomorrah were totally destroyed by fire.[384] The
same fate awaits Babylonia (Isa. 13:19; Jer. 50:40; 50:32 and 51:25-
26). In contrast to Sodom and Gomorrah, Babylonia will be completely destroyed by war.

In the 21ˢᵗ century, we have no difficulty imagining a war which
can destroy a land by fire so completely that, as a consequence, it
can no longer be inhabited. In the times of the prophets Isaiah and
Jeremiah it was completely different. Nevertheless, through divine
inspiration (2 Pet. 1:19), they were able to record this realistic picture which fits the age of weapons of mass destruction.

The final destruction of Babylonia is forcefully presented in the
following verses:

Jeremiah 50:12b-13a:
*"12b ... behold, the hindermost of the nations [Babylonia, seen as*
*"mother"] shall be a wilderness, a dry land, and a desert.*
*13 Because of the wrath of the LORD it shall not be inhabited,*
*but it shall be wholly desolate: every one that goeth by Babylon*
*shall be astonished, and hiss at all her plagues."* (KJV)

Jeremiah 50:3:
*"3 For out of the north there cometh up a nation against her,*
*which shall make her land desolate, and none shall dwell*
*therein: they shall remove, they shall depart, both man and*
*beast."* (KJV)

---

384 Cf. Gen. 19:23-29.

Jeremiah 51:25-26:

*"25 Behold, I am against thee, O destroying mountain,[385] saith the LORD, which destroyest all the earth: and I will stretch out mine hand upon thee, and roll thee down from the rocks, and will make thee a burnt mountain.*

*26 And they shall not take of thee a stone for a corner, nor a stone for foundations; but thou shalt be desolate for ever, saith the LORD."* (KJV)

Jeremiah 51:29:

*"29 And the land shall tremble and sorrow: for every purpose of the LORD shall be performed against Babylon, to make the land of Babylon a desolation without an inhabitant."* (KJV)

Jeremiah 51:37:

*"37 And Babylon shall become heaps, a dwelling place for dragons, an astonishment, and an hissing, without an inhabitant."* (KJV)

Jeremiah 51:43:

*"43 Her cities are a desolation, a dry land, and a wilderness, a land wherein no man dwelleth, neither doth any son of man pass thereby."* (KJV)

Jeremiah 51:62:

*"62 Then shalt thou say, O LORD, thou hast spoken against this place, to cut it off, that none shall remain in it, neither man nor beast, but that it shall be desolate for ever."* (KJV)

The fall of Babylonia will ultimately occur unexpectedly. Babylon will *"suddenly"* come to an end (Jeremiah 51:8-9):

*"8 Babylon is **suddenly** fallen
and destroyed:
howl for her;*

---

385 In this verse the power of Babylonia is equated with a mountain.

*take balm for her pain, if so be she may be healed.*
*⁹ We would have healed Babylon,*
*but she is not healed:*
*forsake her, and let us go every one into his own country:*
*for her judgement reacheth unto heaven,*
*and is lifted up even to the skies."* (KJV)

Since the end of the war in 2003, countless international organizations have attempted to turn Iraq into a democratically functioning country based on Western concepts. They have tried to heal Babylonia, economically, politically, socially, etc. As soon as the fall of Babylon occurs, they will have to say, disappointedly, that all these tremendous efforts unfortunately did not achieve their goal. Babylonia will not recover. The helpers will have to return to their own countries, while the catastrophe ascends to high heaven.

# 8. The Gulf War of 1991 and the "Day of the LORD"

In the examination of Isaiah 13:1-5 above we have just seen that the statements were dramatically and literally fulfilled in the Gulf War of 1991. This was the beginning of the first phase of the judgement of Babylonia.

## 8.1 The Parenthesis in Isaiah 13

From verse 6 Isaiah inserts a parenthesis or excursus up to and including verse 16. This section deals with God's future judgement which will affect the whole world on *"the Day of the LORD."* The horizon of prophecy is totally expanded here. In verses 6-16 the land of Babylonia is not mentioned by name again. The spatial terms are extremely broad. This section deals with humanity in general. "Heaven" and "Earth" are affected. (13:13)

In the face of this divine judgement *"shall all hands be faint"* and *"every man's heart shall melt"* (13:7). The prophet speaks comprehensively of *"man,"* a *"mortal,"* which will be more precious than a *"golden wedge of Ophir"* (13:12). So many people will die in this judgement that the value of those surviving will be dramatically raised. This section deals generally and extensively with the guilty people on Earth, *"the sinners"* (13:9), *"the wicked,"* *"the proud"* and *"the terrible"* (13:11).

The horror which came upon Babylonia, Iraq, in 1991, was an incomplete harbinger of what will soon come upon the whole world. This excursus is of the greatest importance for the entire world!

From verse 17, Isaiah speaks about the last phase of judgement on Babylonia, in which the "Medes" will play an important role, as has already been detailed.

Here is the text of Isaiah 13:6-16:

*"⁶ Howl ye; for the day of the LORD is at hand; it shall come as a destruction from the Almighty.*

*⁷ Therefore shall all hands be faint, and every man's heart shall melt:*

*⁸ And they shall be afraid: pangs and sorrows shall take hold of them; they shall be in pain as a woman that travaileth: they shall be amazed one at another; their faces shall be as flames.*

*⁹ Behold, the day of the LORD cometh, cruel both with wrath and fierce anger, to lay the land desolate: and he shall destroy the sinners thereof out of it.*

*¹⁰ For the stars of heaven and the constellations thereof shall not give their light: the sun shall be darkened in his going forth, and the moon shall not cause her light to shine.*

*¹¹ And I will punish the world for their evil, and the wicked for their iniquity; and I will cause the arrogancy of the proud to cease, and will lay low the haughtiness of the terrible.*

*¹² I will make a man more precious than fine gold; even a man than the golden wedge of Ophir.*

*¹³ Therefore I will shake the heavens, and the earth shall remove out of her place, in the wrath of the LORD of hosts, and in the day of his fierce anger.*

*¹⁴ And it shall be as the chased roe, and as a sheep that no man taketh up: they shall every man turn to his own people, and flee every one into his own land.*

*15 Every one that is found shall be thrust through; and every one that is joined unto them shall fall by the sword.*
*16 Their children also shall be dashed to pieces before their eyes; their houses shall be spoiled, and their wives ravished."* (KJV)

## 8.2 What is "the Day of the LORD?

In verses 6 and 9 we have the expression *"the Day of the LORD"* (Hebr. *yom 'adonai* [*yhvh*]). *"The day of his fierce anger"* is mentioned in 13:13. What is the meaning of this term which is extremely characteristic and important for Biblical prophecy?

*"The Day of the LORD"* refers to the time when the Messiah will return and personally bring about an all-encompassing judgement upon the entire world in order to bring everything ultimately under His rule of peace and righteousness. The 3½ year tribulation period immediately before His return is also a part of this judgement.[386] The following OT passages, read together, give an impressive and clear picture of this prophetic event:

- Isa. 13:6,9; Ezek. 30:3; Joel 1:15; 2:1,11,31; 4:14-15.; Amos 5:18,20; Obad. 1:15; Zeph. 1:7,8,9,10,14,15,18; 2:1,2,3; 3:8; Mal. 4:5

The "Day of the LORD" (= *he hemera tou kyriou*) is also mentioned in the NT:[387]

- Acts 2:20; 1Thess. 5:2; 2 Pet. 3:10[388]

---

386  Cf. its mention in the context of the 6th seal judgement in Rev. 6:17. The 7th seal follows, which consists of 7 trumpet judgements, whereby the 7th trumpet consists of 7 bowl judgements (Rev. 8–16). Afterward, Jesus Christ will return as King (Rev. 19:11ff.) The 7th seal includes the 3½ years of the Great Tribulation (Matt. 24:21).

387  *"The Day of the LORD"* (*he hemera tou kyriou*) is not to be confused with the term in Rev. 1:10 which designates the first day of the week: *he kyriake hemera* = lit. "the day belonging to the Lord." Here, the resurrection day of the Lord Jesus is meant, as is easily demonstrated in early-Christian literature: The letter from Ignatius (35–110 AD; a student of Apostle John!) to the Magnesians, section 9: "We have seen how former adherents of the ancient customs have since attained to a new hope; so that they have given up keeping the sabbath, and now order their lives by the Lord's Day [*kata kyriake*] instead, on which our life ..."; or from Didache: (the Teaching of the 12 Apostles) section 14 (100–120 AD): "But on the Lord's day [*kata kyriaken de kyriou*] gather yourselves together, and break bread, and give thanks ..."; or the Letter of Barnabas, chapter 15 (written between 70 and 132 AD): "Wherefore we also rejoice on the eighth day, on which Jesus also rose from the dead and on which He went up to Heaven." Justin Martyr (100–165 AD), First Apology, Chapter 67: "But Sunday is the day on which we hold our usual gatherings, for it is the day on which God made the world by effecting a change to the darkness of the world, and Jesus Christ, our Redeemer, rose from death on the same day."

388  In 2 Thess. 2:2 this "day" is called *"the day of Christ"* (= "the day of the Messiah") according to the Majority Text.

On the *"Day of the LORD"* Jesus Christ will not come to this Earth as "Saviour of the world" (cf. John 4:42). No, he will appear as "Judge of the world." There will be worldwide destruction. All peoples will come under divine judgement without fail. Then it will be clear that God does not simply pass over the outrageous injustices of this world in silence. At that time the Messiah Jesus will initiate a "new world order" of justice and peace. What mankind, despite all its efforts, has not and never could achieve, the Son of God will bring to perfection.

## 8.3 The Day of the LORD is "at hand"
In Isaiah 13:16 we read:

> *"16 Howl ye; for the day of the LORD is **at hand**; it shall come as a destruction from the Almighty."* (KJV)

Verses 1-5 speak of the events of the Gulf War of 1991. The *"day of the LORD"* is announced regarding this in verse 6 as being *"at hand"*! The Gulf War was an extremely remarkable event for various reasons:
- It points to the soon-coming destruction of southern Iraq (Isa. 13:17-20).
- It announces the *"Day of the LORD"* as an imminent event (Isa. 13:6-16).
- It gives a foretaste of the horrors which will come upon the whole world on the *"Day of the LORD."*

## 8.4 Iraq as an Example for the World
At this point, the question must be asked: Are the Iraqis any worse than the people in the rest of the world? This question must be answered categorically, "no." It is only through God's sovereign mercy that His judgement has not already come upon the entire world. In 2 Peter 3:9 it is explained that the Lord is causing the day of His great intervention against a world ripe for judgement to be stayed for an amazingly long period out of pure longsuffering:

*"⁹ The Lord is not slack concerning his promise, as some men count slackness; but is longsuffering to us-ward, not willing that any should perish, but that all should come to repentance. ¹⁰ But the day of the Lord will come as a thief in the night ..."*
(KJV)

No one has reason to see themselves as better than the Iraqis. But their example is a warning for the entire world: If we do not turn to the Living God, the Lord of History, in repentance and confession of sin, we too must reckon with God's judgement in the future.

In Luke 13:1-5 we find a report of people coming to Jesus Christ, telling Him about Galileans whom Pontius Pilate had killed at the Altar in Jerusalem and mixed their blood with the blood of the animal sacrifices. Jesus Christ's reaction is worth taking to heart. He said (Luke 13:2-3):

*"² And Jesus answering said unto them, Suppose ye that these Galilaeans were sinners above all the Galilaeans, because they suffered such things? ³ I tell you, Nay: but, except ye repent, ye shall all likewise perish."* (KJV)

Jesus Christ also reminded His audience of the catastrophic collapse of the Tower of Siloam in Jerusalem in which eighteen people died (Luke 13:4-5):

*"⁴ ...think ye that they were sinners above all men that dwelt in Jerusalem? ⁵ I tell you, Nay: but, except ye repent, ye shall all likewise perish."* (KJV)

This warning was tragically fulfilled less than forty years later. In 70 AD Jerusalem was conquered by the Romans. The siege began as the city was at the bursting point, full of Jewish people at the festive occasion of the sacrifice of the Passover lambs. The blood of over one million people – this number comes from the eye-witness Flavius Josephus – was, in a way, "mixed" with sacrificial blood. The majestic Temple was totally destroyed; countless worshippers were slaughtered in the Temple area near the Altar. The protective walls and towers were battered down and totally ground down by the Romans. Untold numbers of lives were lost in these acts of war.

Just as the events of Luke 13:1-5 were a forewarning of the Jewish War of 70 AD, so was the Gulf War, in which unnumbered Iraqis lost their lives, a forewarning for the entire world of the forthcoming *"Day of the LORD."*

The victims of the Gulf War were not people with greater guilt than the people of the West, for instance. There is simply no person who, in God's eyes, has not earned death. In Romans 3:22-23 we read:

*"22 ... for there is no difference: 23 For all have sinned, and come short of the glory of God ..."* (KJV)

Every person is guilty before God. No-one has really kept to God's moral standards (cf. for example, Exod. 20; Rom. 1:18-32; Gal. 5:19-21 und Mark 7:20-23). We have all broken God's laws. Our conscience convinces us of this and judges us because of this (Rom. 2:12-16). As a result we have, without exception, earned natural physical death and also eternal damnation as God's judgement. Romans 6:23 explains:

*"23 For the wages of sin is death ..."* (KJV)

## 8.5 Salvation Through Repentance

There is a way to escape God's judgement, however: The way is *"Jesus, which delivered us from the wrath to come"* (1 Thess. 1:10). When a person admits in sincere repentance and acknowledges his personal guilt in prayer to the Lord Jesus Christ, the incarnate Saviour-God, he may receive complete forgiveness (1 John 1:9):

*"9 If we confess our sins, he is faithful and just to forgive us our sins, and to cleanse us from all unrighteousness."* (KJV)

On the cross of Golgotha, Jesus Christ suffered death as a substitute for us. He is the only person who did not deserve this judgement. His perfect life here on Earth clearly proved this. Nevertheless, He voluntarily suffered death in order to give those doomed to death eternal life (John 3:16):

> *"16 For God so loved the world, that he gave his only begotten Son, that whosoever believeth in him should not perish, but have everlasting life."* (KJV)

In the three hours of darkness on the cross, He suffered God's judgement for all the sins of all the people who ever have, or ever will, believe in Him (Isaiah 53:10-12). Therefore, whoever trusts in the perfect sacrifice made by Jesus Christ receives divine forgiveness and may have full assurance of salvation (Rom. 8:1,37-39). We need not fear God as Judge! We need not fear the Day of the LORD, nor the Great White Throne Judgement which will follow the 1,000-year reign of peace (Rev. 20:11-15).

## 8.6 Necessity of Deciding

Today you have the opportunity to make the decision to get straight with God and have peace with God! We do not need to pretend to the Almighty. We have nothing to offer Him. Even our own efforts or any compensation or penances are nothing. These do not count with God. But HE wants to give us everything: forgiveness, eternal life, reconciliation, communion with Himself and much more. Are you ready to accept the way God has shown? On the *"Day of the LORD"* you will not be able save anything anymore, for it will already be too late! In Zephaniah 1:14-18 it is written:

> *"14 The great day of the LORD is near, it is near, and hasteth greatly, even the voice of the day of the LORD: the mighty man shall cry there bitterly.*
> *15 That day is a day of wrath, a day of trouble and distress, a day of wasteness and desolation, a day of darkness and gloominess, a day of clouds and thick darkness,*
> *16 A day of the trumpet and alarm against the fenced cities, and against the high towers.*

244

*17 And I will bring distress upon men, that they shall walk like blind men, because they have sinned against the LORD: and their blood shall be poured out as dust, and their flesh as the dung. 18 Neither their silver nor their gold shall be able to deliver them in the day of the LORD's wrath."* (KJV)

Silver and gold, all the prosperity we have today, and in which we perhaps even indulge, will be of no help to anyone on *"the Day of the LORD."* But those who know the Lord Jesus as Saviour understand the fundamental truth of 1 Peter 1:18-19a:

*"18 Forasmuch as ye know that ye were not redeemed with corruptible things, as silver and gold, from your vain conversation received by tradition from your fathers; 19 But with the precious blood of Christ, ..."* (KJV)

It is only the blood of the Substitute on Calvary which gives freedom from bondage and guilt, also saving us from the judgement of God.

## 8.7 The Great White Throne Judgement

Only those still alive and not yet reconciled to God will be affected by the judgement on the *"Day of the LORD."* What will then happen to those who are no longer alive at this time, who have died beforehand without being reconciled to God?

The return of the Lord Jesus Christ on the Day of the LORD is described in Revelation 19:11ff. This *"day"* lasts longer, however, and encompasses the entire period of the Messianic rule during the following 1000 years which follow (Rev. 20:1-10). During this time, it will clearly be demonstrated that only Jesus Christ can administer a really righteous rule of worldwide peace on Earth.

At the end of the *"Day of the LORD"* the entire creation will dissolve in fire. Peter writes that everything, even the elements of matter, will dissolve or be melted in fire (2 Peter 3:10-13). In Revelation 20:11-15 we are shown that all people who ever lived who were not reconciled to God during their lifetime will rise again to eternal judgement.

We see that even the judgement on "*the Day of the LORD*" is a foretaste of the definitive and eternal judgement at the Great White Throne. God will call to account each person who has not been reconciled and has rejected the offer of forgiveness. We must take into account that following a person's death, there is no longer any opportunity to repent and accept divine forgiveness. The person who has not been reconciled dies just once – and then there is the judgement (Heb. 9:27; Luke16:19-31).

The Bible speaks of "*eternal punishment*" (Matt. 25:46). The Greek word *aionios* translated "*eternal*" really means "eternal" in the absolute sense. God gives us a daunting choice: Eternal life in communion with God or eternal judgement alienated from God! Eternal blessing or eternal curse is dependent on our relationship to the Lord Jesus Christ. What happens to us personally depends upon our decision. When you ask the Lord Jesus, from your heart, to be your Saviour and Lord, to come into your life, eternal blessing will be yours (John 1:12). When you decide to reject Him, you choose your own eternal sorrow.

# 9. List of 56 Fulfilled Prophecies (P91–146)

| Prophecy | Statement | Bible verse | Fulfillment |
| --- | --- | --- | --- |
| P91 | **Flight** of the Babylonian Jews | Jer. 50:8,28; 51:6; Zech. 2:11 | From 1941 mass flight out of Iraq, also following Feb. 1952 |
| P92 | **Exodus** from Babylon | Isa. 48:20; Jer. 50:8; 51:45 | March 1950 – Feb. 1952: official emigration of 104,000 Jews |
| P93 | Rescue of the Jews **before** war catastrophe in Babylon | Jer. 51:45; 51:6 | Most Jews leave Iraq before the Gulf Wars of 1991 and 2003, as well as the Iran-Iraq War of 1980–1988 |
| P94 | Terrible news in the land: You may not leave! | Jer. 51:45 | Coup on 15.09.1950: Nuri comes to power ➔ Rumours: No-one can leave anymore! |
| P95 | Fears are unfounded! Jews shall not fear bad news! | Jer. 51:46 | In the end everyone was able to leave |
| P96 | **Time specification:** One year of good news; the year following: bad news | Jer. 51:46 | Jewish year: 24 Sept. '49 – 11 Sept. '50: You can leave! Jewish year afterward: 12 Sept. '50 – 30 Aug. '51: You may no longer leave! |
| P97 | Violence in the land | Jer. 51:46 | 1951, in the period of the exodus: underground organization discovered and brutally destroyed |

| Prophecy | Statement | Bible verse | Fulfillment |
|----------|-----------|-------------|-------------|
| P98 | Coup: ruler follows ruler | Jer. 51:46 | 1950, in the period of the exodus: coup: Tawfiq al-Suwaidi succeeded by Nuri Pasha as-Said |
| P99 | Trap set | Jer. 50:24 | 25.07.1990: the trap "Kuwait," set by Mrs Glaspie |
| P100 | Babylonia is caught out | Jer. 50:24 | The entire world community views the illegal attack on Kuwait with horror |
| P101 | Babylonia did not plan on being caught out and apprehended ("... *thou wast not aware*"): | Jer. 50:24 | Saddam Hussein did not reckon with the military reaction of the USA and the world community |
| P102 | Babylonia is caught and held prisoner | Jer. 50:24 | Iraq lost the war of 1991 and fell into the hands of the world community. Iraq as a prisoner of war of the UN: 1991–2003 |
| P103 | Babylonia made war against the LORD (cf. Zech. 2:8: "... *for he that toucheth you toucheth the apple of My eye.*") | Jer. 50:24 | 3 times Iraq attempted to destroy Israel: 1948/1949; 1967; 1973 |
| P104 | Babylonia = "*the Land of Merathayim*" = "*the land of double rebellion*" Babylonia = "the proud/ impudent" | Jer. 50:21, 31-32 | Iraq, full of pride and impudence, defies the world community (1990–2003) |

| Prophecy | Statement | Bible verse | Fulfillment |
|---|---|---|---|
| P105 | Unusual weapons used in fight against Babylonia; extremely precise ammunition | Isa. 13:5; Jer. 50:25; 51:27; 50:32; 50:9b | Use of advanced war technology, outstripping all previous wars; use of the most modern precision weapons (laser guided bombs, etc.) |
| P106 | Flight of foreigners | Jer. 50:16b | Thousands of foreign hostages are able to flee Iraq thanks to international mediation during the Gulf crisis |
| P107 | Flag waving to greet those entering | Isa. 13:2 | 27/28.2.1991: reception of the Allies by the Kuwaitis with flags; cf. as proof of fulfilment the photos in TIME Magazine, No. 10, 1991, **this also applies to P108-P110** |
| P108 | Loud cries of greeting, hand waving | Isa. 13:2 | Enthusiastic reception of Allies with loud cries (and chorus of car horns); in Kuwait City the masses waving as Allies enter |
| P109 | Entry into the City of the Nobles | Isa. 13:2 | Entry of the Allies into Kuwait City = city of the noble Emir family of Jaber es-Sabah |
| P110 | The people rejoicing proudly | Isa. 13:2 | See the photos of the Allies' entry 27.02.1991 (TIME Magazine, No. 10, 1991)! |
| P111 | Noise of war in the hills | Isa. 13:4 | The majority of the Allied soldiers push into Kuwait over the hills of southern Iraq with their ground troops' noisy vehicles |
| P112 | A great people **as a gathering of nations** | Isa. 13:4 | 1991: Allies = soldiers from over 40 nations from all five continents |

| Prophecy | Statement | Bible verse | Fulfillment |
|----------|-----------|-------------|-------------|
| P113 | One nation = coming from a far country, **from the ends of heaven** | Isa. 13:2-4 | 660,000 soldiers from the USA |
| P114 | The entire country destroyed | Isa. 13:5 | 1991: 100,000 air attacks by the Allies; destruction of the greater part of Iraq's infrastructure |
| P115 | Babylon's enemies are *"cruel and without mercy"* | Jer. 50:42 | Use of Daisy Cutters, cluster bombs, uranium-enriched ammunition; excessive B52 carpet bombing; use of some 500 MK-77 bombs, despite human-rights and war conventions; brutal embargo by the UN resulting in more than 1 million deaths |
| P116 | Cities and surrounding regions burned with fire | Jer. 50:32 | Daisy Cutters burn everything within a radius of 100 metres; use of some 500 MK-77 bombs, carpet bombing, uranium-enriched ammunition |
| P117 | Israel would fight against Babylonia behind the other nations | Jer. 50:21 | Israel's undercover participation in the Gulf War of 1991 with ultra-modern technology and weapon systems |
| P118 | Babylonia becomes a **horror amongst the nations** | Jer. 50:23 | Millions worldwide are shocked and demonstrate against the war of 2003 |

| Prophecy | Statement | Bible verse | Fulfillment |
|---|---|---|---|
| P119 | Noise of war in the land and great destruction – the world horrified about Babylonia | Jer. 50:22,23 | 2003: 30,000 air attacks |
| P120 | Sudden end of war; courageous men surrender, and become as women | Jer. 51:30 | 2003: After 25 days, Iraq conquered, its resistance broken |
| P121 | Shelters set on fire, locks broken | Jer. 51:30 | Soldiers' quarters and protective shelters, etc., bombed |
| P122 | Capital conquered | Jer. 51:31 | 2003: Baghdad conquered |
| P123 | Bridges taken | Jer. 51:32 | Tigris bridges in Baghdad taken |
| P124 | Palaces burn | Jer. 51:32 | March 2003: Saddam Hussein's palaces set on fire |
| P125 | Babylonia's riches in enemy hands | Jer. 51:13; 50:2,10 | Western firms become rich through oil production |
| P126 | *Many* nations *from the ends of the world* against Babylonia | Jer. 50:41 | 1991 and 2003: Australia, Dominican Republic, El Salvador, Estonia, Fiji, Great Britain, Honduras, Japan, Latvia, Lithuania, Micronesia, New Zealand, the Netherlands, Spain, the Philippines, Portugal, South Korea, Thailand |
| P127 | Destroyers (plural!) from the north | Jer. 51:48 | 1991: Syria, Turkey, USSR, 2003: Turkey, Republic of Azerbaijan, Armenia, Georgia, Ukraine |

| Prophecy | Statement | Bible verse | Fulfillment |
|---|---|---|---|
| P128 | Kingdom of Ararat | Jer. 51:27 | 2003: Rep. Armenia |
| P129 | Kingdom of Minni | Jer. 51:27 | 2003: Republic of Azerbaijan |
| P130 | Ashkenaz (Scythians) | Jer. 51:27 | Ukraine |
| P131 | A *"great nation from the north"* with particular significance | Jer. 50:3; 50:41 | 1991/2003: Turkey |
| P132 | The Medes are awakened | Isa. 13:17 | The Kurds (= Medes), disappointed by the unfulfilled promises of the victorious powers after the First World War, awake to their fight for national rights |
| P133 | The Medes fight | Isa. 13:17-18; Jer. 51:11 | Kurdish-US alliance, 2003, conquers northern Iraqi Medes = Kurds |
| P134 | Medes have *"a land … of dominion"* | Jer. 51:28 | 1991, following a centuries-long period of statelessness, Kurds of northern Iraq receive wide-reaching autonomy. The new constitution also gives Kurds in the north extensive right of self-determination |
| P135 | Self-idolatry of the ruler of Babylon | Isa. 14:13-14 | In one of Saddam's palaces is a golden inscription, "You are the glory"! |
| P136 | Fall into the pit | Isa. 14:12.15 | Saddam Hussein was pulled out from a hole. In FOCUS Magazine, 20.12.2003: "Saddam fell from his throne of power literally into the dust." |

| Prophecy | Statement | Bible verse | Fulfillment |
|---|---|---|---|
| P137 | Everyone beholds him, considers him: *"Is this the man?"* | Isa. 14:16 | The entire world sees the unbelievable pictures of the bearded Saddam, who was taken out of a hole |
| P138 | The man who horrified the entire world | Isa. 14:16 | 1990: Conquest of Kuwait; 1991: ecological catastrophe by setting the oil fields on fire |
| P139 | He shook and beat *nations*. | Isa. 14:6,16 | 1980–88: war with Iran, 1.7 million dead, hundreds of thousands crippled; 1990: conquest and terrorization of Kuwait |
| P140 | He made his country a desert and destroyed it | Isa. 14:17,20 | 1980s: destruction and mining of a large part of Kurdish settlement areas; 1993–94: 90% of southern Iraq devastated |
| P141 | Towns and villages torn down | Isa. 14:17 | 1988: Saddam razed 4,500 Kurdish villages and towns. 1991: innumerable Shiite villages in the south burned |
| P142 | Prisoners not released | Isa. 14:17 | Hundreds of thousands of prisoners are untraceable. Their exact fate is unknown |
| P143 | His own people murdered; nations beaten | Isa. 14:20 | In 1985/86 some 1,000 Kurds executed by Saddam; in 1988 some 300,000 Kurds shot or gassed; 1991 some 100,000 Shiites liquidated during the up-rising and more than 100,000 Iraqis disappeared forever since 1997. At least 1 million dead |

| Prophecy | Statement | Bible verse | Fulfillment |
|---|---|---|---|
| P144 | His sons will be slaughtered so that they do not ever rule. | Isa. 14:21 | His sons Uday and Qusay were shot on 22 July 2003. Rumsfeld says on TV to the Iraqis: "...they're dead ... and they're not coming back." |
| P145 | The ruler of Babylon must die violently | Isa. 14:9-11 | Saddam Hussein was hung by the courts on 30 December 2006 |
| P146 | Foreigners attempt to help Babylonia | Isa. 51:9 | Countless international organizations (public and private) have tried, since 2003, to make Iraq a democratic nation |

# V. Jesus' Olivet Discourse

## 1. Introductory Remarks

The Lord Jesus Christ was in the Temple in Jerusalem all day the Tuesday before Good Friday. It was an extremely demanding day. Various Jewish groups had attacked Him, by trying to trap Him in discussion. These encounters are described extensively in the Gospels (cf. Matt. 21:23–23:39; Mark 11:27–12:44; Luke 19:47–21:4). At the end of this day, one thing was clear: the majority of the Jewish leaders rejected Jesus as Israel's Messiah!

As the Lord was leaving the Temple, He announced the coming destruction of the Sanctuary on Mount Zion to His followers (Matt. 24:1-2; Mark 13:1-2; Luke 21:5-6). This national catastrophe would constitute one of the consequences of rejecting of the promised Redeemer.

After leaving the Temple, Jesus Christ, with His disciples, passed through the Kidron Valley and climbed the west slope of the Mount of Olives.

From here they had a wonderful view of the Temple area. The Mount of Olives is higher than the Temple Mount, therefore the most glorious view of the Temple area can be enjoyed from there.

The disciples were troubled inwardly by Jesus' announcement of the destruction of the Temple and therefore asked four questions:

### 1.1 Four Questions
1. When will the destruction of the Temple take place? (Matt. 24:3; Mark 13:4; Luke 21:7)
2. What will be the sign of the destruction of the Temple? (Luke 21:7)
3. What is the sign of Your return? (Matt. 24:3; Mark 13:4)

4. What is the sign of The Last Days? (Matt. 24:3; Mark 13:4)[389]

These questions can be divided in two groups:
Questions 1 and 2 relate to the destruction of the Temple. Questions 3 and 4 have to do with The Last Days. Questions 1 and 2 deal with events following the 1st coming of Jesus 2000 years ago, while questions 3 and 4 concern things which will happen before the 2nd Coming of Jesus as King of the world. Questions 1 and 2 are connected with the time which the Bible describes as "the beginning,"[390] while questions 3 and 4 refer to "The Last Days."

None of the Gospels record all four of these questions. All the synoptic reports must be viewed as a whole in order to have a complete picture.

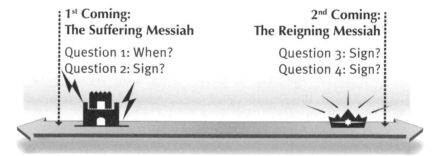

# The Two Comings of the Messiah

**1st Coming:**
**The Suffering Messiah**

Question 1: When?
Question 2: Sign?

**2nd Coming:**
**The Reigning Messiah**

Question 3: Sign?
Question 4: Sign?

*Fig. 24: Questions 1 and 2 relate to the destruction of the Temple. Questions 3 and 4 relate to The Last Days.*

---

389 In Matt. 24:3 it reads literally: "... *what is the sign ... of the end of the age?*" The term "the end of the age" (Greek *synteleia tou anionos*) must be understood in a Jewish context: The ancient rabbis differentiated between "this age" (Hebr. *ha'olam hazeh*) and the "coming age" (Hebr. *ha'olam haba'*) in which the Messiah will set up His kingdom according to Dan. 7:13ff f (e.g. Midrash Koheleth 11,8 [in: BAR ILAN'S JUDAIC LIBRARY]; BABALONIAN TALMUD, Sanhedrin 10,1-3). The disciples' question was this: When does the present age come to an end and when does the Messianic reign begin?

This differentiation between a present and a future age is also clearly retained in the NT in confirmation of the rabbinic point of view (Matt. 12:32, Mark 10:30, Luke 18:30, Ephesians 1:21).

390 The time of Jesus' Coming a little more than 2,000 years ago is designated as "the beginning" in some verses of the NT (1 John 1:1; 2:7,13,14,24,24; 3:11; 2 John 4.5).

## 1.2 From the Beginning to the End

The Lord Jesus gave the so-called Olivet Discourse in answer to the disciples' questions. This is recorded in all three synoptic Gospels (Matt. 24-25; Mark 13; Luke 21), with varying emphases, as is always the case when parallel accounts appear in the Gospels.

Before the Lord addressed the four questions, He warned His followers quite generally of deception by false messiahs (Matt. 24:4-5):

> "*⁴ And Jesus answered and said unto them, Take heed that no man deceive you. ⁵ For many shall come in my name, saying, I am Christ [= the Messiah]; and shall deceive many.*" (KJV)

The word "*Christ*" [Greek *christos*] here in the text is the Greek equivalent of the Hebrew word "Messiah."[391] In Judaism, the promised Redeemer is designated as "the Messiah," the King, Priest and Prophet anointed by God.

According to Matthew 24:5, following the Coming of Jesus Christ 2,000 years ago, there would be many people who would profess to be the fulfilment of the Old Testament prophecy of the Redeemer.

The reference in this verse to false messiahs, first occurring in Matthew 24:24 (cf. Mark 13:22), is not a sign of The Last Days. This is much more a general warning applying to all times, from "the beginning" unto the "Last Days."

The first End-Time sign in the following verse is therefore separated from this general warning by the word "*but*" (Greek *de*) (Matt. 24:6):

> "*⁶ But ye will hear of wars and rumours of wars.*" (KJV)

As a result of the rejection of the true Messiah, more than 50 false Messiahs have appeared in Judaism since the coming of Jesus.

---

391 The Greek word *christos* literally means "anointed one." It is the translation of the Hebrew word *mashiach*. If one did not want to translate this latter word into Greek, but rather transliterate it, the familiar word *messias* resulted.

At times, they have held great masses of the Jewish people under their deceitful spell and ensnared them.

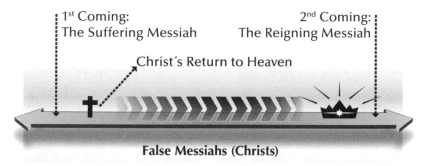

## From the Beginning until the End

1ˢᵗ Coming:
The Suffering Messiah

2ⁿᵈ Coming:
The Reigning Messiah

Christ´s Return to Heaven

False Messiahs (Christs)

*Fig. 25: Over the centuries following Jesus' departure, more than 50 false messiahs appeared among the Jews.*

In the following list there are more than 50 false messiahs from the past 2,000 years. The date of their appearance is noted in brackets (AD in each case).[392]

1. Theudas (44–46)
2. The Messiah from Egypt (between 52–58)
3. The nameless prophet (59)
4. Menachem the Galilean (c. 66)
5. Jonathan the Weaver (after 70)
6. Lukuas (115)
7. Bar Kochba (c. 100–135 AD)
8. The Moses-Messiah of Crete (440–470)
9. The Messiah of Syria (c. 643)
10. Abu Isa of Isfahan, Persia (684–705)
11. Serenus of Syria (c. 720)

---

392 For the topic of false messiahs in Judaism see: GILBERT: Jewish History Atlas, p. 52; RABOW: 50 Jewish Messiahs; http://www.livius.org/men-mh/messiah/messiah00.html#overview ; http://www.jewishencyclopedia.com/view.jsp?artid=581&letter=P#2185 (as of: 25.10.2011). See Roger Liebi: False Messiahs (audio lecture at www.sermon-online.de ).

12. Yudghan of Hamad, Persia (c. 800)
13. Mushka (850)
14. Menachem, Kazakhstan (1000)
15. The Messiah of Leon, Spain (1060)
16. Ibn Ayre of Cordoba, Spain (1100)
17. Chadd, Iraq (1100)
18. Moshe al Dar'l of Morocco (1120)
19. The uneducated Messiah of Yemen (1192)
20. David Alroy of Kurdistan (1120–1147)
21. Abraham Abulafia, Spain (1240–1291)
22. Samuel of Ayllon, Spain (1290)
23. Nissim Ben Abraham, Spain (1295)
24. Moses Botarel, Spain (1393)
25. Rabbi Joseph Karo, Spain (1488–1575)
26. The Messiah of South Yemen (1495)
27. Asher Lemmlein, Reutlingen (1500–1502)
28. Shlomo Molkho, Portugal (1500–1532)
29. Ludovico Luis Diaz, Portugal (1540)
30. Isaac Luria Ashkenazi Safed/Israel (1534–1572)
31. Chaim Vital Calabrese (1542–1620)
32. Shabbetai Zvi, Smyrna (1626–1676)
33. Suleiman Jabal, Yemen (1666)
34. Miguel Cardoso, Crete (1630–1706)
35. Moshe Chaim Luzzato, Padua (1707–1747)
36. Nehemiah Hiya Chajun, Amsterdam (1650–1726)
37. Jacob Filosoff (1650–1690)
38. Mordechai Mokia, Eisenstadt (1650–1729)
39. Jacob Querido, Turkey (? –1690)
40. Berechiah (1740: son of Filosoff)
41. Baruchya Russo (c. 1720)
42. Jacob Joseph Frank, Lemberg (1726–1791)
43. Löbele Prossnitz (? –1750)
44. Rachel Frank (1770)
45. Baal Shem Tov (1700–1760)
46. Rabbi Nachman of Bratslav (1772–1811)
47. Rabbi Israel of Rhuzin (1797–1850)
48. Rabbi Yitzhak Eizik of Komarno (1806–1874)

49. Shukr Ben Salim Kuhayl I, Yemen (1821–1865)
50. Shukr Kuhayl II, Yemen (1867)
51. Rabbi Menachem Mendel Schneerson, New York (1902–1994)

The tragic success of these false Christs in deception demonstrates one thing: When the truth is rejected, there is great danger of falling into error and falling prey to deception (cf. John 5:43)! This is a precept which is applicable to all people.

# 2. The Discourse Regarding the Time of the Beginning

## 2.1 The Answer to Questions 1 and 2

The Lord Jesus does not answer the first two questions in the text of Matthew 24. In the parallel passage of Luke 21, however, there is clear emphasis on the theme surrounding these questions. That is related directly to the fact that the question about the sign of the destruction of the Temple is only mentioned in the Gospel of Luke (Luke 21:7).

The End-Time signs and the beginning of the birth pains heralding the Messianic period, are dealt with in Luke 21:8-1, as well as in the parallel passages in Matthew 24 and Mark 13. However, Luke 21:12 is clearly distinguished from The Last Days. A fundamental reversion in time occurs in verse 12. Verse 12 could be seen as a flash back. The time-markers in this passage must be closely observed:

*"12 But **before** all these, ..."* (KJV)

Verses 12–19 contain statements which were exactly fulfilled for Jesus' disciples in 32–68 AD.[393] There is a very short parallel to this

---

393 A very significant parallel to this flash-back is found in the same Gospel in 17:25. Verse 24 deals with Christ's Second Coming in power and glory. In the following verse, Christ's First Appearance as the suffering Messiah is addressed. The chronological reversion from the Second to the First Coming results from the linguistic indicator at the beginning of Luke 17:25: *"But first ..."*

section in Mark 13:9-11.[394] Otherwise, these verses record an exclusive element of the third Gospel.

Let us examine Jesus' statements in this passage in detail (Luke 21:12-13):

> *"[12] But before all these, they shall lay their hands on you, and persecute you, delivering you up to **the synagogues**, and into **prisons**, being brought before **kings** and **rulers** for my name's sake. [13] And it shall turn to you for a **testimony**."* (KJV)

These statements are added to in the parallel passage of Mark 13 with the reference to "councils":

> *"[9] But take heed to yourselves: for they shall deliver you up to **councils**;[395] and in the **synagogues** ye shall be beaten: and ye shall be brought before **rulers** and **kings** for my sake, for a **testimony** ..."* (KJV)

In answer to the question "When will the Temple be destroyed?", the verses in Luke 21:12ff. describe the events which must happen up until the destruction of the Temple. All of the events prophesied here had to be fulfilled first; only afterwards could there be the destruction of the Temple.

The Lord Jesus announced to his Jewish followers that there would be a difficult time of persecution. This would be persecution coming from the *Jews*. Note the mention of *synagogues* as places of judgement in Luke 21:12, as well as the mention of *councils* (Jewish courts) in Mark 13:9.

There was oppression of Christians by Jews until 70 AD. A fundamental change occurred with the destruction of Jerusalem in 70 AD. From this point on, the Jews themselves were persecuted for centuries.

Following the crucifixion and resurrection of Jesus Christ in

---

394  In this regard, notice the time indicator *"first"* in Mark 13:10. The following verses deal with The Last Days, as is easy to see by a comparison with the parallels in Matt. 24:9 – 10:13.

395  The Great Sanhedrion (Sanhedrin) was a tribunal of 71 men under the leadership of the High Priest at the Temple of Jerusalem. The Lesser Sanhedrion (Sanhedrin) constituted local synagogue courts, distributed throughout Israel, each with 23 judges.

the spring of 32 AD, the Assembly of God, or the Church of God, emerged. Its birth fell on Pentecost of that same year (Acts 2). In the beginning, the assembly or church consisted only of Jewish Christians, i.e. Jews who had come to faith in the Messiah. Many thousands of Jews believed in the Messiah Jesus during the first few decades (cf. Acts 2:41; 4:4; 6:7; 21:20).

Acts Chapters 3–8 (dealing with the years 32–33 AD) describe how the first Messianic Jews were persecuted, how they were brought before the highest Jewish court, the Sanhedrin; how they were taken into custody and how all this provided an opportunity to be able to testify that Jesus was Israel's Messiah (Acts 4:5-22; 5:26-42). Stephen became the first martyr in the history of the church (Acts 7:54-8:1). Before being executed, he was first able to deliver a wonderful speech to the Jewish High Court, glorifying Jesus Christ (Acts 7). Subsequently, persecution against the early church was so extreme that almost all Christians had to flee Jerusalem (Acts 8:1-3). During this period, Saul of Tarsus played a leading role in the persecution of Christians and brought innumerable Messianic Jews before the courts of local Synagogues (Acts 26:11).

In Luke 21:12 and in Mark 13:9 the Lord Jesus spoke not only of Jewish courts (synagogues and Sanhedrins), but also of interrogation before procurators or governors. Acts 23 reports how Paul had to answer to the Roman governor Felix in 58 AD.

This would have been only *one* such case. The Bible speaks of "rulers" in the plural, indicating a minimum of two such events.

In Acts 25 we find the report of how Paul had to answer to Porcius Festus, Felix' successor, in 59 AD.

Luke 21:12 also speaks of court hearings before "*kings.*" That had been lacking up to that point. Yet in 60 AD Paul was presented before King Agrippa. This gave Paul the opportunity to proclaim the Good News of Jesus Christ to this influential man, just as he had done earlier with the governors (Acts 26). This would be evidence of *one* court case before a king; but Luke 21:12 speaks of "kings" in the plural, meaning at least two.

Since Paul had appealed to the highest court in the Roman Empire (Acts 25:11) in order to receive justice, he had to be taken to the Emperor in the capital of the Empire, to the king over all the subordinate kings of the Empire (Acts 25:12 – 28:31). Having arrived in Rome, Paul waited *"two whole years"* (Acts 28:30) for his court appearance, until 62 AD. According to Roman law, the plaintiffs had to act within "two full years" else it would be necessary to acquit the defendant. Apparently, the leading priests from Jerusalem who had accused Paul never appeared in Rome before the Emperor. Therefore, Paul, in his letter written in 62 AD to the Philippians, was able to announce his then directly pending acquittal by Emperor Nero (Phil. 1:12-14,26; 2:24).[396] Paul was able to give testimony of Jesus Christ even before the Emperor, the supreme king of Rome (Phil. 1:12-14).[397]

At that point, all the prophecies from Luke 21:12-13 were fulfilled. In the year 62, the destruction of the Temple was very near which, as we know in hindsight, would finally take place in 70 AD. In His Olivet Discourse the Lord Jesus answered the question of when the Temple would be destroyed by the describing the early persecution of Christians and the various court hearings which would all take place little by little.

While Luke 21:12-19 answers the question "When will the Temple be destroyed?", Luke 21:20 settles the question "What will be the sign of the destruction of the Temple?:"

> *"20 And when ye shall see Jerusalem compassed with armies, then know that the desolation thereof is nigh. 21 Then let them which are in Judaea flee to the mountains; and let them which are in the midst of it depart out; and let not them that are in the countries enter thereinto. 22 For these be the days of vengeance, that all things which are written may be fulfilled. 23 But woe unto them that are with child, and to them that give suck, in those days! for there shall be great distress in the land, and wrath upon this people. 24 And they shall fall by the edge of the sword, and shall be led away captive into all nations: and Jerusalem shall be trodden down of the Gentiles, until the times of the Gentiles be fulfilled."* (KJV)

---

396 Cf. Philem. 1:22; Heb. 13:23.

397 Paul was later brought again to Rome as a prisoner. In 67 AD he was beheaded by Emperor Nero. Shortly before this, Paul wrote the letter 2 Timothy from his prison cell.

History confirms these precise prophecies in every detail:[398]

The Jewish uprising against the Roman occupation broke out in 66 AD. With the dramatic defeat at Masada in 73 AD, the revolt was finally and extremely brutally brought to an end.

It had all begun with a spontaneous popular uprising. The political situation had been exceedingly strained for a long time. The catalyst for the Jewish people's rage was that Gessius Florus, the last Roman governor of Judea, began to rob the Temple treasure in Jerusalem.

To begin with the rebels had amazing success. As a consequence, however, Emperor Nero sent Vespasian, one of his best commanders, with a large army to the rebel area. Vespasian, one-time conqueror of Britain, arrived in the north of the land in early summer of 67 AD.

First, Jodphat in Galilee was conquered, then Gush Halav and, in late summer, Gamla on the Golan.

With the fall of these important towns, Galilee finally came under Roman control again. Vespasian then secured Samaria; in Transjordan, he blocked the connecting roads to Judea. He then went down the coast and conquered Jaffa, Javne and Ashdod. All this took place in 67 AD.

## 2.2 Jerusalem Surrounded

Over the course of 68 AD Vespasian encircled the heart of Judea, the city Jerusalem, more and more. With the exception of the city of Machaerus, he conquered all of Transjordan as well as the western bank of the River Jordan, including Jericho and Qumran. In the west, advancing from the coastal towns, he conquered the entire Shephelah. The towns of Lod, Emmaus and Beth Guvrin also fell into Roman hands. Guards were posted on the main roads in the remaining area of Judea, preventing the Jews from leaving the area.

In the summer of 68 AD, however, Emperor Nero committed

---

398  Cf. KRUPP: Die Geschichte der Juden im Land Israel, p. 30-39; JOSEPHUS: The Jewish War, passim.

suicide.[399] This brought confusion to the Roman Empire, halting the war against the Jews. The conditions of the siege, however, barely changed. In July 69 AD Vespasian was proclaimed Emperor by a large part of the army. Consequently, he left the war zone, in order to return to Rome and from there to establish his claim to the throne throughout the entire empire.

## 2.3 Flight to the Mountains

Jerusalem was thus surrounded by army camps, but there was no progress being made in the war. The war had virtually come to a stand-still. The Jews who had believed Jesus to be the Messiah knew that this situation conformed exactly to the prophecy in Luke 21:20.[400] This led to a mass exodus of the Messianic Jews from Jerusalem and Judea. They fled to the mountains which are primarily in the present day so-called West Bank. In Pella, beyond the Jordan River, in the Decapolis region, they found safety from the horrible final phase of the Romans' war against the Jews. There, they were accepted and protected as freedom-loving citizens by King Agrippa II.[401]

Paul had convinced Agrippa, in his speech preserved in Acts 26, that Christians were not dangerous elements to the Roman state. Though this significant speech, which emphatically bore witness to the Gospel, did not result in the eternal salvation of Agrippa's soul (the King remarked snappily, *"Almost thou persuadest me to be a Christian"* [Acts 26:28 KJV]), it did mean the rescue of the Jews who believed in the Messiah.

There was not one Messianic Jew known to have died in the destruction of Jerusalem in 70 AD! Belief in the Messiah Jesus and in His word in Luke 21 saved the lives of these Jewish Christians!

---

399 Not long before this, Nero had the Apostle Paul as well as the Apostle Peter executed by judicial murder (cf. the writings of these witnesses of Jesus from their death cells. Both letters are to be dated to c. 66/67 AD: 2 Timothy and 2 Peter [cf. MAUERHOFER: Einleitung in die Schriften des Neuen Testaments, Vol. II, p. 183 and 254]). Nero's suicide was, without a doubt, a judgement of divine providence.

400 However, it did not conform at all to Matt. 24:15ff. The signs in Matt. 24:15 deal factually with something completely different than Luke 21:20. While Luke 21:20 was fulfilled in 68 AD, Matt. 24:15 is yet to have its future fulfilment. The signs in Luke 21:20 would take place *before* the End-Time signs, while the signs in Matt. 24:15 will take place only in The Last Days and, in fact, following the signs mentioned in Matt. 24:4-14.

401 EUSEBIUS: Church History III, 5.

The text of the Gospel of Luke was written and published before the year 62 AD.[402] Jesus' prophecy in Luke 21 was obviously known by the Jewish Christians in Israel already before the war of 66–73 AD! This prophecy had saved all their lives.

## 2.4 The Battle for Jerusalem

By July 70 AD, Vespasian was the undisputed ruler on the emperor's throne in the Empire's capital, Rome. He had previously given his son Titus the task of bringing the war against the Jews to an end. Titus arrived in Israel in the spring of 70 AD.

The attack on Jerusalem began from the north. First of all the third wall was broken through. This enabled the outskirts to be taken. Then the breach of the second wall was next. Thus the Roman Army was able to reconquer the Antonia Fortress, then occupied by the Jews and which lay north of the main Temple area. This strategically important point made control of the Temple area possible.

Even before the attack on the Temple, Titus fought for control of the upper city, where the Jewish Quarter is situated today. But in the summer of 70 AD it had come this far: on the 9th Av the Temple went up in flames. The amazing thing is that the First Temple was destroyed by the Babylonians on this same date! 9th Av was already a day of mourning for the destroyed First Temple in the centuries before 70 AD.[403] This date continues to be, after more than 2,500 years, the day of mourning for the loss of the Temple!

## 2.5 Deportation and Dispersion

Following the terrible battle for the Temple, the Romans hunted down the last pockets of resistance in the upper city. After that Jerusalem could be considered to be fully conquered.

Thousands of Jews – Josephus Flavius speaks of 97,000 – were taken away as slaves, to be sold in various places in the Roman Empire (Luke 21:24).[404] There were so many slaves offered that

---

402 For the dating to 59/60 AD cf. MAUERHOFER: Einleitung in die Schriften des Neuen Testaments, Vol. I, p. 163-170.

403 Cf. Zech. 7:1-7; 8:18-23; Av = the 5th month (July/August); JOSEPHUS: The Jewish War VI, 4.8.

404 JOSEPHUS: The Jewish War VI, 9.3.

there was a collapse of prices in the slave trade.[405]

As a result of 70 AD, the Jewish nation began a centuries-long process of dispersion over all five continents (Luke 21:24).

## 2.6 "Jerusalem Trodden Down"

The Messiah Jesus had foretold the painful lot of Jerusalem's history from the 1st until the 21st centuries with outstanding accuracy (Luke 21:24):

> "24 ... and Jerusalem shall be trodden down of the Gentiles, until the times of the Gentiles be fulfilled." (KJV)

The term "the times of the Gentiles" designates the period in which the world empires of man hold power and the Chosen People are under their dictates (cf. Dan. 2 and 7).[406]

These human empires will finally be done away with by the Kingdom of God, the Messiah's Rule of Peace in The Last Days. Thus the Lord Jesus foretold that Jerusalem would be ruled, humiliated and trod upon until The Last Days.

With Luke 21:24 we arrive again at The Last Days.[407] From 21:25 the Time of the End, already addressed in verses 8-11, is taken up once again in order, ultimately, to be able to introduce the theme of the glorious appearance of the Messiah (Luke 21:27):

> "27 And then shall they see the Son of man coming in a cloud with power and great glory. 28 And when these things begin to come to pass, then look up, and lift up your heads; for your redemption draweth nigh." (KJV)

---

405 Deut. 28:68 was hereby fulfilled. Cf. JUBILÄUMSBIBEL, notes to Deut. 28:68.

406 Cf. LIEBI: Weltgeschichte im Visier des Propheten Daniel (English edition in progress by CMV Hagedorn, Germany).

407 As already explained the verses in Luke 21:12-24 are a coherent block, distinguished from the rest of the statements about The Last Days by the words "before" (the beginning) and "until" (its end).

# 3. The Discourse on The Last Days

## 3.1 Answers to Questions 3 and 4

In answer to Questions 3 and 4, the Lord unfolds a whole catalogue of End-Time signs which will occur before His appearance in power and majesty, like, for example, large-scale wars, famines, epidemics, earthquakes, martyrdom of believers, false prophets, lawlessness and love growing cold (Matt. 24:4-13). Furthermore, the Gospel will reach all nations (Matt. 24:14). Then the period of the *"great tribulation"* will come (Matt. 24:21), following the erection of an idol in the Temple by the Antichrist (Matt. 24:15; Dan. 9:27; 12:11; Rev. 13:14-15). This period will be more terrible than any time since the beginning of the world, and will never again be repeated. Following the tribulation of these days, the Messiah will appear in power and great majesty (Matt. 24:29-31).

The disciples asked for *one* sign of the end of the present age and for *one* further sign announcing the return of Jesus as King of the world. But the Lord did not merely give them two signs, but more than twenty!

## 3.2 Sorrows in The Last Days

The Lord referred to His End-Time signs as *"birth pains."* After having given a first series of five signs, He said in summary (Matt. 24:8):

> *"8 All these are the beginning of sorrows [birth pains]."* (KJV)

It is very important to understand why *"birth pains"* are spoken of here. As is well known birth pains occur at the end of a pregnancy. As soon as they begin, it is as if an unmistakable and understandable language (at least for those who understand this "language") announces the end of the long waiting period for the birth. Birth pains are a type of "Last Days sign" following the long period of pregnancy.

Just as pregnancy is a long period of time, the time between the First and the Second Coming of Jesus Christ is quite a long period.

Just as a time of pain occurs at the end of pregnancy, a period of painful events will occur for this world between the First and the Second Coming of the Messiah, at the end of the present age.

At the very end of pregnancy it is like this: after the climax of the pains, following the extremely painful exertion of bearing down, there comes great joy: the longed for and long-awaited person comes into the world! It will be exactly this way with the so-called present age following the Great Tribulation (Matt. 24:21): Jesus Christ, *"the Son of Man,"*[408] will come on the clouds of heaven into this world to the joy to those who believe in Him (Matt. 24:29-30).

The birth pains of pregnancy are not precisely timed. They occur periodically, incessantly recur, tending to become ever more painful and intense. This is an important indicator of the character of The Last Days signs given in the Olivet Discourse. These signs will be events which happen *repeatedly*, in contrast to The Last Days signs dealt with in the earlier chapters of this book.

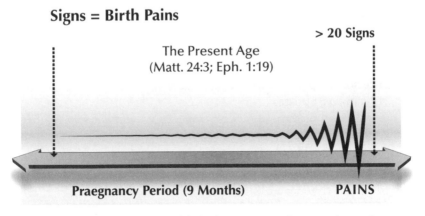

**Signs = Birth Pains**

**> 20 Signs**

The Present Age
(Matt. 24:3; Eph. 1:19)

**Praegnancy Period (9 Months)**        **PAINS**

*Fig. 26: The period of pregnancy and the birth pains at its end is an analogy to the present age, at the end of which there will be painful events for this world without fail.*

---

408 The term *"Son of man"* is a title of the Messiah in the OT (Ps. 8:4; Dan. 7:13). It is precisely this title the Lord Jesus uses in the Olivet Discourse in connection with His return (Matt. 24:29-30).

## 3.3 "The Beginning of Birth Pains"

In relation to the expression "*the beginning of birth pains*" it must be noted that this is a typically rabbinic style of speech. The terrible events preceding the establishment of the Messianic world empire are called "*the Messiah's birth pains*" (Hebr. *chevlo shel mashiach*) in the Talmud.[409]

When the Lord Jesus uses this term in the Olivet Discourse, He is pointing out that the greatest distress will come upon mankind before He returns as King of kings and Judge of the world. It is clear that His words do not relate to the destruction of the Temple in 70 AD, for there were much more terrible times to come than those of the Jewish War of 66–73 AD.

At the beginning of His discourse, the Lord Jesus mentioned five different birth pains, which He designates as "*the beginning of birth pains*." Afterwards there will follow a massive persecution of those who believe in Him, connected with a massive falling away from faith. These are the birth pains:

1. large-scale war
2. revolutions
3. famines
4. epidemics
5. earthquakes

*Afterwards*: persecution of Christians
*Afterwards*: apostasy

Matthew 24:6-9:
"⁶ *And ye shall hear of **wars and rumours of wars**: see that ye be not troubled: for all these things must come to pass, but the end is not yet.* ⁷ *For **nation shall rise against nation, and kingdom against kingdom**: and there shall be **famines**, and **pestilences**, and **earthquakes**, in divers places.* ⁸ *All these are the **beginning of sorrows**.* ⁹ *Then shall they **deliver you up to be afflicted, and shall kill you**: and ye shall be hated of all nations for my name's sake.*" (KJV)

---

409 BABYLONIAN TALMUD, Shabbat 118a and Sanhedrin 98b.

In the parallel passages in Luke and Mark, in addition to Matthew, the sign of *"revolutions"* or *"popular uprisings"* are mentioned:

Luke 21:9-11:
*"⁹ But when ye shall hear of **wars and commotions** [Greek akatastasiai], be not terrified: for these things must first come to pass; but the end is not by and by. ¹⁰ Then said he unto them, **Nation shall rise against nation**, and **kingdom against kingdom**: ¹¹ And **great earthquakes** shall be in divers places, and **famines**, and **pestilences**; and fearful sights and great signs shall there be from heaven."* (KJV)

Mark 13:8:
*"⁸ For **nation shall rise against nation**, and **kingdom against kingdom**: and there shall be **earthquakes** in divers places, and there shall be **famines** and **troubles** [Greek tarachai]: these are the beginnings of sorrows."* (KJV)

In Chapter 1 of this book we have seen that the Jews' return to the Land of their Forefathers from all five continents, an important event in the history of the world, fundamentally defines The Last Days. It follows that the term "Last Days" must be applied quite specifically from 1882 onwards, the year when the first waves of Jewish immigration began If the first five pains in Jesus' Last Days Discourse are called *"the beginning of birth pains,"* then it had to be expected in earlier times that someday in the initial period of Jewish immigration there would be large-scale wars, revolutions, famines, epidemics and earthquakes.

## 3.4 Large-scaleWars
In 1914, the assassination of an heir apparent in the Balkans occurred. Who at that time could have foreseen what a catastrophe this crime would unleash? This event initiated a fatal chain of events. Thus the First World War ultimately broke out, which would last until 1918.

Why do we call this war, this large-scale war the *"First* World

War" instead of, for example, the "27th World War"? It is very simple: In the years 1914–1918 the phenomenon of a world war occurred for the first time in world history which affected all five continents, together with the world's oceans! This was a period of large-scale wars, just as the Lord had described in His discourse: *"nation shall rise against nation, and kingdom against kingdom."*

The geographic extent of this conflict is indicated by the sentence *"And ye shall hear of wars and rumours of wars."* The wars of which one would *hear* would take place near to the hearer, whereas *rumours of wars*, on the other hand, have to do with distant battles.

For the first time in history chemical weapons of mass destruction were used in abundance during the First World War. Altogether this eruption of human madness cost some 17 million lives![410]

Isn't it striking that a few years after the beginning of the first Aliya, the worst large-scale war up to that time in human history erupted?

Following the end of the war, people worldwide took comfort in the decision never again to allow such a catastrophe to reoccur. To this effect the League of Nations was founded at that time which was to actively prevent another similar catastrophe from happening.

Nevertheless, a few years later, the phenomenon of a war affecting all the continents occurred a second time in human history, in an escalation of evil never before known. Nuclear weapons were used for the first time. The war during 1939–1945, would cost some 50–70 million lives.[411]

But this is not the end of it: Dozens of millions of people have been destroyed again in numerous further wars since then.[412]

---

410 http://de.wikipedia.org/wiki/Erster_Weltkrieg (as of: 25.10. 2011).

411 http://de.wikipedia.org/wiki/Zweiter_Weltkrieg (as of: 25.10.2011).

412 http://de.wikipedia.org/wiki/Liste_von Kriegen#20._Jahrhundert (as of: 25.10.2011).

# First World War

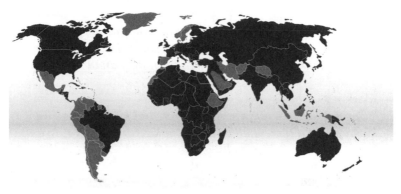

*Fig. 27: The dark areas show all the countries which took part in the First World War (source: Wkipedia, Thomas Hwang, GNU 1.2 or later).*

# Second World War

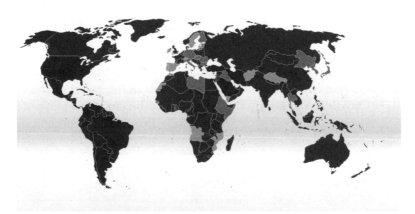

*Fig. 28: The light areas show all the countries which did not take part in the Second World War (source: Wikipedia, GNU 1.2 or later).*

## 3.5 Revolutions

Luke 21:9:
*"⁹ But when ye shall hear of wars and **commotions [revolutions]** [Greek akatastasiai], be not terrified: for these things must first come to pass; but the end is not by and by."* (KJV)

Mark 13:8:
*"⁸ For nation shall rise against nation, and kingdom against kingdom: and there shall be earthquakes in divers places, and there shall be famines and **troubles** [Greek akatastasiai]: these are the beginnings of sorrows."* (KJV)

The Greek word *akatastasiai* translated in Luke 21:9 by "commotions/revolutions" also means "popular uprisings", "insurrections" or "tumults."

The expression *tarachai* used in the parallel passage of Mark 13:8 can also be rendered "mass disorders" as well as "sedition", "confusion", "agitation" or "revolutions."

Of course, there have always been revolutions in human history. One may think of the French Revolution or the Glorious Revolution in England, etc. But we want to especially consider revolutions which have occurred beginning in 1882, in the period of the Jews' return. Then it will be clear that this epoch is both the period of the most numerous and the most geographically encompassing revolutions in world history! A prime reason for this lies in the person of Karl Marx (1818–1883), who, in the 19th century, drew up a theory of revolution which led to terrible upheavals in the 20th century.

- Only a few years after the First Aliya began, the Philippine Revolution took place: 1896–1898. This was an uprising of the secret organization "Katipunan" against Spanish colonial rule.[413]
- The Constitutional Revolution occurred in Iran from 1905–1911.[414]

---

413 http://de.wikipedia.org/wiki/Philippinische_Revolution (as of: 25.10.2011).
414 http://de.wikipedia.org/wiki/Konstitutionelle_Revolution_%28Iran%29 (as of: 25.10.2011).

- In the country from which caused the first waves of Jewish immigration there was an uprising against the czarist regime in 1905–1907. However, this brutally crushed so-called Russian Revolution ended without positive results for the impoverished masses. The czar was able to fully retain his military power in the end.
- At the time of the First Aliya, it was precisely in the Ottoman Empire, to which the land of the Jews' return, "Palestine," belonged, that the association of Young Turks was active from 1876 onwards. This led to a successful revolution in 1908 for these revolutionaries.[415]
- Mexico was plagued by serious rioting and bloody confrontations from 1910.[416] Not until 1920 did this country come to rest from this revolution.
- The Xinhai Revolution broke out in China on 10 October 1911.[417] It led to the end of the Qing Dynasty under the last Manchu emperor Pu Yi. The wave of riots led to the founding of the Chinese Republic on 1 February 1912. This was followed by numerous power struggles and uprisings which eventually led to the Chinese Civil War which would last from 1927–1949. In 1949 the communists seized power in mainland China, founding the People's Republic of China.[418] This resulted in more than 1 million deaths as well as epidemics, catastrophic famines, floods of refugees and terrible devastation. Beginning in 1966, Mao Zedong spurred on the masses to a so-called "Cultural Revolution" which continued until his death in 1976, allowing the Communist state to purge ideological opponents. China was plunged into unspeakably bloody chaos with more than 1 million deaths. Millions of people were injured, denounced and humiliated.[419]
- In Russia, the revolution of 1905–1907 did not achieve the goal it strove for at that time. However, in 1917 there was the

---

415 http://de.wikipedia.org/wiki/Jungt%C3%BCrkische_Revolution (as of: 25.10.2011).

416 http://de.wikipedia.org/wiki/Mexikanische_Revolution (as of: 25.10.2011).

417 http://de.wikipedia.org/wiki/Chinesische_Revolution (as of: 25.10.2011).

418 http://de.wikipedia.org/wiki/Chinesischer_B%C3%BCrgerkrieg (as of: 25.10.2011).

419 http://www.wpluta.de/work/china/kr.htm (as of: 25.10.2011).

February Revolution.[420] This led to the end of czarist rule in Russia. The impoverished and hungry nation was able to overthrow the government of Nicholas II.

- Yet with the 1917 October Revolution the liberal government, which had been installed in the meantime, was overthrown by the Communist Bolsheviks.[421] A terrible civil war followed, lasting until 1920 and costing some 8 million lives.[422] Thus, finally in 1922, the USSR was established as a cruel dictatorship over millions and millions of people.
- In 1916–1918 the Arabs in the Ottoman Empire, with the support of the Western Powers, rebelled against their Turkish rulers. This is known as the Arab Revolt.[423]
- In 1918 Hungary won independence from Austria through the Aster Revolution.[424]
- In Germany, as a result of the immense burden of First World War, the November Revolution took place in 1918–1919. This involved the entire Reich and eventually led to the abolition of the Empire.[425]

The epoch of the Jews' return from all over the world was an age of revolution exceeding all earlier periods regarding number, territorial expanse, number affected (hundreds of millions of people, if the Communist revolutions in Russia as well as China alone are considered) and level of violence. It is clear that a large number of revolutions are related to Marxism and Islam. The following list with dozens of revolutions in the period from 1882 until the present amazingly documents the fulfillment of Jesus' prophecy on the Mount of Olives concerning revolutions and popular uprisings.[426]

1. Philippine Revolution 1896–1898

---

420 http://de.wikipedia.org/wiki/Februarrevolution_1917 (as of: 25.10.2011).

421 http://de.wikipedia.org/wiki/Oktoberrevolution (as of: 25.10.2011).

422 http://de.wikipedia.org/wiki/Russischer_B%C3%BCrgerkrieg (as of: 25.10.2011).

423 http://de.wikipedia.org/wiki/Arabische_Revolte (as of: 25.10.2011).

424 http://de.wikipedia.org/wiki/Asternrevolution (as of: 25.10.2011).

425 http://de.wikipedia.org/wiki/Novemberrevolution (as of: 25.10.2011).

426 http://de.wikipedia.org/wiki/Umsturz (as of: 25.10.2011).

2. Constitutional Revolution in Iran 1905–1911
3. Russian Revolution 1905–1907
4. Young Turkish revolution in the Ottoman Empire in 1908
5. Mexican Revolution in 1910 and subsequent years
6. Chinese Revolution (Xinhai Revolution) 1911/1912
7. Arab Revolt 1916–1918
8. February Revolution in Russia in 1917
9. October Revolution in Russia in 1917
10. November Revolution in Germany 1918/1919, including the Soviet Republics in Bavaria (Munich Soviet Republic) and Bremen (Bremen Soviet Republic)
11. The Aster Revolution of 1918 in Hungary
12. The libertarian revolution in Spain 1936–1939
13. The Great Arab Revolt (1936–1939)
14. August Revolution in Vietnam in 1945
15. Cuban Revolution 1956–1959
16. Hungarian uprising in 1956
17. Zanzibar Revolution, 1964 (Zanzibar = Tanzania)
18. Cultural Revolution in the People's Republic of China 1966–1976
19. Cultural Revolution of 1968 in the U.S. and Europe
20. Carnation Revolution in Portugal in 1974
21. Revolution in Laos in 1975
22. Nicaraguan Revolution in 1979
23. Islamic Revolution in Iran in 1979
24. First Intifada in Israel 1987–1993
25. Romanian Revolution of 1989
26. The revolution in Bulgaria, 1989
27. The Velvet Revolution of 1989 in Czechoslovakia
28. The peaceful revolution in GDR 1989/1990
29. The Singing Revolution in the Baltic states (Estonia, Latvia and Lithuania) 1987–1991
30. The Bolivarian Revolution in Venezuela since 1999
31. Second Intifada in Israel (2001–2005)
32. The Rose Revolution in Georgia in 2003
33. The Orange Revolution in Ukraine in 2004
34. The Tulip Revolution in Kyrgyzstan in 2005

35. The Cedar Revolution in Lebanon in 2005
36. The Jasmine Revolution in Tunisia 2010/2011
37. The revolution in Egypt in 2011
38. Revolution and civil war in Libya in 2011
39. Revolution in Yemen in 2011
40. Revolution in Syria in 2011

In 2011 there were also revolutionary mass protests in Algeria, Bahrain, Iraq, Oman, Iran, Djibouti, Kuwait, Lebanon, Mauritania, Morocco, Saudi Arabia, Western Sahara and Sudan. The so-called "Arab Spring," which has drawn the attention of the whole world has, in fact, great significance for The Last Days. However, it must be seen in regard to the entire list of revolutions since the end of the 19th century.

As well as the revolutions and uprisings already mentioned, there is still a lot more: In the timeframe from 1882–1922 alone there were some 70 revolutions and uprisings altogether, and from 1882–2012 more than 334.[427]

## 3.6 Famines

When looking at the prophecy "... *and there shall be famines, and pestilences, and earthquakes, in divers places*" in Matthew 24:7, we must first of all examine the difference between *acute* and *chronic famine*.

Acute famines occur as a result of wars, unrest or catastrophes. In these circumstances, people often have nothing, or barely anything to eat.

Chronic hunger is the problem of ongoing malnutrition of poor sections of the population. The people do actually have something to eat, but too little to be able to remain healthy.

Acute famines occurred in many countries as a result of the First World War and the Second World War. Masses of people had nothing to eat anymore and perished because of the results of hunger. In connection with both the world wars in which the large part of the directly affected world population suffered from

---

427 http://en.wikipedia.org/wiki/List_of_revolutions_and_rebellions (as of: 30.4.2012).

lack of nutrition, the following catastrophic famines are listed as representative of others:[428]

- 1916–1918: Famine in Lebanon: 100,000 deaths (nearly ¼ of the region's population)
- 1944–1945: Famine in Vietnam during Japanese occupation: 600,000–2 million victims
- 1941–1944: The siege of Stalingrad: some 1 million people died of hunger
- 1943–1944: Great famine in Bengal – worsened by British-Indian conflict in the region: 4 million dead[429]
- 1944/1945: *Hongerwinter* ("Hunger Winter") in the Netherlands
- 1946/1947: "Hunger Winter" in Germany

Furthermore, since the time of the First Aliya and excluding of the years of the two world wars, the following acute famines have occurred:

### China:

- 1892–1894: Famine: 1 million dead
- 1896–1897: Famine: 5 million dead
- 1920–1921: Famine in North China: 500,000 dead
- 1928–1929: Famine: 10 million dead.
- 1959–1961: Famine due to the "Great Leap Forward." This was triggered by a Communist social experiment which resulted in the deaths of 30–43 million people. It was undoubtedly the largest acute famine disaster in human history!

### India:

- 1876–1878: Famine with 5 million dead
- 1896–1897 and 1899–1902: Famine with 100 million people affected; estimates vary greatly over the number dead, perhaps up to 11 million
- 1966 famine in Bihar

---

428  http://de.wikipedia.org/wiki/Hungersnot (as of: 25.10.2011); http://fr.wikipedia.org/wiki/Famine (as of: 25.10.2011).

429  http://en.wikipedia.org/wiki/List_of_wars_and_disasters_by_death_toll (as of: 25.10.2011).

**Africa:**

- 1899: Famine in Central Kenya: 50-90% of the population died.[430]
- 1967–1970: Biafra and Nigeria (triggered by the Biafra war), more than 1 million dead
- 1968–1974: Famine in the Sahel, 1 million dead
- 1973: Famine in Ethiopia
- 1984–1985: Famine in Ethiopia and also in several countries of the Sahel, more than 1 million dead
- 1990–1995: Famine in Somalia (causes: drought and civil war)
- 1990s: Famine in Southern Sudan (cause: civil war)
- 2000: Famine in Zimbabwe
- 2003: Famine in Darfur/Sudan (cause: Darfur conflict)
- 2005: Food crisis in Niger, more than 100,000 dead
- 2006: Food crisis in Ethiopia, northeastern Kenya, Somalia and Djibouti

**Tibet/Vietnam/North Korea**

- 1954: Famine in Tibet (due to failed communist planning)
- 1980s: Vietnam
- 1990s: Famine in North Korea, 1-2 million dead

**Russia:**

- 1891–1892: Russian famine, about 2 million dead (along the Volga, in the Urals, and in regions to the Black Sea)
- 1921: Russian famine, about 5 million dead (particularly in the areas of the Volga and the Urals)
- 1932–1933: Soviet famine, 6-17 million dead.[431] (The collectivization of agriculture under Stalin resulted in catastrophic shortages in many largely agrarian parts of the Soviet Union. Particularly hard-hit was Ukraine. This famine of this time in Ukraine has become known infamously as the "Holodomor.")[432]

---

430 http://de.wikipedia.org/wiki/Hungersnot_in_Zentralkenia_1899 (as of: 25.10.2011).

431 http://en.wikipedia.org/wiki/List_of_wars_and_disasters_by_death_toll (as of: 25.10.2011).

432 http://de.wikipedia.org/wiki/Holodomor (as of: 25.10.2011).

Added to this is chronic world hunger:[433] The Earth's population increased from 1.6 billion people in 1900 to 6.3 billion in the year 2000. Today (autumn of 2011) we have reached 7 billion. This development is directly related to the unique problem of famine in the last decades, which has caused the deaths of hundreds of millions of people. There would be enough food to feed everyone, more than enough. But, because of injustice, selfishness, corruption and serious mismanagement in politics and economics, unimaginable amounts of food are wasted each year and do not reach those who need it so desperately. 1.3 billion tons of food, about one-third of global food production per annum, is destroyed![434] About half of the total spoils on the way from producer to customer. Meanwhile, every day 26,000 children aged 0-5 years die of malnutrition.[435]

The number of hungry people has risen in past years. In 1990, the number was 822 million. Today it is 1 billion![436] For decades now, millions have been dying yearly from hunger. This is a most painful woe of The Last Days!

## 3.7 Pestilences

The Greek word *loimoi* translated in Matthew 24:7 and Luke 21:11 as *"pestilences"* means: plagues, epidemics or illnesses.

A list with an important selection of epidemics in the period from 1882 until today shows the devastating fulfilment of prophecy regarding this in the Olivet Discourse (Matt. 24:7):

*"7... and there shall be famines, and **pestilences** ... **in divers places.**"* (KJV)

- The Russian Flu of 1889/1890 cost approximately 1 million lives.[437] It spread rapidly throughout Russia, Europe, and Asia as well as in North and Latin America.

---

433  http://de.wikipedia.org/wiki/Welthunger (as of: 25.10.2011).

434  http://www.pt-magazin.de/newsartikel/datum/2011/10/06/gegen-den-hunger-auf-der-welt.html (as of: 20.10.2011).

435  AZ (Argauer Zeitung), 17 Oct. 2011, p. 1.

436  http://de.wikipedia.org/wiki/Welthunger (as of: 24.11.2011).

437  http://en.wikipedia.org/wiki/Influenza_A_virus_subtype_H2N2#Russian_flu (as of: 25.10.2011).

- The so-called "Third Plague Pandemic" in history,[438] which occurred in 1896–1945, killed a total of about 12 million people.[439]
- The "Sixth Cholera Epidemic" in world history caused more than 800,000 deaths worldwide (India, Middle East, North Africa, Eastern Europe, Russia, etc.) in the years 1899–1923.[440]
- Towards the end of the First World War, in June 1918, the pandemic "Spanish Influenza" broke out.[441] It expanded in several waves until December 1920. The name stems from the circumstances that it was reported for the first time in Spain. This disaster was triggered by a virulent derivative of the influenza virus. This pestilence brought death to millions and millions of people. No one knows the exact number of victims. We have to reckon with 50-100 million deaths. Most of the victims were healthy young adults. This plague spread throughout the world, infecting more than a quarter of the world's population (27%), about 500 million people. It was one of the worst epidemics in history. By comparison, the devastating Bubonic Plague of the 14th century, which is buried deep in the westerner's historical memory, snatched away some 25 million people in Europe (1/3 of the population).[442] Numerically, however, there were significantly fewer affected victims than with Spanish Flu. In contrast to history's previous pandemics, Spanish Flu affected the entire world, all five continents, and even reached some very remote areas like the Pacific Islands and the Arctic.[443]
- The Russian Typhoid Epidemic of 1918–1922 affected 25 million people and caused 3.5 million deaths.[444]
- The pandemic Asian Flu killed between 1 and 4 million people

---

438  The First Plague Pandemic: 581–8th century; the Second Plague Pandemic: 1347–1352.

439  http://de.wikipedia.org/wiki/Pandemie (as of: 25.10.2011).

440  http://en.wikipedia.org/wiki/Sixth_cholera_pandemic (as of: 25.10.2011).

441  http://en.wikipedia.org/wiki/1918_flu_pandemic (as of: 25.10.2011).

442  Cf. SULGER BÜEL: Der schwarze Tod.

443  http://en.wikipedia.org/wiki/1918_flu_pandemic (as of: 25.10.2011).

444  http://en.wikipedia.org/wiki/Pandemic (as of: 25.10.2011).

during the years 1956–1958.[445]

- The so-called Hong Kong Flu raged from 1968–1969. It led to a worldwide death toll of some 800,000-2 million.[446]
- The Russian Flu of 1977–1978 took about 700,000 lives.[447]
- The AIDS virus was diagnosed for the first time in 1981.[448] The pandemic caused by this pathogen is one of the most destructive epidemics in recorded history. The death toll is now estimated at 37 million.[449] It is assumed that the number of those living today, who are suffering from AIDS, is over 33 million. About 2.6 million become infected each year. The death rate per year is at 1.8 million.
- The highly contagious smallpox disease was responsible for the deaths of 300 million to half a billion people in the 20th century![450] Thus, this disease was several times more catastrophic than the Spanish Flu. The deaths continued over many years, even into the 1980s. In the 1950s about 50 million people were infected every year with smallpox. In each case a large proportion proved fatal.
- Tuberculosis carried off some 100 million people in the 20th century.[451] Today, some 2 million people still die of tuberculosis yearly.
- Over the past 150 years, measles, a highly contagious disease, is estimated to have caused 200 million deaths worldwide.[452]
- Worldwide today, approximately 500 million people suffer with hepatitis B or hepatitis C.[453] Thus, every 12th person on our planet is affected by this devastating disease. Every year about 1.5 million die from this plague.
- The World Lung Foundation's Tobacco Atlas published the

445 http://en.wikipedia.org/wiki/Influenza_A_virus_subtype_H2N2#Asian_flu (as of: 25.10.2011).

446 http://en.wikipedia.org/wiki/Hong_Kong_flu ; http://de.wikipedia.org/wiki/Hongkong-Grippe (as of: 25.10.2011).

447 http://de.wikipedia.org/wiki/Pandemie (as of: 25.10.2011).

448 http://en.wikipedia.org/wiki/HIV/AIDS_pandemic (as of: 25.10.2011).

449 http://de.wikipedia.org/wiki/Pandemie (as of: 25.10.2011).

450 http://en.wikipedia.org/wiki/Pandemic (as of: 25.10.2011).

451 http://en.wikipedia.org/wiki/Pandemic (as of: 25.10.2011).

452 http://en.wikipedia.org/wiki/Pandemic (as of: 25.10.2011).

453 http://en.wikipedia.org/wiki/World_Hepatitis_Day (as of: 25.10.2011).

following shocking figures, accepted by the WHO, in connection with the plague of nicotin addiction:[454] During the 20th century smoking addiction caused 100 million deaths! If present trends continue, 1 billion deaths due to smoking are predicted for the 21st century.

## 3.8 Earthquakes

A horrifying list of some 140 major earthquakes in the 20th century documents the fulfilment of Luke 21:11 and the parallel verses in the other synoptic Gospels:[455]

*"11 ... and **great earthquakes** shall be in divers places, ..."* (KJV)

Throughout the 20th century, earthquake catastrophes claimed well over 2 million lives and caused an even greater number of injuries.

Of course, there have always been earthquakes.[456] All of human history is filled with such events, but there have never been so many people on earth as there are today. The world's population has grown from 1.6 billion in 1900 to 7 billion today (autumn 2011). Therefore, on the basis of population statistics alone, earthquakes are altogether incomparably more devastating than in previous eras. In Jesus' time, the world population is estimated to have been only about 300 million.

Moreover, there is the fact that areas of the world especially vulnerable to earthquakes are, in general, very heavily populated.

Furthermore, most of the affected areas are particularly poor regions where money for technical improvements in constructing earthquake-safe architecture is lacking. The number of deaths from earthquakes in the 19th century was exceeded by four times during the 20th century. The number of victims of the earthquake of 1976 alone probably exceeds the sum total of earthquake deaths

---

454  http://www.tobaccoatlas.org/downloads/TA3-ChineseFactSheet.pdf; http://www.hilfreich.de/raucher-sterben-frueher_2756 (as of: 24.11.2011).

455  http://en.wikipedia.org/wiki/List_of_20th-century_earthquakes; http://it.wikipedia.org/wiki/Lista_di_terremoti_del_XX_secolo; http://de.wikipedia.org/wiki/Liste_von_Erdbeben (as of: 25.10.2011).

456  Cf. in the Bible for example: Job 34:20; Amos 1:1; Zech. 14:5; etc.

throughout the entire 19th century.[457]

The following are the most devastating or most significant earthquakes of The Last Days from 1882 until the present:

- The Ottoman Empire (in Ayvalik, Urla, Chesma), 1883: 15,000 dead
- Iran, 1893: 18,000 dead
- Iran, 1885: 11,000 dead
- Japan, 1896: 27,000 dead
- India, 1905: 20,000 dead
- United States (San Francisco), 1906: more than 3,000 dead, up to 300,000 people lost their homes (¾ of the city), in one of the greatest natural disasters in U.S. history[458]
- Messina/Sicily/Calabria, 1908: 72,000–110,000 dead (varied data given for victims; earthquake *and* tsunami)
- Italy, 1915: 30,000 dead
- China, 1920: 200,000 dead (earthquake of Hayuan)
- Japan, 1923: 143,000 deaths ("Big Kanto Earthquake", earthquake and tsunami with 12 meter-high waves)
- China, 1927: 41,000 dead (earthquake in Gansu)
- Baluchistan (now Pakistan), 1935: 30,000 dead
- Chile, 1939: 28,000 dead
- Turkey, 1939: 32,700 dead
- Turkmenistan, 1948: 110,000 dead (NOAA reports a lower number of victims)
- Peru, 1970: 66,800 dead
- China, 1976: Unofficially to 800,000 dead (The Chinese Communist regime spoke of "only" 242,000 victims. Many experts believe that the number published by the Chinese government was falsified. China refused all foreign aid at that time.) The Tangshan earthquake made 5.3 million houses uninhabitable. This could well have been the most devastating earthquake to date in world history!
- Iran, 1978: 25,000 dead
- Mexico, 1985: unofficially 30,000 dead (government: c. 10,000)

---

457 http://de.wikipedia.org/wiki/Liste_von_Erdbeben (as of: 24.11.2011).

458 http://en.wikipedia.org/wiki/1906_San_Francisco_earthquake (as of: 24.10.2011).

- Armenia, 1988: 25,000 dead (1 million homeless)
- Iran, 1990: 40,000-50,000 dead (½ million homeless)
- Iran, 2003: more than 31,000 dead[459]
- Indonesia, Thailand, India, Maldives, etc., 2004: 243,000 dead
- Pakistan, 2005: over 87,000 dead
- China, 2008: 87,600 dead
- Haiti, 2010: 316,000 dead

## 3.9 Afterwards: Persecution of Christians

Subsequent to the five birth pains we have just examined (large-scale wars, revolutions, pestilence, famines and earthquakes), Jesus warned of massive persecution of Christians (Matt. 24:9):

*"⁹ **Then** shall they deliver you up to **be afflicted**, and shall **kill** you: and ye shall **be hated of all nations** for my name's sake."* (KJV)

And this has been fulfilled precisely: The Last Days began in 1882, as the Jews began to return home en mass to the Land of their Fathers. Afterwards, during the following years, all five of these birth pains occurred in a striking way. Pertaining to these were, among others, the First World War, famines claiming millions of deaths in China, Russia, India and Africa, the Russian Revolution of 1905, the Communist October Revolution (1917); the Spanish Flu (1918–1920) and the especially destructive earthquakes of Messina/Sicily/Calabria (1908) and China (1920).

The exact chronological order must be observed absolutely: *First of all* there would be these five birth pains, and *then* extensive persecution of Christians with affliction, death and hatred would follow. Apostasy en masse would come as a result of this oppression.

The Soviet Union was founded in December 1922. This state was the first in world history to pursue the goal of elimination of religion as ideology. From the 1920s on the Communists had already

---

459 http://de.wikipedia.org/wiki/Liste_von_Erdbeben_des_21._Jahrhunderts (as of: 24.10.2001).

set the elimination of Christianity as one of their goals.[460] Hatred and persecution of Christians had been practiced by the Bolsheviks earlier during the civil war. With the founding of the Soviet Union, however, this objective was thoroughly pursued over the following decades in the whole of its immense domain. The brutal and cruel execution of this plan by modern atheists led to millions of deaths. The only fault of these people was that they held fast to the Christian faith.[461]

The Soviet regime also pursued an unprecedented and ruthless campaign to re-educate people as atheists under their rule, with particular focus on young people and children. Atheism was proclaimed and propagated as "the only scientific truth." The schools were misused as re-education centres. Christians were systematically ridiculed, mocked, harassed and subject to discrimination. But that was just the bearable minimum. Christians were also executed, tortured, as well as detained both in prisons and in work camps. Some were emotionally wrecked by medication in psychiatric institutes. The Soviet Union extended its persecution of Christians to other Communist states in Eastern Europe. This persecution of Christians, which can be divided into different phases historically, continued until the dissolution of the Soviet Union in December 1991.

The free world knew about this systematic persecution of Christians in Communist countries. However, it was never a real issue in western politics. This catastrophe was mostly ignored and abandoned the Christians to the cruelty of these atheistic regimes of injustice. In the Communist hatred and the indifference of the free world the word *"...and ye shall be **hated of all nations for my name's sake**"* was fulfilled.

As the Communists came to power in China in 1949, here, too, began a terrible history of decades-long persecution of Christians.

The persecution by the Communists has affected a significant portion of humanity altogether. It surpassed all earlier persecu-

---

460 http://en.wikipedia.org/wiki/Persecution_of_Christians (as of: 24.10.2011).

461 http://en.wikipedia.org/wiki/Persecution_of_Christians_in_Warsaw_Pact_countries (as of: 24.10.2011).

tion of Christians in extent and organization. Certainly, Christians have been persecuted throughout their entire 2,000-year history. It began with the persecution of Jesus' disciples by Orthodox Judaism and was continued brutally by the Roman Empire up until the change in the 4th century under Constantine. In later centuries there were countless persecutions by Islam and by the Inquisition of the Roman Catholic Church. The storms long ago in Church history were terrible. For 2,000 years countless Christian martyrs have been killed. However, Christian persecution in the 20th century exceeds everything that happened in the past.[462] Here, again, the truth of the Word is confirmed, *"... and ye shall be hated of all nations for my name's sake."*

National Socialists under Adolf Hitler from 1933–1945 and likewise the countries dominated by Islam worldwide have joined the leading role played by the atheistic Communists during the 20th century. According to statistics from Open Doors mission organization, 80-120 million Christians are being persecuted worldwide today.[463] Islam has been primarily responsible for this worldwide since the demise of the Soviet Union.

### 3.10 Afterwards: Apostasy from God en masse

Due to the systematic persecution of Christianity by the Communists in the East and by the unprecedented, decades-long atheistic campaign, in the Soviet Union and in socialist Eastern Europe millions of once professing Christians fell from the Christian faith. This is exactly what the Lord Jesus foretold in His Olivet Discourse. Due to the persecution of Christians, there would be apostasy en masse (Matt. 24:9-10):

> *"⁹ Then shall they deliver you up to be afflicted, and shall kill you: and ye shall be hated of all nations for my name's sake. ¹⁰* **And then shall many be offended, and shall betray one another, and shall hate one another.**" (KJV)

---

462  http://www.factum-magazin.ch/wFactum_de/aktuell/2011_10_06_Mord.php (as of: 25.10.2011).

463  http://en.wikipedia.org/wiki/Persecution_of_Christians (as of: 25.10.2011).

Let the chronological order be noted in verse 10: "¹⁰ **And then** ...*" First this – in the sequence of the five signs of the beginning of birth pains – there would be massive persecution. Afterwards mass apostasy would follow.

The Greek verb *skandalizomai* translated by "*be offended*" also means "to stumble", "to fall" and "to fall away [from the faith]" or just "to abandon [the faith]."[464]

The rulers of Communist states had chosen the following course of action in their strategy for the destruction of Christianity: Their secret services would work with the population. Members of the Communist society were to betray and hand over one another underhandedly. Over the years and decades this course of action destroyed normal interpersonal trust. No-one could be sure, for example, whether the friendly neighbour who always greeted you so nicely in the morning was not an informer and co-operating with the KGB, the Securitate (Romanian secret police), the Stasi (East German secret police) or whatever secret intelligence agency it might be. Teachers at school, colleagues in the workplace, or friends and acquaintances were also potential informers. All this was prophetically foretold in Matthew 24:10.

Even within a family no-one could be certain as to whether someone was working as a informer and a betrayer of the family members. The Communists did not even hold back from breaking in to the family with its methods and destroying the closest family relationships. The Lord prophesied this in Mark 13:12:

*"¹² Now the brother shall betray the brother to death, and the father the son; and children shall rise up against their parents, and shall cause them to be put to death."* (KJV)

---

464 BAUER: Wörterbuch zum Neuen Testament; Sp. 1504; cf. also Standard-Greek Dictionary on the Bible Works CD 8.0.

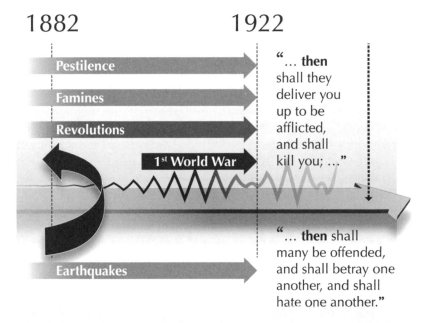

## "The Beginning of Birth Pains..."

1882              1922

Pestilence

Famines

Revolutions

1st World War

Earthquakes

"... **then** shall they deliver you up to be afflicted, and shall kill you; ..."

"... **then** shall many be offended, and shall betray one another, and shall hate one another."

*Fig. 29: Following the "beginning of birth pains" from 1882–1922, mass persecution of Christians began in the Soviet Union. This triggered a mass falling away, together with spying and betrayal.*

### 3.11 Voluntary Apostasy in the West

While the Marxists during 20th century in the East used violence to turn the masses from God and His Word, the Bible, something extraordinary happened at the same time in the free West: millions of people, who earlier had made a Christian profession, turned away from God and His Word totally voluntarily. This has been especially so since *the 1968 Cultural Revolution*, which, seen ideologically, constituted one of the profoundest decisive points in Western history. While before this time Christian values had been part of society's general consensus, with Biblical ethics and a certain fear of God shaping daily life, this was thrown overboard en masse following the Neo-Marxist Revolution of 1968. Those who hold Biblical values today must often reckon with ridicule, ostracism and caustic "pity."

In 2 Thessalonians 2, the Apostle Paul predicted the great apostasy of The Last Days, prior to Christ's return and also before the coming of the Antichrist:

> "³ ... for that Day [i.e. the day of the return of the reigning Messiah] will not come unless **the falling away**⁴⁶⁵ comes first, ..."
> (NKJV)

This prophecy encompasses the coerced apostasy in the East, according to Matthew 24:10, as well as the voluntary apostasy in the West.

Paul expressed this voluntary apostasy, as it was fulfilled in the West, in 2 Timothy 4, for example, with the following words:[466]

> "³ For the time will come when they will **not endure** sound doctrine; but **after their own lusts** shall they heap to themselves teachers, having itching ears; ⁴ **and they shall turn away their ears from the truth**, and shall be turned unto fables. ⁵ But watch thou in all things, endure afflictions, do the work of an evangelist, make full proof of thy ministry." (KJV)

Other passages also speak about this voluntary falling away, Luke 17:26-30, 2 Peter 2 and 3, as well as in Jude, for example.

This great apostasy of the West is also related to the rise of *liberal, Bible-critical theology* which generally permeated theological education in the universities during the 20th century, with Bible Criticism (denial of the inspiration and divine authority of the Bible), denial of the divinity of Christ and the saving effect of His substitutionary death on the cross, denial of the resurrection and return of Jesus Christ, etc. This resulted in an inner erosion of Christianity which was an ideal prerequisite for the seduction '68.

---

465 Greek apostasia = apostasy, abandon, departure, separation, give up, insurrection, rebellion.

466 Note that 2 Timothy 3:1, in the context of the letter, clearly refers to The Last Days.

It must be assumed that a large percentage of pastors in the Evangelical Reformed Church and the Evangelical Lutheran Church no longer believe that the Bible is God's Word. Additionally, many no longer believe in the resurrection of Jesus Christ or in their own personal resurrection. Some even doubt life after death. These revealing conclusions were brought clearly to light by a survey a few years ago.

What can such people preach on a Sunday? What can they pass on during religious education in the schools? Why do such pastors remain in the church? Why don't they do something about it and publically admit that they are not Christians at all and are not standing on the foundation of the Gospel? Who can then be surprised that the masses have lost their belief in the Bible and its truth?

A third important influence, which must be mentioned absolutely in this regard, was *the theory of evolution* made popular among 19th century academics by Charles Darwin. Through its propagation in schools, universities and the media, the theory of evolution became commonplace in Western society during the 20th century.[467] Through this the masses were led to believe that, regarding the origins of the universe and life itself, a Creator could be dispensed with, and this only on alleged scientifically "proven" grounds. The significance of the theory of evolution to Last Days apostasy can scarcely be overestimated!

When Paul speaks in 2 Thessalonians 2:3 of the apostasy, which will pave the way for the Antichrist, the *"man of sin,"* it must be clear that apostasy always means a turning away from Biblical faith. Talk of *"apostasy"* does not relate to the regions of the world where the Gospel is known only to minorities, but rather, to the regions of our planet which have been formed and shaped by a Christian profession over a long historical process. Never before, in the 2,000-year history of Christianity, has there been voluntary mass apostasy. Christianity had always expanded. It had only been pushed back by persecution (cf. the history of Christian per-

---

467  For the intellectual context in connection to the theory of evolution, cf.: OUWENEEL: Evolution in der Zeitenwende. This work also contains a very thorough and extensive refutation of the theory of evolution.

secution through the rise of Islam in the 7th and 8th centuries.)[468]
The phenomenon of mass voluntary apostasy seen in Europe and
North America during the 20th century is a unique occurrence. But
the Bible had also foretold this for the time in which Jews from all
over the world would be returning home.

## 3.12 "But the End is Not Yet"

In relation to the first five birth pains of the Olivet Discourse it
must be clearly noted that the Lord Jesus Christ defined these as
*"the beginning of birth pains,"* by emphasizing that *"the end"* would
not come immediately.

> Matthew 24:6,8.
> *"6 And ye shall hear of wars and rumours of wars: see that ye be
> not troubled: for all these things must come to pass, **but the end
> is not yet.** ... 8 All these are **the beginning of sorrows.**"* (KJV)

> Luke 21:9:
> *"9 But when ye shall hear of wars and commotions, be not terri-
> fied: for these things must first come to pass; **but the end is not
> by and by.**"* (KJV)

Subsequent to the five initial birth pains, there would come
extensive persecution of Christians which was brutally fulfilled by
the rise of the Soviet Empire.

On the basis of the lists set out in the text above regarding the
fulfilment of the five initial birth pains it is necessary to particularly note the events from 1882–1922. The concurrence of all five
signs in such an extreme and dramatic way is remarkable for the
world of history! Precisely in this 40-year period, as the Jews began
to return to their Land after 2,000 years, there was a concentration
of all five birth pains. Note the relationship of all these separate
events! In this way, it will be clear that the events such as the ones
listed below correspond strictly to that which the Lord Jesus Christ
termed *"the beginning of birth pains"* in His Olivet Discourse.

---

468 Cf. the following extraordinarily informative and factual book: BAT YE'OR: The Decline of Eastern Christianity under Islam. From Jihad to Dhimmitude : seventh-twentieth century.

There are voices today which criticise preachers of earlier times, let us say c. 1920, for example, because they had then announced publicly that we would be living in The Last Days and that we should prepare ourselves for Christ's return. Well, these preachers of God's Word were not wrong. That period was, according to the Bible, already "The Last Days." But the Lord Jesus pointed out in His prophetic discourse on the Mount of Olives that *"the end"* i.e. the very end with the Antichrist's appearance, with the apocalyptic judgements during the last seven years[469] and the subsequent visible return of Jesus Christ as Judge of the world in power and glory (Rev. 6:1–19:21) must all be clearly separated from the *"beginning of birth pains."* "The end" had clearly not yet arrived with the signs which had been fulfilled as *"the beginning of birth pains"* in the 40 years from 1882–1922.

Considering all of this, it is helpful to look at an outline of the events listed together once again and see them in connection with one another as *"the beginning of birth pains"* and in full knowledge that *"the end"* was not to follow immediately:

1. **Large-scale Wars:**
   - The First World War (1914–1918): 17 million dead

2. **Revolutions:**
   - Philippine Revolution, 1896–1898
   - Constitutional Revolution in Iran,1905–1911
   - Russian Revolution, 1905–1907
   - Revolution of the Young Turks in the Ottoman Empire, 1908
   - Mexican Revolution, 1910 and subsequent years
   - Chinese Revolution (Xinhai Revolution), 1911/1912
   - Arab Revolt 1916–1918
   - February Revolution in Russia, 1917
   - October Revolution in Russia, 1917
   - November Revolution in Germany, 1918/1919
   - The Aster Revolution of 1918 in Hungary

---

469 The last 7 years before the return of Christ relates to Daniel's so-called 70th week (cf. Dan. 9:27; Rev. 11:2-3 [first half]; Rev. 13.5 [second half]).

### 3. Hunger
- Lebanon: 1916–1918: Famine in Lebanon, 100,000 deaths
- China:
  1892–1894: Famine, 1 million dead
  1896–1897: Famine, 5 million dead
  1920–1921: Famine in North China, 500,000 dead
- Russia:
  1891–1892: Russian famine, about 2 million dead
  1921: Russian famine, about 5 million dead
- India:
  1896–1897 and 1899–1902 great famine, 100 million affected; up to 11 million dead
- Africa:
  1899: Famine in Central Kenya, 50-90% of the population died

### 4. Epidemics
- "Third Plague Pandemic" of 1896–1945: 12 million dead
- The "Sixth Cholera Epidemic" of 1899–1923: more than 800,000 deaths
- The Russian Flu of 1889/1890: 1 million deaths[470]
- The Russian Typhoid Epidemic of 1918–1922: 25 million affected; 3.5 million dead
- Spanish Influenza, 1918–1920: 50-100 million dead

### 5. Earthquakes
- Ottoman Empire, 1883: 15,000 dead
- Iran, 1893: 18,000 dead
- Iran, 1885: 11,000 dead
- Japan, 1896: 27,000 dead
- India, 1905: 20,000 dead
- 1908: Messina/Sicily/Calabria: 72,000-110,000 dead
- Italy, 1915: 30,000 dead
- China, 1920: 200,000 dead

---

470 http://en.wikipedia.org/wiki/Influenza_A_virus_subtype_H2N2#Russian_flu (as of: 25.10.2011).

In this context I would like to direct the reader to consider the following: To some extent certain events were the direct result of an earlier birth pains-event, e.g. hunger as the result of a revolution or the world war. But among the events listed above, there are sufficient dramatic events of all the five birth pains which were independent from one another. Thus, for example, the Russian October Revolution was not absolutely necessarily a result of the First World War. It could have broken out without the war. The Spanish Flu was not a necessary consequence of the First World War. Most of the victims were not people with weakened immune systems (children or the elderly) as is normally the case in flu epidemics. The virus at that time was so amazingly virulent that it was the people with a well-functioning immune system who were the main victims in that the over-reaction of their immune system led to death.[471] The great famines in China and India before the First World War were not the result of revolutions or large-scale war. Yes, the famine in Lebanon (1916–1918) was a direct consequence of the World War. But such dependencies play a role only to a limited extent in all the events listed, through which the prophecy was fulfilled. The destructive earthquakes of 1882–1922, on the other hand, were events completely independent from the other four birth pains. Yet all of these five birth pains occurred, heavily concentrated within a clearly defined time frame of 40 years, and were followed chronologically by extreme Communist persecution of Christians and the associated, coerced mass apostasy in the East. This is an important point to consider for the probability calculation of prophecies given at the end of this book.

## 3.13 Concrete and Practical Commands

In Luke 21:28, the Lord Jesus Christ explicitly points out that the signs of the Olivet Discourse must be discerned well *right from the beginning*. Christians should comfort and convey real hope especially during a period of dark clouds and human uncertainty, because God will ultimately lead those who believe in Him to a wonderful completion:

---

471 http://en.wikipedia.org/wiki/1918_flu_pandemic (as of: 25.10.2011).

*"28 And when these things begin to come to pass, then look up, and lift up your heads; for your redemption[472] draweth nigh."* (KJV)

This verse makes it clear how important it was to observe the initial signs of the end already at the end of the 19th century and to include this in the preaching of the Word of God.

The parable of the fig tree following on from that underscores this thought again:

*"29 And he spoke to them a parable; Behold the fig tree, and all the trees; 30 When they now shoot forth, ye see and know of your own selves that summer is now nigh at hand. 31 So likewise ye, when ye see these things come to pass, know ye that the kingdom of God is nigh at hand."* (KJV)

These statements are very easy to understand: Just as in the land of the Bible, following the winter, from late January to early February, we are able to recognise that summer is at hand on account of the trees budding, so, too, we are able to recognise, with the help of the End-Time signs given in the Olivet Discourse, that Jesus Christ will soon appear as King of the world in order to establish the 1,000-year reign (Revelation 20). It should be noted at this point that there is a *command* given:

*"31 ..., **know ye** that the kingdom of God is nigh at hand."* (KJV)

Among all the trees, the *fig tree* is mentioned by name. Why? In Luke's Gospel, the fig tree had just been used as a picture of Israel in the parable in Chapter 13:6-9. The Lord is speaking here of His three years of public preaching (29–32 AD). During this period, God (*"the owner of the vineyard"*) seeks in vain among His people for fruit (repentance from sin, willingness to receive the Lord Jesus as Messiah). *"The dresser of his vineyard"* (the Holy Spirit)

---

472 In light of later revealed truth about the rapture in 1 Corinthians 15.51 ff. and 1 Thessalonians 4:13-18, it is clear that the Lord was pointing to His coming for the church with the term "redemption."

wanted to give the fig tree a special chance for *one more year*, "I shall dig about it, and dung it." This year speaks of the time from Pentecost in 32 AD until the stoning of Stephen (Acts 7). During this year, the Holy Spirit again provided Israel with a very special testimony through those filled by the Spirit (Acts 2–7). When the Sanhedrin had ultimately rejected Stephen's testimony, this window of opportunity closed. From that time on, the Gospel was not only preached to Israel, but also to the Gentiles (the non-Jews; Acts 8ff.). From that time on the word from Luke 13:9 applied:

*"⁹ And if it bear fruit, well: and if not, **then after that thou shalt cut it down.**"* (KJV)

In 70 AD Jerusalem and the Temple were razed. Sometime later, in 135 AD the Jewish state was completely destroyed.

In connection with The Last Days, the Lord spoke again of the fig tree in Luke 21. In the Olivet Discourse this budding fig tree allegorically symbolizes the clear Last Days signs which are associated with the return of the Jewish people to the Land of their Forefathers, beginning in 1882.

What do the *other* trees in the parable represent? These trees refer to the other, non-Jewish nations. Let it be noted how, at the same time as the Jews began to return to the Land of their Fathers, people groups, which had once played a large role in the Bible but in the meantime had moved into the background in world history, began to attain significance again after centuries or even millennia-long sleep. Let us think of Philistia, Egypt, Syria, Assyria, Arabia, for example.

The Lord Jesus did not just want to satisfy the curiosity of His disciples with His discourse about The Last Days. He actually answered all of their questions far beyond what they had wanted to know. Yet the Lord combined His teachings with important spiritual lessons and edifying, practical exhortations. It is well worth the Bible reader taking all the commands in Matthew 24, Mark 13 and Luke 21 accounts and asking oneself the question for each imperative, what this has to say personally to him/her.

Luke 21:34-36:

*"³⁴ But take **heed to yourselves**, lest at any time your hearts be weighed down with carousing⁴⁷³, drunkenness, and cares of this life, and that Day come upon you unexpectedly. ³⁵ For it will come as a snare on all those who dwell on the face of the whole earth. ³⁶ **Watch** therefore, **and pray always** that you may be counted worthy to escape all these things that will come to pass, and to stand before the Son of Man."* (NKJV)

These admonitions are highly relevant today: Warning against the misuse of drugs and alcohol, which obscure the sight to perceive the signs of the time and warning against being overwhelmed by day-to-day worries which also cloud one's perception, a call to spiritual alertness and a life of prayer in daily living fellowship with God.

## 3.14 False Prophets, Signs and Wonders

Readers from past centuries could know from the Olivet Discourse that in The Last Days, the period of the Jews' return to their homeland, there would be a major outbreak of false prophets who would perform great signs and wonders (Matt 24:11,24):

*"¹¹ And many false prophets shall rise, and shall deceive many.... ²⁴ For there shall arise false Christs, and **false prophets, and shall shew great signs and wonders**; insomuch that, if it were possible, they shall deceive the very elect."* (KJV)

It was precisely during Church history of the 20ᵗʰ century that there were three immense occurrences of false prophecy as well as signs and wonders, and in actual fact to a degree and with a widespread impact which overshadowed everything comparable in earlier centuries.

The first wave broke out in 1906 in Los Angeles, after a precursor which occurred in a Topeka Bible school in 1910, with phenomena such as babbling tongues, false prophecy and uncon-

---

473 Greek *kraipale* = exuberance in intoxication, dizziness, giddiness, light-headedness. The word refers to both the noise and the unpleasant effects of intoxication.

trolled falling. This awakening spread rapidly and was hurriedly brought to Europe. Thus, the so-called Pentecostal movement was born resulting in the establishment of many new churches. From the very beginning this development was not only characterized by healing and speaking in tongues, but also by false prophecy.

In the 1960s the Charismatic movement emerged with the same typical characteristics as those of the first wave. But this movement was not satisfied with the founding of new churches. Rather, the goal was to charismatically "renew" and "leaven" the existing churches. So, this awakening penetrated not only countless independent churches, but also into the Catholic, Protestant and Reformed Church. Countless enormous gatherings for the healing of the sick were held. Masses of people were swept away by such charismatic manifestations.

In the 1980s the so-called "Third Wave" emerged. It was said that now all churches which had previously resisted a "charismatic renewal" were to be reached. This was often achieved through clearly charismatic songs which bear meditative features and characterized by driving pop rhythms. This music is crafted so that, over a period of time, the emotional disposition necessary for charismatic phenomena can be cultivated indeed.

Typical of the Third Wave is the "Toronto Blessing" which, as its name indicates, had its beginnings Toronto, Canada, then spreading over the entire world so that tens of thousands of local churches were gripped by it. With this phenomenon people uncontrollably fall backwards en masse, laughing completely without self-control or crying out like animals, as the case may be. Such phenomena are well known from demonic rituals in Hinduism, Animism and other religions.

Each of these three waves increased in intensity. They increased just as labour pains tend to increase in intensity.

Leading new prophets, world-renowned personalities, had predicted the greatest revival ever for the western world in the year 2000, this despite the Biblical prophecy of 2 Thessalonians 2 to the contrary, pronouncing the End-Time apostasy in Christendom. Today, years later, we can calmly look back and clearly say that all these prophets were false prophets because their predictions have not been fulfilled at all. The Bible commands that a prophet who prophesies something false about the future just once, is clearly a false prophet and must thoroughly be rejected as a prophet (Deut. 18:20-22; Jer. 29:9).

Another characteristic of false prophets, according to the statements in the Bible, is the fact that they spread doctrines which contradict the Word of God, even when certain predictions are fulfilled (Deut. 13:1-18). This characteristic very clearly applies to this movement in each of the three waves. There are many false doctrines and practices which are contrary to the Holy Scripture, such as:[474]

- Spirit baptism as a second experience
- Toronto blessing
- Spiritual Warfare
- Pursuit of ecstatic experiences/encouragement of emotional spirituality in worship
- Powerful, rhythmic music to encourage ecstatic experiences
- Resting in the Spirit (Slain in the Spirit)
- Laughing in the Spirit
- Dancing in the Spirit
- Proclamation with flags and banners
- Visualization
- False teachings about laying on of hands
- False teaching about the meaning of health and illness
- Transfer of gifts
- Inner Healing
- Prosperity Gospel
- Kingdom Theology (Dominion Theology)
- Ecumenical movement
- Spiritual death of Jesus
- Restoration of the office of apostles and prophets in The Last Days

---

474 http://www.vigi-sectes.org/evangelisme/pfingstlich-charismatischen.html#Slain%20in%20 the%20Spirit%20%28Ruhen%20im%20Geist /as of: 25.10.2011).

Instead of turning our backs on these false prophets and false teachers, today we are continuing on in the same vein. Spectacular healing events are still being held. Millions today speak in tongues. But it is not speaking in tongues as in the Bible (Acts 2; 1 Corinthians 14). Biblical speaking in tongues is the mastery of real foreign languages which the speaker has not learned previously. That was a divine miracle. But the speaking in tongues practiced by millions today is merely an imitation. This is a babbling, whereby the one speaking does not even know what s/he is saying. How will he one day – according to Matthew 12:37 – give account to God for every word spoken? In my book "Speaking in Languages or Speaking in Tongues?"[475] I explain the striking difference between the two phenomena. There are clear distinctions which differentiate the counterfeit from that which was exercised in Biblical times.

Presently there are some 600 million Christians who are willing to listen to new prophets or to rely on their own prophetic impressions, visions, "tongues" messages, etc. This strikingly fulfills Matthew 24:11:

*"11 ..., and shall deceive **many**." (KJV)*

The Lord Jesus makes it clear that this seduction is also extremely dangerous for true Christians. By true Christians, I mean those Christians who have actually experienced a conversion, by having repented and confessed their personal guilt before God in prayer and by having consciously accepted in faith the substitutionary sacrifice of the Lord Jesus Christ on the cross for the forgiveness of their sins. The Lord said (Matt. 24:24):

*"24 ... and shall shew great signs and wonders; insomuch that, **if it were possible, they shall deceive the very elect**." (KJV)*

By the *"elect"* the true believers are meant (cf. Eph. 1:3ff.; 1Pet. 1:2). In Matthew 24:11,24 it obviously does not refer to just some clearly recognizable esoteric seducer - the countless gurus, spiritual healers, astrologers and New Agers of our time, although these

---

475 LIEBI: Sprachenreden oder Zungenreden? Bielefeld 2006 (www.clv.de).

verses also include them. In actual fact the boom in esotericism, which has become a billion dollar market with millions of deceived adherents in the western world since the 1960s, is also predicted in Matthew 24:24, but this verse is not limited to this. With gurus and spiritual healers, usually, any true Christian notices from a distance that it is pure seduction. However, this warning deals with *"great signs and wonders"* which obviously look amazingly similar to the genuine miracles done by the Lord Jesus and the apostles, as well as by the disciples Stephen and Philip! Although there is much quackery and fraud in this charismatic mass movement today, not all manifestations can be dismissed as deception. This is what makes this movement so very dangerous for true Christians! But the prophecy in Matthew 24 serves to awaken us all in order to separate and distance us clearly and decisively from this Last Days mass delusion. There are so many true Christians who have been swept away by it and who must now be freed from this deception. This is not about putting ourselves above others. We are all affected by this birth pain! It is most painful when even faithful Christians are swept up in this maelstrom.

In 2 Timothy 3 Paul speaks about The Last Days and the deception through signs and wonders:

*"¹ This know also, that **in the last days** perilous [dangerous/ savage/extreme] times shall come."* (KJV)

A few verses further, the Apostle explains:

*"⁸ Now as **Jannes and Jambres** withstood Moses, so do these also resist the truth: men of corrupt minds, reprobate concerning the faith."* (KJV)

Jannes and Jambres were the two miracle workers in Egypt who contended with Moses by imitating God's miracles (cf. Exod.7-8).[476] Because of this verse, it was known in ages past that one day,

---

476  These names have been preserved and passed on by Jewish tradition (cf. Targum Onkelos to Exod. 7:11 (= Aramaic translation of the 5 Books of Moses). Edition of the Targum Onkelos: in MIQRA'OTH GEDOLOTH or in BIBLE WORKS.)

namely in The Last Days, people would appear who would contend with God's truth by imitating God's signs and wonders.

In the same chapter, Paul also speaks explicitly of seducers who are themselves deceived. He further says that their End-Time works would continue to develop, just as the three waves of deception in the 20th century actually increased in intensity, in seductive potential and in additional new heresies (2 Tim. 3:13):

> *"13 But evil men and seducers[477] **shall wax worse and worse,** deceiving, and being deceived."* (KJV)

How can we protect ourselves from this? In the very next verse Paul exhorts the reader to the hold true to the inspired Word of God. Thorough study of the Bible helps us to keep ourselves protected from these temptations, or to escape from them (2 Tim. 3:14-17):

> *"14 But continue thou in the things which thou hast learned and hast been assured of, knowing of whom thou hast learned them; 15 And that from a child thou hast known the holy scriptures, which are able to make thee wise unto salvation through faith which is in Christ Jesus. 16 All scripture is given by inspiration of God, and is profitable for doctrine, for reproof, for correction, for instruction in righteousness: 17 That the man of God may be perfect, thoroughly furnished unto all good works."* (KJV)

In Matthew 7 the Lord Jesus pointed out prophetically that there would be many deceivers in the future who wrongly think that they are on the right side:

> *"22 **Many** will say to me in that day, Lord, Lord, have we not prophesied in thy name? and in thy name have cast out devils? and in thy name done many wonderful works? 23 And then will*

---

477  The text speaks of miracle workers here, which in reality are "*frauds*" (Greek *goes*). By contrast, in Matthew 24 "great signs and wonders" are spoken of. This corresponds to the present reality in the charismatic movement: many "miracles" turn out to be mere illusion. But there are obviously also true miracles. But in Matthew 24:24 the Lord gravely warns of the dangerous seduction caused by real miracles

*I profess unto them, I never knew you: depart from me, ye that work iniquity."* (KJV)

## 3.15 False Messiahs

In Matthew 24 the appearance of false messiahs is also announced for The Last Days:

*"²⁴ For there shall **arise false Christs**, and false prophets, and shall shew great signs and wonders; insomuch that, if it were possible, they shall deceive the very elect."* (KJV)

The term "Christ" or "Messiah" denotes the promised Redeemer of Israel and all nations of the world as announced in the OT. In The Last Days there will appear not only false prophets and miracle workers, but also individuals who present themselves as saviours.

This prophecy has also been fulfilled in the era of The Last Days (1882 to present). I have listed some examples of such false messiahs and false saviours below. Most of them have provoked headlines worldwide and caused a great stir. Many millions have been deceived by them:

- Oskar Ernst Bernhardt, also known as Abd-ru-shin (1875–1941): He was of German origin. Bernhardt claimed that the work of Christ had failed, and he was now the "true Christ" who would have to bring the Grail Message for the salvation of mankind.
- Jiddu Krishnamurti (1895–1986): In 1910, when he was still a boy, he was announced as the returned Messiah by Annie Besant, President of the Theosophical Society.
- George Baker, known as Father Divine (1880–1965): Baker founded the Peace Mission Movement. He regarded himself as the second incarnation of God. His death is considered by his followers as atonement for their sins.
- Maharishi Mahesh Yogi (1918–1998): This Hindu Guru was generously supported by the Beatles and touted as the greatest spiritual authority. He drew millions under his spell. For many years he had headquarters in Seelisberg, Switzerland.
- Sun Myung Moon (1920–2012): The Korean Moon considers

himself "son of God" and "Messiah." He regarded his fourth marriage in 1960 as "the marriage of the Lamb." He won over some 2 million followers.

- Bhagwan Shree Rajnesh/Osho (1931–1990): He was the founder of the Bhagwan sect. Among his large following there is many a celebrity.
- Guru Maharaj Ji (1957*): The founder of the Divine Light Mission is worshiped as divine and has won millions of followers.
- David Koresh (1959 –1993): He saw himself as a messiah figure. Following a 51-day war-like siege of his sect's property by the US federal authorities, he was killed by a bullet. Another 82 sect members were killed in the catastrophic fire which followed.
- Swami Omkarananda (1930–2000): Omkarananda was an Indian Hindu guru. In Winterthur, Switzerland, he founded the Divine Light Centre describing himself as "God omnipresent Swami Omkarananda."
- Jim Jones (1931–1978): He was the notorious founder of the Peoples Temple. He died in a mass murder, or mass suicide, together with 900 cult members in the jungle of Guyana.
- Marshall Applewhite (1931–1997): He was the leader of the Heavens's Gate cult which staged a mass suicide as the Hale-Bopp comet appeared in 1997. Applewhite propagated a confused belief in UFOs.
- Charles Manson (1934*): He was a US-American criminal and cult leader. Manson preached that blacks would one day make him the "ruler of the world."
- Rebbe, Rabbi Menachem Mendel Schneerson (1902–1994): The world-renowned rabbi of the Lubavitcher sect was proclaimed by his some 400,000 followers to be the Messiah of Israel.

## 3.16 Catastrophes through Tsunamis and Flooding
Another sign of The Last Days is identified in Luke 21:25:

*"25 ... and upon the earth distress of nations, with perplexity; the sea and the waves roaring; ..."* (KJV)

The tsunami disaster in December 2004 shocked the whole world.[478] One of the largest ever recorded earthquakes occurred in the Indian Ocean off the coast of Sumatra, triggering a massive tsunami with waves up to 30 metres high which brought death and destruction to India, Sri Lanka, the Maldives, Indonesia and Thailand. There were further casualties in Myanmar, Malaysia, Bangladesh, the Seychelles, Somalia and Kenya. It is estimated there were over 230,000 deaths. Over 110,000 people were injured. Around the Indian Ocean 1.7 million coastal dwellers were left homeless. This was one of the largest tsunami disasters in world history!

Many people in the West donated generously to alleviate the misery of survivors.

It was not expected that such a thing would soon be repeated, but a short time later the storm surges caused by hurricane "Katrina" ensured worldwide horror (August 2005): New Orleans was catastrophically flooded. It was one of the four strongest hurricanes that have ever been measured in the USA. It caused one of the worst natural disasters in American history.[479] There were 1,800 deaths. The damage is estimated at around 81 billion US dollars. Approximately 80% of the city was inundated, under some 7 metres water.

Then, in September 2005, hurricane "Rita" occurred. This storm possessed a mean wind speed of up to 290 km/hour; Rita caused 6-metre storm surges in Texas. New Orleans had to be evacuated again. President Bush warned:

"We must be prepared for the worst."

He declared a state of emergency. Millions of fearful and panicked people attempted to flee the states of Texas and Louisiana. This corresponded exactly with the statement of Luke 21:25! In the USA "Rita" sparked memories of the deadliest natural disaster in US history: the Galveston hurricane in 1900 with 8,000 dead. The environment was laid waste by "Rita." Entire towns were devastated. Oil pipelines burst and this contaminated water supplies.

478 http://de.wikipedia.org/wiki/Erdbeben_im_Indischen_Ozean_2004; http://en.wikipedia.org/wiki/2004_Indian_Ocean_earthquake_and_tsunami (as of: 25.10.2011).

479 http://de.wikipedia.org/wiki/Hurrikan_Katrina (as of: 25.10.2011).

Many animals were poisoned, forests destroyed and sanitation systems were contaminated, leading to the pollution of lakes and rivers.

In October 2005 came "Wilma," up to now the strongest hurricane ever measured in the Atlantic.[480] It brought tidal waves over Haiti and flooded entire tracts of land. Hundreds of thousands were forced to flee before it. There was also flooding on the Florida peninsula, causing billions of dollars in damages.

The decade from 2000–2010 is recorded as the decade with the most Level 5 hurricanes.[481] There were eight such storms measured at this devastating intensity: "Isabel" (2003), "Ivan" (2004), "Emily" (2005), "Katrina" (2005), "Rita" (2005), "Wilma" (2005), "Dean" (2007) and "Felix" (2007). Next in the rankings are the 1960s in which six such storms were measured.

The tsunami of 2004 had not been forgotten when on 11 March 2011 a new tsunami, caused by an earthquake with a Richter scale magnitude of 9.0, struck Japan's Tohoku coast.[482] Waves with a height up to 23 metres hit the east of the country. The officially confirmed death toll is given as 11,500, but there are still 16,400 people reported missing. The nuclear meltdown at Fukushima was triggered by this terrible natural disaster.

Numerous devastating tsunamis have occurred throughout the entire history of The Last Days from 1882 until today. These catastrophes are a striking documentation of the fulfillment of Luke 21:25:

- 27 August 1883: Java/Sumatra: 40m-high tidal waves, 36,000 dead
- 3 March 1888: German New Guinea: 8m-high tidal waves (triggered by eruption of the volcano Krakatoa)
- 15 June 1896: Japan: 23 metre-high tidal wave, 26,000 dead
- 15 January 1905: Norway: 40 metre-high tidal waves (caused by rock fall), 63 dead
- 31 January 1906: Colombia/Ecuador; 500–1,500 deaths
- 28 December 1908: The earthquake of Messina, Sicily and Ca-

---

480 http://de.wikipedia.org/wiki/Hurrikan_Wilma (as of: 25.10.2011).

481 http://de.wikipedia.org/wiki/Liste_der_atlantischen_Kategorie-5-Hurrikane (as of: 25.10.2011).

482 http://de.wikipedia.org/wiki/Tsunami (as of: 25.10.2011).

labria triggered a devastating tsunami. Messina was almost completely destroyed. This was the biggest natural disaster in Europe in the 20th century with 75,000–110,000 dead

- 18 November 1929: Newfoundland, Canada, 28 dead, over 10,000 homeless
- 2 March 1933: Japan: 28.7 metre-high tsunami, more than 1,500 dead and 1,500 missing
- 1936: Norway: 70 metre-high tidal wave (caused by rock fall) that destroyed two villages. A tourist ship was carried 350m inland
- 1 April 1946: Alaska/Hawaii, 164 dead
- 5 November 1952: Severo-Kurilsk (Russia): 2,336 dead, destruction in Kamchatka and the Kuril Islands
- 9 July 1958: Alaska (triggered by landslide). Flooding reached a height of 520 metres on the opposite hillside
- 22 May 1960: Chile/Hawaii, up to 11 metre-high tsunami, over 1,000 dead
- 27 March 1964: Alaska/West Coast of the USA: the destruction of almost all coastal towns southern Alaska, many dead
- 16 August 1976: the Philippines, 5,000 dead
- 26 May 1983: Japan: 14 metre-high tidal waves, 104 dead
- 2 September 1992: Nicaragua, 10 metre-high tidal waves, 116 dead
- 12 July 1993: Japan: 32 metre-high tidal waves, 230 dead
- 17 July 1998: Papua New Guinea, 2,000 dead
- 21 May 2003: Algeria, earthquake with 2,000 dead, tsunami with local flooding on Majorca and Ibiza
- 26 December 2004: India, Sri Lanka, the Maldives, Indonesia and Thailand, Myanmar, Malaysia, Bangladesh, the Seychelles, Somalia, Kenya, up to 30 metre-high tsunami, more than 230,000 deaths
- 17 July 2006: Java: over 700 dead
- 2 April 2007: Solomon Islands, up to 12 metre-high tsunami, devastation of the islands, 12-20 dead
- 30 September 2009: Samoa Islands: parts of the island devastated, 80–100 deaths
- 25 October 2010: Mentawai Islands, 3 metre-high tidal wave,

flooding up to 600 metres inland, over 272 dead
- 11 March 2011: Japan: 23 metre-high tsunami, 11,500 dead, 16,400 missing, resulted in: Nuclear disaster at Fukushima

## 3.17  Terrorism and Natural Catastrophes

In Luke 21:11 a sign is announced which is not named in the other Gospels:

*"11 ... and there shall be great earthquakes, and in divers places famines, and pestilences; and there shall be **terrors** ..."* (ASV)

The English word *"terrors"* translated from the Greek word *phobêthra* means:
1.  terrible events or
2.  that which strikes fear

If we assume the second meaning, this is exactly what we now call "terror" or "terrorism." Terror is actually Latin and means "fright." With this word we express the use of terror for the systematic dissemination of fear, panic and horror.

International terrorism is a child of the 20th century. There are or were two distinct forms:
- the leftist-ideological, Marxist-inspired terrorism
- Islamic terrorism

Islamic terrorism of the modern era can be divided into 4 phases. Each phase became more intense and horrific than the one before.
1.  From 1920 on: Islamic terrorism against Jewish settlements of Palestine
2.  From 1947 on: Islamic terrorism against the establishment of Israel
3.  From 1967 on: Islamic terrorism as recompense for the defeat in the Six Day War
4.  From 2001 on: Islamic terrorism against Israel and the West

The fourth phase, beginning with 11 September 2001 and the devastating attacks on the Twin Towers in New York, sparked off the global "War on Terrorism."

The long and cruel series of terrorist attacks over the years from 1882 till today is a very painful birth pain of The Last Days according to Luke 21.

The meaning of Luke 21:11 cannot be restricted to terrorism. The sense of the word *phobêthra* is broader. If we take the first meaning mentioned above ("terrible events"), the long list of floods, heat waves, forest fires, flooding, oil spills, volcanic eruptions, nuclear reactor accidents, etc., falls under the signs of The Last Days. Tsunamis, famines and earthquakes are mentioned separately in the Olivet Discourse. But all other types of disasters are summarized under the concept of "terrible events." The signs of the Olivet Discourse are "birth pains" which are cyclical and tend to become more painful. Natural disasters have increased dramatically and steadily from 1900 to the present. This increase over the last decade has been incredible and most frightening.[483] This increase has become a huge problem for the insurance companies!

---

483 http://de.wikipedia.org/wiki/Katastrophe ; http://en.wikipedia.org/wiki/Disaster ; http://de.wikipedia.org/wiki/Naturkatastrophen ; http://www.wissen.toppx.de/2010/03/24/zunahme-von-naturkatastrophen-durch-klimawandel (as of: 25.10.2011).

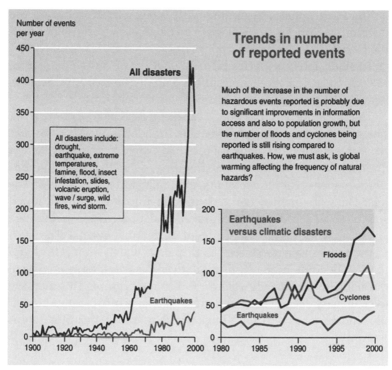

*Fig. 30: The increase of catastrophes in the 20th century according to the United Nations Environment Programme (source: Wikipedia, GNU 1.2 or later).*

## 3.18 Lawlessness and Moral Collapse

The Lord Jesus prophesied in Matthew 24:12:

> *"12 ... and because **lawlessness [Greek anomia] will abound**, the love of many shall grow cold ..."* (NKJV)

The word "lawlessness" is the Greek term *anomia* meaning:

* contempt of law, binding rules and order
* godlessness
* illegality

I've already explained briefly in another context that the revolution of 1968 cannot be overestimated as a turning point in the intellectual history of the West. From that time, the masses in the West made a break with the Christian past of Europe and North America. Millions of people who formerly professed to be Christian turned away from God and His Word. While previously Christian values had been part the consensus of society, and the Bible and a certain reverence for God had shaped societal life, this was indiscriminately thrown overboard with the neo-Marxist mass uprising of 1968. Those who hold such Christian values today must often reckon with ridicule and contempt.

Intellectually, this break was primed by people such as Sigmund Freud, Herbert Marcuse, Erich Fromm, Wilhelm Reich, Alfred C. Kinsey, Jean-Paul Sartre, Simone de Beauvoire, Hermann Hesse, and many others. It was, indeed, a multiple-revolution:[484]

1. *Sexual Revolution* (call for free sexuality without moral restraints [premarital sex, cohabitation, homosexuality, call for abortion rights, etc.])

2. *Drugs Revolution* (propaganda promoting the use of drugs for the alleged expansion of consciousness, call for freedom in the misuse of drugs, etc.)

3. *Feminist Revolution* (call for the abolition of gender-specific tasks, through to gender mainstreaming which claims that the man is not born as a prospective "man" and the woman is not born as a prospective "woman")

4. *Religious Revolution* (propaganda for Eastern religions such as Buddhism, Hinduism, tribal religions [animism], esoteric thought, occultism, through to Satanism)

Morality shaped by Christianity and the Bible was largely destroyed by the 1968 movement. This resulted in Western society being permeated by immorality, with cohabitation, changing partners, adultery, divorce, homosexuality and pornography.

In 1973 abortion, the killing of unborn babies in the womb, was liberalized in the United States. France and Italy soon followed. Then, one country after another joined in this trend.

The family as the nucleus of a healthy social structure came under general attack:

---

484  Cf. REGGLI: Die 68er-Falle, Fluchtwege aus dem Desaster der Neuen Linken, Zürich 2005.

The mother was to be taken out of the family and away from her care of the children and integrated into the workforce outside the home, all in accordance with the teachings of Karl Marx.

The authority of the father was placed under general suspicion. At that time, the age of father hatred began.

The Left's concept of the enemy had three aspects: Children, church and the kitchen. They were to some extent succeeded by three other aspects: crib, coldness, collective. Anti-authoritarian upbringing was introduced. Marriage and family were to be obsolescent models which would be replaced with other, more modern blueprints for long-term relationships. Society would be eroticized.

The use of drugs such as hashish and LSD was propagated, in order to escape bourgeois constraints with the help of "consciousness expansion," falsely so-called. An ideal medium was found in the rock and pop music emerging at that time, with its powerful, ecstatic rhythms, avoiding critical thinking in order to hammer all these neo-Marxist goals into the minds of youth worldwide.[485]

Further, Hinduism, Buddhism, New Age, the occult through to Satanism were actively touted as substitutes for Christianity.

The goal of the neo-Marxists was the overthrow of society ultimately in order to build their communist "paradise," a society of erotic pleasure seekers according to their own anti-Christian ideas, in which there would no longer be anyone laying any claims to personal property. Everything would belong to the collective.

In the years and decades which followed, Western society was greatly destabilized, which would have tangible consequences:

The outbreak of a drug epidemic that is unstoppable, widespread contempt of authority of any kind, increased crime, dramatically increasing violence, abortion as an everyday routine in hospitals, a growing divorce rate, godlessness, esoteric disorientation, involvement in the occult, etc.

After more than five decades, we can look back on the disastrous effects:

• The drug problem has become unsolvable.

---

485 Cf. LIEBI: Rockmusik! Daten, Fakten, Hintergründe, Jugend in einem sterbenden Zeitalter.

- The majority of marriages end in divorce.
- Patchwork families are increasingly replacing the former stable family.
- Countless children are confused and do not know where they belong.
- Many young people suffer from a sense of insignificance and worthlessness.
- Abortion has become a machine to which, according to the WHO estimates, 42 million children fall victim worldwide, each year.[486]
- Since 1973, more than 1 billion babies have been killed in the womb worldwide![487]
- In the tiny country of Switzerland alone more than 10,000 babies (officially) are killed in the womb every year.
- We note a dramatic increase of European welfare cases (in Germany Harz IV recipients), many due to problems such as depression, schizophrenia, AIDS, hepatitis B and C, post-abortion syndrome, etc., due to the lifestyle of the '68ers.

This moral rupture in the Western World has led to the decadence being able to occur which Paul predicted in 2 Timothy 3 for Christianity in The Last Days. Our Western society today is characterized by the 19 distinguishing marks listed in 2 Timothy 3.

In researching trends, it is said that one mega-trend of modern times is the "love of self" (narcissism). We hear such terms as "individualization of society" and "soft individualism," etc. Education in self-love is strongly encouraged nowadays and is praised as a "cure" by psychotherapy. The first item on the list in 2 Timothy 3 speaks of self-love or self-indulgence!

Further, all the other points have become marks of broad sections of society alienated by the neo-Marxists since the '68ers' movement. Each word is a prophetic direct hit on our times (2 Tim. 3):

---

486 http://apps.who.int/rhl/fertility/abortion/CD006712_chengl_com/en/ (as of: 25.10.2011).

487 http://www.zenit.org/article-14360?l=german (as of: 25.10.2011).

*"¹ But know this, that in the last days perilous times will come. ²For men will be*
*lovers of themselves,*
*lovers of money,*
*boasters,*
*proud [arrogant],*
*blasphemers [Greek blasphemos],*
*disobedient to parents,*
*unthankful,*
*unholy [godless/sinful/abhorrent],*
*³ unloving [Greek astorgê; especially designating lack of love of parents for children, of children for parents, or generally within the family]*[488]
*unforgiving,*
*slanderers,*
*without self-control,*
*brutal,*
*despisers of good,*
*⁴ traitors,*
*headstrong [coarse/wild],*
*haughty,*
*lovers of pleasures more than lovers of God;*
*⁵ Having a form of godliness [religiousness], but denying its power ..."* (NKJV)

### Concerning "lovers of money"

While the difficult post-war years meant a modest living standard for most people, the Western nations built a prosperous society that is without parallel in the entire history of the world. This prosperity was at the same time occasion for widespread love of money (cf. James 5:1-6).

### Concerning "blasphemers" [Greek blasphemos]

Since the 1960s the Western world has been engulfed by an unprecedented wave of blasphemy. Blasphemy and profanity

---

488  LOUW/NIDA: Greek-English Lexicon of the New Testament Based on Semantic Domains, Vol. I, 25.42, p. 293.

mean offense against God and the subject of faith.

Within the framework of alleged artistic freedom, God and the Bible were publicly mocked through drama, photography exhibitions, dance performances, films, songs, musicals, etc. In the first half of the 20th century, this would never have been possible, but would have been punished by the state. There are laws in the Western constitutional nations prohibiting blasphemy. But the fact that these laws are now only minimally enforced means that the problem of public blasphemy has been able to spread so freely.

### Concerning "disobedient to parents"

The '68ers' ideology promoted contempt for authority in preparation for the revolutionary overthrow of society. In this context, anti-authoritarian education was also promoted. One consequence of this trend is widespread questioning of parental of authority.

### Concerning "boastful, proud [arrogant]" – "puffed up"

Humility and modesty were once generally regarded as desirable virtues. In the past 60 years, the Left's emancipatory indoctrination has thoroughly turned education in the family and school upside down.[489] Especially these virtues, as seen from the perspective of neo-Marxist ideology, were often ridiculed and portrayed as kitsch. Is it any wonder that the evil tendencies of boastfulness, arrogance and pomposity, which belong to the fallen nature of man in every generation, were able to develop very freely and without hindrance in our modern society?

### Concerning "unloving" [Greek astorgê; especially designating lack of love of parents for children, of children for parents and generally within the family and marriage]

The lack of natural affection is the origin for the widespread practice of abortion since liberalization began in the USA in 1973. 42 million abortions per year, according to the WHO, is a shocking testimony to the fulfilment of this prophecy.

---

489  http://www.johannes-lerle.net/Boehm/SE/body_se.html (as of: 1.11.2011).

Another effect of this lack of love is the megatrend in society of choosing not to have and/or commit to raising children. "Children" were explicitly a part of the '68ers' concept of the enemy. The enormous number of disintegrating marriages and families today is also related to the lack of natural love.

### Concerning "without self-control"
The '68ers promoted the tearing down of all ethical standards in the field of sexuality. This led to widespread sexual promiscuity in society with premarital sex, cohabitation, adultery, homosexuality, paedophilia, pornography, etc.

### Concerning "brutal"
The term "cruel" or "brutal" in 2 Timothy 3 describes the problem of increasing violence in the Western world since the 1968 revolution.

### Concerning "headstrong [coarse/wild]" – "unthankful, unholy [godless/sinful/ abhorrent]" – "unforgiving, slanderers"
In the 1960s, rock and pop music was ascendant throughout the whole world with its characteristic powerful rhythms and volume. Since then, countless different styles have developed which cater to every nuance of musical taste. This was not just a new kind of music. A whole lifestyle is bound up with this music, characterized by the worship of stars in a cult which puts anything comparable to shame. This music also sparked off the massive use of drugs. Since the 1960s, this music has played an increasingly significant role in the brutalization of large groups of young people.[490] Values like hard work, dedication, reliability, loyalty, respect for parents and authorities have been more and more undermined in the home and school.

### Concerning "lovers of pleasure rather than lovers of God"
The pursuit of pleasure and exhilarating entertainment was encouraged by the 1968 movement. The striving for pleasure has

---

490 Cf. LIEBI: Rockmusik! Daten, Fakten, Hintergründe, Jugend in einem sterbenden Zeitalter.

since become an integral part of life for a large part of society. This includes everything from the disco through to consumer electronics with film, music, games, etc., in connection with television, computers, iPods and Smart Phones, etc. Viewed historically, this is an unprecedented social phenomenon in both qualitative and quantitative respects. Having fun on the weekend is central to the thinking of large sectors of society. Many go through the work week thinking of nothing but festivals, parties and amusements at the weekend.

Paul is speaking of apostate Christendom in 2 Timothy, not of the pagan world which is without the Bible and without the Gospel. He speaks of the Christian profession of faith as the "*great house*" in which true and false Christians (v. 20: "*golden and silver vessels*" on the one hand, "*wood and earthen*" on the other) and false teachers (such as "*Hymenaeus and Philetus,*" v.17) exist, mingled together. He calls true believers to separation from evil (2:21- 22).[491] Paul continues with a description of The Last Days where the problem of meaningless, purely external Christian faith is pointed out in chapter 3:5.

Paul had already used certain expressions from the 19-point list given above in Romans 1 where he describes the morally decadent pagan world as it manifested itself in the Greco-Roman culture of his time, for example (cf. the expressions "boasters/proud/ disobedient to parents/unloving" in Romans 1:28ff.) Christianity replaced the pagan consensus of morality with a Christian consensus during the course of the centuries, which had an enormous effect on the nature and development of Western culture.[492] But, Paul makes it clear in 2 Timothy that the old pagan morality will again be expressed fully in The Last Days.

In 2 Peter, which the author had written in 67 AD from his cell

---

491 Verse 21: "to purge oneself" = Greek *ekkathairo heauton* = literally, to cleanse oneself by separating oneself (cf. also 2 Tim. 3:5; 2 Cor. 6:14–7:1; Heb. 13:12,13; Rev. 8:4).

492 The Christians in the Greco-Roman culture were against the widespread killing of children by abortion and abandonment, the bloody gladiator games, the widespread practice of suicide, against perverse sexuality (adultery, paedophilia, homosexuality, etc.) and against the disdaining women. They promoted, on the other hand, love of one's neighbour and mercy, especially in regard to the needs of orphans, widows, the blind, elderly and the sick, etc. (cf. SCHMIDT: Wie das Christentum die Welt veränderte, Menschen – Gesellschaft – Politik – Kunst, Gräfelfing 2009).

on death row in Rome, there is also much stated prophetically regarding the "Last Days" (cf. 2Pet 3:3). In chapter 2 Peter foresaw exactly how sexual immorality would be found in the church, and not just kept in secret. No, it has happened exactly so in the wake of the 1968 movement in Evangelical-Reformed and Protestant-Lutheran pastors, in keeping with their liberal, Bible-critical theology, have declared the sexual morality of the Bible (e.g. regarding premarital sex, homosexuality, etc.) to be outdated and have thus become seducers. This goes so far as to tolerate or even defend and bless the practice of homosexuality within the Evangelical and Evangelical-Reformed Church. These pastors act as if they were proclaiming freedom, but in fact, Peter says, they are "slaves of sin" (2 Peter 2):[493]

> *"¹ But there were false prophets also among the people, even as there shall be **false teachers among you**, who privily shall bring in damnable heresies, even denying the Lord that bought them, and bring upon themselves swift destruction. ² And **many shall follow their pernicious ways**; by reason of whom the way of truth shall be evil spoken of. ... ⁹ The Lord knoweth how to deliver the godly out of temptations, and to reserve the unjust unto the day of judgement to be punished: ¹⁰ But chiefly **them that walk after the flesh in the lust of uncleanness**, ... ¹³ and shall receive the reward of unrighteousness, as **they that count it pleasure to riot in the day time**. Spots they are and blemishes, sporting themselves with their own deceivings while they feast with you; ¹⁴ **Having eyes full of adultery, and that cannot cease from sin; beguiling unstable souls**: ... ¹⁷ These are wells without water, clouds that are carried with a tempest; to whom the mist of darkness is reserved for ever. ¹⁸ For when **they speak great swelling words of vanity, they allure through the lusts of the flesh**, through much wantonness, those that were clean escaped from them who live in error. ¹⁹ **While they promise them liberty, they themselves are the servants of corruption**: for of whom a man is overcome, of the same is he brought in bondage."* (KJV)

---

493  Cf. also the book of Jude.

At the very end of his letter Peter warns true Christians, virtually with his last testamentary bequest immediately before his crucifixion by Emperor Nero in 66/67 AD
(2 Peter 3:17-18):

> *"¹⁷ Ye therefore, beloved, seeing ye know these things before, beware lest ye also, **being led away with the error of the wicked, fall from your own stedfastness.** ¹⁸ But grow in grace, and in the knowledge of our Lord and Saviour Jesus Christ. To him be glory both now and for ever. Amen."* (KJV)

The Greek word *athesmoi* translated "wicked" also means:
* those having contempt for law
* those adverse or contrary to the law
* lawless
* unjust

In Luke 17 the Lord Jesus Christ had foretold that The Last Days would be an era with significant parallels to the days of Noah and likewise Lot:

> *"²⁶ And as it came to pass in the days of Noah, even so shall it be also in the days of the Son of man. ²⁷ They ate, they drank, they married, they were given in marriage, until the day that Noah entered into the ark, and the flood came, and destroyed them all. ²⁸ Likewise even as it came to pass in the days of Lot; they ate, they drank, they bought, they sold, they planted, they builded; ²⁹ but in the day that Lot went out from Sodom it rained fire and brimstone from heaven, and destroyed them all. ³⁰ After the same manner shall it be in the day that the Son of man is revealed."* (ASV)

The Bible describes Noah as a "preacher of righteousness" (2 Pet 2:4, cf. also Heb. 11:7; 1 Pet. 3:19-20 and Gen. 6–9). Noah pointed the people to the coming global judgement. But most people rejected his message. They lived their normal lives with all the usual patterns related to daily food and the establishment of new families ("²⁷*They ate, they drank, they married, they were given in marriage …*"). Quite obviously they did not expect that there would be a sudden break in this cycle through God's direct intervention. Noah's era was, in a certain way, also an "End Time," the end of the antediluvian age. The people of that End Time were just like the people of today's Last Days: The masses do not listen to the divine message. People live their own fairly normal lives. God and His Word are not relevant to them.

Lot lived in the "Last Days" of the history of the cities of Sodom and Gomorrah. The people of these metropoles lived, for them, normal lives with all the usual cares related to daily food and economic aspirations ("²⁸… *they ate, they drank, they bought, they sold, they planted, they builded; …*") In Luke 17:28, in contrast to the days of Noah in the previous verse, marriage is no longer mentioned. The people of Sodom and Gomorrah, in contrast to other cultures of that time, had thrown overboard all moral restraints related to sexuality. In these cities, marriage was no longer "in." Homosexuality and even sodomy had been "normalised" (Gen. 19:4-5; Jude 1:7, Isa. 3:9). Quite obviously they did not expect that an interruption could come in their daily cycle through God directly intervening in the course of history. But finally God's judgement came with fire from heaven and brought an end to these cities near the Dead Sea.

## 3.19 Destruction of Natural Affection

It is clear that these immoral, perverse practices, from promiscuity all the way to abortion, destroy something in us. God has given us natural feelings and valuable feelings, so that we are essentially able to love and make commitments. But all the Neo-Marxists' perversions listed above seriously injure and scar the depths of our souls which can lead to hardness, bitterness and insensitivity. This is evident, for example, in finding that the statement "In Switzerland, more than 10,000 babies are aborted annually" elicits no shock, no outrage, and no real sympathy in most of our contemporaries! Something has perished in the depths of our souls! The Lord Jesus predicted this as follows in Matthew 24:12:

*"12 ... and because lawlessness [Greek anomia] will abound, **the love of many will grow cold."** (NKJV)*

I am again reminded of Paul's statement regarding Christendom's moral state in The Last Days (2 Tim: 3:3):

*"3 ... without natural affection ..."* (KJV)

As I have said already, the Greek word *storgê* means the love of parents for their children and also the love of children for their parents. Yet in this verse, the word is written with the *alpha privativum*: *a-storgê* meaning "**without** natural love."

## 3.20 The Gospel Reaches All Nations
Jesus Christ also predicted that the proclamation of the Gospel, the Good News of the Bible, will reach all nations in The Last Days, when all the signs discussed occur in combination with one another.

Matthew 24:14:
*"14 And **this gospel of the kingdom shall be preached** in all the world **for a witness unto all nations**; and then shall the end come."* (KJV)

Mark 13:10:
*"10 And **the gospel** must first be **published among all nations."*** (KJV)

The term "gospel" (Greek *euangelion*) means "good news". While Mark simply says *"gospel,"* Matthew uses the term *"gospel of the kingdom."* The use of "kingdom" expresses that part of the proclamation of the Gospel referring to Jesus Christ coming again as King and speaking the last word over this world, as Paul proclaimed (Acts 28:30,31; 17:7).

The word translated here "nations" in the King James Bible is the Greek *ethnoi* (= plural of the singular: *ethnos*). According to the standard dictionary by Louw/Nida this word means *the largest social unit*.[494]

The smallest social unit is the marriage (one man and one woman). The next biggest unit is the family with two parents and one or more children. Then come the clan, the tribe, and finally the people (Greek *laos*).[495] Even more comprehensive is the term "nation" (Greek *ethnos*). A nation can be composed of many different peoples, such as in Russia and India. The Lord Jesus did not say that "all men" or even "all tribes" would be reached with the Gospel before the end, he did not even say "all peoples". No, the statement in Matthew 24 relates to "all nations." All *nations* would be reached with the Gospel.[496]

The number of people groups, in the sense of "ethno-linguistic groups,"[497] is estimated at about 12,000 worldwide. Not all people groups, and certainly not all tribes, have been reached by missionary preaching of the Good News of Jesus Christ, even though current efforts are extensive. But it is a fact that the Gospel had been preached to every nation in the 20th century, and is still being preached.

The Bible had been translated into about 70 languages by 1800. At that time, many Christians became aware that the Great Commission from Jesus Christ was directed to all people (Matt. 28:18-20; Mark 16:15; Acts 1:8). This was the epoch of revival in Europe and North America. It was in that era that the ball started to roll. Already by 1830 the Bible had been translated into about 157 different languages. Today, in 2011, the Bible has been translated wholly or in part into over 2,560 languages.[498]

Additionally, there is the work done via audio gospel. These Gospel messages are proclaimed in recordings in about 6,000

---

494  LOUW/NIDA: Greek-English Lexicon of the New Testament based on Semantic Domains, Vol. I, 11.55, p. 130.

495  Some passages in the NT where laoi is found: Acts 4:25; Rom. 15:11; Rev. 10:11; 15:16.

496  Some Bible translations have translated ethnoi with "peoples" in this passage. Unfortunately, this does not express the fact that the Bible differentiates between laoi ("peoples") and ethnoi. laoi designates smaller social units than ethnoi.

497  = any ethnic group in which one defines the identity of the individual person according to his language and ethic affiliation.

498  http://www.wycliffe.net/ScriptureAccessStatistics/tabid/73/language/en-US/Default.aspx (as of: 25.10.2011).

languages and dialects![499] The good news of Jesus Christ and His offer of salvation reaches into countries that are officially closed to the message of the Bible over the radio (e.g. Trans World Radio) and also via the Internet. Today, the statements of Matthew 24:14 and Mark 13:10 are fulfilled! Today, the Gospel is being preached simultaneously in all nations!

Regarding the five initial birth pains, which were fulfilled during the first 40 years of The Last Days (1822–1922), we have seen that the Lord explicitly said (Luke 21:9):

> *"⁹ But when you hear of wars and commotions, do not be terrified; for these things must come to pass first; **but the end will not come immediately.**"* (NKJV)

However, the Lord's message is very different in regard to reaching all nations (Matt. 24:14):

> *"¹⁴ And this gospel of the kingdom shall be preached in all the world for a witness unto all nations; **and then shall the end come.**"* (KJV)

Jesus Christ is coming soon! Are you ready to meet the Judge?

## 3.21 "Peace and Safety"

If the Judge is coming soon we ought to look at an astonishing prophecy in 1 Thessalonians 5:1-3 where the Apostle Paul, describing the final phase of The Last Days, says:

> *"¹ But of the times and the seasons, brethren, ye have no need that I write unto you. ² For yourselves know perfectly that the day of the Lord so cometh as a thief in the night. ³ For **when they shall say [continually], Peace and safety; then** sudden destruction cometh upon them, as travail upon a woman with child; and they shall not escape."* (KJV)

The phrase "they say" (Greek *legousin*) in verse 3 is durative in

---

499 http://audiogospel.ch/index.htm (as of: 25.10.2011).

the original Greek text. The Greek verbal system is an aspect system which distinguishes very precisely whether a particular action is punctiliar, continuous or repeated action (durative) or resulting from a past action (resultative).[500] The exact meaning of the word *legousin* in 1 Thessalonians 5:2 is: "*When they **continually** say: ...*"/"*When they **repeatedly** say: ...*"

Who is meant by "*they*"? In ancient Greek, the third person plural is often used where we would use the impersonal "one."[501] Therefore, it may be justifiably translated as: "*When **one** continually says: ...*" or "*When **one** says again and again...*"

In the context of 1 Thessalonians 5:2-3, this regards "*the day of the LORD*" (v. 2), i.e. the Judgement at the end which will come upon the whole world (cf. Zeph. 1:2-3:14-18). Thus, the word "they" or the word "one" designates the people and nations of the world in The Last Days.

The text says nothing about real peace having come, not even a semblance of peace is indicated. The Bible only says that *people will constantly speak of peace and safety*.

### 3.21.1 Founding of the League of Nations (1919)

Following the First World War, on 28 June 1919, the Versailles Peace Treaty was signed between the USA, the British Empire, France, Italy, Japan, Belgium, Bolivia, Brazil, Cuba, Ecuador, Greece, Guatemala, Haiti, Hejaz, Honduras, Liberia, Nicaragua, Panama, Peru, Poland, Portugal, Romania, the State of the Slovenes, Croats and Serbs, Siam, Czechoslovakia and Uruguay on the one side and Germany on the other side. Part I (Articles 1-26) includes the Statute of the League of Nations adopted on 28.4.1919 by the plenary session of the Paris Peace Conference. The introductory words read as follows:[502]

"In order to promote international co-operation and to achieve international **peace and security** by the acceptance of obliga-

---

500 HOFFMANN/VON SIEBENTHAL: Griechische Grammatik, p. 304ff; WALLACE: Greek Beyond the Basics, p. 494ff.

501 HAUBECK/VON SIEBENTHAL: Neuer sprachlicher Schlüssel zum Neuen Testament, Vol. II, p. 452 (A76).

502 http://www.dhm.de/lemo/html/dokumente/versailles/index.html (as of: 25.10.2011); emphasis by the author (RL)

tions not to resort to war by the prescription of open, just and honourable relations between nations by the firm establishment of the understandings of international law as the actual rule of conduct among Governments, and by the maintenance of justice and a scrupulous respect for all treaty obligations in the dealings of organised peoples with one another Agree to this Covenant of the League of Nations."

When the League of Nations, this completely new type of international organization in human history, began its work on 10 January 1920, its primary mission was to ensure "peace and security" for our world.

### 3.21.2 The Founding of the UN (1945)

It was not long before the Second World War broke out, becoming even more devastating than the First World War. As a consequence, the League of Nations was dissolved in 1946, to be replaced by an organization which would ensure "peace and security." This new organization was the United Nations, whose Charter went into effect on 24 October 1945. The Preamble begins with the following words:[503]

"We the peoples of the United Nations determined to save succeeding generations from the scourge of war, which twice in our lifetime has brought untold sorrow to mankind, and to reaffirm faith in fundamental human rights, in the dignity and worth of the human person, in the equal rights of men and women and of nations large and small, and to establish conditions under which justice and respect for the obligations arising from treaties and other sources of international law can be maintained, and to promote social progress and better standards of life in larger freedom, and for these ends - to practice tolerance and live together in **peace** with one another as good neighbours, and to unite our strength to maintain **international peace** and **security**, and to ensure, by the acceptance of principles and the institution of methods, that armed force shall not be used, save

---

503 http://www.unric.org/de/charta (as of: 25.10.2011); emphasis by the author (RL).

in the common interest, and to employ international machinery for the promotion of the economic and social advancement of all peoples, ..."

A green light was given for the establishment of a Jewish state in Palestine in one of the first sessions of the UN in November 1947.

The Arabs' total war against Israel immediately followed the founding of the Jewish state on 14 May 1948, although Israel had expressly extended the hand of peace to all the Arab states on the day of the founding.

The war ended in 1949 with separate cease-fire agreements between the various belligerent Arab states and Israel. However, no Arab state was prepared to enter into a peace treaty with Israel in the following years.

### 3.21.3 UN Resolution 242 (1967)

A second attempt to totally destroy Israel was made in 1967. Any possibility of a peace treaty with Israel was vehemently rejected at the summit conference of the Arab states in the Sudanese capital, Khartoum, in August, 1967. The future policy with regard to the Jewish state was succinctly formulated:

"No peace with Israel, no recognition of Israel, no negotiations with Israel"[504]

Meanwhile, the United Nations adopted Security Resolution 242 on 22 November 1967. This resolution demanded the right of all states in the region to: "...live in **peace** within **secure** and recognized boundaries free from threats or acts of force; ..."[505]

### 3.21.4 UN Resolution 338 (1973)

The third attempt of total destruction of Israel came in 1973. This also ended in yet another lost war for Israel's Arab neighbours. On

---

504 http://www.hagalil.com/israel/geschichte/kriege-3.htm (as of: 25.10.2011).

505 http://www.hagalil.com/israel/geschichte/kriege-3.htm (as of: 25.10.2011); http://avalon.law.yale. edu/20th_century/un242.asp (as of: 28.8.2012).

22 October 1973 the United Nations adopted UN Resolution 338:[506]
"The Security Council,
1. Calls upon all parties to the present fighting to cease all firing and terminate all military activity immediately, no later than 12 hours after the moment of the adoption of this decision, in the positions they now occupy;
2. Calls upon the parties concerned to start immediately after the cease-fire the implementation of Security Council resolution 242 (1967) [cf. there the right "to live within **secure** and recognized borders in **peace** and freedom from threat and violence."] in all of its parts;
3. Decides that immediately and concurrently with the cease-fire, negotiations shall start between the parties concerned under appropriate auspices aimed at establishing **a just and durable peace** in the Middle East."

### 3.21.5 Peace With Egypt (1979)

Egypt realised that Israel could not be conquered. Therefore, this south-westerly neighbour of the Jewish State was finally ready to sign a peace treaty on 26 March 1979, on the basis of the Camp David I negotiations, in order to get back the whole of the Sinai Peninsula, conquered by Israel, along with its oil sources, c. 80% of the areas Israel had occupied in the Six Day War. This treaty was the work of US President Jimmy Carter, along with Egyptian President Anwar Sadat and Israeli Prime Minister Menachem Begin.

This peace treaty begins:[507]
"Preamble
Convinced of the urgent necessity of the establishment of a just, comprehensive and **lasting peace** in the Middle East in accordance with Security Council Resolutions 242 and 338; ...
Desiring to bring to an end the state of war between them and

---

506 http://de.wikipedia.org/wiki/Resolution_338_des_UN-Sicherheitsrates (as of: 25.10.2011); http://avalon.law.yale.edu/20th_century/un338.asp (as of: 28.8.2012); emphasis by the author (RL).

507 http://www.mfa.gov.il/MFA/Peace%20Process/Guide%20to%20the%20Peace%20Process/Israel-Egypt%20Peace%20Treaty (as of: 25.10.2011); emphasis by the author (RL).

to establish a **peace** in which every state in the area can live in **security**; ..."

### 3.21.6 Madrid Peace Conference (1991)
Following the Gulf War of 1991, the United States fulfilled its promise, which had been given shortly before, to devote itself with increased resolve to the solution to the Middle East conflict. The conflicting parties met at the great Peace Conference in Madrid. The Soviet Union also participated. The US-Soviet letter of invitation to the conflicting parties, dated 30 October 1991, states in conclusion:[508]

"Indeed, only through such a process can **real peace** and reconciliation among the Arab states, Israel and the Palestinians be achieved. And only through this process can the peoples of the Middle East attain **the peace and security** they richly deserve."

### 3.21.7 Peace with the PLO and the Palestinians (1993)
Another consequence of the Madrid Peace Conference was the peace treaty with the Palestinians, represented by the PLO, on 13 October 1993, when Israeli President Yitzhak Rabin shook hands with Yasser Arafat in the presence of US President Bill Clinton on the White House lawn. On that day the Declaration of Principles (Oslo I agreement) was signed by both parties to the conflict. It begins:[509]

"Israel-Palestine Liberation Organization Agreement: 1993
The Government of the State of Israel and the Palestinian team representing the Palestinian people agree that it is time to put an end to decades of confrontation and conflict, recognize their mutual legitimate and political rights, and strive to live in **peaceful** coexistence and mutual dignity and **security** to achieve a just, lasting and comprehensive **peace** settlement and historic reconciliation through the agreed political process."

---

508 http://www.miftah.org/Display.cfm?DocId=430&CategoryId=10 (as of: 25.10.2011); http://www.miftah.org/Display.cfm?DocId=430&CategoryId=7 (as of: 28.8.2012); emphasis by the author (RL).

509 http://avalon.law.yale.edu/20th_century/isrplo.asp (as of: 25.10.2011); emphasis by the author (RL).

### 3.21.8 Peace with Jordan (1994)

On 26 October 1994 Israel, represented by Yitzhak Rabin, and Jordan, represented by King Hussein, agreed to peace in the presence of US President Bill Clinton. This peace treaty was signed explicitly on the basis of the Washington Declaration of 25 July 1994. In the declaration it reads:[510]

> "B 1. Jordan and Israel aim at the achievement of **just, lasting and comprehensive peace** between Israel and its neighbours and at the conclusion of a Treaty of **Peace** between both countries.
>
> ...
>
> B 5. The two countries desire to develop good neighbourly relations of cooperation between them to ensure **lasting security** ..."

### 3.21.9 Oslo II (1995)

On 24 September 1995 the "Israeli-Palestinian Interim Agreement," also named Oslo II, between Israel under Yitzhak Rabin and the PLO under Chairman Yasser Arafat was signed in the presence of US President Bill Clinton and other political witnesses from Russia, Egypt, Jordan, Norway and the EU[511] in Taba (on the Sinai Peninsula, Egypt). This agreement was very important for the future of the Gaza Strip and the West Bank. It was based on UN Resolutions 242 and 338 which call for peace and security. Here is the opening text of this 1995 document:[512]

> "PREAMBLE
> WITHIN the framework of the Middle East **peace** process initiated at Madrid in October 1991;
> REAFFIRMING their determination to put an end to decades of confrontation and to live in **peaceful coexistence**, mutual dignity and **security**, while recognizing their mutual legitimate and political rights; ..."

---

510 http://www.kinghussein.gov.jo/w-declaration.html (as of: 25.10.2011).

511 http://de.wikipedia.org/wiki/Interimsabkommen_%C3%BCber_das_Westjordanland_und_den_Gazastreifen (as of: 25.10.2011).

512 http://www.jewishvirtuallibrary.org/jsource/Peace/interim.html (as of: 25.10.2011); emphasis by the author (RL).

This treaty from 1995 became the basis for further agreements such as the Hebron Protocol (1997), the Wye Agreement (1998) and the Roadmap (2002).

### 3.21.10 The Hebron Agreement (1997)

The Hebron Agreement governed the redeployment of Israeli military forces in Hebron[513] in accordance with Oslo II and was signed by Benjamin Netanyahu and Yasser Arafat in the presence of US Secretary of State Warren Christopher in January 1997. An integral part of this agreement was a letter from Christopher to Netanyahu in which he writes:[514]

"… the United States' commitment to Israel's **security** is ironclad and constitutes the fundamental cornerstone of our special relationship. The key element in our approach to **peace**, including the negotiation and implementation of agreements between Israel and its Arab partners, has always been a recognition of Israel's **security** requirements…I would like to reiterate our position that Israel is entitled to **secure** and defensible borders, which should be directly negotiated …"

### 3.21.11 The Wye River Memorandum (1998)

The Wye Agreement,[515] signed on 23 October 1998 by Benjamin Netanyahu and Yasser Arafat in the presence of King Hussein and Bill Clinton, was to have governed the withdrawal of Israeli

forces from the West Bank while tangibly implementing the concept of "**security**" within the framework of the **peace** process.

### 3.21.12 Camp David II (2000)

Prime Minister Ehud Barak made a sensational offer to Yasser Arafat at the Middle East Peace Summit at Camp David which exceeded all past Israeli offers. Yasser Arafat categorically rejected it, however. Yet the warring parties, together with Bill Clinton, at

---

513 http://en.wikipedia.org/wiki/Hebron_Protocol (as of: 25.10.2011).

514 http://en.wikipedia.org/wiki/Hebron_Protocol (as of: 25.10.2011); emphasis by the author (RL).

515 The original wording: http://www.state.gov/www/regions/nea/981023_interim_agmt.html (as of: 25.10.2011).

least signed the "Trilateral Statement," in which, referring to UN Security Council Resolutions 252 and 338, "**peace** and **security**" would be sought.[516] Shortly afterwards the Second Intifada, the second Palestinian uprising, erupted.

### 3.21.13 The Roadmap (2002)

The "*Middle East Quartet*" (UN, US, EU and Russia) developed a comprehensive peace plan in the new millennium. The principles of this plan were presented by US President George W. Bush in a speech from 24 June 2002. In it, he expressed:[517]

> "My vision is two states, living side by side in **peace and security**."

There was no rest, no peace and no security in the Middle East even with these peace agreements. Arab terrorism continued, year after year, and caused countless deaths.

International efforts for peace and security continue. The US, UN, EU and Russia are presently attempting to end the conflict through countless efforts. Countless speeches are held on the international stage, numerous appeals addressed to the conflicting parties. Those who have followed this note that "peace and security" is a constant phrase. This formula has been constantly repeated on the international political stage, much like a prayer-wheel mantra, especially since the peace agreement at the Madrid Conference of 1991. If you have 1 Thessalonians 5 in front of you, it may well bring you out in a sweat.

Only a few examples from recent times will illustrate this. Here is the Middle East Quartet's statement in London, 1 March 2005:[518]

> "The Quarter commends the Israeli cabinet's recent approval of the initiative to withdraw from Gaza and parts of the West Bank, and reiterates that withdrawal from Gaza should be full and complete and should be undertaken in a manner consistent

---

516 http://en.wikipedia.org/wiki/2000_Camp_David_Summit (as of: 25.10.2011).

517 http://articles.cnn.com/2002-06-24/politics/bush.mideast.speech_1_palestinian-state-borders-and-certain-aspects-palestinian-parliament?_s=PM:ALLPOLITICS (as of: 25.10.2011). http://edition.cnn.com/2002/ALLPOLITICS/06/24/bush.mideast.speech/ (as of: 28.8.2012).

518 http://www.un.org/news/dh/infocus/middle_east/quartet-1mar2005.htm (as of: 25.10.2011); emphasis by the author (RL).

with the Roadmap, as an important step toward the realization of the vision of two democratic states, Israel and Palestine, living side by side in **peace and security.**

... The Quartet remains ready to engage actively, reaffirms its encouragement and support for both sides for the progress they have made in recent weeks, and reiterates its commitment to the fulfillment of the vision of two states, a **safe and secure** Israel and a sovereign, contiguous, democratic Palestine, living side by side in **peace and security.**"

The Middle East Quartet's statement in New York 15 December 2008:[519]

"The Quartet expressed its considered view that the bilateral negotiations process launched at Annapolis is irreversible and that these negotiations should be intensified in order to put an end to the conflict and to establish, as soon as possible, the State of Palestine, living side by side in **peace and security** with Israel."

A communication from President Obama, during his press conference at the White House on 24 March 2009:[520]

"... that it is critical for us to advance a two-state solution where Israelis and Palestinians can live side-by-side in their own states with **peace and security.**"

The Israeli Prime Minister Benjamin Netanyahu in Jerusalem on 25 March 2009 declared that:[521]

The Palestinians "should understand that they have in our government a partner for **peace**, for **security** and for rapid development of the Palestinian economy, ..."

---

519  http://www.un.org/News/Press/docs/2008/sg2147.doc.htm (as of: 18.10.2011); emphasis by the author (RL).

520  http://blogs.suntimes.com/sweet/2009/03/president_obamas_press_confere.html (as of: 25.10.2011); emphasis by the author (RL).

521  http://www.nytimes.com/2009/03/26/world/middleeast/26mideast.html (as of. 25.10.2011); emphasis by the author (RL).

US President Obama spoke to the Turkish Parliament on 7 April 2009:[522]

"Let me be clear, the United States strongly supports the goal of two states, Israel and Palestine, living side by side in **peace and security**. That is a goal shared by Palestinians, Israelis, and people of good will around the world. That is a goal that the parties agreed to in the road map and at Annapolis. And that is a goal that I will actively pursue as president."

President Obama also said that the Israelis and the Palestinians "must overcome longstanding passions and the politics of the moment to make progress toward a **secure** and lasting **peace**."

## 3.22 Jerusalem at the Centre of the Conflict

It has been attempted by all possible means and treaties to create peace in the Middle East. And yet peace has not succeeded. We have already seen that Al Mawardi's Islamic doctrine of Dar ul-Islam always precludes compromise. According to this doctrine, no Jewish state may exist on Islamic territory. Therefore, the Middle East conflict has not only existed since 1967, when Israel occupied Gaza along with the Sinai Peninsula, the West Bank and the Golan Heights. The conflict began in the period of the first Aliyah (1882–1903).

In international debate on the Middle East conflict the issue of the occupied territories is more important than the issue of the Israeli heartland. But the hottest issue of all is "Jerusalem"! Today's struggle for Jerusalem is concentrated especially on the Temple Mount in the Old City, in the centre of which soars the golden dome of the Mosque of Omar. Years ago, the "New York Times" correctly described this piece of land on Biblical Mount Zion as "the most explosive square metre in the world."

This raises the question: Why is there such tremendous interest in this patch of ground?

The Jewish Temple stood here on Zion (I), Mount Moriah, for some 1,000 years, from the 11th century BC to the 1st century AD.

---

522 http://www.turkishweekly.net/news/71058/-obama-we-are-committed-to- annapolis.html (as of: 25.10.2011); emphasis by the author (RL).

According to instructions in the Torah, the Law of Moses, the Temple may only be located on this site (Deut. 12:13-14). The Temple is the geographical centre of Israeli worship, which includes animal sacrifice in particular. The Jewish people have deeply yearned for the restoration of the Temple for some 2,000 years. The huge stone blocks, known as the "Wailing Wall," on the western side of Mount Zion are a remnant of the formidable walls which once protectively surrounded the Jewish Temple.

Jews have here lamented their lost sanctuary for two millennia. No one can count the tears which have been shed and how many prayers have ascended for the restoration of the Temple here, by this wall. For Judaism, these stones are a symbol of lost glory and, at the same time, a sign of hope of future redemption.

On the other hand this area also plays an important role in Islam. Since the 7th or 8th century AD, the Al-Aqsa Mosque and the so-called Dome of the Rock (= "the Mosque of Omar") have stood here. This area, situated above the Wailing Wall, with its ten doors and four minarets, is called "the noble sanctuary" (Arabic: *haram esh-sharif*) by Muslims. Jerusalem is considered the third most important city in Islamic hierarchy. Only the pilgrimage cities of Mecca and Medina are more important.

According to popular Islamic interpretation of the 17th Koranic sura, Mohammad rode his white-winged steed, Al-Burak, whose every leap carried him as far as the eye can see, during his night journey north from Mecca "to the most distant (Arabic *'al-'aksa*) place of worship," the Temple area in Jerusalem. The founder of Islam dismounted and prayed at the rock where the Al-Aqsa Mosque is now located. Following this, Mohammad ascended from there into heaven. After he learned from Allah how to correctly pray, he then returned to the Temple area. According to Islamic tradition, Mohammad quickly came back to Mecca on the back of Al-Burak, arriving before dawn.

Furthermore, Islamic tradition states that Abraham planned to sacrifice his son Ishmael (!) on the rock which is today found in the interior of the Dome.

This background information explains why Muslims will never give up their claims to this site.

Jerusalem was abandoned to an uncertain fate by the so-called peace agreement of 13 September 1993 between Israel and the Palestinians. The Gaza-Jericho Agreement provided that the future status of East Jerusalem would be negotiated within a foreseeable period of time – even though in late 1980 the Israeli Parliament had declared "all of Jerusalem to be the undivided, eternal capital of Israel."[523]

The Arabs, and especially the Palestinians, demand possession of Jerusalem, especially East Jerusalem with the Temple Mount. This coveted place will be, from their point of view, the capital of the future Palestinian nation – and will include the Temple Mount. Scheich Isam'il Al-Nawadah stated in his sermon in the Al-Aksa Mosque Friday, 3 April 1998:

"Jerusalem is at the top of cities sacred to Islam. No city equals its holiness, except Al-Medina and Mecca ... Jerusalem is ours and not yours [i.e. Israel]; this city is more important to us than to you ... Jerusalem is the key to both war and peace [but] if the Jews think that force will allow them [to keep] both the land and the peace –they delude themselves"[524]

Jerusalem has always been at the centre of all the wars since 1967, the thousands of rocket attacks and the countless terrorist attacks with suicide bombers against Israel. Iranian President Ahmadinejad's statement, "... this regime occupying Jerusalem must vanish from the page of time,"[525] makes clear that, for him, the battle for Jerusalem is central. This claim will enforce Iran's insane pursuit of the atomic bomb, a move which threatens the whole world. The Hamas terror organization, allies of Iran, also calls for Israel's annihilation. The Al-Aqsa Mosque is pictured on their logo, clearly showing what is most important to them.

Hezbollah in Lebanon, supported by Syria, is another of Iran's allies. This terror organization has frenziedly armed itself with missiles in the past years, in order to destroy Israel in the future.

---

523  MAY: Israel heute – Ein lebendiges Wunder, p. 96.
524  PRICE: The Coming Last Days Temple, p. 177. Original source: MEMRI's Media Review of April 6, 1998.
525  http://fr.wikipedia.org/wiki/Mahmoud_Ahmadinejad (as of: 25.11.2011).

From a purely human point of view, who would ever have thought centuries ago that the city of Jerusalem, whose name means "foundation of peace" would one day put the peace and safety of the entire world at risk, by its neighbours becoming slaves to thoughts of sheer madness? Yet, this is exactly what was to happen, according to Biblical prophecy. The ETERNAL ONE, with The Last Days in view, stated in 520 BC in Zechariah 12:2:

*"² Behold, I will make Jerusalem a **cup of trembling** [Hebr. saph ra'al] unto all the people round about, ..."* (KJV)

The Hebrew term for *"cup of trembling"* can also be translated with *"cup of bewilderment."* This concerns a vessel for alcohol which makes clear thinking impossible by intoxication. Jerusalem would, thus, become the trigger for the insanity of the surrounding nations in The Last Days. Today, we are eye-witnesses of this fact and are all very much affected by it.

In the next verse of Zechariah 12 Jerusalem is compared to a *"burdensome stone"*:

*"³ And in that day will I make Jerusalem a **burdensome stone** for all people: all that burden themselves with it shall be cut in pieces ..."* (KJV)

The Hebrew term *'even ma'amaseh* designates a heavy stone with which young men test their strength. A strong man may be able to lift the stone to chest height and stronger men, over the head. But woe betide when the stone is then dropped ...! Zechariah says that Jerusalem will become a test of the military strength of the surrounding nations, but with a disastrous end. We can see the mad build-up of weaponry in the Middle East today. At the same time we can know that the end will be catastrophic.

### 3.23 What Happens Next?

The aim of this book is to present the more than 175 already fulfilled prophecies regarding The Last Days. This is not an explanation of what is yet to come according to the Bible. I have covered this topic in many lectures[526] and in other books.[527]

However, to briefly comment on the Olivet Discourse, the events of Matthew 24:15ff, Mark 13:14ff. and Luke 21:26-27 (by and large already in verse 25) are all still future.

Matthew 24:15 and Mark 13:14 speak of the image of the Antichrist in the Temple in Jerusalem.[528] This will be the initial spark for the following 3½ years of Tribulation (Dan. 7:25; 9:27; 12:7; Rev. 11:2,3; 12:7,14; 13:5), at the end of which Christ will return in power and great glory (cf. Matt. 24:15-31; Mark 13:14-27; Luke 21:25-27).

The incident of the speaking image of the Antichrist (cf. Rev. 13:11-18), the *"abomination of desolation"* according to Matthew 24:15,[529] will take place after the rapture of the Church (cf. 1 Cor. 15:51ff; 1 Thess. 4:13-18). The Church will be saved from *"the hour of temptation"*[530] (Rev. 3:10), i.e. from the period when the Antichrist will appear as the greatest seducer of all times.[531]

Following the rapture of the Church, Israel will again take its place as witness for God and His Word, just as it once did in the OT. There will then be revival in Israel (Isa. 10:20-22; 37:31-32).

---

526 At www.sermon-online.de there are many lectures by Roger Liebi free to download. See particularly:
· Die Bibel in der Vogelschau. Die 7 Bündnisse und die 7 Heilszeitalter
· Abriss der kommenden prophetischen Ereignisse
· Jerusalem – Hindernis oder Chance für den Weltfrieden?
· Einführung in die Offenbarung

527 Cf. the author's bibliography in the Appendix.

528 The sign of the image (*"abomination of desolation"*) is quite different from the sign of the army camps around Jerusalem (Luke 21:20). While the sign in Luke was fulfilled in 68 AD, the sign of the image points to a still future event. Both signs are followed by flight to the mountains. Those fleeing in Luke 21:21 were the Jewish Christians in the 1st century, while in Matthew and Mark, the future flight of the believing remnant of Israel who believe in Messiah Jesus (cf. Isa. 10:20-22) following the rapture of the Church is meant.

529 The term *"abomination that maketh desolate"* designates in the fulfilled prophecy of Dan. 11:32 an image that Antiochus IV Epiphanes set up in the Temple during the 2nd century BC. This parallel helps us to clearly understand that an image is meant with the still future *"abomination of desolation"* in Matt. 24:15.

530 *"The hour of temptation"* designates the period of deception by the Antichrist. It will be the worst period of deception in the entire history of mankind (cf. Rev. 13:11ff).

531 There are people who wish to translate Rev. 3:10 with *"saved out of the hour of temptation"* instead of *"saved from the hour of temptation."* The isolated Greek word *ek* can mean "out of" as well as "from." But the intended meaning in a particular context is understood in each case by the sequence of words in the text. Here, we have the combination *tereo ek*. This can only mean "protect from." Someone is protected *from* a danger, not *out of* a danger. If the word *sozo* (= "to save") instead of *tereo* were used, then this could rightly be translated "saved out of." The combination *tereo ek* occurs one other time in the NT, in John 17:15. This would never be translated with "keep them *out of* evil." It is clear to everyone that this means "keep them *from* the evil."

The "remnant of Israel" will come to belief in the Messiah Jesus, initially 144,000 (Rev. 7:1-8) as a vanguard, the so-called *"first fruits"* (Rev. 14:4). Afterwards – but only during the Great Tribulation – ⅓ of the Jewish population of Israel will come to repentance (Zech. 13:8).

As soon as the believing remnant of 144,000 see the image of the Antichrist in the Temple (Matt. 24:15), they will take flight to the mountains (Matt. 24:16-20) to find refuge in Moab (central Jordan, beyond the Dead Sea) (Isa. 16:3-4; Rev. 12:6-7,13-14).

Then the *"king of the north"* will begin his attack on Israel and overrun the Promised Land (Dan. 11:40-45; Joel 1–2; Isa. 28:14–29:8; Zech. 12–14; etc.).[532] Thus, the most devastating world war of all times will be unleashed, bringing mankind to the brink of self-destruction. The Lord called this period *"the great tribulation"* in Matt. 24:21-22. God has fixed, or limited, this interval to 3½ years (Matt. 24:21,22; Rev. 12:6,14; 13:5; Dan. 7:25; 12:7).

The term *"the king of the north"* referred to in the fulfilled prophecy in the book of Daniel (Dan. 11:1-35) always designates "Greater Syria," i.e. the entire territory of Syria, Lebanon to Pakistan, and including areas which are presently part of Azerbaijan, Turkmenistan, Uzbekistan, Kyrgyzstan, Tajikistan, Afghanistan, Iraq, as well as Turkey and Iran.[533] It is obvious that *the Islamic world* will strike a mortal blow against Israel.

The rapture of the Church could happen at any time. There is no remaining prophetic event which must necessarily take place before the rapture.

In this connection, I want to stress that the people who have heard the Good News of Jesus Christ and, nevertheless, have not turned to God – will have no further opportunity of repentance. They will be lost forever. 2 Thessalonians 2:11-12 testifies that they will all fall victim to the Antichrist's seduction:

> *"11 And for this cause God shall send them strong delusion, that*

---

532 *"The king of the north"* is designated in Isaiah and Micah as *"Assur"/"Assyria,"* in Joel as *"the one coming from the north."*

533 Cf. LIEBI: Weltgeschichte im Visier des Propheten Daniel, p. 79ff (English edition in progress by CMV Hagedorn, Germany).

*they should believe a lie: [12] That they all might be damned who*
*believed not the truth, but had pleasure in unrighteousness."* (KJV)

The rapture corresponds as a parallel event to the time prior
to the flood, when Noah entered the life-saving ark (Gen. 7:1,5).
God then sealed the door (Gen. 7:16; cf. Job 12:13). From then on,
no one could be saved (cf. Matt. 24:38: *"until the day that Noah
entered into the ark ..."*). No one could get into the ark any longer.
The period of grace was definitively concluded.

Shortly afterward the flood came as the global judgement of
mankind (cf. Matt. 24:39: *"... and knew not until the flood came,
and took them all away..."*). The present period of grace, *"the day
of salvation,"* will have its end with the rapture of the Church (cf. 2
Cor. 6:2; Isa. 26:9b-10a).

Daniel's 70th week will take place only following the rapture of
the Church.[534] This still future period of 7 years will be begun by
an alliance with the leader of the restored Roman Empire (Dan.
9:27). This covenant will be a security agreement with Israel (Isa.
28:14-18). The Great Tribulation will occur during the second half
of this 7-year period.

The seven seal judgements of Revelation will occur only after
the rapture of the Church. The first six will occur *after* the rapture, but *before* the Great Tribulation (Rev. 6). The 7th seal will
begin the Great Tribulation (Rev. 8:1). This consists of seven trumpet judgements (Rev. 8:6–9:21), with the 7th trumpet judgement
(Rev. 11:15) consisting of seven bowl judgements (Rev. 16). The
Lord Jesus Christ will then appear as King and Judge of the world
(Rev. 19:11ff), to establish the 1,000-year Reign (Rev. 20:1-10) and
to deliver Israel from all distress (Zech. 14).

The 1st seal judgement includes the coming of the Antichrist
(Rev. 6:1-2). The Antichrist can only be revealed when the Holy
Spirit, together with the Church, departs. God the Holy Spirit is,
according to 2 Thessalonians 2:1-12, *"**that** [neuter] which restrains
[the evil in its last expression]."* (The Greek word for "Spirit"
[*pneuma*] is grammatically neuter.)

---

534 For Daniel's 70 Weeks see Dr Roger Liebi: Die Bibel in der Vogelschau. Die 7 Bündnisse und die 7
Heilszeitalter (audio lecture) at www.sermon-online.de .

Among the signs from the Olivet Discourse the following six still refer to the future:

1. The image set up in the Temple (Matt. 24:15; Mark 13:14)
2. The darkening of the sun (Matt. 24:29; Mark 13:24; Luke 21:11,25)
3. The darkening of the moon (Matt. 24:29; Mark 13:24; Luke 21:11,25)
4. Asteroids (stars)[535] falling from heaven (Matt. 24:29; Mark 13:25; Luke 21:11,25)
5. Powers of the heavens will be shaken (Matt. 24:29; Mark 13:25; Luke 21:11,26)
6. The sign of the Son of Man in the heavens (Matt. 24:30; Luke 21:11)

The image in the Temple will be erected, as stated earlier, in *"the hour of temptation"* and is therefore still in the future.

It is understood from Matthew 24:29 that signs 2–6 will take place directly before the Second Coming of Christ as King of the World. This applies especially to the period after the rapture of the Church. Therefore these signs are not in operation at present.

The so-called Tunguska explosion deserves special mention as a forerunner in this context: On 30 June 1908 a meteorite, or fragment of a comet, some tens of meters in diameter crashed on Earth and exploded in Siberia, 65 km north of the city Vanavara.[536] It is estimated that some 60 million trees were snapped and/or uprooted in an area of 2,000 km². Doors and windows in Vanavara were shattered. A bright, fiery glow and strong shaking, accompanied by a shock wave and thunder could be perceived more than 500 km away. The energy released by this explosion was approximately 1150 times that of the atomic bomb dropped on Hiroshima

---

535 Matt. 24:29 does not say that stars in the sense of "suns" will fall to Earth. For instance, in the Tajik language asteroids or meteors which fall to Earth are called "falling stars." The Greek text of the Olivet Discourse is to be understood in this sense. Our word "asteroid" comes from the Greek word *aster* (= star) and the Greek component *eides* (= similar). There are now well over 1,000 asteroids with a diameter of over 1 km which could be dangerous to Earth because of their orbit. One such impact would cause an unimaginable catastrophe for our planet. (http://de.wikipedia.org/wiki/Meteoriteneinschlag [as of: 25.10.2001]).

536 http://en.wikipedia.org/wiki/Tunguska_event ; http://de.wikipedia.org/wiki/Tunguska-Ereignis (as of: 25.10.2011).

(1945). Can one imagine the devastating consequences if this had happened in a densely populated area of the Earth?

## Prophetic Plan of the Last 7 Years

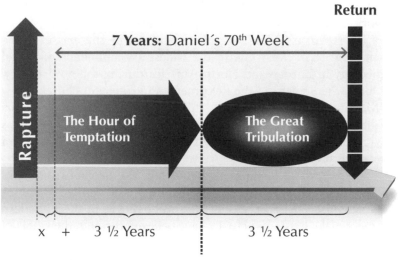

The Antichrist desecrates the Temple. He sets up the image (Matt. 24:15) and sits in the Temple (2 Thess. 2:4).

*Fig. 31: Overview of the upcoming events from the Rapture until the Coming of Jesus Christ as King and Judge of the world.*

### 3.24 Second Coming of Christ Rejected

We have already seen how Jesus Christ's statements regarding End-Time events are wonderfully supplemented in 2 Timothy and 2 Peter. Therefore, a few more points can be added here.

Peter prophesied that belief in the return of Jesus Christ would be mocked and ridiculed in The Last Days (2 Peter 3:2-4):

*"²... that ye may be mindful of the words which were spoken before by the holy prophets, and of the commandment of us the apostles of the Lord and Saviour: ³ knowing this first, **that***

***there shall come in the last days scoffers,*** *walking after their own lusts,* ⁴*and* **saying, Where is the promise of his coming?**" (KJV)

For nearly 2,000 years of Church history, people in the Christian West took for granted that Jesus Christ rose again on the third day and that He will come again in The Last Days as Judge of the world.

The return of Jesus Christ is now denied by the masses in the once-Christian West due to the widespread influence of liberal theology in Europe and North America during the 20ᵗʰ century. Liberal theologians of the Reformed and Protestant churches say: "Modern man" cannot believe in the bodily resurrection of Jesus Christ, and even less in His return. They say that these are myths which can no longer be accepted at face value in an era dominated by scientific thought.

Anyone who still explicitly believes in the Second Coming of Christ must reckon with the fact that he will be derided as a "fundamentalist Christian," because he still believes in these modern times what Christians actually have believed through the whole of Church history of almost 2,000 years.

This development had to come about and precisely in that epoch in which the Jews returned to the Land of their Fathers.

Peter explains in the following verses of Chapter 3 why the scoffers cannot believe in the Second Coming of Jesus. They assume that everything, from the beginning on, has always followed the exact same principles. They say God has never intervened in history. Therefore, it is inconceivable that this will happen in the future. Furthermore, Peter states that these mockers are convinced of the consistent passing of time without God because they neither believe in God's direct intervention in Creation, nor in His supernatural act precipitating the Flood.

It follows that belief in creation by God, according to the Biblical account in Gen. 1–2, and belief in the Flood as a worldwide historical event, according to Gen. 6–9, would be abandoned in The Last Days (2 Peter 3:3-6):

*"³... knowing this first, that there shall come in the last days scoffers, walking after their own lusts, ⁴ and saying, Where is the promise of his coming? for since the fathers fell asleep, all things continue as they were from the beginning of the creation. ⁵ For this they willingly are ignorant of, that by the word of God the heavens were of old, and the earth standing out of the water and in the water: ⁶ whereby the world that then was, being overflowed with water, perished"* (KJV)

Verse 5 refers directly to the creation account, which begins with the words *"In the beginning God created the heaven and the earth."* (Gen. 1:1; cf. *"... that by the word of God the heavens were of old, and the earth ..."*).

Furthermore, the apostle focuses in particular on the third day of creation, Gen. 1:9-10. In the creation account the land is first completely covered by water. Only on the third day, the Creator causes the land (Hebr. *yabbashah* = "dry") to appear by upthrust out of the water through His commanding call, His Word, while the water, from then on, will surround the mainland as an ocean (cf. *"... by the word of God ... the earth standing out of the water and in the water ..."*).

This same water, which covered the planet before the third day of creation, again completely covered the whole of the earth in the Flood, as *"all the fountains of the great deep"* broke up (Gen. 7:11; cf. *"whereby [i.e. by water] the world that then was, being overflowed with water, perished"*).[537]

The beginning of verse 5 states that the scoffers reject the Creation and Flood accounts because they don't want to know this. They willingly reject this (*"For this they willingly are ignorant of ..."*). Things can be unknown because people do not desire to know them!

The mockers' statement in verse 4, *"for since the fathers fell asleep, **all things continue as they were from the beginning of the creation**"* does not necessarily mean that they believe in the Creator God. This expression can be used even by atheists! Ste-

---

537 The total quantity of water existing on Earth would be enough to cover the entire planet to nearly 3 km depth if the surfaces of the land and the ocean bottom were evened out.

phen Hawking, one of the most important Big Bang theorists of our time, said that the universe was *created* out of nothing in his book "The Grand Design," published in autumn 2010. The reason why "there is something rather than nothing" is because of "spontaneous *creation*."[538] Hawking outs himself clearly as an atheist for the first time in this book. Nevertheless, he used the term "*creation*"! For him the Creator is effectively the not-yet-existing universe, which created itself, and the law of gravity, which existed prior to matter. The statement that the universe created itself is patently absurd, going against all principles of logic and reason. Something that does not exist cannot create itself, or it would have existed before it existed... If Hawking intended something else, then he would have to say it differently.

Moreover, the idea that matter and energy originated out of nothing without a Creator God is contrary to the 1st Law of Thermodynamic.

## 3.25 The Flood Account Rejected

Until 1800, most geologists believed that the Biblical account of the Flood played a crucial role in explaining the origin of the strata and the fossils they contain.

A new perspective developed in 1830 as Charles Lyell (1797–1875), a lawyer who was also interested in geology, rejected the possibility of the Flood. A global flood includes the idea that there is a holy God who does not allow mankind's sins to go unpunished, but Who is willing to interrupt and directly intervene in the course of history. This thought was unacceptable to Lyell. Therefore, he invented "the principle of uniformitarianism" which states that the processes of nature are always uniform and that there have never been great catastrophes. Things have been the same since the beginning of the world. This is exactly the scoffers' argument in 2 Peter 3:4b:

> "*4b ...for since the fathers fell asleep, **all things continue as they were from the beginning of the creation.**" (KJV)

---

538 http://de.wikipedia.org/wiki/Stephen_Hawking ; http://www.giessener-zeitung.de/giessen/beitrag/37888/schoepfung-ohne-evolutions-theorie-etoe-weltformelq/ (as of: 25.10.2011).

Of course, the strata and the huge variety of fossils they contain can obviously be explained by catastrophic floods. Gigantic layers of earth, such as are found and impressively documented in the Swiss Alps, for example, do not develop under normal circumstances. But for Lyell, it was important not to speak of disasters. No, in his opinion, the strata were formed by the ordinary processes of erosion; wind, rain, heat and cold, etc. without catastrophic events. The eroded material was transported by streams and rivers, just as is seen today, and the strata very slowly formed, millimeter by millimeter, centimeter by centimeter. Clearly, if this were the case, there would be no layers filled with mass graves of fossils such as are found worldwide; but for Lyell, his principle of uniformitarianism was more important than such objections.[539]

Since the notion of a non-catastrophic emergence of huge layers of earth within a short time frame doesn't work, Lyell introduced the idea of enormously long periods of time into geology.

The principle of uniformitarianism was widely disseminated in the 20th century through lessons at school. The Flood was generally no longer taught as the explanation for the formation of strata and fossils. Now, the average person has turned his back on the Flood; this event has become a myth, a fairy tale. But, it had to come to pass exactly in this way! The Flood would be denied in the period when the Jews were returning to their homeland.

Charles Lyell published his three-volume work "Principles of Geology" in the years 1830–1833.[540] When Charles Darwin set out on his five-year-long journey around the world in 1830, the captain of the Beagle, a British government survey ship, gave him Volume I of Lyell's series on geology. This publication would be of crucial importance to Charles Darwin. In it Lyell presented him with the idea of enormously long geological time periods which Darwin desperately needed to explain the random, gradual development of living things. In this way, the rejection of the Flood account became the basis for the rejection of the Creation account.

---

539 Objections to evolutionary geology which can be understood by all can be found in the following publication: HAM, K.: The New Answers Book [in three volumes], Green Forest, Arizona, 2006.

540 http://en.wikipedia.org/wiki/Principles_of_Geology (as of: 25.10.2011).

## 3.26 The Creation Account Rejected

Most people in the West believed in the truth of the Creation (Genesis 1–2) and the Flood (Gen. 6–9) accounts until the early 20th century.

Charles Darwin published his first book on evolution, "The Origin of Species" in 1859. The purpose of this book was to make clear that a Creator God was not necessary to explain the diversity of plants and animals. Everything evolved according to natural laws, without God.

Another influential book, "The Descent of Man," followed in 1872. Here, Darwin explained that what he had written in the 1859 book also applied to mankind. Man was also the product of a slow natural development (evolution), not requiring a Creator.[541]

At the time, these books were met by an extremely positive and enthusiastic response in academic circles. The spirit of the age was ripe for such ideas. 50 years earlier this would not have been the case. But, it took some time before these thoughts and ideas of evolution became common knowledge in Western society. Throughout the 20th century the theory of evolution was accepted and assimilated by the masses, thanks to the schools and mass media. Today, anyone who still believes in the Bible's Creation account must be prepared to be dismissed as a "stick-in-the-mud" and an "anti-scientific fundamentalist." But this had to happen; Peter had prophesied the deliberate rejection of the Creation account in The Last Days (2 Peter 3:5):

> "⁵ For this they willingly are **ignorant of, that by the word of God the heavens were of old, and the earth standing out of the water** and in the water ..." (KJV)

Peter says that they are "*ignorant of*" the knowledge of the Creation and the Flood accounts. It is noticeable that the opponents

---

541 For scientific criticism of evolution see: OUWENEEL: Evolution in der Zeitenwende. LIEBI: Herkunft und Entwicklung der Sprachen. Lingusitik contra Evolution. See the following audio lectures by the author at www.sermon-online.de :
· Charles Darwin und seine Evolutionslehre: Wahrheit oder Irrtum?
· Herkunft und Entwicklung der Sprachen
· Spuren Gottes im Weltall (also on YouTube).

of the doctrine of Creation generally do not know what is actually in the Bible text. They do not know what it says precisely or what it does not say. They know even less about the significance of the statements in detail.

The rejection of Biblical truths, such as the Second Coming of Christ and the Creation and Flood accounts is not restricted to small groups, but pertains to the masses. This is linked to the mass apostasy according to 2 Thessalonians 2:3 already discussed!

## 3.27 Hunting for Myths

We have seen that 2 Timothy has The Last Days, *"the last days"* of Christendom, in mind (2 Tim. 3:1). Another prophetic detail that we have not yet addressed is found in chapter 4 of this NT letter:

> *"³ For the time will come when they will not endure sound doctrine; but after their own lusts shall they heap to themselves teachers, having itching ears; ⁴ and they shall turn away their ears from the truth,* ***and shall be turned unto fables.*** *⁵ But watch thou in all things, endure afflictions, do the work of an evangelist, make full proof of thy ministry."* (KJV)

Today's modern, enlightened man rejects the Bible as God's Word. He sees the Bible as a collection of myths, at best providing information about the thinking of people in so-called pre-scientific times. But he rejects any relevance the Bible has for modern times.

The German theology professor, Rudolf Bultmann (1884–1976) once developed a program to demythologize the Bible. He claimed that the modern, scientifically-minded person could no longer believe that Jesus Christ rose from the dead and that He will return. He also claimed that it was not possible to take the Bible seriously as a historical record. Bultmann exerted an incredibly strong influence, not only in theology, but far beyond.

We can counter him: It is possible for us to provide evidence that the Bible is historically, absolutely reliable! It is also possible for us to disprove the theories of liberal theology and reveal their false presuppositions and methods.[542]

Incidentally, Rudolf Bultmann came to saving belief before his death. He asked for forgiveness, in view of his students, for the dissemination of false teaching. His former student, Prof. Dr. Eta Linneman, who also experienced a very radical conversion to Jesus Christ, testifies to this.

We can now perceive an interesting paradox: Although modern man sees himself to be above the myths of the Bible, we observe, especially in the wake of the 1968 movement, that there has definitely been a run by the masses on mythology, science fiction, UFO-belief, fantasy and horror. This applies to all sorts of areas such as film, literature, music, computer games, and even children's toys, etc. Mythological films such as "Star Wars," "E.T.," "The Unending Story," "Lord of the Rings" and "Harry Potter" have brought in hundreds of millions of dollars. This is connected to the continuing esoteric wave. Esoteric is a billion dollar market. On one hand, there is the widespread rejection of the Bible, (*"For the time will come when they will not endure sound doctrine [the Bible]; ... and they shall turn away their ears from the truth [the Bible]"*), and on the other hand, openness for all sorts of irrational, religiously-inspired nonsense that somehow tickles the ear (cf. *"...and shall be turned unto fables"*). It is just as Napoleon said:

"People will believe anything; as long as it's not in the Bible."

---

542 Cf. for example: ARCHER: G.L.: A Survey of Old Testament Introduction, updated and revised ed., Chicago, 1994; KITCHEN: Ancient Orient and Old Testament; KÜLLING: Zur Datierung der «Genesis-P-Stücke»; LIEBI: Weltgeschichte im Visier des Propheten Daniel (English edition in progress by CMV Hagedorn, Germany).

# 4. List of 32 Fulfilled Prophecies (P147–178)

| Prophecy | Statement | Bible verse | Fulfillment |
|---|---|---|---|
| P147 | **Large-scale wars** | Matt. 24:6-7; Mark 13:7-8; Luke 21:9-10 | First and Second World Wars (1914–1918/1939–1945) |
| P148 | **Revolutions** | Mark 13:8; Luke 21:9 | C. 40 revolutions from 1882–2011 |
| P149 | **Famines** in various places | Matt. 24:7; Mark 13:8; Luke 21:11 | 20th century = century of famine; presently: 1 billion chronically hungry; long list of acute, devastating famines since 1882 |
| P150 | **Plagues** in various places | Matt. 24:7; Luke 21:11 | Third Plague Pandemic (1896–1945); Spanish Flu (1918–1920); Smallpox (300-500 million dead); AIDS; Hepatitis B and C, etc. |
| P151 | **Earthquakes/ massive earthquakes** in various places | Matt. 24:7; Mark 13:8; Luke 21:11 | Approx. 140 serious earthquakes with over 2 Million dead and many more injured (1882–2011) |

| Prophecy | Statement | Bible verse | Fulfillment |
|---|---|---|---|
| P152 | **Chronological relationship:** *"beginning of birth pains"*: large-scale wars; revolutions, famines, pestilence, earthquakes, **then** Christian persecution | Matt. 24:8-9 | First World War, Russian Revolution, Chinese Revolution, February Revolution, October Revolution, famines in China and India, earthquakes in Iran, Japan, China, Messina, Spanish Flu, **then** Soviet persecution of Christians (1922–1989) |
| P153 | Massive Christian persecution: *"affliction"* for Christians | Matt. 24:8-9 | Persecution of Christians in the Soviet Union and Eastern Europe (1922–1989): **Oppression and discrimination, prison, labour camp, psych. hospitals** |
| P154 | Massive persecution of Christians: *"they shall kill you."* | Matt. 24:8-9 | Persecution of Christians in the Soviet Union and Eastern Europe (1922–1991): **Millions of Christians killed** |
| P155 | Massive persecution of Christians: *"ye shall be hated of all nations for my name's sake."* | Matt. 24:8-9; Mark 13:13 | Persecution of Christians in the Soviet Union and Eastern Europe (1920–1991): **The entire free world largely ignored the persecution of Christians in the Soviet Union and Eastern Europe** |
| P156 | The masses are forced to give up the faith. | Matt. 24:10 | As a consequence of persecution many professing Christians in the Soviet Union and Eastern Europe fall away from God and His Word (the Bible) and are re-educated as atheists. |
| P157 | People will betray one another | Matt. 24,10 | Co-operation between secret police and society: mutual spying and betrayal |

| Prophecy | Statement | Bible verse | Fulfillment |
|---|---|---|---|
| P158 | Even **family members** will turn against each other | Mark 13:12 | Infiltration of the family by the secret police |
| P159 | They will hate one another ➜ **interpersonal trust destroyed** | Matt. 24:10 | Mutual trust is destroyed by the informant system in the Communist countries. Love gave way to hatred |
| P160 | General **voluntary apostasy** in Christendom (without persecution) | 2 Thess. 2:3; 2 Tim. 4:3-4; 2 Pet. 3:3-6; Jude 1:11,17-18; Luke 17:26-30 | 20th century, especially since 1968: Millions in the West turned their backs on Christianity. Liberal theology rejects the basics of Christianity |
| P161 | Immorality taught in the churches and called freedom | 2 Pet. 2; Jude 1 | Protestant and Evangelical Ref. churches are infiltrated by the immorality of the 1968 revolution: Premarital sex, homosexuality tolerated or defended |
| P162 | Many false prophets | Matt. 24:11,24 | Three charismatic waves: from 1906; from around 1960; from around 1980: Masses of false prophets worldwide; numerous false teachings disseminated worldwide; the esoteric wave beginning in the 1960s |
| P163 | Many will be deceived | Matt. 24:11 | About 600 million follow new prophets and charismatic heresies; also: millions have turned to esoteric teachings |

| Prophecy | Statement | Bible verse | Fulfillment |
|---|---|---|---|
| P164 | **Great (real) signs and wonders**, presenting danger of deception also for the true believers (*"the elect"*) | Matt. 24:24; 2 Tim. 3:8 | Mass gatherings for healing the sick, millions who speak in tongues, Toronto blessing; also: Spirit healing by esoteric practioners , etc. |
| P165 | Progressive deception through **charlatanry** | 2 Tim. 3:13 | Many wonders of the Charismatic movement prove to be charlatanism |
| P166 | False messiahs | Matt. 24:24 | Oskar Ernst Bernhardt alias Abd-ru-shin (1875–1941); Jiddu Krishnamurti (1895–1986); George Baker alias Father Divine (1880–1965); Rabbi Menachem Mendel Schneerson, Rebbe (1902–1994); Maharishi Mahesh Yogi (1918–1998); San Myung Mun (1920–2012); Swami Omkarananda (1930–2000); Jim Jones (1931–1978); Marshall Applewhite (1931–1997); Bhagwan Shree Rajnesh (1931–1990); Charles Manson (1934*); Guru Maharaj Ji (1957*) David Koresh (1959–1993) |
| P167 | Tsunamis and flooding | Luke 21:25 | Long list of major floods: 1882–2011; Tsunami 2004: 230,000 dead; 2005: New Orleans flooded; Japan 2011: Tsunami und nuclear disaster |
| P168 | *"Terrorism"/ "terror events"* | Luke 21:25 | Islamic terrorism worldwide problem in 20th and 21st centuries/dramatic increase in natural disasters in 20th and 21st centuries |

| Prophecy | Statement | Bible verse | Fulfillment |
|----------|-----------|-------------|-------------|
| P169 | Moral collapse among the masses in the West | Matt. 24:12; Luke 17:28-30; 2 Tim. 3:1-5; 2 Pet. 2; 3:17; Jude 1:4-23 | Moral collapse in the West due to 1968 Revolution, teachings of evolution, liberal, Bible-critical theology |
| P170 | "The love of many shall wax cold." | Matt. 24:12; 2 Tim. 3:3 | More than 40 million babies aborted yearly; this leaves the masses unmoved, cold. Natural feelings destroyed by perverse/sinful life styles |
| P171 | The Gospel reaches all nations. | Matt. 24:14; Mark 13:10 | Preaching of the Gospel reaches all nations (not all tribes) in the 20th century (also via the radio, internet, etc.) |
| P172 | They continually say: *"peace and safety!"* | 1 Thess. 5:1-3 | The phrase used constantly in the Middle East peace process from 1974 – today is: "Peace and safety!" |
| P173 | Jerusalem = *"cup of trembling"* (alcoholic drink clouding all reasonable thinking) and *"burdensome stone"* to gauge the military strength of the surrounding nations | Zech 12:2.3 | East Jerusalem with the Temple Mount is at the heart of the Middle East conflict. Iran wants to liberate Jerusalem with the nuclear threat. The liberation of Jerusalem = the main objective of the terrorism of Hamas, Jihad, Hezbollah, etc. The Palestinians claim East Jerusalem as the capital of their future state |

| Prophecy | Statement | Bible verse | Fulfillment |
|---|---|---|---|
| P174 | Christ's return rejected | 2 Pet. 3:2-4 | Liberal theology rejects the return of Christ as a myth. Millions in the once-Christian West have discarded the expectation of the Coming of Christ |
| P175 | It has always been the same from the beginning in the natural world. No worldwide catastrophes! | 2 Pet. 3:4-6 | The principle of uniformitarianism replaced the catastrophic principle in geology for the masses in the 20th century |
| P176 | The Flood account rejected | 2 Pet. 3:4-6 | In the 20th century the masses see the Flood as a myth |
| P177 | The Creation account rejected | 2 Pet. 3:4-6 | In the 20th century belief in the theory of evolution has replaced belief in the Creation account of the Bible |
| P178 | Hunting for myths | 2 Tim. 4:3-4 | Boom of mythology, science fiction, belief in UFOs, fantasy and horror in film, literature, music, computer games, esotericism, occultism |

# VI. Conclusions

## 1. The Prophetic Test for Religions

On the basis of fulfilled prophecy, we can demonstrate that we are indeed living in The Last Days and that Jesus Christ will come again soon. This now raises the question: Are you ready to meet the Eternal Judge?

Do you have peace with God? It would be terrifying to face the Judge of the world without being at peace with God!

We have seen, in detail, how more than 175 prophetic statements about The Last Days were fulfilled in the years from 1882–2012. These are astonishing facts. This phenomenon of fulfilled, detailed prophecy is found in no other religion in the world, except in the Bible. You can verify this for yourself. Ask representatives of other religions if they can produce a list of 175 prophecies relating to our times, including very detailed statements which have been precisely fulfilled, after millennia or, at the very least, centuries. You won't be given such a list. But in this book, you have lists of 178 fulfilled prophecies altogether.

And that's not all, by any means. The entire Bible, from Genesis 1 through to Revelation 22, is abounding with fulfilled prophecies, not only affecting our times, but also other ages.

In the book of Daniel alone you will find over 200 fulfilled prophetic statements regarding world history (Babylon, Medo-Persia, Greece, Rome, Israel, Syria and Egypt) which have been unerringly fulfilled and proven by historical sources in world history.[543] I systematically enumerated these prophecies in the book of Daniel years ago.

---

543 In my book, "Weltgeschichte im Visier des Propheten Daniel" (English edition in progress by CMV Hagedorn, Germany) I discuss over 200 prophecies, and give scientific proofs of the authenticity of the book of Daniel.

Over 300 Messianic prophecies were fulfilled by the Coming of Jesus Christ 2,000 years ago.[544]

Taken together, we already have over 675 fulfilled prophecies. Yet, the Bible contains many more such prophecies which have been fulfilled!

The Bible is the only book in the world which can make absolutely reliable and detailed statements regarding the future!

By comparison, humans are generally unable to accurately predict the distant future. This follows from the fact that we, as created beings, are subject to time and space. Man has the possibility of making reliable statements in terms of the present and the past. In view of the distant future, man fails miserably when attempting to make reliable statements. The following examples illustrate this:

At the 1893 Chicago World's Fair scientists, actually social experts, declared what society would look like in 100 years. They claimed:

1. People would live to be 150 years old.
2. Governments would have it increasingly easy, because true greatness always results in simplicity.
3. Prisons would hardly be needed.
4. Divorces would no longer be necessary (because men and women would then know how to solve problems in a socially competent way before it ever came to failure).

All these predictions have proven to be completely wrong. Another few examples from the recent past: The following are cited in the newsletter of the trend research company, "Trend Alert":[545]

- **CD:** Philips executive Jan Timmer said: "Who needs these silver discs" when the CD was introduced. Since then more than 200 billion CDs have been produced.
- **Computer:** Thomas J. Watson was convinced there would be no need for more than five computers worldwide ... in 1980 Bill Gates was still of the opinion that 640 kilobytes of storage

---

544  Cf. LIEBI: Der verheissene Erlöser (English edition in progress); MELDAU: The Prophets Still Speak: Messiah in Both Testaments.

545  Received per email on 1.11. 2011.

was sufficient for every purpose ...

- **TV:** Darryl F. Zanuck, chief of film company 20th Century-Fox expressed the following thought about "television," "People will soon get tired of staring at a plywood box every evening."
- **Cars:** Gottlieb Daimler, founder of Daimler Motors Corporation was convinced: "The worldwide demand for automobiles will not exceed a million – if only for lack of available chauffeurs."
- **Telephone:** "Perhaps Americans need the telephone, but we don't. We have a lot of express messengers." William Preece, chief engineer of the British Post Office, expressed this assessment of the unchangeability of his business when questioned about Alexander Graham Bell's invention of the telephone ...

Comment on these "prophecies" is unnecessary.

How can it be that the Bible is so accurately prophetic, even though people – and scientists are among them – cannot know the distant future?

The Bible says of itself that it is the inspired Word of God (2 Tim. 3:16):

*"16 All scripture is given by inspiration of God ..."* (KJV)

Of course, many different *people* wrote down the Bible text, but as 2 Peter 1:21 explains:

*"21 For the prophecy [the Scriptures] came not in old time by the will of man: but holy men of God spake as they were moved by the Holy Ghost."* (KJV)

The Bible says that God, in contrast to all created beings,[546] is not subject to time and space. Several thousand times in the Bible God is called by the Hebrew word "Yahweh," which means "the

---

546 According to Biblical statements, angels, i.e. spirits (Heb. 1:14) are subject to time and space (cf. Job 1:7; 2:2; Dan. 10:12-14,20).

Eternally Existing One," the Unchangeable" or, to be succinct, "the Eternal One." In Hebrew this name is written with four consonants, *yhwh*:

$$\text{יהוה}$$

In his translation Martin Luther expressed this Hebrew name of God with the name "LORD" printed in capital letters each time, quite in the Jewish tradition, where this name is not spoken, out of reverence to God, but replaced with *'adonai* ("LORD") when read aloud in the synagogue.

In German language Jewish translations of the OT *yhwh* is very beautifully rendered "der EWIGE" ("the ETERNAL").[547]

In Jeremiah 23:24 God says:

*"24 ... Do not I fill heaven and earth? saith the LORD [the ETERNAL]."* (KJV)

This expresses that God is omnipresent. He is simultaneously present in the entire universe (Acts 17:28: *"28For in him we live, and move, and have our being"*). Furthermore, the Bible declares that God is not only present in the universe, in this world now, but is also present in the hereafter (Joshua 2:11). He is the immanent (present in this world) and the transcendent (present in the hereafter) God. He is not subject to time and space. That is why, in God's view, it says in 2 Peter 3:8 that: *"one day is ... as a thousand years, and a thousand years as one day."* 2,000 years ago it was much more difficult to understand this statement. "How can that be?" one may have asked. "The passage of time is objective. How can God be excluded from it?" However, since Einstein's Theory of Relativity and the subsequent 20th-century scientific revolution in the field of physics, we know that space and time are inseparable. Time is relative. It depends on space, speed and gravity. Now it is clear: For Someone who is omnipresent and omnipotent (Rev. 1:8),

---

547  E.g. TUR-SINAI: Die Heilige Schrift; ZUNZ: *thorah, neviim, kethuvim*, Die vierundzwanzig Bücher der Heiligen Schrift.

they are not subordinate to space, speed and gravity. So it is absolutely, logically consistent that for God, 1,000 years is like a day and a day like 1,000 years!

How can we know that the eternal God was directing the writers of the Bible as its inspirational Author? The proof of this is in the accuracy of prophecy. It is clear that this information came from someone not subject to time and space. Fulfilled prophecy demonstrates that the Bible was inspired by the eternal God. It is possible to acknowledge God through fulfilled prophecy. The following refrain, with 77 variations, is found in the book of the prophet Ezekiel:[548]

*"...ye shall know that I am the LORD."* (KJV)

We have encountered this refrain several times during our study of the texts in Ezekiel in previous chapters.

The book of Ezekiel is brimming with prophecy. Here, it is repeatedly attested that, as soon as a prophecy is fulfilled, we should recognize that the God of the Bible is "the ETERNAL ONE."

The very fact that this proof of prophecy is not found in the Muslims' Koran, the Hindus' and the Buddhists' writings, in the traditions of the tribal religions (animism) or in any other religion is most important! It becomes clear that YAHWEH, the eternal God, is not behind these other religions.

In the book of Isaiah, the God of the Bible challenges the gods of other religions. They are challenged to give a prophecy, such as is found in the book of Isaiah and other books in the Bible. They are called to pass the test of prophecy (Isa. 41:21-24):[549]

*"[21] Produce your cause, saith the LORD; bring forth your strong reasons, saith the King of Jacob.*

---

548 Ezekiel's refrain of the knowledge of God ("... *and ye shall know that I am the LORD!*"): 77x (with every variation): *yada '+ ki ani YHWH* (= know + that I [am] the ETERNAL ONE): 71 verses: 5:13; 6:7,10,13,14; 7:4,9,27; 11:10,12,15,16,20; 13:9,14,21,23; 14:8; 15:7; 16:62; 17:21,24; 20:12, 20,38,42,44; 21:10; 22:16,22; 23:49; 24:24,27; 25:5,7,11,17; 26:6; 28:22,23,24,26; 29:6,9,16,21;30:8,19,25,26; 32:15; 33:29; 34:27,30; 35:4,9,12,15; 36:11,23,36,38; 37:6,13,14,28; 38:23; 39:6,7,22,28; + 6 variations: 2:5; 14: 23; 21:4; 25:14; 33:33; 39:23, cf. in the OT(18x): 8x: Exod. 6:7; 7:5; 10:2;14:4,18; 29:46; 31:13; 2x: Joel 2:27; 4:17.

549  Cf. Isa. 43:8-13; 44:6ff; 46:8-13; 48:2-16.

*<sup>22</sup> Let them bring them forth, and shew us what shall happen:*[550] *let them shew the former things, what they be, that we may consider them, and know the latter end of them; or declare us things for to come. <sup>23</sup> Shew the things that are to come hereafter,*[551] *that we may know that ye are gods: yea, do good, or do evil, that we may be dismayed, and behold it together. <sup>24</sup> Behold, ye are of nothing, and your work of nought: an abomination is he that chooseth you."* (KJV)

In contrast to this, the God of the Bible is a God of fulfilled prophecy:

Isaiah 46:8-10:
*"<sup>8</sup> Remember this, and shew yourselves men: bring it again to mind, O ye transgressors.*
*<sup>9</sup> Remember the former things of old: for I am God, and there is none else; I am God, and there is none like me,*
*<sup>10</sup> Declaring the end from the beginning, and from ancient times the things that are not yet done, saying, My counsel shall stand, and I will do all my pleasure ..."* (KJV)

Isaiah 14:24:
*"<sup>24</sup> The LORD of hosts hath sworn, saying, Surely as I have thought, so shall it come to pass; and as I have purposed, so shall it stand."* (KJV)

Isaiah 34:16:
*"<sup>16</sup> Seek ye out of the book of the LORD, and read: no one of these shall fail, none shall want her mate: for my mouth it hath commanded, and his spirit it hath gathered them."* (KJV)

Fulfilled Last Days prophecy is a blow to anti-dispensationalism. All the arguments of this thought system are refuted and dismissed by the fact of fulfilled prophecy.

---

550  I.e. short-term prophecy.

551  I.e. long-term prophecy.

# 2. Coincidental Fulfilment?

Can the fulfillment of Biblical prophecy simply be coincidence?

Probability relegates such an assumption to fairyland. We will work with the probability of 1:2. In reality, most events are much less likely to happen. The return of the Jews from all over the world to the Land of their Fathers is an event without parallel in world history. The probability of this event is therefore drastically less likely than 1:2 or 50%. Similarly, the revival of Hebrew after more than 1,000 years is a unique phenomenon in history. It is clear to everyone that this event, too, cannot have a probability of 1:2 or $p = 0.5$. Nevertheless, we will use 1:2 in the following calculation. Thus, I am challenging critics of Biblical prophecy in a "generous" way.

The probability $p$ of several (independent) events is calculated as follows:

$$p = 1 : x^n$$

It would also be possible, of course, in the cases of prophecies where there are interdependencies in the different statements, to take account of these individually. But that would be extremely complicated! Therefore, using some simple examples with *independent* events, it will be shown that the idea of a coincidental fulfilment of Biblical prophecy is simply absurd.

When we use a probability of 50% (1:2) for each prophesied event, we must place the number 2 for $x$ in the formula given above. $n$ stands for the number of prophecies we want to calculate. Let us calculate the probability of only 25 prophecies, each an independent event. This gives $p = 2.8 \times 10^8$. Dr. Werner Gitt, Professor Emeritus of the National Institute for Natural and Engineering Sciences [Technische Bundesanstalt Braunschweig], Germany, illustrated a case of probability with his famous ant model:[552] Imagine a bath tub, filled with black ants (= 36 million average-sized ants, each with a volume of 10 mm³). Among all these ants

---

552  http://www.werner-gitt.de/down_deu/Factum_Gottesbeweis.pdf (as of: 25.10.2011).

is *one* red ant. The probability of picking out the red ant in *one* attempt, blindfolded, is as unlikely as the probability of the fulfillment of 25 prophecies with a probability rate of 1:2.

Let's now choose 78 independent events from our list of fulfilled prophecies. With $p$ = 1:2 this would give a probability of 1:2 x $10^{24}$. For comparison, we can imagine the entire surface of the earth of 510 million km² (oceans and land together), covered 10 metres deep with black ants. Among all these ants there is *one* red ant. The possibility of picking out that red ant in *one* attempt is the same as the probability of the fulfilment of 78 prophecies with a probability rate of 1:2.

The more prophecies we include in the calculation, the more striking the improbability. If we start with exactly 160 prophecies, we obtain the following probability:[553] $p$ = $0.5^{160}$ = 6.84 x $10^{-49}$. If we use the reciprocal value of $p$, we arrive at the following number of black ants: $n$ = 14.6 x $10^{48}$. If an ant has a volume of 10 mm³, all these creatures combine to create an "ant hill" of 14.6 x $10^{30}$km³. Our sun has a volume of 1.41 x $10^{18}$ km³. The volume of the ant hill just mentioned corresponds to the volume of 10 million million suns. So, we arrive at the following comparison: The probability of a coincidental fulfilment of 160 prophecies is equal to the probability of picking out, in *one* attempt, one single red ant, hiding itself in a hill of black ants the size of 10 million million suns.

I think that these modest reflections on probability theory suffice to make clear to any thinking person that fulfilled Biblical prophecy proves beyond doubt that the Bible is inspired by the eternal and unchangeable God!

# 3. Death Blow for Atheism

Fulfilled prophecy clarifies not only the question of truth, in connection with the religions of the world, but also in connection with atheism. The fulfilled prophecy of the Bible is actu-

---

553 This example goes back to a personal communication from Prof. Dr. Werner Gitt to the author (15.2.2011).

ally the final death blow for atheism.[554] According to atheism, there cannot be detailed and demonstrably true prophecy. This fact fundamentally contradicts this ideology. This phenomenon of the Bible is verified, however, as we have seen. It proves:

- that an eternal God exists,
- and that this God speaks to us through the Bible.

When we acknowledge that the Bible is God's Word, we also recognize that He holds the whole of world history in His hand. He knows the future and can also direct it according to His purpose (Isa. 46:8-13). This means that He not only has the history of the world, as such, in His hands, but also my personal life. God is so great that we are not too small for Him!

In the Bible, we find God speaking to us personally. The Bible is like a letter to mankind, but also to every individual. It is worthwhile to read the Bible regularly in order to encounter God's message for you in a very personal way. Anyone who prays to God for help in understanding His Word before reading will experience wonderful things.

In the Bible we learn that we must turn to God. We must be reconciled to Him. It is absolutely necessary to recognize that Jesus Christ died for us, personally, on the cross! The Just One came into this world to take the punishment substitutionally that we deserved due to our disobedience to God and His commandments (1 Peter 3:18). When we lay open our guilt and sin to God in prayer, in full conviction and repentance, and acknowledge that of which we are aware and put our complete trust in Jesus Christ, the Son of God, as our Substitute, He will forgive us completely and give us eternal life (John 3:16):

*"[16] For God so loved the world, that he gave his only begotten Son, that whosoever believeth in him should not perish, but have everlasting life."* (KJV)

---

554 See the audio lecture by the author at www.sermon-online.de : Ist Gott eine Projektion des Gehirns?

1 John 1:19 testifies:

*"⁹ If we confess our sins, he is faithful and just to forgive us our sins, and to cleanse us from all unrighteousness."* (KJV)

# VII. Appendix

## 1. Bibliography

AEBI, E.: Geheimnis Israel, Zürich 1961.

ALEXANDER, J.: L'Apocalypse, Geneva 1979.

ARCHBOLD, N.P.: The Mountains of Israel, The Bible & The West Bank, Second Edition, 1993.

ARCHÉOLOGIA, No. 266, March 1991, BP 90, 21800 Quétigny.

ARCHER, G.L.: A Survey of Old Testament. Introduction, updated and revised ed., Chicago, 1994.

ARIEL, Y./RICHMAN, C.: The Odyssey of the Third Temple, Jerusalem 1993.

AZ (Aargauer Zeitung), 17 October 2011.

BABYLONIAN TALMUD:

* Hebrew – Aramaic Basic text Edition *talmud bavli*, 11 Vols, Yerushalaiyim, n.d.

* Hebrew – Aramaic edition with English translation: THE SONCINO TALMUD, Classic Judaic Library, CD-ROM, Version Iic3, Judaic Press, Inc. Brooklyn, New York.

* Hebrew – Aramaic edition in: BAR ILAN'S JUDAIC LIBRARY, Bar Ilan University, Responsa Project, CD-Rom, Version 5.

* Complete German translation: GOLDSCHMIDT, L.: Der Babylonische Talmud, neu übertragen durch L. Goldschmidt, 12 Bde., 2. Auflage, Berlin 1964-1967.

BAR ILAN'S JUDAIC LIBRARY, Bar Ilan University, Responsa Project, CD-Rom, Version 5.[555]

---

555 A comprehensive collection of rabbinic works from the past 2,000 years, more than 400 volumes: Hebrew Bible, Targum Onkelos, Bible Commentaries [Even Ezra, Rashi,Ramban, Radaq, Ralbag,

Metzudath David, Metzudath Ziyon], Mishnah, Toseftha,Masekhthoth Qetannoth, Talmud Bavli, Rashi on the Talmud Bavli, Tosfoth on the Talmud Bavli, Talmud Yerushalmi, Halachic Midrashim, Haggadic Midrashim, Zohar, Rambam, Tur, Beit Yosef, Shulchan Aruch, Kitzur Shulchan Aruch, Mishnah Berurah, medieval Responsa, Responsa of the 16th century, Responsa of the 17th–19th century, Responsa of the 20th century.

BAT YE'OR: The Decline of Eastern Christianity: From Jihad to Dhimmitude; seventh-twentieth century, 1996, Fairleigh Dickinson University Press.

BAUER, W.: Griechisch-Deutsches Wörterbuch zu den Schriften des Neuen Testament und der frühchristlichen Literatur, 6., völlig neu bearbeitete Auflage, im Institut für neutestamentliche Textforschung / Münster unter besonderer Mitwirkung von Viktor Reichmann, herausgegeben von Kurt und Barbara Aland, Berlin, New York 1988.

BECK, H.W.: Genesis, Aktuelles Dokument vom Beginn der Menschheit, Neuhausen-Stuttgart 1983.

BERGSTRÄSSER, G.: Einführung in die semitischen Sprachen, Sprachproben und grammatische Skizzen, im Anhang: Zur Syntax der Sprache von Ugarit, von Carl Brockelmann, München 1963.

BIBLIA HEBRAICA STUTTGARTENSIA, Stuttgart, 4th ed. 1990.

BIBLEWORKS 8.0, Software for Biblical Exegesis & Research (http://www.bibleworks.com/).

BRIERRE-NARBONNE, J.-J.: Exegese talmoudique des prophéties rnessianiques, *hamashiach batalmud*, Paris 1934.

BLASS, F./DEBRUNNER, A.: Grammatik des neutestamentlichen Griechisch, bearbeitet von F. Rehkopf, 16. durchgesehene Auflage, Göttingen 1984.

BOTTERWECK, G.J./RINGGREN, H.: Theological Dictionary of the Old Testament, Translated by J.T. Willis, Vol. I, Revised Edition, Grand Rapids, Michigan 1974.

BRIERRE-NARBONNE, J.-J.: Les prophéties messianiques de l'Ancien Testament dans la littérature juive en accord avec le Nouveau Testament, avec une introduction sur la littérature messianique juive apocryphe, targoumique, midrachique, zoharique et rabbinique, Paris 1933.

BROWN, F./DRIVER, S./BRIGGS, C.: The Brown-Driver-Briggs Hebrew and English Lexicon, Peabody, Massachussetts, Fourth Printing 1999.

BURKHARDT, H./GRÜNZWEIG F./LAUBACH F./MAIER G. (eds.): Das grosse Bibellexikon, Wuppertal / Giessen, Vol. I, 1987, Vol. II, 1988, Vol. III, 1989.

BÜHLMANN, W./SCHERER, K.: Sprachliche Stilfiguren der Bibel, Von Assonanz bis Zahlenspruch, ein Nachschlage werk, 2. verbesserte Auflage, Giessen 1994.

CARTA-REDAKTION/AUMANN, M.: Geschichte Israels, Marburg, Lahn 1985.

COMRIE, B. (ed.): The World's Major Languages, London 1989.

DARBY, J.N./KELLY, W.: Betrachtungen über das Buch Daniel, Nachdruck, Neustadt / Weinstrasse 1967.

DAVIDSON, B.: Analytical Hebrew and Chaldee Lexicon, London n.d.

DAVIS, L.J.: Israels Überlebenskampf, Neuhausen-Stuttgart 2. Auflage 1989.

DER SPIEGEL, Nr. 35, 27. Aug. 1990: Saddam Husseins Vorbilder: Die Herrscher von Mesopotamien.

DER SPIEGEL, 12/2003.

DIO, C.: Roman History, (translated by Ian Scott-Kilvert), Penguin Classics, Reprint edition, 1987.

DYER, CH. H./ HUNT A.: The Rise of Babylon: Sign of The End Times, Wheaton, Illinois 1991.

EBAN, A.: My Country: The Story of Modern Israel, London: Weidenfeld & Nicolson, 1972.

ELBERFELDER BIBEL, Wuppertal-Elberfeld 1905.

ELLENBERGER, H.: Die Leiden und Verfolgungen der Juden und ihre Beschützer in chronologischer Reihenfolge, Prag, 2. Auflage 1882.

ENGEL, J.: Die Juden in Babylonien unter den persischen Königen während des zweiten Tempels bis nach dem barkochbäischen Kriege. Inaugural-Dissertation zur Erlangung der Doktorwürde an der hohen philosophischen Fakultät der Universität Bern, 1907.

EUSEBIUS: Church History from A.D. 1–324, Translated with Prolegomena and Notes by Arthur. Cushman McGiffert, in: THE MASTER CHRISTIAN LIBRARY, loc. cit., The Nicene and Post-Nicene Fathers, Second Series, Volume I, by Philip Schaff.

EISSLER, H./NÄNNI, W: Israel – Heimkehr eines Volkes, Neuhausen-Stuttgart 1993.

JOSEPHUS, F.: The Jewish War, (in three volumes; translated by H. St. J. Thackeray), Cambridge, Massachusetts, 2004.

JOSEPHUS, F.: The Jewish Antiquities, (in nine volumes; translated by Ralph Marcus), Cambridge, Massachusetts, 1998.

FOCUS, 20 December 2003.

FRIBERG, T. and B.: Analytical Lexicon to the GNT, in: BIBLEWORKS 8.0, a.a.O.

FRUCHTENBAUM, A.G.: Jesus was a Jew, Tustin, California, 1981.

GAUTHIER, J.P.: Sovereignty over the Old City of Jerusalem, A Study of the Historical, Religious, Political and Legal Aspects of the Question of the Old City, Thèse présenté pour l'obtention du grade de Docteur ès Science politiques (Droit international), Université de Genève, Institut Universitaire de Hautes Etudes Internationales, Thèse N° 725, Genève 2007.

GEMOLL, W.: Griechisch-deutsches Schul- und Handwörterbuch, neunte Auflage, durchgesehen und erweitert von Karl Vretska, mit einer Einführung in die Sprachgeschichte von Heinz Kronasser, Nachdruck, Müchen 1991.

GEO: Probleme und Chancen in Nahost, Aktueller Wegweiser durch eine Region, deren Konflikte die Welt in Atem halten, March 1991 (GEO-Extra nach p. 180).

GEO, Nr. 10, 19. 10. 1990, p. 78-79.

GESENIUS, W./BUHL, F.: Hebräisches und aramäisches Handwörterbuch über das Alte Testament, 17. Aufl., Berlin, Göttingen, Heidelberg 1962.

GESENIUS, W. /MEYER, R./DONNER, H.: Hebräisches und Aramäisches Handwörterbuch über das Alte Testament, bearbeitet. und herausgegeben. von Meyer, Rudolf und Donner, Herbert, 18. Aufl., Berlin, Heidelberg, New York, London, Paris, Tokyo, Vol. I: 1987, Vol. II: 1995.

GILBERT, M.: Israel, A History, London 1999.

GILBERT, M.: Jerusalem, Illustrated History Atlas, 2nd revised Ed., Jerusalem 1978, reprinted 1987.

GILBERT, M.: Jewish History Atlas, second edition, London 1976.

GILBERT, M.: The Arab-Israeli Conflict, Its History in Maps, fifth edition, Jerusalem, Tel Aviv, Haifa 1992.

GIBERT: The Routledge Atlas of the Arab-Israeli Conflict, Eighth Edition, Abingdon, Oxfordshire 2005.

GOLDFISHER Y./SACKS, E.: The Wine Route of Israel, second edition, Jerusalem 2008.

HAM, K., et al.: The New Answers Book [in three volumes], Green Forest, Arizona, 2006.

HAREUVENI, N.: Desert and Shepherd in Our Biblical Heritage, Neot Kedumim 1991.

HARRIS, R.L./ARCHER, G.L./WALTKE, B.K.: The Theological Wordbook, Illinois 1980.

HAUBECK, W./VON SIEBENTHAL, H.: Neuer sprachlicher Schlüssel zum Griechischen Neuen Testament, Matthäus bis Apostelgeschichte, Vol. I, Giessen/Basel 1997.

HAUBECK, W./VON SIEBENTHAL, H.: Neuer sprachlicher Schlüssel zum Griechischen Neuen Testament, Vol. II, Römer bis Offenbarung, Giessen/Basel 1994.

HEIJKOOP, H.L.: Die Zukunft (Die Zukunft derer, die an den Herrn Jesus glauben, Die Zukunft Westeuropas, Die Zukunft Russlands, Der Richterstuhl des Christus), Die Versammlung Gottes (9 Vorträge, 76 Fragenbeantwortungen), Schwelm und Winschoten 1975.

HEIJKOOP, H.L.: Die Zukunft nach den Weissagungen des Wortes Gottes, Winschoten 1951.

HERLITZ, G./KIRSCHNER, B. (eds.): Jüdisches Lexikon. Ein enzyklopädisches Handbuch des jüdischen Wissens in 4 Bänden, Königstein /Ts. 1982.

HETZRON, R.: Hebrew, in: COMRIE: The World's Major Languages, loc. cit., pp. 686-704.

HILLEL, SH.: Le souffle du levant. Mon aventure clandestine pour sauver les juifs d'Iraq, 1945 – 1951, Bruxelles 1989.

HILLEL, SH.: Operation Babylon: The Story of the Rescue of the Jews of Iraq, London 1988.

HIRSCH, E.: Israel von A-Z, Daten, Fakten, Hintergründe, völlig überarbeitete Neuausgabe, Jerusalem 1993.

HIZAK, S./EKEROTH, G.: Hier in Israel, April 1991.

HOEKEMA, A.A.: Der siebte Tag, Bielefeld 1995

HOFFMANN, E.G./VON SIEBENTHAL, H.: Griechische Grammatik zum Neuen Testament, Riehen 1985.

ICE, TH./PRICE, R.: Ready to Rebuild: The Imminent Plan to Rebuild the Last Days Temple, Eugene, Oregon 1992.

ICE, TH./DEMY, T.: When the Trumpet Sounds: Today's Foremost Authorities Speak Out on End-Time Controversy, Harvest House Publishers 1995.

JOHNSTONE, P.: Operation World: Handbook for World Intercession, imprint unknown 1981.

JUBILÄUMSBIBEL, Die Bibel oder die ganze Heilige Schrift des Alten und Neuen Testaments nach der deutschen Übersetzung Martin Luthers mit erklärenden Anmerkungen, Stuttgart 1981.

KEIL, C.F. /DELITZSCH, F.: Commentar über das Alte Testament, Erster Teil: Die fünf Bücher Moses, Bd. I: Genesis und Exodus, Frankfurt a.M. 1858.

KEIL, C.F. /DELITZSCH, F.: Commentar über das Alte Testament, Dritter Teil, Die prophetischen Bücher Vol. I, Biblischer Commentar über den Prophet Jesaja, Leipzig 1889.

KEIL, C.F.: Commentar über das Alte Testament, Dritter Teil: Die prophetischen Bücher, Vol. II: Biblischer Commentar über den Propheten Jeremia und die Klagelieder, Leipzig 1872.

KITCHEN, K.A.: Ancient Orient and Old Testament, InterVarsity Press, Downers Grove, Illinois 1978.

KITTEL, G./FRIEDRICH, G.: Theological Dictionary of the New Testament, 10 Vols. (Vol.10: Index, compiled by R.E. Pitkin), Reprinted 1978, Grand Rapids, Michigan.

KLEIMAN, R. Y.: DNA & Tradition, The Genetic Link to the Ancient Hebrews, Second Edition, Jerusalem, New York 2004.

KÖHLER, L./BAUMGARTNER, W.: Hebräisches und aramäisches Lexikon zum Alten Testament, 3. Auflage, Leiden, Lieferung I, 1967, Lieferung II, 1974, Lieferung III, 1983, Lieferung IV, 1990, Lieferung V (aramäisches Lexikon), 1995.

KÖNIG, E.: Hebräisches und aramäisches Wörterbuch zum Alten Testament mit Einschaltung und Analyse aller schwer erkennbaren Formen, Deutung der Eigennamen sowie der massoretischen Randbemerkungen und einem deutsch-hebräischen Wortregister, Leipzig 1910.

KRUPP, M.: Die Geschichte der Juden im Land Israel, Vom Ende des Zweiten Tempels bis zum Zionismus, Gütersloh 1993.

KÜLLING, S.R.: Zur Datierung der «Genesis-P-Stücke», namentlich des Kapitels Genesis XVII, Riehen, 2. Aufl. 1985.

LANGE, J.P.: Theologisch-homiletisches Bibelwerk, Die Heilige Schrift Alten und Neuen Testaments mit Rücksicht auf das theologisch-homiletische Bedürfnis des pastoralen Amtes in Verbindung mit namhaften evangelischen Theologen bearbeitet und herausgegeben von J.P. Lange, Bielefeld 1857 – 1877.

LANDMANN, I. (ed.): The Universal Jewish Encyclopaedia, Vol. 2, New York 1940.

LAVY, J.: Langenscheidts Handwörterbuch Deutsch-Hebräisch, 6. Auflage, Berlin, München, Wien, Zürich 1990.

L'EXPRESS, 20.3.2003.

LIDDELL, H./SCOTT, R.: A Greek-English Lexicon, revised and augmented throughout by Sir Henry Stuart Jones, with the assistance of Roderick McKenzie, and with the co-operation of many scholars, with a supplement, Oxford 1992.

LIEBI, R.: Chronologie der Könige Israels und Judas, Excel-Datei, 2007.

LIEBI: Das neue Europa – Hoffnung oder Illusion? 5. Auflage, Berneck 2002.

LIEBI, R.: Der verheissene Erlöser, Messianische Prophetie – ihre Erfüllung und historische Echtheit, veränderte Neuauflage, Zürich 2007.

LIEBI: Herkunft und Entwicklung der Sprachen. Sprachwissenschaft contra Evolution, zweite Auflage, Holzgerlingen 2007.

LIEBI, R.: Hesekiel, Ezra Studienreihe, Düsseldorf, Pfäffikon 2011.

IEBI, R: Introduction à la poésie hébraïque, Caillers des REBS, No. 8.

LIEBI, R: Poesie im Alten Testament, factum, Berneck Mai 1988, p.189-191.

LIEBI, R.: Rockmusik! Daten, Fakten, Hintergründe, Ausdruck einer Jugend in einem sterbenden Zeitalter, 4. Auflage, Zürich 1995 (Erstauflage 1987).

LIEBI, R.: Weltgeschichte im Visier des Propheten Daniel, Bielefeld 2009.

LIEBI, R.: Zur Chronologie des Alten Testaments, e-Skript, 2007 (downloadable at www.rogerliebi.ch).

LIETH, N.: Die letzten 75 Tage, Nachrichten aus Israel, Nr. 3, March 1993.

LOUW, J.P./NIDA, E.A. (eds.): Greek-English Lexicon of the New Testament Based on Semantic Domains, 2 Vols., 2nd Edition, New York 1988.

MAIER, G.: Das Buch Esther, Wuppertal 1987.

MAUERHOFER, E.: Einleitung in die Schriften des Neuen Testaments, 2 Vols., Neuhausen / Stuttgart 1995.

MAY, F.: Israel heute – ein lebendiges Wunder, Ein aktueller Streifzug durch die Gegenwart

MAY, F.: Israel zwischen Blut und Tränen. Der Leidensweg des jüdischen Volkes, Asslar 3. Aufl. 1990.

MAY, F.: Israel zwischen Weltpolitik und Messiaserwartung, 4. Aufl., Moers 1976.

MAY, F.: Von Saba nach Zion, Die dramatische Rettung und Heimkehr der äthiopischen Juden nach Israel.

MEDEMA, H.P.: Europa, Der Alptraum von einem Supermarkt, Bielefeld 1992.

MELDAU, J.: The Prophets Still Speak: Messiah in Both Testaments, Friends of Israel Gospel Ministry 1988.

MICHAEL, C.: Der Zionismus. Entstehung, Fakten Hintergründe, Neuhausen-Stuttgart 1985.

MILLARD: Pergament und Papyrus, Tafeln und Ton, Lesen und Schreiben zur Zeit Jesu, Giessen 2000.

MIQRA'OTH GEDOLOTH, Vols. I–VIII, *yerushalajim* 1972.[556]

---

556 Hebrew rabbinical Bible with Aramaic translations (Targumim), standard medieval commentaries and prayers.

MITTELLAND-ZEITUNG, 9 September 1994.

MOORE, H. (ed.): Pass the Word, 50 Years of Wycliffe Bible Translators. California 1984.

MOULTON, H.K.: The Analytical Greek Lexicon, London, Reprinted 1973.

MOULTON J.H./MILLIGAN, G.: The Vocabulary of the Greek Testament illustrated from the Papyri and other non-literary Sources, Grand Rapids, Michigan 1980.

NACHRICHTEN AUS ISRAEL, 11/2011.

NEGEV, A.: Archaeology in the Land of the Bible, Schocken 1977.

NESTLE-ALAND: Novum Testamentum Graece, 27th revised edition, Stuttgart 1993.

NEUE ZÜRCHER ZEITUNG, 9 September 1994.

NIRUMAND, B.: Sturm im Golf, Die Irak-Krise und das Pulverfass Nahost, erweiterte Ausgabe, Reinbek bei Hamburg 1991.

OUWENEEL, W.J.: Das Buch der Offenbarung, Bielefeld 1995.

OUWENEEL, W.J.: Das Lied der Lieder, Schwelm 1976.

OUWENEEL, W.J.: Die Zukunft der Stadt des grossen Königs, Neustadt/ Weinstrasse 1977.

OUWENEEL, W.J.: Evolution in der Zeitenwende, Neuhausen-Stuttgart 1984.

PAUSANIAS: Description of Greece, (in five volumes; translated by W.H.S. Jones and H.A. Ormerod), Cambridge, Massachusetts, 1989.

PETERS, B.: Geöffnete Siegel, Leitlinien der Zukunft im Buch der Offenbarung, Berneck 1990.

PETERS, B.: Mit Saddam in den «Heiligen Krieg»? factum, Bemeck Nov./ Dez. 1990, p. 456-459.

PETERS, B.: Die Sprache der Propheten, ethos Nr. 2, 1990, pp. 31ff.

PETERSON, P.: PLO kontra Israel, Berneck 1979.

PFISTERER, R: Israel oder Palästina? Perspektiven aus Bibel und Geschichte, Wuppertal und Zürich 1992.

PRICE, R.: Fast Facts on the Middle East Conflict, Harvest House Publishers 2003.

PRICE, R.: The Coming Last Days Temple, The Latest Developments in Bible Prophecy, Eugene, Oregon 1999.

PROD'HOM, S.: Der verheissene König und sein Reich, Eine Hilfe zum Studium des Evangeliums nach Matthäus, Zürich 1964.

RABOW, J.: 50 Jewish Messiahs, Jerusalem 2002.

RIESNER, R.: Essener und Urgemeinde in Jerusalem, Neue Funde und

Quellen, 2. erweiterte Auflage, Giessen 1998.

ROBINSON, M.A./PIERPONT, W.G.: The New Testament in the Original Greek according to the Byzantine / Majority Textform, Introduction and appendix by the editors, executive editor W.D. McBrayer, Atlanta 1991.

ROSENTHAL, F.: A Grammar of Biblical Aramaic, Wiesenthal 1983.

ROSE PUBLISHING: Then and Now Bible Maps, Torrance, California 1997.

ROSSIER, H.: Betrachtungen über die Psalmen, Neustadt/Weinstrasse 1978.

ROSSIER, H.: Die symbolische Sprache der Offenbarung, Neustadt/Weinstrasse 1972.

ROSSIER, H.: Le livre du prophète Osée, 4e édition, Vevey 1978.

ROSSIER, H.: Le livre du prophète Joel, 4e édition, Vevey 1977.

ROSSIER, H.: Le livre du prophète Amos, 2e édition, Vevey 1974.

ROSSIER, H.: Le livre du prophète Abdias, 4e édition, Vevey 1980.

ROSSIER, H.: Le livre du prophète Jonas, 4e édition, Vevey 1973.

ROSSIER, H.: Le livre du prophète Amos, 2e édition, Vevey 1974.

ROSSIER, H.: Le livre du prophète Michée, 4e édition, Vevey 1978.

ROSSIER, H.: Le livre du prophète Nahum, 3e édition, Vevey 1970.

ROSSIER, H.: Le livre du prophète Habakuk, 4e édition, Vevey 1979.

ROSSIER, H.: Le livre du prophète Sophonie, 4e édition, Vevey 1979.

ROSSIER, H.: Le livre d'Agée et son application au temps actuel, 4e édition, Vevey 1972.

ROSSIER, H.: Le livre de Zacharie le prophète prophète Amos, 4e édition, Vevey 1976.

ROSSIER, H.: Le livre du prophète Malachie, 4e édition, Vevey 1976.

SCHIRRMACHER, CH.: Der Islam, Band I, Neuhausen-Stuttgart 1994.

SCHIRRMACHER, TH./CH.: Die Kurden: Ein staatenloses Volk als Spielball islamischer Mächte, factum, Berneck Mai 1991,S. 24-29.

SCHMIDT, R.: Wiedergeburt einer Nation, 50 Jahre Israel und danach, 2. Aufl., Berneck 2001.

SCHMIDT, A.J.: Wie das Christentum die Welt veränderte, Menschen – Gesellschaft – Politik – Kunst, Resch-Verlag, Gräfelfing 2009.

SCHRUPP, E.: Israel in der Endzeit, Heilsgeschichte und Zeitgeschehen, Wuppertal und Zürich, 2. Auflage 1991.

SEPTUAGINTA, ed. Alfred Rahlfs, Stuttgart 1935.

SEPTUAGINTA DEUTSCH, Das griechische Alte Testament in deutscher Übersetzung, Stuttgart 2009.

SIDDUR SCHMA KOLENU, Basel, 2. Auflage 1997.

ST. JOHN, R.: Die Sprache der Propheten, Die Lebensgeschichte des Elieser Ben-Jehuda, des Schöpfers der neuhebräischen Sprache, Bleicher-Verlag, Gerlingen 1985.

ST. JOHN, R.: Tongue of the Prophets: The Life Story of Eliezer Ben Yehudah, Wilshire Book Co., U.S. 1972.

SULGER BÜEL, E.: Der schwarze Tod, ethos, Berneck März 1991, p. 48-51.

TAPERNOUX, M.: Einführung in das Studium der Prophetie, 2. Auflage, Zürich 1976.

THAYER, J.H.: A Greek-English Lexicon of the New Testament, being Grimm's Wilkes's Clavis Novi Testamenti, translated, revised and enlarged by Joseph Henry Thayer, D.D., Grand Rapids, Michigan 1988.

THE GREEK NEW TESTAMENT, United Bible Societies, Fourth Revised Edition 1993.

THE MASTER CHRISTIAN LIBRARY, CD-ROM,[557] AGES Software, Albany, Oregon 1998.

THIEDE, P.C./STINGELIN, U.: Die Wurzeln des Antisemitismus, 5. Auflage, Basel und Giessen 2003.

THOMPSON, J.A.: The Bible and Archaeology, Paternoster Press 1969.

TIME, March 11, No. 10, 1991

TITZE, W. (ed.): Lexikon der Geographie, Braunschweig, Vol. 1 1968, Vol. 2 1969.

TUR-SINAI, N.H.: Die Heilige Schrift, zweite Auflage, Neuhausen Stuttgart 1995.

UNGER, E.: Babylon, Berlin 1970 (Nachdruck der Ausg. von 1931).

UNGER, M.F.: Unger's Bible Handbook, Moody Press 1995.

VANGEMEREN, W.A.: New International Dictionary of Old Testament Theology & Exegesis, Vols. I-V, Carlisle, Cumbria 1997.

WALLACE: D.B.: Greek Grammar Beyond the Basics, An Exegetical Syntax of the New Testament, Grand Rapids, Michigan 1996.

WALVOORD, J.F./ZUCK. R.B.: Bible Knowledge Commentary – Old Testament, Victor Books 2003.

WALVOORD, J.F.: The Nations in Prophecy, Grand Rapids, Michigan 1978.

WISEMAN, D.J.: Assyrien, in: BURKHARDT/GRÜNZWEIG/LAUBACH/MAIER: Das grosse Bibellexikon, Vol. I, p. 126-134, Wuppertal/Giessen 1987.

---

557 Collection of over 400 classic works of theology.

WISEMAN, D.J.: Babylonien, in: BURKHARDT/GRÜNZWEIG/LAUBACH/
MAIER: Das grosse Bibellexikon, Vol. I, p. 159-160.

WISEMAN, D.J.: Shinar, Logos Bible Atlas 1.0a, Logos Research System 1994.

WISEMAN, D.J.: Ur in Chaldäa, in: BURKHARDT/GRÜN-ZWEIG/LAU-
BACH/MAIER: Das grosse Bibellexikon, Vol. III, p. 1617-1618, Wuppertal/
Giessen 1989.

ZUNZ, L.: *thorah, neviim, kethuvim*, Die vierundzwanzig Bücher der Heiligen Schrift, übersetzt von Leopold Zunz, Basel 1995.

# 2. The Author

**Dr. Roger Liebi** (M. Mus., B.Th., M. Th., Th.D.),
born 1958, married to Miriam, six children,[558] studied
music (at the Zurich Conservatory and Zurich Musik-
hochschule violin and piano), Biblical languages
(Greek, classical and modern Hebrew, Aramaic, Akkadian) and theology. At Whitefield Theological Semi-
nary in Florida (USA), he completed a doctor-
ate degree in the fields of Jewish Studies and
Archaeology with a dissertation on the Second Temple in Jerusalem. As a
university lecturer, he has taught Archaeology of Israel and the Middle East
from 2004–2011. He works as a Bible teacher and speaker in various countries and has been involved in three projects as a Bible translator. A number
of publications have resulted from his years of involvement with the Scriptures and related fields.

# 3. Publications by the Author

Der Verheissene Erlöser, ihre Erfüllung und ihre historische Echt-heit, 7. Auflage, Bielefeld 2007 (online: clv.de). Entspricht dem früheren Titel: Er-
füllte Prophetie, Messianische Prophetie - ihre Erfüllung und historische
Echtheit, 5. Auflage, Berneck 1990 (Erstauflage 1983). Translations: French,

---

558  His eldest son, Nathan Eljoenai, died in 2009 in a tragic sports accident on the River Aare.

Dutch, Italian, Hungarian and Tajik (English edition in progress by CMV Hagedorn, Germany).

Weltgeschichte im Visier des Propheten Daniel, 8. Auflage, Bielefeld 2009 (Erstauflage 1986). Translations: French, Spanish, Polish, Russian, Slovak, Bulgarian and Hungarian (online: clv.de). (English edition in progress by CMV Hagedorn, Germany.)

Rockmusik! Daten, Fakten, Hintergründe, Ausdruck einer Jugend in einem sterbenden Zeitalter, 4. Auflage, Zürich 1995 (Erstauf-lage 1987).

Introduction à la poésie hébraïque, in: Cahiers des REBS. No. 8, 1994 (= Übersetzung eines factum-Artikels von Mai 1988).

Einführung in die vier Evangelien, Zürich 1990. Translations: Italian and Hungarian.

Der Mensch - ein sprechender Affe? Sprachwissenschaft contra Bibel, Berneck 1991.

New Age! Kritische Bemerkungen zum gegenwärtigen Esoterik-Boom, Zürich 1991. Translations: French, Hungarian, Russian, Slovak, Spanish (English edition in progress).

Wolfgang Amadeus Mozart, Zwischen Ideal und Abgrund, Berneck 1991.

Défendre la foi chrétienne, in: Cahiers des REBS. No. 14, 1995 (Seminar 1991).

Israel und das Schicksal des Irak, Unruheherd Nahost im Licht der Bibel, 5. Auflage, Berneck 2003 (Erstauflage 1993). Translations: Italian, Spanish and Hungarian.

Das neue Europa - Hoffnung oder Illusion? 6. Auflage, Berneck 2004 (Erstauflage 1994).

Ist die Bibel glaubwürdig? Die Bibel ihre Autorität und Zuverlässigkeit, Zürich 1995. Translation: Hungarian.

Jerusalem - Hindernis für den Weltfrieden, Das Drama des jüdischen Tempels, 5. Auflage, Berneck 2003 (Erstauflage 1994). Translations: French, Dutch and Hungarian.

La Palabra de Verdad – Unidad y Diversidad de la Biblia, Porto Alegre 2003.

Hesekiel, Ezra Studienreihe, Pfäffikon / Düsseldorf 2001 (Koautor: Joël Prohin). Entspricht weitgehend dem französischen Original: Le prophète Ezéchiel, in: Sondez les Ecritures, Bd. 9, Koautor: Joël Prohin, Valence 1995.

Livre des Proverbes, in: Sondez les Ecritures. Bd. 5, Koautor: Joël Prohin, Valence 1995.

So entstand das Christentum: Die Welt der Evangelien und der Apostelgeschichte völlig neu erlebt. In: R. Liebi, D. Hunt, A. A. Seibel, N. Lieth: Prophetie – zeitnah – zeitwahr – zeitklar. Pfäffikon 2000, S. 9–39. Translation: Portugese.

Ein neuer Blick auf die Passionswoche und ihren jüdischen Hintergrund, Das Schönste kommt noch – die himmlische Herr-lichkeit im Buch der Offenbarung, in: L. Gassmann, N. Lieth, R. Liebi: Was uns die Zukunft bringt, Pfäffikon, 2002, p. 8–75.

The Messiah in the Temple. The Symbolism of the Second Temple in Light of the New Testament, CMV Hagedorn, Düsseldorf, 2012. Der Messias im Tempel. Die Symbolik des Zweiten Tempels im Licht des Neuen Testaments, 2. Auflage, Bielefeld 2007 (Erstauflage 2002; online: clv.de). Translation: French.

Herkunft und Entwicklung der Sprachen - Linguistik contra Evolution, 2. Auflage, Holzgerlingen 2007 (Erstauflage: 2003).

Vertaling van Hosea, in: G. de Koning: Hosea actueel, Gods liefde en trouw, Doorn 2003, p. 8-36.

Vertaling van Joël, in: G. de Koning: Joël actueel, God bestuurt de geschiedenis, Doorn 2003, p. 8-19.

Vertaling van Amos, in: G. de Koning: Amos actueel, Gods toorn over de zonde, Doorn 2006, p. 9-28.

Sprachenreden oder Zungenreden? Bielefeld 2006 (online: clv.de).

# 4. Homepage

The author's personal home page with schedule, download offers of lecture texts, etc. at:

www.rogerliebi.ch

Email at: info@rogerliebi.ch

# 5. Lectures

Most of the author's lectures can be obtained on CD at www.nehemia-edition.ch. More than 400 files can be downloaded for free, partly with transcripts or PowerPoint presentations at www.sermon-online.de, www.clkv.ch, www.bibelklasse.de.

# 6. Liability

We assume no liability for the content of links listed in this book. The operators of the sites are solely responsible for the content. Further information regarding picture/image licencing given as GNU and CC can be found at:

- http://en.wikipedia.org/wiki/Wikipedia:Text_of_the_GNU_Free_Documentation_License
- http://en.wikipedia.org/wiki/Creative_Commons

# The Second Temple

Roger Liebi

THE MESSIAH
IN THE
TEMPLE

The Symbolism and Significance
of the Second Temple in Light of
the New Testament

– the sanctuary at Jerusalem during the time of Jesus Christ – plays a very significant role in the New Testament. Matthew to Revelation teems with references to this glorious edifice of Antiquity.

Many readers of the Bible do not understand much by the terms such as "pinnacle of the Temple", "the Beautiful Gate", "Solomon's Porch", "the Sheep Gate" and "the Sanhedrin". These, and many other buildings of the Temple area, come alive in the present publication. They are connected to Messiah Jesus so that the life of faith may be refreshed and enlarged by it.

During the years 1967-2003 modern archaeology on the Temple Mount made huge progress. Through this, knowledge of the Second Temple could be extended in a grandiose way and reached a high point never before attained. The present work builds upon the rich fruits of these efforts and considers them profitable for the study of the Bible.

To date, there has not been a book written in which all the passages of the NT, which refer in some way to the Temple, have been synthesized extensively.

This book is dedicated especially to all those who are enthused by the same desire, as were those Greeks who came to the sanctuary in Jerusalem in those days, to encounter the historical Jesus there. They asked of Philip of Bethsaida (John 12:21): "Sir, we wish to see Jesus."

Author: Roger Liebi
$ 39.95 / € 29.95
Published: 2012
Pages or Length: 656
Binding: Hardcover
ISBN: 978-3-943175-05-9
Christlicher Medienvertrieb Hagedorn
www.cmv-duesseldorf.de

Christlicher Medienvertrieb Hagedorn
Postfach 300430
40404 Düsseldorf
Germany

www.cmv-duesseldorf.de
info@cmv-video.de